Consuming Innocence
Popular Culture and Our Children

Consuming Innocence

Popular Culture and Our Children

KAREN BROOKS

UQP

First published 2008 by University of Queensland Press
PO Box 6042, St Lucia, Queensland 4067 Australia

www.uqp.uq.edu.au

© 2008 Karen Brooks, T/A Beyond the Rainbow Creative Productions Pty Ltd

This book is copyright. Except for private study, research, criticism or reviews, as permitted under the Copyright Act, no part of this book may be reproduced, stored in a retrieval system, or transmitted in any form or by any means without prior written permission. Enquiries should be made to the publisher.

Text design and typesetting by Pauline Haas, Bluerinse Setting
Printed in Australia by McPherson's Printing Group

Cataloguing-in-Publication Data
National Library of Australia
    Brooks, Karen.
    Consuming Innocence: Popular Culture and Our Children.

    Bibliography.
    Includes index.
    ISBN 9780702236457 (pbk.).

    1. Children – Australia – Social conditions. 2. Popular culture – Australia. 3. Child rearing – Australia. 4. Mass media and children – Australia. 5. Children in popular culture – Australia. I. Title.

305.230994

To my own very savvy and no longer tortured (I hope) children, Adam and Caragh, who continue to forgive my parenting mistakes and unreasonable demands, as well as the numerous times I've embarrassed them, and who, in their own not-so-subtle ways, have taught me how to be a better parent and mother.

To my partner in everything, Stephen, who showed me the path and continues to walk with me no matter how rough the journey.

contents

introduction   The Toxic 'Truth' About Our Tots, Tweens and Teens   1

chapter one   Back to the Future: Childhood Through the Ages   11

chapter two   'Bling, Bling, Why Don't You Give Me a Ho?': The Commercial Theft of Childhood   37

chapter three   Fashion Victims: The 'Celebrification' and Sexualisation of Children Through Clothing   66

chapter four   Toy Stories: Growing Up in a Material World (written with Lisa Hill)   87

chapter five   Boys and Their Toys: Guns, Swords and Testosterone   109

chapter six   The D'oh of Homer: The Questionable Wisdom of the Electronic Babysitter   124

chapter seven   Sense and Censorship: Film and the Uncomfortable Question of Parental Guidance   152

chapter eight   Once Upon a Time: Disney, Harry Potter, Hans Christian Andersen and Other Grimm Tales   173

chapter nine   Give Me Some MySpace: The Cyberlution of Social Networking and Electronic Games   200

chapter ten   My Little Prince/ss: Why Kids Don't Always Have to Feel 'Special'   231

conclusion   The Parent Trap   252

Notes   265
Select Bibliography   299
Acknowledgements   315
Index   317

The concentration of control over the means of producing, circulating, and exchanging information has been matched by the emergence of new technologies that have transformed culture, especially popular culture, which is the primary way in which youth learn about themselves, their relationship to others, and the larger world.

Henry Giroux
The Mouse That Roared: Disney and the End of Innocence

introduction

The Toxic 'Truth' About Our Tots, Tweens and Teens

Sugar and Spice and All Things Vice

Remember the nursery rhyme that described what little boys and girls were made of? You know, the one we'd chant that made science teachers and politically correct parents rip their hair out by the roots. Boys were made of slugs and snails and, very cruelly, puppy dogs' tails, while girls were a pathetic mix of sugar and spice and all things nice. Yawn. No wonder so many of us hated being girls. It wasn't penis envy. It was all to do with ingredients. Nowadays, however, when referring to what makes little girls, well, little girls, the eponymous 'sugar and spice' is a bit more interesting than some sweeteners and herbs from the kitchen pantry. These days, for example, 'Sugar and Spice' is the sexy brand name given to a pair of baby dolls named Phoebe and Roxxie who are being marketed to kids as young as three. These aren't your ordinary Baby Born kind either. These are your leather and lace, heavily made up, pouting kind, à la JonBenet Ramsey. Think I'm kidding? Take a stroll down to your nearest department store and check out the toy aisles. There, among the Barbies and Bratz (and I'll get to those later) and other dollies, are the new kids on the shelf: the nappy-trash of toys. I'm talking about the latest must-have phenomena: Bratz Babyz. And the kids love them. In 2006, sales of the Bratz range topped $48.7 million in Australia (compared with Barbie's meagre $40.8 million)[1] while the California-based company that makes the dolls, MGA Entertainment, earns about $4 billion a year worldwide.[2] The dolls have been called immoral by the Australian Family Association, and there have been cries to take the lingerie-clad, diminutive dolls with enormous heads and milk bottles on chains off the shelves. Parents are being warned not to buy these 'sexualised images of children' by such august bodies as the American Psychological Association.[3]

Another story that hit the media around the same time revolved around a new character introduced on that stalwart of children's television *Sesame Street*. The spotlight shone very brightly on the newcomer, a fairy-in-training named Abby Cadabby — only the fifth female character to be included in the show's 37-year history. Abby is a vibrant pink with little wings, carries a frayed wand, has purple hair tied in bunches at the side of her head and wears a pretty blue dress. She's three years old and is learning about magic, yes, but also friendships and how to cope with new environments such as kindergarten. Innocuous, you're thinking. Harmless. A wonderful antidote to the baby Bratz of this world.

Instead, critics are sharpening their claws on tiny Abby as well, determined to clip her wings. The cute Muppet has been described by one New York columnist as 'toxic to little girls', because she's an amalgam of Lindsay Lohan and Paris Hilton. Another claims she's a 'sugar and spice stereotype'.[4] And there we have it. Those words again: sugar and spice. Who would have thought they could carry so much baggage? Meant to imply something completely inoffensive and benign, depending on which toy or character they're aligned with, they bear connotations of forbidden desires, sexiness and paedophilia, or stereotyped notions of passivity and femininity. No matter how hard we try, when it comes to our kids it doesn't seem to take much to ring those clarions and start a whole range of contradictory and often hypocritical warnings and messages flying around the ether and cyberspace, confusing parents, teachers and other adults in the process.

Corporate Conspiracies and Parental Responsibility

Listening to the media and other reports circulating, you'd be hard-pressed not believing that our kids are just one doll, song, website, TV show, film, Muppet or outfit away from being sexually corrupted or, worse, abused. In other words, what we refer to very broadly as popular culture (that is, TV shows, music, films, books, internet sites, fashions, toys and advertisements) is having such a toxic effect on our kids that it's stealing their childhoods. We're constantly being fed the notion that those invidious evil beings from another planet called 'marketers' or even, in a parody of Disney, 'marketeers', along with the business corporations, are out to kidnap and consume our children's innocence one way or another and if it's not through sex, then it's by making them fat, lazy, disrespectful and downright rude or by stereotyping them.

It would be easy to believe that there's a global conspiracy by a bunch of misanthropic corporate leaders and child-hating executives to build the metaphoric equivalent of a giant gingerbread house, stocked to the brim with sex, drugs and rock 'n' roll, designed to lure our children inside and make them sexy, savvy before their time and, ultimately, tortured and dysfunctional.

Or is it all the fault of parents?

Because, if reports from other sources are to be believed, then parents are a bunch of self-indulgent, time-poor, narcissistic, materialistic go-getters who never should have had children in the first place. Just ask Supernanny, because the message out there is that, honey, we're killing the kids. Instead of nurturing the next generation, we're substituting our presence with presents (or junk food) and reaping the consequences of our neglect.

In fact, hand in hand with the corporations, we're responsible for stealing childhood.

Or is this a load of paranoid and utter nonsense?

Well, the truth is, there's no complete 'truth'. All notions, from money-hungry corporations to baffled, indifferent adults, contain elements that are patently false while also bearing mute and very valid witness to society's failings. Society, in this case, is you, me, our kids and the wider familial, social, media, educative and friendship networks of which we're all a part – including those marketers. While it may not be deliberate, we have to face facts: we're all complicit in the erosion of childhood.

Do you remember back when we were kids how well behaved we were compared with this generation? We sat at the dinner table, ate everything placed in front of us and minded our manners. We kept our clothes and rooms clean and never said 'boo' until we were spoken to by an adult. We were seen and not heard. We also played contently outside for hours on end, climbing trees, running sticks along walls whether it rained, hailed or shined 40 degrees Celsius. And we certainly *never* demanded presents or 'things' from our parents, even on birthdays or Christmas. In fact, we never demanded or grizzled: full stop. Remember those days?

No. Neither do I.

There's a good reason for that: they never existed. But for some reason I'm yet to fathom, reaching adulthood means you acquire selective memory and you start to view the past through a set of very rosy-coloured lenses. It also means that your judgement begins to suffer; common sense is strained; and, worst of all, you start to sound like your own parents. You literally hear the phrases and warnings that used to make you roll your eyes spewing out of your mouth. And then you become convinced by what I call frog logic – leaping from one conclusion to another until you assume, as Bree (played by Marcia Cross) from *Desperate Housewives* does in the show's first season, that because your child wants to dye his or her hair, get a piercing, wear black clothes and purple lipstick, or paint their nails, they're soliciting for sex and doing drugs.

While our common sense should tell us there's no corollary between hair dye and prostitution, images of various sub-cultural groups such as Goths, Emos (Emotionals) and Punks, music videos and every other report on tabloid TV tries to persuade us otherwise. We become nervous whenever our kids want to adjust their appearance – even minor changes. What does it mean? Where have I failed? Who are they hanging around with? What are they doing? Oh, God, they're going to end up unemployed, on the streets, doing drugs and fat. And it's *my* fault!

To a degree, these fears are normal and start long before our kids reach puberty. They begin the day our children first reject the toys that, for months, if not years, they'd contentedly played with, or screw up their noses at a show they'd previously adored. Suddenly, what used to amuse them and shape their world is 'childish' – that's when, as parents, we start to fret and look for the maturation handbrake. The abandoned baby doll (even a Bratz), the rusting Matchbox car, the doll's house or robot left out in the rain, the after-school cartoon rejected in favour of time spent surfing the web or in a chatroom – these become signifiers of something we cherish being outgrown. It makes us upset; it makes us anxious. It makes us want to resist and rail and stop our kids doing what we cannot stop them from doing: growing up.

The good news is that once we give ourselves a reality check, we realise we don't want to prevent that process – slow it down perhaps, but not call it to a halt. But that's the problem. While most of us lament the maturing of our kids, it's the speed at which it's happening today and the age that it's starting that's giving us cause for concern. It's referred to as KGOY (Kids Growing Older Younger),[5] and most of us don't like what it signifies or that it seems to have become an accepted attribute of childhood today.

Mind you, we don't need the marketing notion of KGOY and the panic around Bratz Babyz or Abby Cadabby to set off the playdars and make us reach for the phone to call the Childhood Protection Agency (that doesn't actually exist). Walk down your average suburban street; sit down on a Saturday morning and watch some music television; hang around the local mall; view a G-, PG- or M-rated film (though they're clearly for 15 and over, kids as young as six are being taken to them); and you'll see evidence that what passes for imaginative play, dress ups and boy-girl interactions today is very different to what it was 10, 15 and certainly 30 years ago.

Why is that? Are we really so different?

Well, yes. And so is the world.

Cybertots and Computeens

Unlike us, our children are born into a world that not only has TV, but also CDs, DVDs, computers, mobile phones, the internet and the world wide web, and where words like cyberspace, SMSing and Google are in the dictionary. They wear iPods and other MP3 players, build a 'treehouse' in MySpace, create an avatar or second identity to 'play' in an online world or game, upload clips (sometimes of themselves) on YouTube, and are more likely to have a friendship with someone they've never physically met than they are to travel.

They're also born into a world where girls shave their legs and pluck their eyebrows before puberty; where dyeing a child's hair is as common as plaiting; and where piercings on all parts of the body are birthday presents and so, more often than not, are tattoos. Tattooing no longer (or should no longer) carries the stigma that it once did. Whereas tattoos were signifiers of a particular experience (prisoners of war, prison) or subculture, or of 'loose morals', they're now private and public expressions of individuality – or conformity. Our kids have also entered a world where personal grooming for men is a booming industry and where five queer guys made 'style' a straight guy's passport to heterosexual romance. In other words, traditional gender roles have been turned, literally, inside out.

Kids these days are much savvier about the visual and technological culture around them than we ever were, engaging and processing it with an ease that astonishes. Reciting slogans and wearing them while surfing the net and listening to the bubblegum pop of Nelly Furtado or the angst of Lily Allen, kids can swoop to levels of triviality and mimicry that is mind-numbing and in the same breath start discussing politics, environmental issues, divorce rates and third-world poverty. Information about anything and everything is literally a microsecond away. Assaulted by images, words and ideas, kids take it in their stride – strides that leave the older generations lagging behind and more than a little worried.

We Live in a Mediated World

Whereas many of us were born into a world where the TV occupied one room in the house, kids these days are born into homes where not only are there multiple TVs, but houses are now redesigned to acknowledge the role the media (in the broadest sense) and entertainment plays in our fast-paced, stranger-danger, double-income, time-poor world. I'm talking about the appropriately named Media Room.

The fact is that for 97 per cent of children aged between five and 14 years, their favourite pastime is watching TV or DVDs. At least 85 per cent access the internet, while 79.5 per cent play a range of electronic games. Of the 2,664,700 children who watch TV or videos, about half watch for 20 hours or more per fortnight while more than one-third watch for 10 to 19 hours.[6] But it's not just the seemingly unlimited access to TV and other technology, including mobile phones and computers, that makes this generation of children unique. Nor is it the abundance of merchandise that accompanies films and popular TV shows (and books), or the pressure to have cool toys, the latest accessories and clothes, a mobile phone or two; to collect and trade (for money) cards; and to have your own email address and personal computer. It's the *degree* to which they engage with all forms of popular culture simultaneously and the anticipated influence, if not control, over our children's minds that these media have that scares us and makes us believe they're being emotionally and psychologically damaged and missing out on childhood.

Because of technological advances and the forces of globalisation, never before have television, film, magazines, advertising, music and other cultural influences such as food and fashion had the power to persuade, seduce, shape, control and manufacture imaginations and identities: not just of children, but of adults as well. Pop culture, in all its myriad forms, surrounds and bombards us with visions, ideas, facts and fictions about ourselves and the world we live in – whether it be on buses and trains, or in hospitals, schools, cinemas, shopping plazas and even our own homes. But, instead of working with these diverse forms and the culture that produces them and using it to both our own and our children's advantage, we've decided (or the media has decided for us) that not only is popular culture toxic, but it's making our kids toxic as well. Like one of Doctor Who's Daleks, it's exterminating sense, manners and respect; killing our children's precious innocence; making them sexy and savvy too young; and poisoning them against the people who love them and care about their wellbeing most: parents, families, friends and teachers.

At least, that's what most of the media reports and some research (usually that which gets the most publicity) would have you believe.

Absorbent Children: Soaking Up the Information Overload

Culture – popular and unpopular – does not function in a vacuum. Neither do *we*. Regardless of whether we are five weeks old or eighty-five years old, we gain our ideas about each other and culture, gender, sexuality, ethnicity, masculinity, femininity, prejudice and stereotypes from everywhere. We're all bower birds who collect and build. Only what we're building is not just a nest, it's the uniform we wear for life – our identity, ethics and morals.

The only thing is, while we acknowledge the lessons that our parents, family, friends, religion, teachers and employers have taught us, we don't thank (or blame) Rupert Murdoch, CNN, the Packer family and George Lucas, or the Simpsons, Britney Spears, reality TV, Google or JK Rowling. Okay, perhaps a few of us do thank her.

Our children and their imaginations are like sponges that absorb the information flowing around them. But don't make the mistake of believing that, just because that information isn't being delivered in a formal situation like school or a finger-wagging telling-off from mum or dad, it's not being processed. On the contrary, it means it's being quickly consumed and stored. It's the ideological equivalent of fast food – only, unlike fast food, and despite what we're being told by everyone from politicians to the guardians of education to concerned parents and grandparents, it *is*, when filtered through the right processes, full of nutrients. Our tendency is to take popular culture for granted. We don't think very deeply about what we're learning from the music we listen to, the films and TV shows we watch, or the magazines we read. After all, it's often done in our own time, it's usually fun, sometimes cheap and ubiquitous – and it's everywhere. Yet, the fact is, we *do* learn. And, the younger we are, the more we absorb and learn.

Sexy Tots and Savvy Teens?
Popular culture has been accused of everything from turning our children into sex-obsessed, mindless, witless, toxic, deviant sociopaths, to dumbing down society. To read, listen and watch the information circulating about popular culture, it would be easy to believe that it's *the* enemy against whom we should arm ourselves and our children.

As a mother of two children, a consumer and teacher of culture, a newspaper columnist and a media commentator, I've experienced the love-hate and contradictory relationship we have with all things trivial and significant. From the perspective of parent and educator, I've watched, listened to and participated in the arguments for and against popular culture. I have seen them gain momentum and be diffused. I've read, heard and participated in the debates about its role in education. I've watched, ducked and even been behind the finger pointing and accusations about its influence in and out of the home.

I wouldn't blame any parent (single, de facto or married), grand-parent (biological or pseudo), teacher or professional working with children for believing that the heady cocktail of popular culture that our kids engage in is responsible for everything from their attempts (and successes) to look sexy, to temper tantrums and distorted body image.

That's why I've written *Consuming Innocence: Popular Culture and Our Children*. Like the majority of people out there, young and old, I live and breathe this culture. I wake up to radio – music and talkback. I watch morning television while getting ready for work and switch it back on when I get home to wind down. I pick the longest queue in the supermarket so I can read the latest gossip magazines (with my husband's reminder ringing in my ears – 'this isn't a library you know').

I see waiting at the doctor's as a chance to either indulge in last decade's issue of *Cosmopolitan* or a few chapters of a novel I'm reading. I surf the net, watch films and DVDs, read *Time* magazine and the *Bulletin*, watch lots of commercial TV and ABC as well as SBS and I have set up a shrine to that satellite dish on my roof that beams pay TV into my house during the cricket season.

I can quote from the Simpsons and Shakespeare, from John Keats and KISS, from Stephens Hawking and Spielberg. So-called popular culture is the soundtrack, the screenplay, the megabyte, the gimmick, the pleasure and the pain of my life. And whether you like it or not, it functions that way in yours too. I adore aspects of pop culture and loathe others. Our kids do as well. And while you might be able to tell your friends, your kids' teachers and relatives what TV shows, films, music, games and websites your kids love, how often do you sit down and actually watch, play, or listen *with* them? You probably don't have time – I know I didn't always when my kids were younger. But that's dangerous. After all, how can you understand your kids if you don't understand the variety of people, images and stories that shape their world and, in turn, them?

This book will help give you access to their sometimes overwhelming and complex world. It will help reduce the risk of your child's innocence being consumed and, subsequently, their childhood disappearing. It will not only provide a historical and social context for the multimedia we take for granted, but also teach you how to work with the children in your lives to keep those lines of communication open from tot to tween, from tween to teen and beyond. It will help you feel in control about providing or denying access to various elements of popular culture and more relaxed about discussing this with your child. You'll understand the power pop culture has – good and bad – to influence your children's ideas about other people and the world; and you'll also learn what it's saying about *you*. You'll learn how not to react too quickly or too harshly when the latest scandal over a fad, toy, film or music clip breaks; you'll discover *how* to talk to your kids about the culture that consumes them, that defines them. And your kids will love you for it.

chapter one

Back to the Future: Childhood Through the Ages

History Always Repeats

Leafing back through the musty pages of history, it's clear that the childhood of our ancestors was very different to that experienced by kids today. Different historical accounts tell us that children in the past were considered 'imperfect adults' or miniature ones, or were possessed of mystical, dream-like qualities and romanticised.[1] They were viewed as works-in-progress as opposed to individuals with rights, voices and specific needs. Depending upon which era they lived in and the conditions of their birth and family, they were loved, chastised, abused, spoiled and exploited – much the same as now. Today we seem to have clear notions of childhood and just who is a child, yet up until around the late 1600s and early 1700s[2] any coherent understanding of 'childhood' as a special life-stage with privileges and public acknowledgement appears to be lacking, but that doesn't mean we can't piece together what adult society felt about it. As historian Robin Lane Fox argues, 'the absence of a general word for something is certainly not evidence that the thing did not exist'.[3]

With this in mind, I'm going to take a quick trip back through history and examine some of the arguments posited by historians and sociologists to look at the ways children were spoken of and treated so we can get a sense of 'childhood' in the past. I'm going to briefly discuss some of the art and literature and then explore childhood today to see if we've inherited or learned anything from our ancestors and their experiences or if we've thrown the baby out with the bathwater. Contrary to what you might think, there's evidence to suggest that when it comes to childhood and kids, we're returning to a model of childhood that existed for hundreds of years before TV, the internet and other pop cultural demons took possession of our children.

Where Have All the Children Gone?

There have been a number of scholars who have whet their intellectual appetite by examining the way children have been depicted in history. One very influential account that's cited in many books on childhood was written by Phillippe Ariés. In his book *Centuries of Childhood*, published in 1962, Ariés basically argues that in the past childhood, as we understand it today, didn't exist. It is, he believes, a modern category that emerged to reflect changing social circumstances, such as the advent of literacy, education and work conditions. Whereas once the boundaries between child and adult were blurred, they became distinct as children lingered on the border of adulthood learning the tools to become socially recognised as grown up and to function as adults. Adolescence, according to Ariés, evolved to define this threshold period.

To defend his hypothesis, Ariés (among other examples) looks at medieval art. He notes that throughout the medieval period (roughly between 500 and 1500 CE (the Common Era), also known as the Middle Ages), there are no pictures of children except the baby Jesus, who is mostly painted in his mother's arms with a wizened old face – one of those 'miniature adults' I mentioned above.[4] While it may seem strange to arrive at 'facts' based on the study of pictures alone, in some ways it makes sense. This was a period in which the overwhelming majority of people were illiterate and so, to record what was meaningful and significant at the time, artists, the 'photographers' of the era, were called upon. Ariés believes that the absence of children in the art suggests they were taken for granted at best and unimportant at worst. He also says that because children were dressed in smaller versions of what the adults wore, childhood didn't exist. Children were simply mini-adults.[5]

While there was no Baby Gap in the Middle Ages, it seems a long stretch to base a theory about childhood first on pictures and then the fashion portrayed in them. But Ariés takes it further. Throughout different historical periods, he continues, no distinction was made between kids and adults in work *or* play.[6] Labour was shared, as were stories and games, and the fashions reflected this lack of distinction. Children morphed into adults and, from a social perspective at least, it seems to have been a relatively seamless transformation. Yet, as we move forward through time, artistic representations of children slowly alter. Not only do children start to appear in artwork looking more like children, they even begin to have their own wardrobe.

Childhood: A Cultural Artefact

What Ariés concludes from this is that, while childhood didn't originally exist, it did gradually develop (remembering that he draws a distinction between 'child' and 'childhood'), but it's not a naturally occurring phenomenon. Ariés believes that, because there were no words (such as 'adolescent') to distinguish a child from an adult and the terms 'boy' and 'girl' could apply to people of any age, there was no concept of 'child'.[7]

In his book *The Disappearance of Childhood*, Neil Postman also explores the meaning and understanding of childhood through the ages, tending to agree with many of Ariés's findings. He argues that 'childhood' as a 'social artefact' is less than 400 years old and says that, in North American society, formal recognition of childhood has only been around for 160 years.[8]

Historian Barbara Hanawalt, however, disagrees with Ariés, explaining that because much of his findings centred on not only the absence of distinct representations but also the language of the period, his argument is flawed. Hanawalt is not alone in challenging Ariés and writes quite humorously that 'it is preposterous to argue that people woke up on the morning of January 1, 1500, and found their family structure and social values about the little adults or little monsters in their households had undergone a revolution'.[9]

Another critic, Chris Heywood, agrees that, while children *were* largely absent from medieval art, that's because regular scenes of everyday life were as well. Medieval times are renowned for their focus on the divine rather than the secular, on the holy family as opposed to *the* family. Just because 'kids' *per se* aren't featured in the art doesn't mean they weren't acknowledged in the social sense or that what we refer to as childhood wasn't a known and understood stage in life development.[10] Numerous other sources support this view, pointing to the proliferation of child-rearing books during the Enlightenment (the period around the 18th to the 19th century, also known as a rationalistic movement), the rise of universal education (with a strong religious focus) and the manufacturing of toys.[11]

The Tender Years

In her book *Growing Up in Medieval London*, Hanawalt writes that, contrary to popular belief, the 'Middle Ages did recognize stages of life that correspond to childhood and adolescence ... Londoners, when they contrasted these ages with adulthood, spoke of youth as "wild and wanton" and adulthood as "sad and wise"'.[12] She argues that, even though dominant historical views of the past claim that childhood as an official life-stage didn't really exist, other literature from the time and evidence from social records begs to differ. For example, Hanawalt discusses the importance of apprenticeships, fostering and squirehood, which were essential to children's development in medieval times and which in themselves suggest both a recognition and formalisation of a particular life-stage between 'child' and 'adult'.[13]

According to Hanawalt, the Middle Ages were also a time when English society became obsessed about rearing children 'correctly' and preparing them for adulthood. Pamphlets and advice manuals were prolific and even the laws began to accommodate young people.[14] A sentimentality crept into reflections on childhood and phrases such as 'tender years' and 'I was but a child then' began to be used.[15] Jan Kociumbas believes that while various life-stages were recognised, up until the 15th century in Europe, 'childhood was not seen as an intrinsically separate condition but rather a period of defective adulthood from which children had to be wrenched as soon as possible'.[16] Postman quotes Elizabeth Eisenstein who, when writing on education from the 1600s onwards, points to the segregation of the sexes at schools, the use of special printed materials geared to distinct stages of learning and the appearance of separate 'peer groups' as markers that a distinctive 'youth culture' was rising.[17]

Up until around the 17th century and the beginnings of the Industrial Revolution (from the mid-1600s onwards – in many respects coinciding with the Enlightenment), children lived in what Kathleen McDonnell describes in her book, *Honey, We Lost the Kids*, as extended-family homes.[18] Forget the nuclear family, these were homes bursting with generational differences, relatives, conversation, smells, noises and germs. Privacy was non-existent. Boys, girls, men and women shared beds, ablutions, meal times and labour. It wasn't until the 1600s that houses were divided and rooms with specific functions such as sleeping or eating were created. Even then, depending on a family's economic status, those rooms, if they existed at all, were cramped and sometimes only separated from the main living areas by flimsy curtains.

What this meant was that adult matters, particularly those pertaining to sex, were common knowledge to children. They weren't protected or shielded from what was a fact of life: mum and dad had sex to make babies (and perhaps, sometimes, for pleasure). Sharing a bed with your kids was not a call to abstain. Kids were conceived and delivered in the family bed – often witnessed by children.[19]

This is quite shocking to modern sensibilities, but to the children of yesteryear it was a fact of life. They saw and heard things that adults said and did, but they had it drummed into them that they were not to be emulated or repeated. Respect for parents and adults generally was a given. The philosopher John Locke described the ideal relationship between child and parent as one where children 'should look upon their parents as their lords, their absolute governors, and as such stand in awe of them; and that, when they come to riper years, they should look on them as their best, as their only sure friends, and as such love and reverence them'.[20]

What happened in the adult world stayed there, and more fool children if they were caught imitating their elders before they were the 'right' age.

While debates about the existence of an identifiable stage called childhood in the past still continue today,[21] it's clear that even those who disagree on aspects of understanding childhood as a life-stage concur with historian Martin Hoyles's contention that childhood, in any period, is 'a social convention and not just a natural state'.[22] That is, childhood is culturally formed through the actions and ideas of adult society.[23] It's also important to realise that childhood cannot be discussed without considering social, political, gender and class differences and contexts. This means it will always evolve and change according to a range of cultural and historical conditions.[24] As Chris Jenks writes:

> Childhood is not a brief physical habitation of a Lilliputian world owned and ruled by others; childhood is rather a historical and cultural experience and its meaning and interpretations and its interests reside within such contexts.[25]

The fact that a notion of childhood as distinct from adulthood has always existed in some form is persuasive, particularly when we look at other evidence from different eras. It may have been briefer and for many, many children much tougher, but there are just too many examples from history, legislation, social practices, literature, poetry, drama *and* fairytales – in essence the popular culture of specific periods – to believe that childhood wasn't recognised by adult society, despite what Ariés, Postman and others might argue.

Let's look at some of these examples in the hope that they'll offer insights into not just the way children were thought of and treated in the past, but some ideas about contemporary attitudes to children and parenting practices as well.

Things Were Better Then

Did Aristotle, the Greek philosopher who lived between 384 and 322 BCE (Before the Common Era), have a childhood? And what about Homer, creator of the epic poems the *Iliad* and *Odyssey*, who dwelt in Classical times, when people wandered around in togas, philosophising, exploring, worshipping a fractious and sensual bunch of gods and creating timeless works of art; did he have what we would call a childhood? There's evidence to support that they both did, and from some of the finest minds in the ancient business; minds that readily distinguished between children, youth and adults. Back in 800 BCE, the Greek poet Hesiod wrote:

> I see no hope for the future of your people if they are dependent on the frivolous youth of today, for certainly all youth are reckless beyond words. When I was a boy, we were taught to be discreet and respectful of elders, but the present youth are exceedingly wise and impatient of restraint.

While 300 years later, Plato's wonderful mouthpiece, the philosopher Socrates, famously said:

> Children now love luxury. They have bad manners and contempt for authority. They show disrespect to their elders and love to chatter in places of exercise.

And his complaints didn't end there, as he also said:

> Children today are tyrants. They contradict their parents, gobble their food, and tyrannize their teachers.

Socrates should know. He's arguably the most famous teacher in Classical times. Certainly these two grumpy old men saw children as not only different from their adult counterparts, but as rebellious, impertinent and in need of some boundaries. Popular historian Tom Holland writes that in Roman times 'children were too weak to be idealised, and the highest praise a child could be given was to be compared to an adult'.[26]

We all know that being a child is transitory and brief in life's great schema. While today we seem to imbue childhood with so much significance, in ancient times, through to the 1800s and even beyond (with the exception, perhaps, of the Romantic era), it was uncomplicatedly viewed as a means of getting somewhere else – to adulthood. But as Hesiod and Socrates demonstrate, children were definitely identified as bumps in an all-too-brief journey. By the time the Renaissance flowers, however, children are firmly in the artist's eye, suggesting, despite what Ariés contends, that childhood is too.

Domenico Ghirlandaio's *An Old Man and his Grandson* (1480) is fairly typical of the art of the period in the way it represents a child. The work depicts a seated, benign, old man gazing into the upturned face of his cherubic grandson. The child is smaller, rounded, with golden locks and the hand he presses against his grandfather's chest is both reassuringly loving and a gesture that acknowledges the old man's mortality. It's not the meek that will inherit the earth the child seems to be saying, but the young – who in turn pass it to their children.

In 1560, Pieter Brueghel's painting *Children's Games* depicts a busy scene with dozens of children in the throes of play, interweaving with the adult life humming around them. It's a lively painting, with kids rolling hula-hoops, doing handstands, straddling a fence and dancing. In the background there's what looks like a child receiving a terrible beating and others sharing drinks with adult counterparts. It's a work of art that clearly distinguishes between adult 'work' and children's 'play', while at the same time blurring them by illustrating that children didn't need to be separated from the mainstream activities and rhythms of adult life. Importantly, the 'play' in the painting is unfettered and unstructured.[27]

Throughout the Renaissance, there are many examples of children in art. Most were the offspring of nobles, but some were anonymous sitters. What all the images have in common is a genuine effort on the part of the artist to paint them as distinct from the adults. Their smooth faces are naive, their eyes trusting. But, as Ariés notes, their clothes are still smaller versions of what the adults are wearing.[28]

If the art isn't persuasive, other examples from the popular culture of other periods illustrate how children were imaginatively represented and, therefore, socially understood.

Children's Stories

Stories written exclusively for children are a relatively modern phenomenon. Since ancient times, stories of heroes and villains, magic and gods, were told to young and old to impart morals and values, fire the imagination and soothe the soul. The most popular tales reveal a great deal about how children and childhood were regarded across time.

Homer's *Odyssey*, an epic poem believed to have been crafted around 1200 BCE, features the much set upon King Odysseus,[29] absent from his homeland of Ithaca for 20 years, pining for his wife, Penelope, and son, Telemachus, who has grown up without him. Throughout the tale, the listener/reader is made to feel aware of what an absent father actually means to the family who, at the end of the tale, are well and truly threatened by outside forces, usurpers to the titles king and husband, and who want to murder young Telemachus.[30]

The idea of a missing parent and the impact of this upon the developing child is a common theme that recurs throughout literature in many periods, with orphans and motherless or fatherless children featured often. In Greek and Roman myths alone, these young characters abound: there's the crippled god, Hephaestus, thrown out of Olympus by his mother, Hera, and raised by the sea-nymphs; never mind the countless young women Zeus impregnated (as a swan, golden shower and bull among others forms) and abandoned, pregnant, and left pretty much to their own fate to raise his kids. Lots of heroes result from these liaisons – Perseus, Achilles and Hektor to name a few.[31] In the tragedy *The Orestian Trilogy*, by Aeschylus, the young characters,

Orestes (and later, Electra), enact revenge for the death of their father by killing their mother and face terrible consequences for their actions. King Arthur was an orphan; Hamlet is rendered fatherless; Cinderella, Oliver Twist, David Copperfield, Peter Pan, Bambi, Luke Skywalker, Peter Parker (Spiderman), Bruce Wayne (Batman) and Harry Potter are also parentless characters whose childhood is dramatically shortened (but arguably also made more poignant) by having their parents taken away. Rudely flung into the adult world, these 'kidults' learn to survive without adult nurturing or in spite of other, unwelcome adult interference.[32]

There's also Hansel and Gretel, Little Red Riding Hood, Sleeping Beauty, the Little Mermaid, Aladdin and the Little Match Girl – children who survive, celebrate, or are victims of the good or bad intentions of the adult world. Hans Christian Andersen's biographer, Jens Andersen (no relation), believes that Andersen especially was responsible for enabling children, for the first time, to appear in literature on their own terms. He writes that Andersen 'allowed children of all ages and both sexes ... to speak in magnificent dialogues and lines that turn everything upside down and see right through the essential lies of adults'.[33]

As much as we talk about protecting our kids from the vagaries of life, it's the harsher elements and the unkindness of strangers endured by fictive kids, and the lessons we've learned from those, that we remember. I'll discuss these in much more detail in Chapter Eight.

It's not just myths and fairytales that acknowledge 'childhood' as a stage. Just as wonderful folktales and fairytales were being whispered around the fireplaces and bedsides of families of all classes, Shakespeare also paid homage to childhood in one of his most famous soliloquies. In his pastoral, cross-dressing comedy, *As You Like It*, the character Jacques reflects on the seven ages of man. It's a very well-known soliloquy (and particularly pertinent in this era of reality TV and celebrity culture) if for no other reason than the opening lines:

> All the world's a stage,
> And all the men and women merely players,
> They have their exits and entrances,

> And one man in his time plays many parts,
> His acts being seven ages.

Shakespeare then defines childhood by breaking it into at least three stages: infancy, the school-aged child and then adolescence, when that first rush of hormones and sexual awareness occurs:

> At first the infant,
> Mewling and puking in the nurse's arms.
> Then, the whining schoolboy with his satchel
> And shining morning face, creeping like snail
> Unwillingly to school. And then the lover,
> Sighing like furnace, with a woeful ballad
> Made to his mistress' eyebrow.[34]

Shakespeare writes of stages of growth and change that are distinguishable from each other and that we all go through in order to age and finally die – sans teeth, eyes, taste. We end as we begin – gummy, blind and unable to savour life. It's not a very appealing picture. Still, the stages he describes are not blurred, but quite discrete, marking the passage of time and maturation. Dante Alighieri, author of *The Divine Comedy*, describes the same process in the late 1200s but, unlike his English counterpart, places all children in Limbo.[35] So how could Shakespeare, writing in the 1500s, so clearly define childhood (and let's not forget the tragic impetuousness of Romeo and Juliet, both in their early to mid-teens) if it wasn't already a recognised life-stage? Like Hanawalt, Jenks and others, I would argue that he couldn't.

Romancing Childhood

From the late 1700s, the birth of what I referred to earlier as the 'mystical child' in fiction occurs. This was the Romantic view of children as mellifluously described by the great poets and essayists William Blake, William Wordsworth and Samuel Taylor Coleridge – who, when he wasn't high on opium, was opining about kids. The Romantics basically believed that children, because of their youth and innocence, were closer to God than adults; they were spiritually in tune. The older they grew, the more they fell into knowledge and therefore sin, as if they kept biting into Eve's apple and having their eyes and minds opened to the unpleasantness and cruelties of the world. To be born into this world was to experience another Fall from Paradise.[36] It's a very Christian, upper-class notion and incredibly maudlin and unrealistic. As a result kids were described as little lambs, angels and just so sickly sweet. These types of descriptions, which focused on 'innocence', ignored the harsh realities of many children and rendered their voices mute, something that Andersen and Charles Dickens strove to redress in their fiction.[37]

From Socrates to Shakespeare and then on to the Romantics, we have diverse pictures of young people. They are alternately represented as frivolous, reckless, disrespectful, impatient, bad-mannered children who chatter far too much and have a healthy contempt for authority, or as little cherubs who wouldn't dream of putting butter in their mouth let alone melting it. They're described quite differently to adults, suggesting that though it wasn't called 'childhood', it was nonetheless understood as a life-stage that, once successfully survived and traversed, led to adulthood.

All Work and No Play

Sex, birth and death were everyday occurrences in the life of the historical child. So were chores and, from about the age of seven (though there are many reported instances of children much younger), work. Why seven? Because, according to Neil Postman, that's when children had command over speech. They could communicate with adults like adults – though, as Hanawalt wisely points out, 'it is very difficult to set children of seven to skilled labour such as smelting, ploughing or carpentry. They may be set to some tasks and may even be married at such a young age, but no one really anticipates that they will have the physical capacity to perform adult roles'.[38] To emphasise her point, she discusses the work of Arnold van Gennep who, in his studies on rites of passage from child to adult, distinguishes between 'physical puberty' and 'social puberty'.

Physical puberty is characterised by sexual development whereas social puberty is a cultural phenomenon. Hanawalt and van Gennep agree that both play a part in initiating young people into the adult world and often converge and diverge.[39] This is particularly evident with girls, who develop much earlier than boys and therefore, in terms of 'physical puberty', have different expectations placed upon them.[40]

What is clear is that, from what would now be considered a young age, children in the past were given some kind of work and often indentured into trades – some very unpleasant and demanding. Apprentices cut their familial ties and joined the home and thus family of their masters and for many years became a part of a different household with its own rules, mix of ages, sexes and hierarchy and concomitant mix of professional and personal roles. Hanawalt states, 'With such close living and such potential for deep emotional conflict and attachment, it is not surprising that archival sources record both terrible abuse and close friendships within the apprenticeship arrangements'.[41] If children remained at home, they worked in the fields or family business alongside the adults.[42] Not much evidence exists to suggest that their hours or tasks were made shorter or easier just because they were children, but the expectations placed upon them in terms of specific labour most likely would have been.

The nursery rhyme 'Boys and Girls Come Out to Play', published in about 1708, reveals much of childhood during that period and points to the notion that youth was no barrier to hard work:

> Boys and girls come out to play,
> The moon does shine as bright as day;
> Come with a hoop, and come with a call,
> Come with a good will or not at all.
> Loose your supper, and loose your sleep,
> Come to your playfellows in the street;
> Up the ladder and down the wall.
> A halfpenny loaf will serve us all.
> But when the loaf is gone, what will you do?
> Those who would eat must work – 'tis true.[43]

The second line indicates how long the working day was for kids. 'The moon does shine', so it's night-time. It also reveals that children, who are workers, also need and want to play. The last line, however, is a poignant reminder of the harshness of life for the child: 'Those who would eat must work'. Talk about adult worries being placed on young shoulders.

The important point here is that children weren't simply a biological imperative, they were an economic necessity as well: not just to the family, but to society as a whole.[44] Under the watchful eye of either parents or masters of particular trades, children learned a series of life-skills that equipped them for a future. Girls mostly learned how to run a household while boys learned how to earn a living that would provide for a family: as a farmer, blacksmith, cobbler, baker, cooper or miller – the list is almost endless. In turn, these skills would be passed to the next generation.[45] Adult society needed children and children needed adults to ensure a workable and, in every sense of the word, sustainable future.[46]

Just because a person is needed, however, doesn't mean they were always treated well. Despite high infant mortality, the children who survived weren't all treasured. As a society, we despair about the cruel tales of child abuse that make the news. This type of treatment is not exclusive to our time. In the past adults both exploited and abused the children in their care – sexually, physically and emotionally – prompting 17th-century French cleric Pierre de Bérulle to describe childhood as the 'the most vile and abject state of human nature, after that of death'.[47] But let's not assume from this bleak picture that children weren't also loved, valued and cared for deeply; as Ariés notes, 'the idea of childhood is not to be confused with affection for children'.[48]

While some children may have been doted upon, as history and literature records, others were freely beaten. Lloyd deMause discusses a 13th-century law that brings child-beating into the public domain: 'If one beats a child until it bleeds, then it will remember, but if one beats it to death, the law applies'.[49] He believes that based on the evidence he collected, 'a large percentage of children born prior to the eighteenth century were what would today be termed "battered children"'.[50] Corporal punishment was a sign of the times and a way of controlling children by instilling fear and pain as the adage 'spare the rod and spoil the child' attests.[51] Something all too familiar to workhouse kids.

Exploiting Children

Born of the Industrial Revolution and movingly portrayed in Dickens's *Oliver Twist*, the realities for orphaned/abandoned/unwanted children raised in government workhouses, were ruthless. These children existed on poor diets with no adult succour or comfort and endured working days of up to 16 hours. Shoved up chimneys, down mines or into factories and mills, sometimes as young as five and six,[52] the life expectancy of these children was pitiable. Due to the high infant mortality rate, combined with appalling work conditions, the average lifespan of most of these kids was 23.[53] The type of knowledge that these children would have been privy to would no doubt shock and appal adults today. But the reality is that the children of yesteryear, rightly or wrongly, were not sheltered in the way that most children are today. They entered the adult world at a very young age and managed it to the best of their ability. Their childhood was brief and most likely bitter, marked by control, beatings, exploitation, sexual depravity and very hard work.

Hans Christian Andersen was determined to emphasise the harsh realities of life for orphans and dispossessed children (and adults) through his creative works. In his poignant tale 'She Was No Good', published in 1852, about a drunken, single mother, a washerwoman who hoists her skirts to stand in the freezing river and clean the clothes of the upper classes, we are presented with a realistic portrayal of the cruelties for not only the female proletariat but, as biographer Jens Andersen suggests, an insight into the life of Andersen's mother, Anne Marie Andersdatter, as well.[54]

Likewise, Andersen's tale 'The Little Match Girl' is another tragic story of a young girl who, in an effort to keep warm and recapture memories of a happier childhood, lights a series of the precious matches she's meant to sell so her family can put food on the table. The story ends with her death, alone and in the bitter cold.

Child prostitution during this period has been well documented and there is evidence to suggest that the Little Match Girl, who is alone on the streets with her paltry wares, may also have been (or was certainly destined to be) a prostitute.[55] Andersen's fable of the poor child both alludes to and mourns this situation.[56]

While Hans Christian Andersen wrote about children as victims of adult abuse and neglect who were ultimately rewarded by going to heaven, children's writer Lewis Carroll (the Reverend Charles Dodgson) not only created magical adventures for them, but photographed them as well.

Carroll's most famous work is, arguably, the logic-lover's delight *Alice in Wonderland*. The magical story of the inquisitive girl who fell down a rabbit-hole gave to the world characters such as the Mad Hatter, the Queen of Hearts, the Dormouse, the White Rabbit and, of course, Alice. What many people don't realise is that Alice was based on a real person. Alice Liddell was the daughter of one of Carroll's friends. When she was still very young, Carroll developed what we would now describe as an unhealthy obsession with her. Though there's no proof he ever touched her inappropriately, he did bribe her to allow him to photograph her.[57]

Carroll took a picture of Alice in an orchard. Alice is holding an orange balanced in the palm of her hand and her dishevelled dress and pose in the photograph suggest more than a child caught stealing a piece of fruit. Her head is tipped, her look knowing. Her hand is placed on her hip and one leg is raised, lifting her skirts and revealing a tiny bit more flesh. Reading the photo in light of contemporary culture, it's difficult to view Alice's pose except in a very Lolita-like way. She appears as Carroll's nymphet, the object of his desire.

This photo alone is probably not enough to convict Carroll of any transgressions. The public overall has trouble thinking of someone who wrote such timeless tales for children as having anything but the best of intentions towards them. But other photos and, indeed, diary entries that Carroll left to posterity suggest otherwise. They're more than clear about his desires and wishes. Stephanie Lovett Stoffel, in her book *Lewis Carroll and Alice,* is very firm in her conviction that Carroll's obsession with child nudes and the female form generally has to be read in the context of the times and Carroll's tendency to romanticise children according to the Victorian ethos. She stresses the Reverend's devout Christianity. Even so, she acknowledges that, viewed through modern lenses, Carroll's interest can appear 'odd'.[58]

Lewis Carroll, *Peter Pan* author JM Barrie (who also enjoyed the company of children, a fact made into something much more wholesome in Johnny Depp's portrayal in the movie *Neverland*), and, in our lifetime, pop star Michael Jackson all have huge question marks hanging over their heads regarding the relationships they had with the children they encountered and, in Jackson's case, in their care; relationships that blur the lines between children, sex, exploitation and adult responsibility. But more on that in the next chapter.

In the foreword to his edited book *The History of Childhood*, deMause writes that, for centuries, 'children ... were the victims of forces over which they had no control, and they were abused in many imaginable and sometimes unimaginable ways'.[59] That's a huge and very disturbing statement. But is it true? Looking at the evidence of physical and sexual abuse uncovered by numerous historians,[60] the jury is in and I'm afraid adults stand convicted. While there's no doubt that deMause examines history through a very myopic lens (despite awful conditions, the majority of children grew up into reasonable adults), the picture he paints is one that arouses guilt and horror in equal measure.

A Declaration of Rights

Changes in perceptions and understandings of childhood began to occur as late as the 1950s, when a few advocates started speaking about children's rights.[61] The notion of children's rights was an outrageous suggestion to begin with – after all, what rights can or should children have except those dictated by their adult carers? Children are immature, inexperienced and lacking in worldly knowledge and physical abilities; to what rights could they be entitled? As shocking and innovative as the idea initially seemed, the rights of children slowly became legislated and accepted. These days, we take it for granted that children have rights – of course they do. But, in the process, we seem to have lost sight that some of those rights include the right to feel safe, secure and protected from seemingly benign forces; to have consistency and boundaries; and to be raised to become functioning, healthy adults.

History Lessons

Looking back through history, it's clear that certain perceptions of children and even childhood are shared, while others appear to be completely foreign and even disturbing. So what *does* history teach us about childhood? First, what it tells us is that while childhood wasn't privileged in the ways it is today, it was recognised as a stage that leads to adulthood. It was in childhood that the blueprint for life was drafted. It was then that children were trained in various life-skills, manners, morals and ethics that enabled them to function in adult society. They were taught to survive and, hopefully, thrive. Childhood was a means to an end, not an end in itself. It was also, to use the words of contemporary cultural critic Henry Giroux, 'not a natural state of innocence; [but] … a historical construction'.[62] Marked clearly by abuse of all kinds, the history of childhood also provides enough evidence to suggest that many children were loved and even, in later centuries, coddled.[63]

What's also evident is that from Ancient Greece through to the Western world in the new millennium, attitudes to children have remained pretty consistent. Sadly, there's an 'us' and 'them' mentality that places children on the outer with disgruntled and judgemental adults who seem to have conveniently forgotten they were once young as well. As Hanawalt notes, there has always been a

> natural tension [that] exists between the aspirations of youths and the demands of adults. The adult population wants to

> establish a transition from adolescence to adulthood and consequently seeks to direct, train, and control adolescent behaviour. The adolescent on the other hand, seeks to establish a personal identity and independence.[64]

Henry Giroux sees this tension as divisive and political and as creating a social arena where children are represented as either in danger or dangerous;[65] they're encouraged to 'act like adults ... and then condemned for appropriating' adult behaviours.[66] But as McDonnell rightly states, 'what children *do* need to be shielded from is not the painful realities of life so much as a sense of hopelessness about them'.[67]

Herein lies the fundamental difference between the past and the present – arguably, it's attitudinal. It's the way adult culture constructs, discusses, represents and manages childhood that has undergone a dramatic shift. This has been facilitated by, over time, the decline in mortality and the rise in education, literacy, health, human rights, politics and, most recently, modern digital and visual technology and our increasing reliance upon them, the explosion of information and ready access to it and, very importantly, the influential role of pop culture and peer groups in children's lives.

To test if this summation is accurate, let's briefly have a look at childhood today.

Those Were the Days

According to numerous reports and stories, when it comes to social notions of parenting, the current generation are hopeless, useless and not nearly as good as their parents or grandparents. With all the attacks on modern parenting in the media, it's difficult to locate the exact problem. Raising kids is a natural process, we're told – people have been doing it since they first slithered out of the primordial ooze. Well, if it's so 'natural' how come so many fail miserably? Clearly they do as there is now a veritable industry spawned on the guilt and self-doubt of contemporary, caring people who want to be better than 'good enough' when it comes to bringing up their children. A survey done by the Australian Childhood Foundation in 2004 revealed that more than half the respondents said they 'lacked confidence in their child-rearing ability'.[68] The fact is, while we used to *raise* children, nowadays (like a catch phrase in a TV show or shout-line from a movie poster) we 'parent' them. And thus a new identity is born – the 'parent' – one that is embraced, rejected and criticised. It requires certain skills and knowledge; and, like most identities, is fuelled with self-doubt and anxieties. As Hugh Mackay describes, 'Parenting has become a job or, at least, a job description … [it] used to be something that happened … by example'.[69] Perhaps this is why Catherine Lockhart, mother of five young children, is able to earn $100 an hour as a 'Mum Coach' – a new growth-industry that relies on mainly middle-class parental fears and uncertainties to flourish.[70] Child development researcher at the Australian Institute of Family Studies, Sarah Wise notes that there has been a generational variation in attitudes towards childhood. She states that 'It's definitely a culture shift – valuing children to the extent that they overtake your life'. She further argues that 'parents feel the need to sacrifice absolutely everything, putting their children's needs before their own to be seen as doing an adequate job'.[71] A Melbourne psychologist and family therapist, Andrew Fuller, describes contemporary childhood as a race,[72] one that most parents want their child to win, no matter what the cost to themselves or their child's innocence and long-term happiness.

Regardless of how we approach raising our children now, one assumption that's continually made, by parents, grandparents, many professionals who work with kids, and the general public, is that this brief period referred to as 'childhood' was better in the past. Not the historic ones discussed earlier, but the childhood experienced by the last generation or the one before. You know, during the Depression, the world wars, Vietnam, the 1970s or the 1980s. That was when we were left (mercifully) to our own devices, unsupervised and outside rain, hail or shine, and given punitive and sometimes extreme punishments for any wrongdoings, not just by our parents. We were force-fed all sorts of horrible, boring concoctions, and told to sit still and not utter a word in ill-fitting, sweltering clothes whenever adult visitors invaded. We were also given domestic chores, sent to shops to buy groceries and walked or caught public transport to many destinations. If we were part of a one-parent or another type of family structure, or we were from a divergent ethnic or religious background, we had to endure the social stigma of difference. And that's just for starters. Yes, they were great times.

Oh, how quickly we forget. These days, as soon as childhood is mentioned, it's as if we all don our rose-coloured glasses and revisit the past through a lovely Barbie-pink haze, opining and preaching to bewildered kids that 'things were so much better then'. It's not at all healthy for the current generation of children to keep hearing the adults they respect and love moan about everything and anything to do with childhood today. Instead of making the best of what's going on in these fast-paced cyber times, and setting limits and boundaries around various elements of culture that kids access, adults stand there like a giant tut-tut brigade, wagging fingers, denigrating and becoming anxious about kids and every single element of the childhood they're experiencing. What we seem to forget is that together, parents and other adults, along with wider social and cultural forces, create the conditions for and the realities of our kids' childhoods. If we're unhappy with what's on offer, then we not only *have* to change it, we *can*.

Right Here, Right Now
'I'd hate to be raising a child today' – overheard on a bus, 2006.

The more I read about kids and childhood in the past, the more I'm convinced we're heading back to the future – returning to a time when children were miniature or imperfect adults and were open to all kinds of exploitation. Let's look at the evidence.

For a start, we're dressing children like adults again. Instead of fashions that acknowledge and celebrate childhood (or are age-appropriate), we have racks of clothing in department stores and boutiques that turn our children into 'Mini-Me' – tiny versions of ourselves.[73] Tots and tweens (children aged between 7 and 12) are now, through clothing, being turned into adults and sexualised – from bralettes to little French knickers. This is accentuated by multiple industries such as advertising, music, fast food, toys, TV and films that use children's bodies and the sexualisation of these to market a whole range of goods back to children and adults.[74] There will be more on this in the following chapter.

Alongside the powerful and influential marketing forces are seemingly harmless social activities such as children's dance and other creative competitions that encourage very young children to perform 'sexiness' in public and reward them (and their parents who dress, drive, pay the fees and champion their little troupers from back or front of stage). Criticise these, draw attention to the deeply disturbing representations and performances of sexiness and you find yourself labelled a wowser, as someone who is trying to spoil what is healthy, good for the children's self-esteem and promoting clean family fun. I discuss this in greater detail in Chapter Three.

Children of the past accessed the adult world through exposure to grown-up concepts, conversation and ideas. There's no doubt that this is happening again as well. Only this time, the information isn't being filtered through or coming from parents, family, friends and neighbours alone. It's not the collective wisdom of generations being passed down for our children to process. It's random, fast and furious. It's coming from faceless strangers who make all sorts of irresistible promises. Bombarded with messages and contradictory ideas from everywhere, kids are being persuaded that by looking older, prettier, being more feminine, masculine, sexy, famous or being the first to follow a trend, purchase this and that, a passport to social acceptance, popularity and success is theirs. Being a 'winner' as opposed to a 'loser' has become a psychological threat that hovers over children's and parents' heads. Journalist Marly Harris writes that the 'massive restructuring of the economy creates a winner-take-all society in which parents believe that if kids don't end up as one of the few winners they will join the ranks of the many losers'.[75]

While peer groups existed in the past, children today are exposed to and influenced by the opinions and tastes of their age group in ways that were unheard of and unavailable in the past. As Hanawalt records:

> No full-fledged youth subculture in which peers were the chief influence on an adolescent's life existed in the Middle Ages. While youth occasionally rioted, dressed in distinctive styles, and had some holidays reserved for its own fun, these activities were neither organized nor pervasive cultural events, as they became in late-nineteenth-and-twentieth-century Europe and America.[76]

The peer groups our children are a part of these days have expanded to include virtual groups via the internet and mobile phones, celebrities and other media and pop culture idols. These are often people we've never met and, though we read about and see them, we're not always aware (until it's too late) of the kind of influence they're wielding.

Lots of parents have been persuaded to believe that keeping up with the Joneses, especially visible and famous ones, is a way to guarantee their kids a house on Easy Street. The problem is that all of this escalates until childhood has evaporated and we are left with children who look like adults but lack the common sense, emotional nous or experience to match.

Why We Need Childhood

Childhood has always been the foundation upon which we build adult lives. It's the time in life when morals, values and ethics are formed and most likely set. It's a time for exploring, imagining, testing and taking risks; where kids can try on a variety of identities for size. However, instead of setting boundaries and controlling to the best of our ability the level of information and thus imaginative and mental stimulation our kids are accessing, we're throwing up our hands, admitting defeat and looking for someone else to blame.

While our children are young, there's no-one else to blame. Not the teacher, the babysitter, the childcare centre, the marketers who target us and our children with unrealistic promises, the media or popular culture. The buck stops with us. And that's the difference between the past and present. Just because children are once again being treated as miniature or imperfect adults doesn't make it right. We have learned from history – or we should have. But just as we don't want to return to a 1950s family model, neither do we wish to go back to a 1350s model. We know that it's important to value our children and childhood and protect their innocence, not in the maudlin way the Romantics did or in an unrealistic manner that lacks respect and awareness, or as a way to deny abuse and exploitation, but in a sensible and responsible way that takes into account children's rights and their cognitive and physical development. After all, it's important we learn from the past, not replicate its mistakes. Through a combination of factors, ranging from exposure to adult and other worlds, and associated ideas, sexualisation, material goods and confusion over the roles of parents, teachers and adults, childhood today *is* disappearing: it's being consumed and consequently stolen from our children and us. It's being made sexy, toxic and hard work and we need to do something about it now.

I don't think it's at all useful to try to build off-ramps along the information highway, creating detours and cocooning our kids from the real world. Society can be a terrible worry for adults, parents and children, but it's not helpful for anyone to hear continual criticism and denigration of, first, parents and, second, children's culture specifically and more broadly popular culture. Television, computers, iPods, the internet and all those other technologically amazing products we fill our lives with are not going to go away. They are here to stay and we either have to learn to live with them or *through* them. Because, no matter how much we whinge and wish them gone, unless you join an Amish community, you won't be able to live without them.

What we need to do, even for a while, is cast aside our negativity and imagine a world in which screen and popular culture are our friends – not the enemy they're made out to be. I'm constantly bewildered by the number of adults I meet who will rage against various forms of popular culture (from Harry Potter and pop music to *Big Brother*) without having read a word, listened to a lyric, watched the program or, more importantly, asked kids why they like it and what they're getting out of it. If you do, you might be surprised what you learn. Used correctly, popular culture can give you access to a child's world and, believe it or not, to your children as well. All you need is time, patience and a bit of knowledge.

Childhood Protection

I believe in protecting childhood – not in the walled garden or stifling way, but in a responsible manner that allows children to imaginatively and intellectually grow into a world where, for the overwhelming majority of their lives, they will be adults. That's where we can take a valuable leaf out of history's book: we need to raise our children with the knowledge that they're growing into adults. As simple and obvious as that seems, I think we've lost sight of that. We've become so caught up in the apparently complex notion of 'parenting', so anxious and obsessed with making childhood magical; or imbuing it with advantages, adult messages, ideas and lessons; or cramming everything into those few years and getting it out of the way as fast as possible that we're not only spoiling it, we're stealing it away. I can tell you now our kids won't thank us for it. They won't thank us for the computers, five TVs and four mobile phones that all our hard work and absences provided. They won't thank us for the after-school and weekend lessons and competitions that meant we never saw them. But they *will* thank us if we spend time with them and, through example, teach them how to have functional, loving relationships with other adults and children, to respect others, animals and the environment and to reflect on, ponder and tune out of this fast-paced digital world occasionally. They will also thank us if we teach them good manners and how to critically think about culture, and instil in them a sense of dignity, a good work ethic and the ability to function as part of a team or individually.

By giving children some of our 'precious' time, prioritising their needs – not over ours, but over the other demands that life makes of us – then we will return childhood to our children. In the following chapters, I help you understand all those other media and cultural forms – those so-called enemies – that our children engage with, adore and feel are essential to their sense of self and wellbeing. I'll show you how to restore balance to your life and theirs and how to stop your children becoming sexy tots who grow into savvy tweens and tortured teens – in other words, young people who have had their childhood consumed.

chapter two

'Bling, Bling, Why Don't You Give Me a Ho?': The Commercial Theft of Childhood

The Corporate Takeover of Childhood

While we're busy worrying about whether we're seeing the end of childhood as we know it, the corporate giants who produce and distribute all the adult and sexy 'stuff' our children engage with are turning a tidy profit. Acknowledging young people as a lucrative demographic, they're aiming advertising and entire campaigns straight at our children. By appealing to children's insecurities (and ours) and persuading them that, by owning, using, wearing, eating or listening to certain brands or artists, they'll be popular and, most importantly, 'fit in', they've turned our tweens and teens (and there's even a new corporate demographic emerging, which I'll explore in Chapter Four) into some of the biggest spenders in the world. Using what they call 'age compression',[1] which Susan Gregory Thomas defines as 'the imposition of older children's cognitive, emotional and cultural issues onto younger ones',[2] marketers are deliberately pushing teen attitudes and adult concepts onto children. Recognising that children influence between $600 billion[3] and $1.8 trillion[4] a year in spending, this drive 'to make advertising more relevant to kids'[5] is not about to stop. And that's only referring to the money children pester us into spending on everything from their clothes and toys to the family car, not their actual pocket money, which is estimated for the tween age group in the UK at US$2.7 billion a year and in the US at US$121 billion.[6] In Australia, the tween market is worth over A$4 billion dollars per year.[7] Now that's a big market indeed.

Prior to the mid-1960s, parents mediated and facilitated their children's expenditure. This has all changed and accelerated over recent years – through direct advertising to children, particularly during children's TV shows, but also through mobile phones, the internet and children's magazines, and that's just for starters. In all these spheres, marketers get to speak directly to our kids and this is orchestrated by, as Phillip Adams writes, 'highly paid executives who recognise no age of consent'.[8] Michael Brody, from the American Academy of Child and Adolescent Psychiatry, provocatively states, 'Marketers have become child experts, just like paedophiles'.[9]

Research from the US says that not only are children bombarded with over 40,000 commercial messages a year on television alone,[10] but also they're requesting brands as soon as they can talk.[11] This suggests that, even though they don't have the words, tots are developing positive feelings towards toys and licensed merchandise from TV and films. As soon as they *can* speak, they ask for specific brands. Forget 'da-da', now it's 'Elmo' or 'Dora' or 'Dolce and Gabbana'. It's called grabbing a 'mind share' of the market – our children's minds – and while they're still in nappies.[12] Corporations are lodging themselves in our kids' psyche and establishing a loyal fan base on which future spending can be built. That's pretty scary. It's also part of the reason the American Academy of Pediatrics opposes any TV programs that target children under the age of two. Their view is that these shows may also be designed to market products,[13] and very young children are unable to recognise persuasion. Susan Gregory Thomas reassures us that a child's inability to discern a marketing tactic has nothing to do with his or her level of intelligence; on the contrary, 'it's indicative of a developmental milestone corresponding with age level'.[14] Experts generally agree that it's not until a child is eight that they're able to understand (and, indeed, be critical of) a commercial and its often abstract narrative but clear intentions.[15]

Once a child reaches their tweens, however, they're very much in the corporate eye. Establishing brand recognition and preference becomes, for commercial enterprises, paramount. As Martin Lindstrom, the author of the book *Brand Child* (basically a marketers' guide to capturing the lucrative tween demographic), states, 'Brands have become an integral part of the way tweens define themselves'.[16] The process of 'branding' is a serious business. Independent marketing and branding consultant Matt Haig describes it as an important 'art' and likens it to religion because it possesses characteristics such as faith, omnipresence, gurus, goodness, purity, places of worship (for example, Disneyland and Nike Towns), icons (such as Paris Hilton and David Beckham) and miracles (new bodies, friends and happiness).[17] The more 'converts', the more successful the brand and, consequently, the business.

While *we* may be able to ignore all the logos and brands that smother us, children either don't want to or can't. Don't believe me? Ask your kids to recite the number for Pizza Hut, Eagle Boys or Dominos – I can and I *never* eat takeaway pizza. Kids can also tell you the current slogan for Coca-Cola, Nike, McDonald's and a whole range of other products I'll bet you didn't even know existed. Brands, logos, toys, clothes and other 'stuff', and everything they represent in children's lives, define their world and, as they get older, their friendship groups as well. According to *New Internationalist* magazine, an 'international marketing survey (which included Majority World countries like India and Brazil) found that half of urban eight- to 14-year-olds thought that their clothing brands described who they are'.[18] Lindstrom quotes an 11-year-old girl who declares, 'I love brands. Brands are my life. Brands not only tell me who I am, but also protect me from problems with others in my class'.[19] This child is not alone in uttering these sentiments – they are shared among her peers and by those in other age groups.[20]

Children will plead with parents, grandparents and other adults in their lives to buy certain brands because either someone else also has them or they'll look stupid or be left out and possibly picked on if they don't own a specific product. More importantly, we surrender to our children's demands and buy the brand-name product even though our wallet is anorexic and our credit cards are wailing as they're swiped through the machine. This ready (or reluctant) capitulation has created what Monash University psychologist Dr Simon Crisp describes as 'a culture of instant gratification'.[21] The commercial world is aware of this and structures campaigns to grab the attention of both children and parents – especially mothers who, with children in the zero to three age range (never mind older age groups), are not only the primary purchaser of the products, they're also the 'gatekeeper'. Filled with guilt about being career-focused or determined to fill their children's lives with 'things' they lacked when young, these parents and carers are, to big business, little more than a relatively easy and lucrative target.[22]

In many ways, we're making it so easy for the corporations. Not only do we buy the stuff but, as a society, we clamp down on public spaces where kids, especially teens, can socialise and just 'hang out', like neighbourhood parks or streets, and push them into sprawling malls where, on the one hand, we think they're safe but, on the other, they're continually exposed to consumer culture. In our ever-expanding universe of shopping malls, kids get to see, taste, touch, hear, smell and experience new products, people and thus ideas about themselves. Of course, these ideas come with a caveat: they have to own the product to really have the experience and fulfil their dreams. This is called 'shoppertainment',[23] an unhealthy conflation of shopping and fun, where buying becomes a form of self-discovery. Kids don't climb trees anymore, they shop.

Susan Gregory Thomas takes this notion even further. She identifies the change in the relationship between shopping, popular culture and family/child interactions as coinciding with wider cultural changes that occurred in the late 1970s and early 1980s (including the toy-licensing phenomenon started by George Lucas's *Star Wars*), such as single working parents and 'latch-key children'. She argues that this period 'marked the start of a permanent change in kids' marketing … advertisers actively strove to separate parent and child, aiming to divide and conquer. To marketers, it was the birth of the "nag factor". But in the broader social context, the chief point of the connection between parents, children, and toys was no longer in playing together: it was in buying something'.[24]

Aware of the importance of shopping in children's lives, major corporations such as Rupert Murdoch's News Corp, Disney, Viacom (which owns Nickelodeon and MTV), Universal Vivendi, and AOL/Time Warner (referred to as the 'Merchants of Cool' because they 'are responsible for selling nearly all of youth culture'[25]) and Mattel[26] hire groups of savvy, mid-twenties to mid-thirties men and women, along with child psychologists, whose sole purpose within the organisation is to discover and invent trends for kids and work out ways of selling these. Given the name 'Cool Hunters',[27] they perceive their mission as being akin to an ethnographic study as they interview carefully selected tweens and adolescents, often going into their homes, in an attempt to understand what makes them tick.[28] Then, armed with various bits of information and some pseudo-science, they create an appealing campaign for a product luring our kids into believing that certain brands really do equal 'cool' and that filling any void in your life with things is the way to achieve contentment and success.

Paramount in all of this is the notion of sex. Not necessarily the act, though that's there too, but the associated ideas and imagery. Sex sells and not just to adults. Children are being exposed to notions of sex, sexuality and sexiness, often before they're old enough to understand what it is they're seeing, hearing and learning. In his provocative documentary *Decadence: Part Two – Sex*, Pria Viswalingam says that, 'sex has been hijacked from the bedroom and made to sell everything to every man and his dog. It's the great prostitution of intimacy, the seduction of innocence'.[29] What's of concern is that it's our children's innocence that's being both seduced and consumed.

Sexessorising 101

What children are being taught, whether it's through buying clothes, gadgets and other paraphernalia that are marketed directly to them, is that not only is shopping an important act in itself, but being sexy is too.

As US critic Dr Jean Kilbourne noted on her visit to Australia in 2006, 'teach a seven-year-old that sex is about accessorising and you've secured a life-time of lingerie buying. If you dissociate sex from non-market feelings – pleasure, desire, intimacy – and associate it with consumable superficialities, you'll not only keep the rabble in line, you'll have them lined up at the mall'.[30]

Without even knowing what 'sexy' is, our children are buying 'it' – purchasing the products (or begging their parents to) that their 'sexy' peers and older counterparts in the advertisements, magazines, TV shows, films and music are selling – and it's the corporations that are collecting. It doesn't help that young pop stars are unapologetic about their overtly sexual personas or that they use terms like 'empowering' to justify their raunchy image. Former Disney Mouseketeer, songstress Christina Aguilera says that 'it's really empowering for a woman in this day and age to come across as overtly sexual in a strong way and be unashamed'.[31] While being comfortable with your sexuality is important for men and women of all ages, that's a completely different notion to inviting tweens and young teens to both watch a celebrity flaunting a version of 'sexiness' in the public arena and adopt his or her style – particularly when it's a very reductive understanding of the concept.

In the introduction to their book *Packaging Girlhood: Rescuing Our Daughters from Marketers' Schemes*, Sharon Lamb and Lyn Mikel Brown claim that the number of sexual scenes on TV has doubled since 1998.[32] Children, particularly teens, are being exposed to a range of benign and loving sexual acts and often sensitive discussion about whether or not and when to have sex, but they're also confronted with sexually sadistic practices, sexual crimes (including murder), 'girl-on-girl' action (usually performed by 'straight' characters to titillate male characters (and the audience), and sex toys, never mind gratuitous and unfulfilling sex where women and men 'perform'. Lamb and Brown are blunt when they state that children are learning about sex from two sources: friends and the media.[33] The problem is that what they're learning from these sources is basic and stereotyped and removed from the all-important context of emotions and pleasure. But this doesn't seem to matter. This is because knowledge about sex and a specific performance of 'sexiness' give even very young people power and social currency in their peer groups.

When asked if she ever used the word 'sexy', 11-year-old Jessica said 'yes'. She explained that her friends would talk about each other and celebrities such as Hilary Duff that way. When asked what 'sexy' meant, she immediately answered, 'pretty, hot and popular'. I thought this was a very good definition, suggesting that, while young children rarely associate the word 'sexy' with the sexual act, they nonetheless link it to attitudes and perceptions that are important in their clique-ridden world. I also asked Jessica what 'hot' meant; after hesitating (and I had to reassure her that this wasn't a test – there was no right or wrong answer), she said 'pretty and popular ... in fact, sexy and hot mean the same thing'. She's right.

Lamb and Brown state that 'the beginning of a genuine movement to give girls more power and more choice got co-opted and turned into a marketing scheme that reinforced age-old stereotypes'. They add that both boys and girls are now 'ready to be sold a version of mini-teendom that eclipses the wonderful years of childhood which truly belong to them'.[34] The marketers have done their work. From an increasingly younger age, children (little girls especially, but not exclusively) are negotiating ways in which they can be perceived by their peers as pretty and popular because in their minds these secure them a place with the exclusive 'in' crowd.[35] Acting and talking like they're older, these kids are both playing and seriously trying on adult identity for size. While at one level this is something we've always done, at another it's being enacted outside family boundaries, upon each other and in public. The cost of the loss of adult safety nets and role models to children's emotional and psychological development is potentially very high.

Professor Michael Carr-Gregg, child psychologist and author, warns us that kids today are 'being prematurely empowered by a combination of physical maturity, powerful peer groups and a mass marketing machine that makes them feel more sophisticated and more able than they actually are. They look like young adults but they don't have the skills to match'.[36] Through the advertising and media surrounding them, and because of accommodating, well-meaning parents, kids are being fast-tracked through childhood before they have the emotional, psychological and cognitive skills to cope. It's a contemporary paradox – they're not old enough to drink, drive or vote, but young people are old enough to drive adult desires and invigorate a jaded marketplace.[37]

What must children be thinking and dreaming about these days to even want to begin playing in the adult world or try on 'sexiness' for size? There seems to be a quantum leap from dolls to *Dolly* magazine, from trucks to truckin'. The rite of passage that saw kids slowly segue from cute cuddly toys or Matchbox cars to Barbie and Ken, to dreams of being swept off their feet by a romantic hero and loved and adored (for girls) and the first shag (for boys and probably some girls) is a gap that in youngsters' play and speech at least appears to be rapidly closing.

These are the fears I believe many adults are really expressing when they bemoan the loss of childhood. Not that their sexy tots will attract paedophiles (they'll be around no matter how we dress our kids – remember, they sexualise them regardless), but that they are *thinking* about sexiness (being pretty and popular by dressing and acting a particular way and through owning certain things) and all the concomitant pressures this implies in the first place. Some of those fears can be irrational and misguided, but there are a few professional voices being raised to dismiss parents, teachers and other citizens concerns as trivial. This is unfair and invalidates very genuine worries.

As American psychologist Susan Linn writes, 'the sheer volume of advertising to which children are exposed, the values embedded in the marketing messages, and the behaviours those messages inspire'[38] can be quite overwhelming for parents and carers and they can feel very alone. Hugh Mackay also acknowledges that 'parents ... are members of a community dealing with a generalised sense of anxiety, and anxiety about the well-being of children is bound to be one of the most vivid forms of its expression'.[39] Voices that dismiss these worries without examining the social, cultural and psychological context or offering explanations as to where and why these anxieties arise are simply voices in the wilderness, exacerbating the fears, guilt and embarrassment of adults, instead of extinguishing them.

In many ways, our society is so hypocritical; *we* are hypocritical. We rail and despair against stories about paedophiles – the fact they exist and that after serving too short a time they're released back into our communities, possibly to threaten the safety of our children and families. Together, we gather and talk in shocked whispers about the JonBenet Ramsey case, about teachers, clergy and family members abusing trust and hurting and defiling those in their care. We express outrage, disgust and demand justice. We generate what some commentators refer to as a 'sexual panic' around kids, their sexualisation and paedophiles.[40]

Then, we go to the shops and buy bralettes and French knickers for our three-year-old daughters. We allow our nine-year-old to wear make-up and a midriff top to the mall. We think it's amusing when our seven-year-old son imitates his favourite rapper and wears bling around his neck and describes girls as 'bitches' and 'hos'. We also encourage our sons and daughters to participate in dance competitions and mock-idol contests at school where they swivel, pout and sing of lost love, wanting to touch someone and sexual desperation. They're usually dressed in skimpy clothes, wearing cosmetics and adopting facial expressions that mimic sexual promise. To gain some 'me' time or grab an extra few minutes in bed on a Saturday morning, we allow them to watch an M/MA movie or a music video show filled to the brim with images of women and men being sexual, or to surf the net unsupervised. But that's okay – after all, what harm is there in any of that, especially when they're at home?

Potentially, a great deal.

When paedophiles or abuse cases hit the headlines, we're horrified that these things can happen. But at the same time, we're complicit in eroding childhood through the sexualisation and marketing to and of kids in all sorts of other ways. From the way we dress them in public, to the reading and viewing material we enable them to access, to the kinds of examples we set ourselves by approving and buying one sort of display, clothes and products and decrying others.

We pay lip-service to the loss of childhood, and yet do very little in real terms to prevent it from happening. It's as though we believe 'innocence' and 'child' exist in a symbiotic relationship whether we interfere or not. This isn't true. Innocence is something that adults have to protect and preserve. It's not natural. In fact, these days, it's as much a marketing ploy as it's an adjective. It's used to return to adults a sense of lost childhood and reassure them that no matter what the marketers throw in our kids' direction, they'll be fine – they're innocent.[41] Not for long. 'Innocence' and 'innocent' are terms used to mask the exploitative intentions and a range of very problematic and sexual images of children in our culture regardless of their age or cultural background.

Corporate Paedophilia

In 1996, *The Australian* columnist Phillip Adams wrote a very disturbing piece about the way large corporations deliberately target young people and sexualise them, through clothes, films and a range of other products and ideas. In 2006, he addressed the same problem again, this time in conjunction with the Australia Institute Report, written by Dr Emma Rush and Andrea La Nauze, which I'll discuss in more detail in the next chapter. Describing what he calls 'corporate paedophilia', Adams writes, 'The targeting of ever-younger children by marketers determined to turn kids into customers, into little economic units, [is] a new form of child labour. Whereas children in Victorian England had been sent down coalmines and shoved up chimneys, we sent ours into the satanic mills of the shopping malls – to influence what their parents bought, or to buy junk in their own right'.[42]

Adams's comments are a call to arms for all adults concerned about our children's imaginations and their childhoods. But what has happened? Not much. Instead, we've all become complacent and even indifferent to what's happening under our very noses. Critics of Emma Rush and her colleagues were quick to retaliate against the report and, indeed, Rush herself. It was a case of shooting the messenger rather than heeding the message. Why? We've become so accustomed to the marketing to our children and their corporate sexualisation that we not only ignore or defend it, we unwittingly (or knowingly) participate in it. So much so that we engage in what I call 'cultural paedophilia'.[43]

Cultural Paedophilia

Instead of labelling specific abnormal individuals, paedophiles, as being responsible for the sexualisation of our kids, or corporate culture for that matter, the term 'cultural paedophilia' inculcates the whole of society: you, me and everyone else. This may seem unfair, but let's think about it for a moment. Every time we buy our kids the sexy clothes their 'friends are all wearing', and allow our tweens to wear make-up, display 'attitude' and emulate adult role models and celebrities in public, we're complicit in the sexualisation of our kids. By inadvertently turning our young girls and boys into nymphets and inviting other people to look at them this way, we engage in and endorse cultural paedophilia. But it gets worse. In devouring the multiple images of 'sexy' boys and girls, purchasing the products, and watching the programs and films alongside our kids, we're giving the market forces justification for perpetuating them as well. This is our problem. This is cultural paedophilia.

We have to stop right now. We have to stop the commercial theft of our kids' childhood through sexualisation before it's too late.

Corporate culture has taken over childhood and youth and turned them into products that people of any age – from six to 66 – can buy and own. Adults are encouraged to embrace their 'inner' child, whether it be through what they wear, the games they play, the self-help books they buy, the food they eat (think of the McDonald's campaign where various adults, in the midst of their workday, are frozen in time and their 'inner child' literally emerges from their chests (hearts) and searches for fast food to succour them), or through plastic surgery. Certain clothing outlets market T-shirts, underwear and pyjamas in adult sizes, sprinkled with SpongeBob SquarePants, Mr Men and Little Misses, or well-known Dr Seuss and Warner Brothers characters.[44] The advertisements are cutesy, colourful and feature women with their hair tied in bunches and looking decidedly 'adulescent'. Called 'retro' or 'newstalgia'[45] it's also a way of recapturing for adults their younger years.

Fond memories are being turned into an expensive commodity.

We've become caught up in what has been described as 'generational blurring', where the boundary between adult and child has all but dissolved.[46] While this might be fun for the adults (though that's debatable too – I mean, how 'good' is it for a 30-year-old to still be living at home), it's incredibly damaging for children who are being emotionally and psychologically accelerated into adulthood before they're ready and then have to watch the adults enjoying revisiting their own childhoods in all sorts of ways.

While it's all right to remain 'young at heart', it's not all right to remain stuck in a time warp, abrogate adult responsibilities to the kids in your life and refuse to grow up. There can only be one set of kids in a family and those kids need adults to act as role models and provide guidance. Those adults need to be sensible (but not draconian) and ensure that what their children are getting access to is developmentally and age-appropriate as best as they can. And that means resisting the promises and allure of the advertisers and marketers, controlling your child's exposure to sexy notions and redefining those generational boundaries.[47] Hugh Mackay believes that many parents forget to draw the line between themselves and their kids. He writes that 'we need to remember that, in the end, parents are not obliged to be their children's friends (and, by the way, they're not obliged to be sporting or academic coaches either); they're parents and discipline is part of their responsibility to their children. Loving our kids doesn't mean giving in to them, pretending to share their taste in music, fashion or even friends, or refusing to express legitimate feelings of irritation, disappointment or outrage'.[48] And that includes saying 'no' to stuff.

Cradle-to-Grave Consumerism

Another strategy corporations deploy is developing brand loyalty in consumers. They use all sorts of tactics to instil a cradle-to-grave devotion.[49] While I mentioned it earlier in relation to tots and a mindshare, the intention is more invidious and much longer lasting. Cradle-to-grave refers to having potential consumers think about and desire a product so much that they become convinced they can't 'live' without it and develop a loyalty towards the brand that they'll not only pass on to friends, but eventually to their own children as well.

What also happens, as Susan Linn observes, is that 'the culture of marketing that pervades all our communities, from the poorest to the richest, is similar in that it competes with parental values for children's hearts, minds and souls'.[50] This is why the 'nag factor' is such a potent tactic for marketers to nurture. Understanding that most adults want to please children, marketers deliberately educate children on how to pester them. Elana Morales has found that 'children's nagging is assessed as up to 46 per cent of sales in key businesses that target children'. In one study, 150 mothers of children aged three to eight years kept diaries noting their children's requests for toys and other objects over a fortnight. There was a total of 10,000 nags – an average of 66 per mother or 4.7 a day. Another survey with 750 children aged 12–17 found that on average, kids nag nine times before their parents cave in and give them what they want.[51] (Think Bart and Lisa Simpson. They nag their father so often – for example, 'Can we go to Mount Splashmore?' – and Homer says 'no'. They ask again and again until he concedes. The questioning, which becomes a common theme in the series, is actually rhetorical. The kids know Homer will acquiesce to their demands.) This nagging and subsequent resistance (or capitulation), also called pester-power, causes conflict in so many families. Disputes between adults and children and between adults themselves are inevitable, as mothers, fathers, grandparents and other relatives and friends have very different responses to nagging and purchasing requests. The tension this can cause is enormous and the only victors are the corporations competing for children's hearts.[52] This is something advertisers are more than aware of, otherwise, as Linn states, they wouldn't spend so much money on it.[53]

Three books that clearly exploit advertising-speak, pseudo-psychology and children's (and adult) insecurities are *The Kids Market*, *The Great Tween Buying Machine* and one I've already mentioned, *Brand Child*. These books (and there is a veritable library of them – these are simply a selection) are written to educate and coach advertisers and corporations about how to access the lucrative twin markets of kids and tweens. That's right: our children. The tween book discusses such issues as how advertisers can relate to specific tween needs such as 'power, fun, freedom or belonging'.[54] The books also acknowledge that kids (four to seven) and tweens (eight to 12) have different goals, warning that 'you can't create a campaign for one and hope it will work for the other, because you'll fail'.[55] *Brand Child* offers gems such as informing marketers that brand loyalty can be established in children as young as two, and that 'each lifetime consumer is worth US$100,000 to a retailer, making effective cradle-to-grave strategies extremely valuable'.[56] The author also enthusiastically declares that communities based on a shared appreciation of brands 'may very well become the preferred virtual playground of tomorrow ...'.[57]

Brand Imprinting

Instilling brand awareness, or 'imprinting',[58] is occurring at a younger and younger age. As stated earlier, recent research reveals that children are asking for brands as soon as they can speak – often based on beloved characters from TV shows such as *Sesame Street*, *Hi-5* or *The Wiggles*, but also superheroes, even though they may never have seen a superhero movie, TV show or read a comic. For example, in a recent issue of the magazine *Little Friends*, which describes itself as 'The no. 1 learning tool for preschoolers', there is a full-page advertisement for an 'itsy bitsy Spider-Man' doll that sings and dances. It's marketed to adults as a way of encouraging children to join in and learn to sing. The songs it plays are, appropriately, 'Itsy Bitsy Spider' and the 'Spider Man and Friends

Theme'.[59] Even before our kids are old enough to attend school let alone watch a superhero movie, they're inculcated in the Marvel brand and know the theme song, and we all feel positive about it. Alissa Quart quotes advertising 'guru' James McNeal, who advises those trying to attract the kid market to understand that, 'If children are made to feel warm and fuzzy about a store or brand or product, they will bond with it. When they reach market age for that store or brand product, they will logically migrate toward it'.[60] Because memories of childhood are now comfortably interwoven with the 'friendly neighbourhood Spiderman', our kids become trapped in a marketing web.

Brands are everywhere, from children's underwear, clothing, toys, food and other consumables such as drink, to general merchandise like books, school bags, plastic bags and something as mundane as wallets and iPod covers. They're also associated with places, from stationery chain-stores, such as the very popular Smiggle brand to Disney shops, related film merchandise outlets and theme parks. Celebrities are also linked with brands – from the Hollywood star Hugh Jackman spruiking the benefits of Fox satellite television, to Hilary Duff's 'Duff Stuff' or Kylie Minogue's 'Love Kylie' underwear range made by Holeproof (now also available for kids). It's very difficult for a brand-conscious parent to avoid buying one let alone exposing their children to the variety available. We dress, eat, purchase, drive, travel, entertain ourselves and even make choices according to brands. It's no wonder we also, to varying degrees, define ourselves and others through the same visual and aesthetic system. It's ubiquitous. And we're all, both children and adults, becoming walking billboards for the corporations as we work, think, study, play and even dream in brands.

The Power Is Yours

Susan Linn persuasively argues that 'a few giant corporations control much of what children eat, drink, read and play with each day'.[61] She'd have us believe we can do very little about this.

She's wrong.

The corporations don't control *anything* our kids do – not our tots and not our tweens ... and, if we've instilled a strong sense of self and good values and ethics in our kids, the corporations don't control our teens either. Not in any lasting sense anyhow. We control what our kids eat, drink, read and play with each day. And, while it may have originated from the corporations somewhere along the line, it's filtered through us – or it should be. Just because our kids recite the logos, sing the jingles, ask for the trendiest gear, or try to copy the antics of Paris Hilton or maybe even Nikki Webster, in the end it's us they look up to and, for a good portion of their childhood, listen to as well. As a recent Australian survey proves, the overwhelming majority of kids see their parents as heroes and role models.[62]

The verdict is in: we have the power. Now let's use it.

Fortunately, this is a conclusion that a number of people and organisations in the Western world have reached. In Greece, toys can't be advertised between 7 a.m. and 10 p.m.; Quebec bans advertising to children under 13; and Norway and Sweden ban advertising aimed at children under 12.[63] There is also the American Psychological Association's Task Force on the Sexualization of Girls[64] and the Campaign for a Commercial-Free Childhood (CCFC), which is located at the Judge Baker Children's Center in Boston.[65] Sue Palmer's book *Toxic Childhood* lists many organisations in Britain[66] and Susan Linn notes websites and organisations in the back of her book *Consuming Kids*.[67] There is also the Parents Jury[68] and, most recently in Australia, the Kids Free 2b Kids (kf2bk) campaign, established in 2007 by a Melbourne mother of two, Julie Gale.[69]

Disturbed by what she describes as the 'bombardment and saturation' of sexualised imagery to kids through billboards, toys, magazines, clothing and advertising, Gale decided to be proactive. For Gale, 'when the community remains silent, they are effectively condoning the sexualised environment, and the subsequent impact this has on children'. Launching her kf2bk campaign, Gale was overwhelmed by what she describes as 'passionate emails from people who are extremely concerned with the ways children are being influenced and manipulated by the media and popular culture'. She says that so many report feeling 'powerless to make a difference, but want their voices heard nonetheless'. Her ultimate aim is to follow models successfully practised in other countries where direct marketing to children under 12 is banned. A comedian by profession and an articulate and forthright person, Gale is strong in her convictions that 'children need to be left alone to experience childhood in all its complexities as children ... not as commodities'.[70]

From Pester-Power to Parent Power

Are our kids being sexualised through marketing? Yes. Are they being filled with adult ideas before they're cognitively or developmentally ready? Yes. But to make the corporations and popular culture alone responsible is to deny *us* the power to change anything. We helped it happen and we can change it.

And here are some sensible, easy strategies as to how we, as parents, teachers and adults, can bring about these changes.

While your children are still tots, it's important to get in the habit of sharing their world, but not in a smothering or dominating sense – I use the term 'sharing' very carefully here. As Sue Palmer states, 'Parenting is not just about looking inward, at the children in the centre of the family; it's about looking outward at the world where those children, and successive generations of children, will grow and live'.[71] Spend time reading, watching their TV shows (but don't expose them to too much TV before they're two years of age; see Chapter Six), surfing the net, playing games, and just chatting with them. As you talk, discuss the messages – both positive and negative – that these things relay. Think about what values they're reinforcing or undermining and be supportive or critical of them in ways your kids understand. Laugh about what's being shown; mock it if necessary. Reinforce that it's *who* you are and not what you look like or *have* that counts. If you start this early in a child's life, it will continue. There may be gaps when they retreat into their tortured teen world, but they'll return. Don't suffocate them with questions. As they get older, respect their need for space. They'll know that they can come to you and discuss anything – whether it's the latest Gameboy on the market or another celebrity exploit.

If your kids insist on a particular brand and you're happy to pay the money for it, think about what values you're establishing. Kids these days identify with brands and feel very strongly that their social status is affected if they don't have the right 'look', toy or object. As much as we might reassure them this is superficial and unnecessary, and also controlled, we don't live in their world. Point out to them just what the corporations are doing, but also ask them why they want that specific T-shirt or brand of underpants. Remember, it's also all right to say 'yes'. Just be aware of what you're saying yes to.

For those of you who can't afford to buy 'brand' names, do what I did. I told my daughter (from the age of nine and up) that if she wanted a brand-name shirt, well, she'd have to pay the difference between what it would have cost me in Target and what it cost in the boutique. She did extra tasks around the home, saved her pocket money and paid the gap amount. While she learned the value of money, I learned just how important brands are to kids' sense of self in group situations. Needless to say, by the time she was 15, brands were no longer important.

Where Are the Milestones?

In allowing ourselves to be influenced by corporate promises and our children's plaintive demands, we often fail to set age-appropriate milestones. They have nothing to look forward to any more. They have no sense of having reached a physical or psychological target, of having achieved a mini life-goal. They get what they want, when they want it, regardless of their age. We reward them for just being kids – sometimes not very nice ones. So, by the time they do get to important ages, like double figures, our kids have already played with every toy suitable for their age group and then some. For example, there are aisles in every discount and high-end department and speciality store with shelves stocked with lip gloss, lipsticks, nail polishes, mascaras, eye shadows and ever other bit of face paint for kids two years and older. Wearing make-up used to be a milestone for a young girl; now it's a part of a child's sense of self. Maria Puente states that every year 'more cosmetic, hair and nail products aimed at tweens appear on store shelves'.[72] Even boys are buying into this, prompting one salon owner, who decided to cater to the tween market by creating a hair and make-up line for self-conscious young males, to refer to this as the 'mini-metrosexual phenomenon'.[73] That's because we buy for five-year-olds what's more suitable for 10-year-olds, for 10-year-olds what's more appropriate for 15-year-olds – and on it goes. Not only do we buy them sometimes inappropriate toys and 'things', but to justify our expense and lack of sense, we champion them wearing and playing with our purchases, even though a part of us recognises that something is askew. Through aspirational marketing, we're encouraged to think of young children as the new tweens and tweens as the new teens, but that doesn't make it right. They might be considered the new 'teens' by marketers, but they're not. It's a marketing category that's been applied by the corporations to target our kids more precisely, arouse and attempt to sate desire in our kids and encourage them to nag the adults in their life. As the website MarketingSherpa states:

> Kids aged 4–7 and tweens aged 8–12 directly influence hundreds of billions of CPG [consumer packaged goods], entertainment, apparel and travel sales each year. Now, learn how you [marketers] can influence them ...[74]

Marketing expert Lindstrom declares: 'There is no difference for grown-up brands and tweens, except that needs and expense take a back seat to appeal'.[75] He also discusses how important it is for a product to appeal to as many senses (sight, touch, taste, sound, smell) as possible to 'indulge the tween imagination' and inculcate life-long brand preferences.[76]

As all adults with kids in their lives know, no two 10-year-olds are the same. Marketers tend to homogenise them into large age groups (tweens and teens), actively urging kids through marketing to think of themselves as older; as Donna Sabino, a group director of research and market development for the Nickelodeon Magazine Group claims,

'Tweens want to think of themselves as teens'.[77] Not only do corporations encourage this, but they want us and our kids to think like a herd. But individually, our kids differ enormously – physically, emotionally, intellectually and cognitively – and it's the adults in the child's life who know this better than anyone, not a suit in an office projecting sales figures or some expert making millions educating marketers through books and the speaking circuit. We need to set the milestones. We shouldn't let ourselves (or our children) get carried away by the seductive promises in an advertisement, logo or jingle, on the back of a cardboard box or in a kids' magazine. Nor should we allow our guilt, usually aroused by an acute awareness of the way long working hours, perpetual tiredness and absence impact upon our kids, to undermine our common sense (though it's understandable why even the most sensible of us sometimes do). Just like Haig, academic James B Twitchwell describes advertising as the 'new' religion, because it promises in this life (the rewards of success and happiness through the purchasing of material goods) what used to be reserved for the hereafter.[78] Guilty, time-poor, overworked and stressed, we fall for the corporate promises and worship at the quick-fix altar of materialism. After all, it keeps the kids quiet and happy (until next time) and gives us a momentary high.

Kids' Magazines

In discussing the reach and influence of various corporations, it wouldn't be right not to devote some space to the growing business of children's magazines. For over 10 years, tween and teen magazines have been in the marketplace. Kids can now have their own glossy printed versions of grown-up magazines, usually strategically placed at supermarket exits and on the lower shelves in newsagents and other stores. Alissa Quart describes them as the 'training wheels of the glossies, [designed to] prepare girls and boys for the day when they move onto *People*, *Vogue*, and *Elle*'.[79] She also calls them 'magalogs' – a cross between a catalogue and a magazine, traversing the line between editorialising and selling.[80] Academic Alan A Block describes them as 'the culture of adults organized for children',[81] with the intention of making a profit. Is this acceptable? Well, that depends on what messages and ideas kids are gleaning from these publications – publications that are, fundamentally, designed to expose kids to fads, fashions and 'things', make them believe that certain looks equate to success and popularity, and make adults part with money to appease the kids.

A range of magazines targeting girls as young as six are very popular. According to the Australia Institute, 'Each month, twenty per cent of six-year-old girls and almost half of ten- and eleven-year-old girls read at least one of the most popular girls' magazines – *Barbie Magazine*, *Total Girl* and *Disney Girl*'.[82] Disturbingly, the Institute also found that, in 2006, '75 per cent of the content of *Barbie* magazine – aimed at five- to 12-year-olds – is sexualising material, as is half of *Total Girl* (eight to 11 years), and *Disney Girl* (six to 13 years)'.[83] There are the magazines pitched to boys, such as *K-Zone* and *Disney Adventures* (also read by girls if the letters sent to the editor are any indication), while *Girl Power*, *Little Angel*, the ones listed above and other magazines of this type are aimed mainly at girls. Produced in a small format, making them convenient for storage (in school bags particularly) and easy to read, they're covered with pictures of pop stars, celebrities and animated or film characters, sheathed in plastic and contain a ubiquitous 'free gift'. Of the 50 or so tween and teen magazines I've bought over a period of three years, the gifts range from a stopwatch, 'Uglies' biscuits (with 70 grams of sugar per 100 grams!), Ovalteenies and a Batman gadget, to bracelets, bobby pins, key rings (including a mobile phone lip gloss keyring), tote bags, make-up purses, necklaces, and the list continues. There are also film promotions (and, in *K-Zone*, a separate book promotion too).

Between the covers of the girl-oriented mags, there are numerous pictures, captions and short stories on celebrities, pop stars, fashion, make-up and films, and even advice on how to conduct friendships and relationships. Post Paris Hilton's well-publicised stint in jail and Lindsay Lohan's time in rehabilitation for alcohol and drug abuse, there are multiple references to those women. In the June 2007 issue of *Total Girl*, Paris is described as 'so hot' (page 46). *Disney Girl's* cover screams 'fun, fashion, friends', and then invites young readers to enter various competitions to be a 'pop star for a day', 'win a phone call from Vanessa [Amorosi]' or become the third member of the singing sisters group The Veronicas. Barbie and Bratz feature heavily, including in segments on fashion and fashion design. Fashion, shopping, celebrities, BFFs (Best Friends Forever), advice, gossip, embarrassing moments, food favourites and advertisements appear throughout all the magazines, which are mostly coloured in a pastiche of pastels.

Looks and the acquisition of things predominate in all these magazines for girls ages six and up, along with celebrities from film, music and TV.

In the boy-oriented equivalents, there are 'facts', jokes, 'weird' information about celebrities, puzzles (which some of the girl mags have as well), and promotional material for films, TV shows and electronic games. Readers are encouraged to send in photos and reveal aspects of themselves as well as write in to ask for help in managing aspects of their lives – in the girls' magazines, this seems to be in relation to friends, boys and parents.

In the 'girl' mags, it's not uncommon to see terms like 'biatch' (bitch) used in reference to other girls or to read about sexual matters. Terms like 'sexy' sprinkle the pages like confetti. While many of the topics covered and images shown are more than appropriate for a teenager, there are years of emotional, psychological and physical difference between a six-year-old and a 14-year-old – yet girls, particularly, between these ages read them (judging by the photos and letters).

Gossip about 'stars' and how to emulate their look and style permeate these mags, blurring the child's world and that of the older celebrity. Susan Hopkins suggests that through these magazines, 'fame has replaced romance as the dominant female fantasy'.[84] Our girl heroes (and, arguably, boys as well) are supermodels, pop stars and actors. Celebrity is the new social currency in the tween world – being able to talk about them, look like them and offer the latest scandal about them. Thus, these mags are the new Bible, the basis of the secular religion of celebrity worship.

Hopkins discusses how in the late 1990s many of the models in these magazines were offered as contemporary girl heroes: 'in control of their own objectification and exploitation'.[85] However, in the June 2007 issue of *Dolly*, there's a double-page spread (pages 39–40) that claims to know 'Which Look Guys Like Best' and reduces girls to four basic stereotypes, making any sense of 'empowerment' contingent on male attention and conformity. The 'look' that men like best was judged to be the 'Boho Babe' – short for Bohemian. In this same issue there's advice on how to be 'schoolyard pretty', including make-up recommendations (despite the fact that the wearing of make-up is discouraged in many schools), as well as 'hottest celeb videos', 'livin' dolls' where you're invited to match a specific celebrity to a doll, and pages of clothes, accoutrements and make-up. There's also a directory at the back (this appears in *Girlfriend* as well), which tells girls how to 'hook up' with strange guys via SMS. Pictures of happy, clean-shaven, good-looking young men and attractive women dominate the advertisements. One even describes linking up with anonymous people as 'flirty, safe and anonymous'. In an era where we continue to express concern about digital relations and our lack of control or knowledge about our kids' access to and maintenance of these relations, ads like these directly undermine parental and adult desire to know with whom and when their children are communicating. Placing them in a magazine with a relatively positive reputation like *Dolly* imbues them, for the young reader, with a sense of safety and legitimacy. For adults, it should make us question the supposed good intentions of the producers who demand a great deal of revenue for such product placement – but at the potential expense of young people's emotional, psychological and even physical welfare.

Dolly is not the only magazine to construct girls and young women as fashion plates who exist only for a diet of celebrity gossip, competitive purchasing and dressing, and a desire to please the opposite sex at the expense of their own.

The June 2007 issue of *Girlfriend* contains an overwhelming emphasis on fashion and shopping, which was supported by a quote from much-admired actor Jessica Alba (star of *Fantastic Four: Rise of the Silver Surfer*) who declares: 'I can't go more than 72 hours without shopping, but I don't think I'm excessive'. *Girlfriend*, a magazine with readers as young as eight, advertises a Playboy giveaway competition where a 'lucky' reader can win one of 10 prize packs featuring two different styles of Playboy T-shirts, stating that 'Playboy is one brand you should include in your wardrobe'.

Playboy is a corporation that, among other interests, produces a men's 'girlie' magazine, which prides itself on 'appreciating' the female nude – that is, paying huge sums of money for women to strip and, thus, objectify themselves by inviting the predominately male gaze (now appropriated as 'empowering', although quite how remains to be adequately explained) – is well known in adult culture. Yet, a magazine designed to appeal to young girls not only aligns itself with this very adult and semi-pornographic brand and thus all it embodies, but also encourages young girls to compete with each other to win prizes from the company. Not only does this normalise what Playboy represents, but it facilitates its benign entry into children's culture and conflates adolescence and a very specific and arguably salacious adult sexuality.

Believing that these mags are harmless and mini versions of what the adults read, many well-meaning parents and other grown-ups purchase them, hoping they'll keep their kids occupied and entertained for a few hours. They do – but they can also, in combination with all the other images and ideas out there, feed children's insecurities and undermine their self-worth and sense of what's important in life. Lamb and Mikel Brown believe that these types of magazines are not only superficial but are harmful to our children, especially our teens:

> The research on girls reading magazines supports this. Psychologists have shown that even with elementary school girls the more they realize that thin and sexy is the ideal, the more they want to attain it, and the less happy they are with themselves.[86]

The number of adults I spoke to who purchased these mags without ever having read a story or even leafed through the contents was astonishing.

Yet again, with parents thinking that because the magazines are marketed to kids they must be all right, the publishing world gets away with producing what many grown-ups would perceive as vacuous and irresponsible rubbish and we buy it to keep our kids happy. Especially our girls.

I'm Just a Girl

Employing the term 'girl' so as to ensure the broadest possible appeal and maintain their status as a 'symbol of cool and a girl's close confidant',[87] the larger format mags aimed at a slightly older audience, such as *Elle Girl, Dolly, Cosmopolitan* and *Vogue Girl*, still try to cast their net as widely as possible. Aware there is a huge gap in their readership (anywhere from under 10 to over 24), the editors nonetheless press home their advantage, exploiting young people's desire to grow up, look older and, concomitantly, be thought older too. As Camille Alarcon notes, 'while six-to-13-year-olds may not be the core readership of the teen magazines, these young, trend-setting early adopters make up a large percentage of the readers for a title such as ... *Girlfriend*'.[88] Social trends that have seen the rise in double-income families and higher rates of pocket money and part-time employment for young people have also meant that teenagers have cash – lots of it – and it's burning a hole in their pockets.

Raised in a commodity culture where identity is as much contingent on what you wear, eat and buy as it is any other less tangible quality, teens are not only keen to participate in this world of facades but to be seen doing so. Taught to be discerning shoppers, they have a veritable smorgasbord of choices.

Mia Freedman, former editor-in-chief of ACP's *Cosmopolitan, Cleo* and *Dolly*, readily admits that the magazines are competing for girls' hard-earned dollars.[89] Nicole Sheffield, youth titles publisher of Pacific Magazines, which publishes *Girlfriend*, acknowledges that 'these kids have moved on from becoming influencers to purchasers'.[90] Harold Mitchell, owner of Australia's biggest media ad space buyer firm, says that Australia's 1.9 million children aged seven to 14 years are worth $1.3 billion dollars annually.[91] Is it any wonder that companies are keen to buy space in these 'tween' mags? Or that the magazines are prepared to tread the very fine line between editorialising and blatant selling?

Quart argues these 'tween' magazines 'construct an unaffordable but palpable world of yearning for girls. We are all too familiar with the negative effects of the model body on girls' self-images, but these new magazines do something new: They help to solidify feelings of economic and taste inadequacy in girls'.[92] Particularly, as Sheffield unashamedly states in one interview, young readers engage 'with ads and enter competitions because "they see advertising as an information source"'.[93]

Pretending to be socially responsibly because they place a story about depression or why diets don't work between their covers, while using the language of sociology and psychology to create appeal and concern, they continue to 'educate' our young about the superficial world of appearances, turning them into 'victims of the contemporary luxury economy'.[94] As Quart writes, raised in 'a commodity culture from the cradle, teens' dependably fragile self-images and their need to belong to groups are perfect qualities for advertisers to exploit'.[95] And they do, FPC magazines sales director Catherine Baglin stating that 'Vogue Girl reflects … how younger and younger girls have developed an appreciation for the value of brands'.[96] This appreciation has been cultivated and honed by corporations, advertisers and their new bedfellow, the growing market of 'children's' magazines.

Of course, not all young people are victims. Raised beneath the watchful eye of corporatism, they're also capable of turning that unrelenting gaze back upon the fiscal vultures or using, as Catherine Lumby and John Hartley astutely note, the representations in an active, not passive way to shape an external (and internal) sense of self.[97] Being young is also about rebellion and rejection of the forces that seek to shape and mould and many young people subvert the market by refusing to be lured by its promises. However, there are still too many very young people, not-so-savvy tweens and tortured teens out there who are becoming caught in a vicious cycle of labour: dollars earned quickly become dollars spent in an effort to keep up with not only wealthier peers, but with a corporate world that promises if you buy this, eat that, discuss this and possess knowledge of that, you'll be popular (with your own sex and, most importantly, the opposite one) and successful and, consequently, accrue a range of rewards. This notion is fostered by the 'free gifts'. But, as the adage goes, nothing in this life is for free, especially when it comes with a price tag.

Magazines like *Elle Girl*, *Dolly*, *Girlfriend*, *Barbie Magazine* and *Vogue Girl* diminish our young through their promises by reducing them to adolescent clothes-horses and telling them that it's all right to focus on the self – outside and in – and forget about others, unless it's how they look. Dr Emma Rush believes that the emphasis on 'ideal' appearances as promoted by so many of these magazines brings forward the agonies of adolescence.[98] So should you buy these magazines for your kids? Again, that's up to you. On the positive side, these magazines can introduce topics for discussion among mothers and daughters, fathers and sons and across the generational and gender divide. Used this way they can facilitate communication and give you the opportunity to offer your version of what's important in relationships, role-models and even looks. But of course, this can only happen if you read the magazine too.

Sex Talks

Whether you read the magazines or not, make sure you discuss issues around sex and sexiness with your children. This is so important. If they know how you feel about it, then that will be reflected in their attitudes. Don't be alarmist and condescending. Thinking and talking about sex is normal for children and it's essential you create a comfort zone around the topic. Very young kids seem to know it's a word that pushes parents' buttons and they'll play with it, in all sorts of ways. Don't overreact, simply respond. Ask them what they know and think about it. Be blunt, but gentle. You'll find very young kids – five to 10 years old – generally roll around the floor laughing and think it's ridiculous or are completely grossed out. But that's better than making it some mystery they want to solve.

Older kids (from about the age of 11 or 12 onwards) actually both long to and loathe having these conversations with the adults in their lives. Their ambivalence may well be reflected back to you as embarrassment or even conflict. As the adult, you have to walk a fine line here – a line between turning it into a science or pornography lesson. I know of many parents and adults who throw books, CDs or DVDs in their kids' directions and say, 'Ask me any questions afterwards!' Teens will have surfed the net, talked to friends and seen or tried many 'things', such as mutual masturbation and oral sex, long before you get around to talking about sex with them, but that doesn't mean you don't have the conversation. It's as much a rite of passage for parents as it is for kids. Don't be too graphic, but do emphasise emotions and feelings. Sex isn't just about reproduction, it's about physical and psychological bonds, pleasure and respect. Part of the problem of sexual representations these days is that too many young girls and boys are taught to think that sex is something that they can have (and frequently) outside a relationship. In the corporate world of products and advertising, sex and objects are combined. Kilbourne warns of the psychological side-effects of using sex to sell products to kids. She believes that 'children learn to associate physical appearance and buying the right products not only with being sexy but also with being successful as a person'.[99]

One study found that one in five young people are having sex before age 14.[100] A survey of 300 Australian young people done by Joan Sauers in 2007 revealed that, by the age of 11 or 12, 3 per cent had experienced oral sex. By 13 or 14 years of age, the figure rose to 24 per cent and, by age 16, more than 50 per cent of girls and 65 per cent of boys had given or received oral sex or both.[101] Learning about the act from popular culture, they naturally want to experiment and earn boasting rights with friends. Oral sex is viewed as better (and safer) than intercourse, even though it can also lead to sexually transmitted diseases, and kids feel they can still claim 'virgin' status. In sex education classes, oral sex is discussed with children in grades six and seven asking about it and wanting to know what it entails. This survey also revealed that our tweens and teens don't like the sex education they're being given. They actually want more emphasis on the non-clinical aspects of sexual relations. As one 18-year-old boy commented, 'They should warn you in school how bad you feel after a one-night stand'.[102] I would suggest that it's not up to the school to deal with these sorts of issues – certainly not in isolation.

It's vital we talk about love and connection – even if we've had bad experiences in our own relationships. We can use them as examples of what not to do. It's also important that we don't leave these types of discussions to school teachers alone. Parents particularly must start these talks with their children and while they're still in primary school. Fearing that raising the topic will destroy your child's innocence is really a myth. As the author of the survey Joan Sauers so poignantly states, 'The fact is that young people don't lose their innocence learning about sex. Innocence is freedom from moral wrong, not freedom from information'.[103] We can only empower ourselves and our kids by talking about sex with them.

Understanding what your kids think about something as banal as the clothes they wear, celebrities they like, the toys and electronic games they play with, the TV shows and films they watch, the books they read and the music they listen to, the brands they value and sharing with them how you feel too is the way to open up communication, to express your values and morals. It will also ease the way for those all-important conversations about sexual practice, drugs, alcohol and personal responsibility when they're older.

Knowing your attitudes to life and the various people and things that fill it also helps kids to understand why you deny them certain objects. Don't be pressured by the corporations. Don't be pressured by what your neighbours, friends or their kids possess or think. As Susan Linn says, 'conformity, impulse buying and defining self-worth by what you own ... seeking happiness through the acquisition of material goods'[104] are not values we want to pass on to our kids.

Neither is the message that in order to get ahead in this world and be accepted, kids have to be sexy.

chapter three

Fashion Victims: The 'Celebrification' and Sexualisation of Children Through Clothing

Millennium Lolitas

As discussed in the last chapter, debates around children, fashion and commercialisation in society take many forms – mostly negative. We read about how kids are being sexualised through clothing, dressing as adults, being influenced by celebrities and obsessed with brand-name clothing; how various corporations are targeting them; and finally, somewhere in the midst of all the alarm, we also hear how important it is to kids and their sense of self and group status to be perceived at best as trend-setters and at the very least as fashionable. We also read (and hear) so much about the influence adults have on children's dress sense and the relationship they develop to fashion, style, appearances and, subsequently, themselves. Whether we're dedicated followers of fashion or not, we have an idea of what's in style; so do our kids. The combination of adult awareness and market and media forces creates a heady cocktail of influence. As a result, kids today are more than fashion conscious: they've become fashion victims ... and we're letting them.

The adage 'clothes maketh the man' has always resonated in our culture. Only now, they maketh the woman and our children too. As far back as Greek and Roman myths to more recent Grimm fairytales, appearances, centred on clothes, have played a very important role in how characters were understood and treated. Heroes and heroines in popular stories are transformed through the clothes they wear into kings, queens, princes, princesses, suitable husbands and wives and desirable commodities – see Cinderella, the Goose Girl, George Bernard Shaw's *Pygmalion* and even Aladdin. As we know, appearances deceive and often the deception occurs through dress – not just in stories, but in real life as well. Kids learn this from a very early age. They see the adults in their lives 'dress' for work, parties and slumming around on the weekends, and associate certain 'looks' and styles with particular occasions. They start to understand that we not only dress to impress, but choose clothes that project private and public images of who we are and how we want to be perceived and treated.

Clothing and a concern with fashion and trends have always been regarded as superficial and relatively meaningless, even in our image-saturated culture. But as academic Joanna Finkelstein argues, 'to regard fashion as only a frivolity playing over the surface of human existence is to underrate it as a social force … it fiercely imposes a value system on private desires'.[1]

Most of us care, to varying degrees, about how we look and what we wear and, in this day and age, so do our kids. With children's magazines promoting style and fashion sense as important to girls' social wellbeing, even toys – such as Barbie and her endless accoutrements and the Bratz whose boxes scream they're the 'only dolls with a passion for fashion' (more on them in the next chapter) – play a role. According to Patrizia Calefato, the lessons children learn through the act of dressing and undressing Barbie and other dolls are the establishment of taste and aesthetic sense.[2] Celebrities such as the Olsen twins and Hilary Duff have become global brands with their own fashion labels (Mary-Kate and Ashley, and Duff Stuff). The Australian singing sisters The Veronicas have also released a clothing range for tweens. Mischa Barton (formerly from the TV show *The OC*), Jessica Simpson and hosts of Hollywood and Australian stars have pages of tabloid space devoted to what they're buying and wearing. They're labelled 'best' and 'worst' dressed or given a score out 10. The Celebrity Best and Worst Dressed List is national news annually. The Oscars, Emmys, and Grammys all feature red-carpet events where discussion centres on what the women and, increasingly, the men, are wearing. Closer to home, focus on fashions is no less intense. National events such as the Melbourne Spring Racing Carnival, the AFL Brownlow Medal dinner, the Logies and the Arias emphasise how important it is to 'look good'. Terms like 'fashion disaster', 'fashion police' and 'fashion icon' are laden with significance.

In fiction and fact, clothes and accessorising have always been important markers of both individuality and conformity to social values. As Joanne Entwhistle writes, 'dress or adornment is one of the means by which bodies are made social and given meaning and identity'.[3] Just because those bodies belong to our kids doesn't mean clothes and accessories are any less important – arguably, they're more.

Judging Books by Their Covers

In this visual, judgemental world, we look at what people wear, regardless of age, and make assumptions about them. Just like in the fairytales, clothes can endow adults and now children with social status, elevating them beyond their class; they can make suggestions about their personal principles and economic power, both of which reflect upon (rightly or wrongly) their families as well. To kids, clothes and, more particularly, the labels attached to them allow them to 'fit in' by indicating their worthiness as a peer and even their future potential.

Finkelstein writes that 'fashion is a language of group identification – the shared language of logos'.[4] Understanding this goes a long way to tolerating why children as young as six obsess over their clothes and work hard, particularly once they hit their tween and teen years, to establish a style, insisting adults buy them certain brands. It also explains why so many of us have to watch in despair as our once semi-reasonable kids decide to dye their hair black and wear purple lipstick, black nail polish and dark clothing as the character Bree did in the Australian soap opera

Neighbours. They want to establish their individuality and belong at the same time. For kids, clothes and looks are a means of doing this.

The irony is that while many kids, even tweens, believe that they are creating an individual 'look', it's often a prefabricated corporate mould that doesn't shout 'Look at moi, I'm different!' as they might intend. On the contrary, it suggests mindless conformity dressed up as individuality. I call this 'resistance conformity'.[5] We think we're resisting, making a personal statement, but in reality we're all conforming to some business idea of what tots, tweens and teens (never mind adults of various ages) should look like. Finkelstein explains this drive to follow fashion trends, this 'keeping up with the Joneses, [as] a way of keeping life simple and predictable', and as a way of avoiding the 'new and confrontational'.[6] We see it all the time in subcultures such as 'Punks', 'Goths', 'Emos' and so on. It used to be that these subcultures (think back to your childhood and the Punks, Skinheads, Mods or further back to Bodgies and Widgies) really did express their alienation and wilful separation from mainstream society through dress, language and behaviour. It was a 'do it yourself' ethos that embraced recycling and invention and political subversion. Today these subcultures are catered for by businesses that recognise that kids who identify as a minority often have the cash to ensure everyone knows this.

Hal Niedzviecki, in his book *Hello I'm Special: How Individuality Became the New Conformity*, writes about how young and old are 'looking for outfits and accessories that can make them who they want to be. They don't want pre-packaged. They want *special* … here, the conformity of individuality is obvious'.[7] He argues that certain companies are addressing this need by manufacturing clothes, such as jeans, that look ripped, torn and faded, slapping a huge price tag on them and then laughing as they walk off the hangers. How many times have we looked at (or bought) these for ourselves or our children, aware that, while we don't appear to be getting value for money in terms of product (who wants *new* jeans that look like they've been worn for years or already worn out?), what we're paying premium price for is more than clothes – it's a look and all the meaning that comes with appearing a particular way. It gives us and our kids a certain kudos and hip-ness. We conform, we buy, we wear. It's no wonder our kids do as well. Through our own purchasing and wearing habits, we're teaching them about the importance of the fashion stakes.

Adults by Design

For at least three years now, I've made a point of wandering in and out of children's sections in stores like Myer, David Jones, K-Mart, Target, Best and Less and Big W, as well as children's boutiques and speciality shops, to get a sense of the types of children's clothing available, specifically for children from two to about 13. Having spent years in these areas out of necessity when I was raising my own children, I find it interesting and sometimes quite alarming (and amusing) to revisit them and gaze upon the laden racks and shelves with different eyes and ideas. From bralettes, French knickers and bikinis in sizes 2 and up, to T-shirts with slogans claiming that the wearer is a 'princess', has 'attitude', is a 'brat', or is even a 'drama queen'; from evening dresses in slinky, flowing fabrics starting at size 8 (though long white formal dresses in satins and gauzes, presumably for a religious ceremony, are available in much smaller sizes, as well as miniature suits for boys), to designer gear that costs so much it makes Armani seem like a budget brand,[8] some of the clothing available for kids today is stereotyped, diverse, colourful and very 'adult' as well.

In saying this, there are degrees of 'adultness': sometimes the fashions are diminutive versions of what's in the grown-up sections, such as strappy handkerchief tops, jeans, jackets, polo shirts or dresses that can all be quite tasteful, to midriff-baring tops or plunging necklines, much too short shorts and skirts, leather jackets, macho gear and high heels (I found 'strappy black stilettos' with three-centimetre heels in children's size 7, and cork shoes in children's size 13 with five-centimetre heels in Myer, as well as little suede boots with rouched ankles and wedge heels in David Jones). On the one hand, as Alison Lurie reasons, young girls wear completely non-functional training bras as a sign that they will eventually become women[9] but, on the other, we have to ask, do our kids really need to wear adult styles as a sign they're going to 'grow up'?

In June 2007, pop icon Kylie Minogue launched 'underwear' for tweens in her Holeproof 'Love Kylie' range called the Love Kylie Princess Club. Bordered with sparkles and with tiny bejewelled LK initials dangling from between ridiculously small triangles of fabric, the little bralettes are extremely attractive to younger and older consumers alike. Matching briefs offer a boy leg or normal cut as well as a string version. Designed for young girls with or without breasts (depending on their size and weight), the styles have been described as 'lingerie for children'.[10] Adolescent psychologist Michael Carr-Gregg feels that in putting her name and status to such garments Kylie is 'associating herself with what represents, in my view, this ongoing campaign to erode childhood'.[11] The Australian Childhood Foundation CEO, Dr Joe Tucci, agrees and believes that these types of campaigns and products contribute to the increase in problem sexual behaviours in children.[12] While there's a general reluctance to criticise Minogue because of her popularity and an awareness of her personal health and emotional battles, which arouse sympathy and support from the public, the tough questions have to asked. Is this type of 'lingerie', and other similar tween fashions, really appropriate for our tots and tweens?

Carr-Gregg doesn't believe they are. He argues that there has been the effective eradication of early adolescence. Where once there used to be clothing in an eight to 13 age range, this is now an eight to 16 age range with nothing in between.[13] Kids younger than 10 are being encouraged, by the market, adults and each other, to wear push-up bras, body-hugging low-slung pants, scooped necklines and make-up. Carr-Gregg feels that the lack of distinction between tweens and teens in clothing carries over into their emotional and psychological lives whereby what used to be considered appropriate for a 16-year-old to dream about and emulate is now being 'sold', through fashion and popular culture, to tweens to act on *now*. 'Kids are being lured out of childhood by unscrupulous marketers and the media avalanche …

I find a hip and sexy 10-year-old disconcerting'.[14] He contends that 'no self-respecting eight-year-old wants to be eight. They want to be 13'.[15] As Ellen Warwick, author of *Planet Girl* lifestyle books, states, 'a lot of the products are scaled-down versions of adult things. You end up dressing 13-year-old girls in the clothing of 25-year-olds'.[16]

This isn't surprising when you consider the age of the celebrities behind the tween and early teen clothing ranges; many of them are often well out of their teens when promoting certain styles. Warwick also believes that because 'some celebrities are the same age as their fans [or appear to be] … some girls view their favourite star's style not as something to aspire to, but as something they can and should imitate'.[17]

Many children are physically developing at an earlier rate (World Health Organization figures cite 10 as the median age for puberty[18]), but this isn't matched in their psychological and emotional growth. Parenting expert Michael Grose believes that 'ten is the new 15',[19] something Canadian writer Kathleen McDonnell agrees with when she says that 'tweens are the new teenagers'.[20] But even though a child may look and act like a teenager, it doesn't mean they have the internal coping skills or maturity to match. And it's in this growing gap that problems for both adults and kids arise.

I'm Too Sexy for *That* Shirt

Dr Jean Kilbourne, a US academic and media critic, visited Australia in 2006. Throughout a range of talks and interviews, she continued to reiterate how the exposure children have to sexual imagery is being 'delivered without emotion or consideration of the consequences on young minds'.[21]

Importantly for adults, she notes that 'it's the corporate exploitation of children's sexuality that is disgusting and dangerous, not the sexuality itself'.[22] We have to keep this in mind when we discuss the relationship our children have to fashion, sex and the realm of appearances. Too often, whether intentionally or not, critics of the sexualisation of kids come across sounding like wowsers and as if sexuality is the demon. It isn't. Sexuality is completely natural – even in young children. It's the commodification of sexuality – and turning children's exploration of what it means to be sexual into something that can only be expressed through clothes and other forms of consumerism – that's a growing problem.

So much so that when American columnist John Tirman wrote a piece on kids and clothes for his book *100 Ways America is Screwing Up the World,* he referred to US children's clothing as 'Hooker Couture'. When he mentioned to a friend and mother of two what he was writing she said don't forget to mention the 'fuck-me clothes for eight-year-olds'.[23]

The report by Dr Emma Rush and Andrea La Nauze, released by the Australia Institute in 2006[24] and mentioned earlier, discusses how even in something as benign as a David Jones catalogue, children were being posed and dressed in provocative and sexy ways. Reactions to this report were fascinating. Throughout the media, the young, earnest Dr Rush was criticised and practically taken to task for daring to 'read' so much into the chosen images.[25] Some nasty aspersions were cast upon her. David Jones and other companies threatened legal action and other experts claimed Rush and company were exaggerating. On the other hand, Rush and the Institute were flooded with emails and letters from concerned adults who agreed with the message the report tried to get across: that through a range of contemporary media such as TV, films, and especially fashion, young children are being catapulted into the adult world before they're ready.[26]

Into the Wardrobe

One of the fondest memories I have of my childhood was raiding my mother's wardrobe, slipping on an oversize dress, tripping around the carpet in a pair of far-too-big heels, spreading lipstick crudely over my lips and hanging some really tacky piece of jewellery around my neck. Or, better still, looping one of my father's business ties around my throat and donning a cumbersome jacket before stomping down the corridor and bellowing various demands. I felt grown up; I was playing at being my mother or father, at being an adult. I was no different to most children my age then or now.

After all, children want to grow up and fast. Unlike Peter Pan, they can't wait to enter that forbidden world of adulthood and enjoy everything it promises. Only, these days, it takes very little imagination to enter that world.

For young people it's their *own* clothes – the ones we buy for them – that allow them to cross the threshold from child to adult, whether they're ready or not. Journalist Jessica Rudd wryly notes that for '10 year olds, the modern alternative to the enchanting world of Narnia is literally only a wardrobe away, as simple as sliding on a pair of stilettos, smearing on some foundation and singing songs of exploitative relationships. Suddenly you're transformed into Britney or Claudia or another deliciously naughty taboo'.[27]

The 'naughty taboo' has extended to include make-up, mannerisms and other popular cultural forms. Shoe manufacturer Candies, who use Ashlee Simpson (Jessica Simpson's younger sister) as a spokesperson, also produce T-shirts for their mainly tween consumers. Imprinted upon them is the phrase 'Be sexy: It doesn't mean you have to have sex'.[28] This is a message Simpson promotes as well. But why do kids have to be sexy? The answer is they don't. But try telling that to them.

In her book *Honey, We Lost the Kids: Rethinking Childhood in the Multi-media Age*, Kathleen McDonnell suggests that much of our problem with sexualised childhood lies in the way adults see it. She argues that just because kids dress up like their favourite pop star and copy their sexy routines it doesn't mean they want to be sexual. That's what *we* call it because we're projecting our perceptions and anxieties onto what, to a degree, are normal behaviours.[29] According to McDonnell, kids don't actually understand that they're acting in a sexy manner and, for the most part, she's right. They're just indulging in childish fantasies, accessing the adult world and role-playing at being, to use 11-year-old Jessica's words, 'pretty and popular'. Dressing up and performing like an adult has long been a game of choice for young people. So is it any different today?

Yes. It is. If for no other reason than a lot of the 'trying on' happens in public – even for a global public – and it's taken very, very seriously. Consider the examples of two young Gold Coast models, Morgan Featherstone and Maddison Gabriel.

In 2003 pictures of eight-year-old Morgan were published that depicted her heavily made up, staring straight down the camera lens and pouting provocatively. They made the Calvin Klein 'Heroin Chic' look of a few years earlier appear positively tame. Young Morgan looked both post-coital and as if she was soliciting sex. Outrage ensued. Her parents defended their daughter's images (images that her father, as her manager, had both taken and made sure were distributed), stating that for Morgan they were just 'dress-ups'. But the point is dress-ups are fine in the privacy of your own home – even dress-ups that explore sexuality. But, once those images circulate in the public domain, their meaning changes. No longer was Morgan just an eight-year-old daughter: suddenly, she was a sexy, young 'thang', whose look attracted attention and invited desire. Her pictures weren't just sexy, they were sex personified.

The images were taken for a Japanese company to promote swimming pools; however, when the images were lifted and reproduced on T-shirts being sold over the internet (and worn usually by middle-aged European men) in South-East Asia and Germany, then the original intention behind the images became irrelevant. Any sense of innocence was lost and was certainly exploited for every cent it could muster.[30]

What did her parents do? Her mother, Amy, said, 'I didn't find anything alarming about it because it was just a photo of Morgan that's been in newspapers anyway and I didn't see anything wrong with it in the first place. I thought it was very flattering having my daughter's picture on a T-shirt, but at the same time a bit bizarre. When we found out about it we did get them removed from the website because it wasn't something we'd orchestrated and we didn't like the idea of strangers making money from Morgan's image'.[31]

In September 2007, another media furore erupted when 12-year-old Maddison Gabriel was announced as the 'face' of Gold Coast Fashion Week. Quick to deflect criticism, organisers (and her parents) said that not only was she turning 13 within a few days, but also she would be 'almost 14' by the time she took up her duties in 2008.[32] Public outcry followed. The fact that numerous European catwalks had set an age limit of either 15 or 16 for their models and that Melbourne Fashion Week, on discovering that their chosen face was only 15, had given the title to another, older girl seemed to be dismissed.[33]

The accusations of sexualising young Maddison, however, struck a nerve. Organisers said that the judges 'didn't know how old she was. They just saw her as a model against other women'.[34] Nonetheless, on discovering her age, the decision was not reversed; instead, they said 'we're not exploiting this girl. We're not promoting sex'.[35] These types of claims are disingenuous in the extreme: modelling is a sexualised profession – bodies are on display and sometimes the clothes are secondary to the nubile flesh that is carefully chosen to complement the fashions. Drugs, eating disorders and sex are generally regarded as having a symbiotic relationship in the modelling world – and by those who have the experiences to prove it, such as Kate Moss.[36]

Concerns over Maddison's age and the appropriateness of her involvement were legitimate. Regardless of her apparent 'maturity' and life-long ambition to be a model,[37] she was, quite simply, a child. After a few days of relentless media attention and public scrutiny, Maddison's mother was quoted as saying that her daughter 'just needs to be 13'.[38] Yet, a few days earlier, being 13 meant revelling in and celebrating the fact that Maddison had beaten adults at their own game: winning an adult competition, gaining a modelling course as a prize and being asked to stand in as the 'face' of a fashion festival for one week. Suddenly, after criticism, 13 is about being left alone to reap the rewards for getting away with masquerading as an adult, and turning the acrimony of others into everyone else's problem.

In the end, the debates around Maddison and fashion week were not about whether this young beauty should or shouldn't be a clothes-horse;

they were about the context in which she was given the opportunity to realise those dreams and the age at which it happened. Maddison may have always wanted to be model, but what she needed was adult role-models to guide, teach her patience, and prepare her emotionally, psychologically and physically for the time when she's ready to step forward and be an adult – not only on a catwalk, but beyond.

In 2004, 16-year-old Nikki Webster was voted one of the 100 sexiest women by the readership of the adult male magazine *FHM* (*For Him Magazine*). Public fury followed.[39] Nikki was a teenager on the cusp of womanhood. How dare the men's magazine sexualise her so overtly (never mind the fact that in 2003 she also had a mention – the editor noting that she 'wasn't yet legal' so he couldn't 'officially' include her, excusing the inclusion of her name by stating the readers nonetheless voted for her).[40] In 2006, Nikki, our 'Olympic Moppet', with a fan base of predominantly five- to eight-year-olds, celebrated her 18th birthday by appearing in the same magazine – dressed as a cross between a dominatrix and a boudoir madam.

To me, Nikki's drive to represent herself as a 'woman' is indicative of what happens to kids who are exposed to ideas about sexiness before they really understand what it is or how to wield it. To legitimate her career and mark her transition from 'child' to 'woman', Nikki possibly felt she had to be perceived as grown up and 'sexy'. Posing for a men's magazine gave her that much needed entrée into the adult world she'd been playing on the periphery of through her music, fashion and make-up line for years. From Dorothy to Dominatrix.

I find that very sad – philosophically and ideologically. Is this what's in store for future generations?

Another case that raises disturbing issues about children and sexiness is that of brutally murdered American beauty queen JonBenet Ramsey.

Night after night, images of little JonBenet Ramsey were beamed into our homes. Parading across the television with her bouffant-blonde hair, heavily made-up eyes and little red cupid-bow mouth, JonBenet was living proof that sexualising young children and taking delight in how they look is not exclusive to a bunch of perverts and sexual deviants living in the shadows of society. She was found dead in her basement the day after Christmas – arguably, the one day of the year dedicated completely to children. It wasn't just her parents who failed her that day, but a society that allows the sexualisation and display of children to thrive in any guise.[41] Richard Goldstein, in the American magazine *Village Voice*, wrote that the JonBenet case 'brings to the surface both our horror at how effectively a child can be constructed as a sexual being and our guilt at the pleasure we take in such a sight'. He also said that, 'Only in a nation of promiscuous puritans could it be a good career move to equip a six-year-old with bedroom eyes'.[42]

The JonBenet Ramsey case is, in many deeply disturbing ways, an indictment on a society whereby 'dressing kids up' as adults and parading them in a public arena is still seen as harmless play.[43] Those who dare to critique it or express concern are positioned as the ones with the problem – as the Maddison Gabriel case confirms. But there's nothing healthy or normal about sexualising young children and then, on top of that, making them compete for prizes to see who's the prettiest and sexiest. Training them to pout, blow kisses and swing those little hips … but it's not just in children's beauty pageants that this very process is occurring. It's endemic in our culture. Don't believe me? Attend a dance concert in any state on any given weekend and watch kids as young as six in full facial make-up sway their hips with come-hither lips. And then burst into tears when they don't win a trophy.

Mini-Me

When it comes to buying clothes for kids, our common sense often deserts us and we succumb to temptation and buy something that they would look so cute in. We also take more than a bit of pleasure if what we're buying resembles our own clothes. Dr Prue Aherns, who specialises in children's fashion, states that, 'Children are now the insignias of the leisure classes'.[44]

I recently saw a tiny polka-dot bikini in size 2 hanging from a rack in a major department store. It was more than cute – it was ridiculously gorgeous. So were the tiny My Little Pony bralettes (size 2–3), chiffon skirts, halter-necks and diamante-studded tops you could buy for tots and tweens. Next to these were also lovely dresses, tops, skirts and shorts for girls, and delightful shirts and pants or shorts for boys. In fact, boys' clothes generally, no matter where I looked, tended to be just that: clothes for boys. Sometimes extraordinarily fashionable in terms of brands and style (torn hems, cut-off sleeves, latest layered colours), but also practical. Boys could play in their outfits or be seen and not heard (yeah, right) at a family or social function.

Girls' clothes were a completely different story. Not only were they often impractical for play, encouraging adults to discourage girls from running around outside lest they damage the clothes or expose their underwear (reinforcing the stereotype that girls are passive and boys active), there wasn't much fabric in them. The clothing may have been fashionable, but who wants fashionable on a child? A self-conscious adult, that's who – one who consciously or unconsciously feels she or he is in a parenting competition and that their child is their trophy.

What really struck me was that we live in a climate where 'slip, slop, slap' is a daily mantra, and yet clothing for girls exposes more skin than ever. Especially tiny bikinis for babies. Why on earth would you want to put these tiny pieces of (expensive) fabric on a child with baby skin, who probably isn't toilet-trained and who just wants to get into the water to splash and get cool? The bikini is meant to appeal to adults – not children. Like all the clothing for tots and certainly a great deal for tweens, it's designed to cater to adult tastes, desires and the sense of style they want their kids to project. It's all about *them*.

Women particularly channel the inner-little girl (the one who would have loved to have worn this stuff when she was that age) and buy our six-year-olds the little padded Bratz bralettes from Target, or leopard-skin print tops and leather skirts, heels and jewellery, and then parade our kids in public. In the final episode of the British comedy *Absolutely Fabulous*, the irrepressible fashion-conscious Edina (a drunken throwback from the hippy-trippy 1960s) discovers that not only is she going to be a grandmother, but her grandchild has an African father. She declares, 'A mixed-race baby is the finest accessory anyone in my position could ever have! Oh my God! It's the must-have of the season … the Chanel of babies!'⁴⁵ Edina's shocking racial comment aside, we also dress our kids like they're our accessories, making a statement about us and usually our own sense of taste and what's chic.

Journalist Alison Rushby writes about the range of baby T-shirts she saw framed in a children's store window at a shopping centre. They sported phrases like 'I'm having a f@#%ing bad day', 'I hide my crack in my nappy', 'spit happens', 'I must not chase boys' and 'Captain Stinky Pants'. She even saw a three-month-old baby boy wearing a T-shirt stating 'I love tits'.⁴⁶ It's not uncommon to see boys, between seven and 10, wearing T-shirts with pictures of cars on them proclaiming 'My other hot rod is in my pants'. These T-shirts say a lot more about the parents than the child who wears them. Arguably, some are very funny and appropriate, while others are tasteless. They reveal an adult's sense of humour but, instead of using a child as a walking comic billboard, adults should choose other ways of demonstrating their humorous bone is intact.

While these T-shirts and Edina's tacky exclamations take the notion of children-as-personal-fashion-statements to the extreme, the fact is that kids *are* our accessories – not just in that trivial, disposable and interchangeable way that various fripperies are. They're accessories in that, when they accompany adults anywhere, or represent the family in public space, how they look speaks volumes about us: as adults, as parents and as a society. This is why adults and kids clothes are getting so much bad press. Society, generally, doesn't like what kiddie fashions are saying about *us*.

Dressing little girls and boys to look like mum, dad or a celebrity might be 'cute' as a one-off but, if it happens continually, it functions to erase our kids' sense of self, both within and without. As Finkelstein argues and as the fairytales also reveal, appearances have been used to deceive for centuries.⁴⁷ Tweens and teens might use fashion as a means of deceiving others about their age, class and economic status (just like adults) and adults might dress young kids to present a certain version of their parenting, social and financial status to the world, but we all have to be careful that, in doing so, we don't deceive ourselves.

Fashion Sense

The number of adults who moan that their little boy or girl demanded to wear a particular item of clothing, threw a tantrum and desperately wanted or nagged to be bought a specific brand doesn't surprise me. What does is the number of very sensible adults who succumb to the least bit of pressure from their kids. Clearly kids get a thrill out of dressing up like mum or dad – we've all been there, done that. That's partly why we give in. We believe we're indulging our kids in a type of wish-fulfilment. Yes, we are. It's ours.

Buying our children gear we wished we'd had in our wardrobes, allowing them to make style choices when they're still very young, and dressing them 'like us', let alone allowing them to enter, through dress, into the adult world, are all potential time-bombs. If we don't set ground rules around clothing and accessories when our children are young, how can we expect to suddenly wrest control when they reach adolescence and flounce or storm out of the house in the skimpiest of attire or looking like they're an extra in an American R&B music shoot?

We can't.

By placing appearances – through fashion, style, make-up and accessories – in a family and social context, and making sensible as opposed to nostalgic, inappropriate or selfish purchases while the kids are still very young, we can set boundaries and limits that can be expanded and negotiated as our kids grow older and make their own 'style' decisions. By doing this, clothing becomes *part* of what it means to establish a public identity – not the *only* means.

Formals

It wouldn't be right to discuss fashions without dealing with the fraught question of school dances and formals. Instead of being nights that mark a significant milestone in our kids' lives, primary school graduation ceremonies and dances, never mind those at high school have become, for children and parents alike, burdened with costs, despair and, above all, meaning. What our kids wear to these occasions, which are meant to be celebratory and fun, ends up causing endless anxiety and arguments because of the emphasis we place on fashion, style and brands – an emphasis our kids (regardless of age, it seems) emulate. For our kids, from tween to late teens, what they wear to these public rituals announces their style, their social positioning within particular cliques and, too often, their parents' bank balance as well.

Even so, adults often go 'over-the-top' with expense and emphasis.[48] Arguably, this is partly because of the lack of rites of passage for young people in contemporary culture, and the decline of marriages; certainly fewer parents are bearing the cost of weddings these days as we wait until we're older and economically more secure to wed. As a result, many don't mind reaching deep into their pockets for a mere dance. Regarding high school formals, debutante balls (where they still exist) and even Bat or Bah Mitzvahs as the *major* milestone in their kids' lives, many parents and grandparents feel this is the last time they'll be able to control or contribute to their sons' and daughters' threshold moment: where they cross from child to adult in a very public way. As a result, parents can over-indulge and be excessive. It's important to put these events into perspective. Whether a child is a tween or teen, it's only one event in a life we hope will enjoy many. But you wouldn't know it from the lack of restraint being practised at primary and high school levels. The question is, will the kids really thank us? After all, how can a boy or girl relish their wedding, first trip overseas, birth of a child, first house, car or graduating from university if they've already been lavished with gifts, money, gowns, suits, flowers, cars and more. And all because they did what most kids do anyway – graduate from primary or high school, turn 13 (which in Jewish culture is a delightful and very significant ritual, but some parents are paying enormous sums to ensure what was always going to be extraordinary is even more memorable), or attend a formal dance. It's not that I'm saying don't make the moment special – of course it should be. There's just no need to be *so* extravagant and thereby diminish other equally (or more) important milestones. If you arrive by helicopter to your first school formal (as one couple on the Sunshine Coast did recently), how can a trip in a nice car to the chapel on your wedding day compare?

Class

Another topic that has to be dealt with is class – that is, the ways in which family bank balances affect clothing and appearance choices. It's clear that the discount stores lack the clothing choice and quality of their more expensive counterparts. Best and Less and other similar chain stores stock affordable clothes but also tend to have the most T-shirts with attitude slogans, shorter skirts, slinky dresses in polyester or jersey fabrics and diamante tops for very young kids. This isn't to say that the higher end of the market doesn't have these – they do – but they also have greater options in terms of fabric, cut, colour and style.

For those adults in the lower socioeconomic range, it's difficult to avoid buying kids' clothes that aren't mimicking adult style or that aren't sexy. But it's not impossible. The point is to make time to look and hunt down the bargain, especially during sales, and avoid succumbing to the cuteness factor or kids' demands to 'look like everyone else'. Search for better quality materials (if you can) that will last the vigorous washes and perhaps opt to have less choice in your kids' wardrobe. I remember how hard it was when I was a single mum, but it can be done.

No matter what economic strata you're in, don't be fooled by the corporate promises that by dressing your kids in a certain style, you're keeping them in (cheap) fashion. Sometimes, you're just making your kids look cheap.

Beauty

Fashion isn't only about clothes. It's also about overall appearance and this is something corporations (in league with celebrities) have muscled in on in a huge way.

The beauty industry is undergoing a bit of a tween boom of late, with many businesses targeting young, insecure kids and offering temporary solutions to their body-image dilemmas. Honing in on kids' lack of confidence about their looks or bodies, beauty salons are promoting waxes, plucking and other treatments to help them deflect the inevitable teasing about their bodily differences. Many of these salons claim they're empowering kids and helping their self-esteem, not to mention pocketing the money of anxious parents who don't want to see their kids targeted in the playground (more on this in Chapter Ten).

How depressing that instead of teaching our tweens to understand their differences (including cultural, ethnic, gender and sexual), and those of others, we rip off the excess hair, pluck away the 'mono-brow' and make them all look the same. Once a girl or a boy reaches puberty (at whatever age) and their hormones begin to run amok, then it's important to be aware of their self-consciousness and as parents and carers look at beauty interventions if we have to, but not before time. Tolerance, understanding and appreciation of difference are far more beautiful attributes to possess.

A British report in 2004 claimed that three out of five 7–10-year-olds wore lipstick and perfume regularly. Analyst Claire Hatcher said, 'the kids' interest was fuelled by teen magazines, peer groups and their mothers'.[49] In the US, the Hyatt Regency Hill County Resort in San Antonio opened a spa for kids under 17, three years ago. What they didn't expect was that their main clientele would be, on average, eight- to 10-year-olds.[50]

With tweens emulating celebrities who maintain and change their looks on a daily basis, as well as their mothers and fathers who also take pride in their appearance, beauty regimes for tweens are a growth market. While mums claim it's lovely to do the mother-daughter thing by attending a salon together, consider what I said earlier about milestones and giving your kids something to look forward to. How can they look forward to their first facial, let alone first moisturiser, if they've been having them since they were seven, like Kate Beckinsale's daughter, Lily.[51] As Jean Kilbourne warns, emphasising grooming and appearance teaches girls that their value depends on what they look like as opposed to who they are.[52]

Celebrities such as Raven-Symoné, Britney Spears, Paris Hilton, Mary-Kate and Ashley Olsen, and Nikki Webster all have their own perfumes or make-up lines that target very young consumers. Again, adults need to be sensible about how much they allow *themselves* to be influenced by the seductive promises surrounding these products and how much their enthusiasm will affect their kids.

Young children shouldn't be wearing make-up in public. In private space, within the home (or a relative's or friend's house), it's the parents' prerogative. Kids should be encouraged to dress up and wear make-up. They can even be taught how to apply it appropriately, ready for the time when they can step out into the world with painted faces. However, as your child gets older, you should negotiate with them what they can and can't use on their faces when they leave the house. From age 10 and up, for example, you might allow them to use lip gloss and a little eye shadow, and then up the ante from there. Set reasonable boundaries – ones that suit your values and the ones you want to instil in your kids. As for spas and beauty treatments – if you spoil your kids with these then, first, make sure they deserve it. But at the same time consider what you're teaching them and do it in an informed way. It's not wrong to want these for your kids – it is wrong to not think about the consequences.

Mirror, Mirror

We live in a world where appearances are important. In this makeover culture, we're taught to continually reinvent ourselves through our appearance: the clothes we wear, the accessories we buy and the look we adopt. Fashion and appearances are interchangeable, deceptive and emulative and have too much emphasis placed on them. While at one level we know and decry this, at another we fall victim to fashions – and so do our children.

At younger and younger ages, children are using fashion as a means of slipping into the adult world and trying on new identities. They also use fashion as a means of making public statements about their private selves. Understanding this goes a long way to managing it – not just for our kids, but for us as well. It's an irony that, while we worry about how the kids in our culture are dressing and acting, we've forgotten to self-reflect. We need to recognise that we mostly influence the attitudes our kids have to their appearance. In the way we dress, spend, discuss fashion and appearances and how we emphasise our children's, we instil in them a context for understanding themselves and looks generally.

While our culture might want us to believe we are what we wear, we're not. Clothing and fashion might be symbolic but they should be fun and partial reflections of who we are, not absolute statements.

Written with Lisa Hill

chapter four

Toy Stories: Growing Up in a Material World

Not Just Child's Play

The role of toys in children's lives is simultaneously complex and straightforward. Kids use toys in imaginative and practical ways. They project versions of themselves, the world and the life they want to live onto their toys. Robots, blocks, dolls, games, cards and dress-ups allow kids to experiment with who they're becoming in safe and reassuring ways.

Sometimes, the type of play children engage in can worry parents. When boys run around shooting each other with plastic weapons or sticks, wrestle, start World War III between Voltron and Optimus Prime or trade a monster Yu-Gi-Oh card for a magic one so they can duel; or when girls 'marry' their Barbies to each other, give them mixed families and non-mainstream sexualities, or start to demand to look like their Bratz dolls, parents become alarmed. Believing they're raising a sexually confused girl or an aggressive boy (or vice versa), parents can blur the line between valuable fantasy play that contributes to a child's psychological, social and emotional development and the reality that some toys aren't as creative, positive or educational as the marketing spin leads us to believe.

Adults often impose their own criteria on children's play instead of understanding that, through fantasy, kids are testing boundaries and dipping their toes in the grown-up world of which they're on the periphery. A few adults discourage or even ban play that appears sexual, violent or threatening to their family and social values. But is it? Can (un)dressing Barbies or Bratz, wedding them to each other, or 'killing' monsters in card duels or through superhero play damage our children or inculcate skewed values in them?

Some experts believe it can.

This is why parental input into the world of children's toys is so important, from birth to teen. We need to know what our children are playing with and why. Succumbing to kids' demands, commercial hype and pressure from other adults that 'it's okay' are no longer excuses. Certainly, understanding and moderating the relationship between kids, their toys, the commercial world and us is like walking a tightrope between control and disregard and over-indulgence and imaginative deprivation. Your daughter may have seven Barbies, but is she the right age for them, does she *need* that many and, if so, *how* does she play with them?

The Genderation of Toys

In this day and age of abundance, the role of toys has never been more important. So much so, I decided to allocate two chapters to the topic. While it may seem odd to separate chapters on girls and boys, it reflects the way toys are so specifically sexed these days.

Despite all the advances in gender equality, the toys of the new millennium persist in reconfirming very conservative stereotypes. Take a walk down a toy aisle in any department store and you'll see they're clearly divided into 'toddlers', 'board games', 'boys' and 'girls'. The 'girl' shelves are weighed down with boxes of pastel-coloured dolls, complete with numerous outfits and accessories. They come in sets so parents can't just buy one or two. Not when there are 10 to own and an entire friendship group or family to be collected as well. After all, you don't want an unpopular doll (or child), do you? There are also rainbow-coloured, cutesy animals, dogs in handbags à la Paris Hilton, and Polly Pocket with her natty little bits and pieces. There are miniature ironing boards, vacuum cleaners and cooking sets ready to domesticate the girls, as well as dolls with paraphernalia linked to celebrities and classic tales. And let's not forget the book, comic, TV and movie tie-ins that also accompany many of these. The lack of variety is so disheartening.

Over in the 'boy' aisles, you'll find building blocks from Lego and Meccano, logic puzzles, assembly kits of all shapes and sizes, Transformers, Teenage Mutant Ninja Turtles, action figurines from wrestling or films, cars, trains, weapons, knights, swords, dinosaurs and light-phasers. The colours in these aisles are bolder, darker and more mysterious. There's no sign of femininity; it's all designed to harness boys' masculinity and braggadocio. Whereas you feel inclined to waltz up the girl aisle (really, you do), you want to stride boldly down the boy aisle – but more on this in the next chapter.

In the real world, girls might be able to do what boys do and boys might feel more comfortable being in touch with their 'feminine' side, but when it comes to toys and play (apart from some non-gender-specific board games), the gender and sexual boundaries we fought so hard to topple are being firmly erected around our kids. Susan J Douglas writes about how her four-year-old daughter could differentiate between the genders through toys: 'she never calls me when they're selling Killer Commando Unit G.I. Joe, and all the other Pentagon-inspired stuff obviously for boys. She knows better. She knows she's a girl, and she knows what's for her. Twenty years of feminist politics and here I am, with a daughter who wants nothing more in the whole wide world than to buy Rollerblade Barbie'.[1]

Whether this very specific gendering of our kids through toys is something contemporary adults should be worried about or whether we can relax because all this gender stereotyping and cliché-ridden nonsense comes out in the Barbie car-wash is something I'm going to explore.

Brand Power
At the forefront of this toy battle of the sexes are the leading brands. Just as clothes have brands that attract attention and have currency

in children's social circles, so too do toys. Companies work hard to associate their logo and products with specific sexes – for example, Mattel's Barbie and MGA Entertainment's Bratz are clearly designed for girls and Matchbox cars are for boys. We might buy them for the opposite sex, refusing to bow to corporate dictates, but in the colours, packaging and advertising it's clear which sex most brands of toys are targeting.

Identifying toys as appropriate to one sex or the other is not all that 'branding' does. Saturated by advertising, adults and children are also persuaded that only a certain make of toy is good enough. Nagged by their kids (especially as birthdays or annual events such as Christmas approach) for a specific brand of toy, adults will go out of their way to purchase them – even when the bank account is protesting. It's predicted that in the 2007/2008 financial year alone, Australians will spend around $561 million on toys and games.[2] For those who can't afford the 'branded' toy and choose a cheaper but, to their eyes, admirable alternative, the disappointment the children feel (and consequently, the adults for letting their kids down) is simply not worth it. As Alissa Quart points out, 'the heavy-duty marketing from the cradle onward has warped the social lives of today's teenagers and exacerbated caste snobbery in the classrooms'.[3] One 13-year-old wistfully claimed, 'Brands designate social position'.[4] For teens, this happens with clothes and other gadgets; for our tots and tweens, it starts with toys. And we inadvertently buy into this, believing that we're either advancing (through buying) or retarding (through denying) our kids' social standing in the process.

As I explained in Chapter Two, corporations rely on these fears and tap into them to sell their products. For example, Miuchiz, an electronic handheld communication device made by MGA Entertainment (Micro Games of America[5] and maker of Bratz) declares on the back of the packaging: 'It's your choice to get connected. Do you belong?'

Talk about hard sell. These marketers know exactly how to poke the bruises of stigma and stroke the egos of kids (and parents) desperate to fit in. If being accepted in kid culture these days occurs through 'things' then, as far as the corporations are concerned, that's great news. They make lots of pretty, bright and expensive 'things' and then persuade us and our kids that we 'need' them. And we've bought this message – hook (the advertising and outrageous promises), line (the attractive packaging combined with children's plaintive demands) and sinker (the product, the toy). Because we all seem to do it, we take comfort. But it's cold comfort. Why do we keep buying into the hype, the false promises of happiness for ourselves and our kids, knowing it's a vicious cycle? Psychologist Gabriel Tarde believes that society is made up of 'a group of beings who are apt to imitate one another ... and imitation is a kind of somnambulism'.[6] Keeping up with the Joneses has never been such a serious or expensive business but, when it comes to our kids, it's time for us to wake up.

A generation ago, we amused ourselves outside. Recently, we've developed an indoor lifestyle, which means we have a greater focus on toys and objects that entertain and distract our kids. We also live in a society gripped by fear: we're too scared to let our kids go outside in case they get kidnapped, molested, hurt or sunburnt. The natural environment, if you believe all the reports out there and many of us do, is now one of the biggest threats to our kids' wellbeing. What do we do? Create the greatest unnatural environment within our homes, fill them with more unnatural toys and then whinge about our kids' 'unnaturally' bad behaviour. But that's all right. The toy companies are thanking us.

Toying with Emotions
Far from simply being expendable objects enjoyed or neglected by generations of kids, toys are also an important part of the social, emotional and psychological landscape of the family and society as a whole. Sherri A Inness writes, 'you might ... assume that dolls and other toys simply don't matter ... But toys do matter, and they do convey ideas about how adult life should be run'.[7] What we buy for our children and encourage them to play with (or don't know they are) suggests a great deal about how we value or dismiss the relevance of childhood,

play and possessions as a part of a person's overall development. Child psychologist Susan Linn writes:

> Because children use play to understand the world, the toys we provide for them serve as lessons and reflections of society's values. That's why it's legitimate to ask questions about the impact of Barbie dolls on girls' expectations about their lives or feelings about their bodies, or about the impact of excessively and explicitly violent toys on children's attitudes and behaviour.[8]

This is why toys such as the 'sexy' Bratz range of dolls, as well as Barbie, cause such a furore in the media. This is why young boys in particular become captivated by, first, Pokémon, then Yu-Gi-Oh, causing some schools to ban the exchange of these 'monster' cards as their students turned into Wall Street traders, akin to the unscrupulous Gordon Gecko (beautifully parodied in an episode of *Lizzie McGuire*). This is why some pre-schools forbid superhero play and why we all wince at the presence of toy guns in the toy box. On some level we're aware that what our children play with and how they play with these objects really does matter. It impacts upon who our children become, and their toys and play reflect our values and concerns. And we don't want to come across as 'bad', failed or indifferent to our children's needs, do we?

So, what values, if any, are toys instilling in our children? This is the type of question adults should ask before purchasing. It's the kind I'd like to discuss by looking at some of the most popular girls' toys: first, the Barbie range and then the new dolls on the shelf, Bratz.

Barbie: 'The Bitch Who Has Everything'

Described as the 'queen of consumer heaven',[9] 'the most potent icon of American popular culture in the late twentieth century', the 'one toy that stands for the modern day toy industry',[10] Mattel's Barbie has been praised, vilified and accused of changing the nature of play for generations of little girls around the world.[11] Examining the impact of Barbie on global culture gives us an idea of the role toys play in the social and emotional lives of not just girls, but boys and adults as well.

'The bitch who has everything' – that's how cultural critic, Shirley Steinberg, entitled an article she wrote on Barbie for a collection of essays in the book *Kinderculture*.[12] Now, while Steinberg's Barbie and, indeed, Mattel's 'Barbie' line may have everything, I distinctly remember my Barbie (and I only had one) was rather a deprived toy. She drove around my bedroom in one of my mother's slippers, lived in an old shoebox and camped under a large handkerchief, which also doubled as a dress on occasions. But, these days, for a child to own a single Barbie is more the exception than the rule.

Ever since Barbie was introduced in 1959, she's had an impact on generations of young girls and boys in ways her maker could never have foreseen. More than a doll, those who love her appreciate her role as a go-getter, shattering the glass ceiling, and as a fashionista who has worn the clothes of some of the world's great designers. For those who detest her, she represents the worst of racism and capitalist consumer culture. And it's not only Islamic fundamentalists (who imposed a fatwa on her in 1995) who despise her either.[13] For many adults, the problem with Barbie lies not so much in her unrealistic physical dimensions (if she was a real woman her dimensions would have been 40-18-32; now these proportions have been modified), or in that she 'gives the appearance of sexuality without the sex itself',[14] but the fact that she's the ultimate materialist. Burdened with far too many outfits and possessions for one girl to handle, from cars, boats, horses, accessories and even friends, critics fear she's teaching our kids that more means not enough. This is particularly relevant considering Mattel's boast that Barbie is not simply a toy, she's a 'lifestyle brand'.[15]

So who is this fantastic plastic, pneumatically enhanced blonde who arouses envy and wrath in equal measure? Who is this 'she-devil' who has spawned movies, TV shows, CDs, computer games, make-up, linen, clothes, books, perfume, underwear, shoes, handbags and anything else that can be placed in a shop and be seen and desired by our children (and some adults who collect her with zeal)? Who is this eternally youthful 'bimbo' who has inspired academics, songwriters, artists and filmmakers? Who is this 'bitch who has everything'?

Barbie, or Barbara Millicent Roberts, was the brainchild of Mattel co-founder Ruth Handler.[16] On a trip to Germany in 1956, her daughter, Barbara, came across a doll named Bild Lilli in a shop. What Barbara didn't realise was that Lilli was actually a semi-pornographic novelty item for adults based on a character, a prostitute, in a risqué comic strip in a German newspaper, *Bild Zeitung*. According to cultural sociologist Steven Dubin, Handler had been thinking about developing an adult doll for little girls. While baby dolls were all well and good, she wanted to give girls the chance to imagine what it would be like, through play with a doll, to have a womanly body, accoutrements and fashions. Lilli was her inspiration.

The rest, as we say, is history.

Handler then employed the design skills of Jack Ryan, a former husband of Zsa Zsa Gabor, and the inventor of the bodies of the Hawk and Sparrow missiles during the Cold War. With his input, Barbie was born. A mixture of porn and violence was behind the creation of a toy that came to represent middle-class affluence and hope.

Barbie: A weapon of mass instruction; a real bombshell.

Boyfriend Ken (named after Handler's son) followed in 1961 along with other friends, cousins and a multicultural array of Barbies, some lifted straight from classic tales, Disney films, iconic TV shows and any other commercial tie-in you can imagine (including African-American 'Nichelle', which was the first name of the actor who played Lieutenant Uhura in the original *Star Trek* TV series). According to Dubin, if you lined up every Barbie sold in the first 30 years, from the tips of their moulded toes to the ends of their fibre locks, you'd circle the world four times.

Now that's a lot of Barbie.

When Barbie first appeared, there were numerous protests. Not only did corporate buyers 'hate' this woman-doll, but mothers felt she had 'too much of a figure'.[17] Pre-orders for the doll were cut and her projected sale figures reduced. But, as Eric Clark notes, Mattel had discovered the power of advertising – specifically, the power of TV to bypass adults and target children directly.[18] It no longer mattered what the adults thought; kids loved Barbie and began to let the adults in their life know how much. So much so, Barbie is now considered the most valuable 'toy brand in the world'.[19]

One of the reasons she has been so successful is that she keeps reinventing herself. From model to astronaut to teacher, Barbie is a doll on a mission – even a lunar one. While she has had a few bumps along her journey – including her infamous talking phase where one of her pre-recorded lines was 'Math class is tough', setting feminist ire alight; a brief exchange of her voice box with GI Joe's by a protest group; and the fact the Japanese makers of her body kept putting nipples on her breasts (which were filed off) – she's survived.

For Ken, however, the ride hasn't always been so easy. Unable to share Barbie's box, the poor guy has had to endure slights on his sexuality, rumours about Barbie and GI Joe, and her brief fling with Aussie surfer, Blaine.

Once appealing to girls of all ages, Barbie was the doll of choice for a few generations. (She even appealed to some grown-ups – there are a number of women (and at least one man) who have paid hundreds of thousands of dollars to have their bodies and faces sculpted to resemble Barbie,[20] while in 2006 Marina Raebel sold her mother's Barbie collection for over $200,000.[21]) These days, Barbie's popularity is waning. According to psychologist Michael Carr-Gregg, 'Nowadays, even eight-year-olds deem dolls and other playthings babyish'.[22] In his book *The Princess Bitchface Syndrome: Surviving Adolescent Girls*, he describes how a 'UK study in 2005 revealed that girls aged 7–11 felt such hostility towards Barbie dolls of their earlier childhood that they were torturing, maiming and even decapitating them'.[23]

Arguably, this is because of the new dolls on the shelf: the Bratz, the dolls that challenged Barbie's dominance and in doing so altered the playing fields for ever.

I'm Not a Barbie Girl

Originally designed for girls up to their early teens, Barbie now has fans aged from three to six.[24] Built into this age range is the notion that young girls project their fantasies and ideas about being a teen – even one who sometimes acts like an adult – onto the doll. But, as seven-year-old Carrie pointed out to me when I asked her how old she thought Barbie might be in the computer-generated Disney movie *Swan Lake*, Barbie is 'a teenager'. When I asked if she was sure, pointing out that Barbie gets married in the film, Carrie patiently explained, 'Yes, but that's because she's a teenager *acting* as an adult'.

This sentiment is echoed by many other young girls. To them, Barbie is the eternal teenager 'acting' as an adult. Projecting their dreams onto the doll, young girls can also 'act', through play with Barbie and company, as 'teenagers' or adults in a safe and reassuring environment.

With Bratz, however, a different type of play emerges. Bratz have targeted that lucrative tween demographic – roughly seven to 13. Disenchanted with Barbie, girls in this age group now describe her as 'boring', or as reminding them of their mothers.[25] They also note that she doesn't have outfits, hairdos and accessories, as eight-year-old Jacinta says, 'as good as the Bratz ones'. Sweet-faced, smiling Barbie doesn't have attitude either.

Rising to the challenge that Bratz presented, Mattel introduced a new line of dolls: 'My Scene', which includes Street Scene Barbie and My Bling Bling Barbie. In both ranges, the mono-coloured locks have been streaked, the covered torso is now very taut and on display. It's also tattooed and the dolls' navels are pierced. Barbie's once (by comparison) demure outfits are out, and bustiers, faux fur jackets, low-slung hipsters, extremely short skirts, high heels, knee-high boots and jewellery are in. Even her eyes are bigger and layered in eye-liner and eye shadow. Her lips have had the plastic equivalent of collagen treatment and her chin seems more pointed, jutting. These 'Barbies', with names like Nolee, Madison and, of course, Barbie, are the 'skanky-hos' of the Barbie world, set to give pop star Pink attitude and then some.

What all the Barbies have in common is a set of moulded plastic underpants (lacking in earlier models), slim proportions, long legs with moulded toes, and lots of accessories. The packaging is styled to resemble shop fronts, celebrity lifestyle and, generally, project glamour. Turn them over and there's a picture that looks like a still from a music video, with the 'girls' gathered around a sleek vehicle or posing for a fashion shoot. In the corner is a picture of a potential owner, a tween girl, also showing how to wear the included piece of jewellery, tattoo or hair extensions and so match her doll.

Ironically, to keep up with their Bratz competitors, Mattel it seems, have returned Barbie to her inspirational roots. Marketing her as 'Hooker Barbie' doesn't quite appeal to a broad demographic. I guess 'Street Scene' is about as close as Mattel dare get. As for 'Bling, Bling', I'm convinced that's a bit of fun being poked at parents who are sacrificing a great deal of 'bling bling' in order to sate their children's desires while also appealing to an urban culture of affluence.

Something the dolls with a 'passion for fashion', the Bratz, do with zeal.

The Bratz Pack

In 2001 the toy world changed forever. MGA Entertainment produced the Bratz line of dolls and Barbie was toppled off her plastic pedestal.[26] While there were only eight Bratz to start with, including one called Yasmin, named after CEO Isaac Larian's own daughter, there are now dozens. Multicultural, of various ages and created in both sexes, with nicknames to boot, the dolls took the world by storm. By 2003 they had overtaken Barbie in sales; in 2005 in Australia alone the Bratz doll range netted over A$44 million – that's two million dolls sold.[27] Allan Tiest, merchandise director of Toys 'R' Us Australia, acknowledges that, while the dolls have the biggest share of the girls' market, 'our buyers are mostly mums, and the mums are obviously liking it'.[28]

With bigger heads, detachable feet (with shoes), pouting lips and, as essayist Nancy Gibbs wrote, so 'heavily made up, they look jaded, bored, if not actually stoned'.[29] Bratz dolls have captivated kids and the market share. The face-painting of the dolls, which is done in China, takes 16 layers, all done by hand.[30] Journalist Marea Reed describes them as embodying 'some of the ugliest clichés of the all-pervasive hip-hop culture'.[31] They have incredibly funky accessories and partake in the pop-star and fashion lifestyle. Even their names are 'cool'. Cloe, Roxxi, Kobe and Jade have attitude by the mouthful. In the 'Birthday Bratz' range, the girls sport tiny little T-shirts (revealing the obligatory bit of stomach) with Bratz Jade's T-shirt stating, 'No present for me, No cake for you!' Bratz Cloe's T-shirt reads, 'My birthday doesn't end till I say so!' These girls (and boys) don't mess around; they have Bratitude. Gibbs sums up the fascination when she writes that, while 'you may want to play with them ... they don't want to play with you...'.

Their packaging is vibrant and eye-catching. These dolls are out to party, well past bedtime for their owners, as the Midnight party range declares, and embrace the big wide world. Forget fairy princesses and domestic dreams, these girls understand how keeping up with popular culture trends and attracting the attention of the opposite sex gives kids kudos in this day and age. This is why the Bratz line keeps reinventing itself – as Angelz, Rock Starz, Candyz (bright colours), Pixiez and in 2007 in a 'real-life' film, *Bratz: The Movie*. Laden with stereotypes and clichés, the film focuses on friendship, fashion and 'fitting in' (not necessarily in that order) and within narrowly defined cliques, which is mostly parodied. There's the obligatory villain (the school principal's arrogant and spiteful daughter) and banal dialogue. The main characters, for example, make proclamations such as 'Fashion is like your superpower ... you shouldn't have to hide it from the world'.[32] The film is one long promotion for the Bratz brand and another way of establishing and reinforcing brand allegiance.[33]

The doll range even has 'petz' you can purchase – not only your ordinary dog or cat, but a foxz (that happen to look like a poodle) as well. Once again, the names and style blur the line between fun and sex as the 'foxy ladyz' have pets that define their image.

Not content with just giving Bratitude, the MGA dolls also have a princess line. Bratz don't care if Rapunzel has let down her hair, and Mattel's Beauty, well, she's just skin deep. The Bratz princess says: 'Who needs a castle? Being a modern day princess isn't about glass slippers! It's about never bowing to pressure and knowing you're a princess on the inside'.[34] This is the script that appears on the back of Bratz Princess Yasmin's packaging. The sentiment might even be empowering if it wasn't for the overriding message in every single range of Bratz boxes and in the accompanying pamphlets, which is to purchase more of the products and to accessorise!

Aiming for an even younger market, there are also the Bratz Kidz for ages four and over. The Kidz range is simply yet another marketing strategy. Kidz appeal to adults and kids. Adults uneasy about buying their young children sexy Bratz, but understanding their children's desire to be part of the Bratz scene and earn points with friends, can buy these more conservative and younger looking Kidz and feel confident they're not sexualising their tots. They're still Bratz, but they're into 'fun' (as opposed to fashion). In effect, MGA have created a new market: kweens (between kids and tweens). Before Bratitude, it seems we have drama kweens. And don't our wallets know it. I can hear the 'ker-ching' of the registers from here.

Finally, there are the youngest dolls (I'm not dealing with the miniature versions of most of these ranges, but they're there too), the Bratz Babyz, recommended for ages four plus. To me, they're wrong and sexual in a way that makes me deeply uneasy. I don't understand why MGA made baby dolls that look like they sleep (and work) in a boudoir as opposed to a nursery. I would hold these dolls up as evidence that we are sexualising our kids – through their toys and play. I'm not alone. The American Psychological Association, Dr Jean Kilbourne, Professor Michael Carr-Gregg, Julie Gale from the 'Kids Free to Be Kids' campaign and numerous others have all expressed their concern about these dolls, their look and the potential impact they can have. I am also concerned about the problematically named 'Teen Tees' range of dolls – a double entendre and the most blatant announcement of kids' sexual desirability I've ever heard. Why call them that ('teen tease') if not deliberately playing on words? Why not just give the range a name without a double meaning? But, just like the Bratz Babyz, kids like them and parents buy them.

It's true that, to most little girls, the Babyz aren't sexy – they're convenient, trendy and cute. I couldn't understand the appeal until I asked. Six-year-old Lexie likes the fact she can hold them in the palm of her hand, fit a couple in her bag and use household items as cars and houses to build worlds for her Babyz to play in. Not surprisingly, they also give her social kudos because, in her age group, Bratz are 'the' doll to own. Girls want to play with Lexie, who comes from a working-class, single-parent background and this means a great deal to her and to her mother.

Just like Barbie, the Bratz in all their guises arouse controversy and praise in equal measure. Lauded for their multiculturalism and for introducing a range of boy dolls, the makers have also been criticised for being immoral by sexualising kids and encouraging materialism.

This doesn't seem to have deterred the manufacturers who have not only taken Bratz to DVD but also to electronic games. In the various animated movies, they attend high school (around Year 8 – which makes them about 14), write for a fashion magazine while being dogged by an older, jealous fashion editor and her twin sidekicks, the twevils – think 'The Bratz wear Prada' and you get the drift. They travel overseas, date, become rock stars and hang out in nightclubs, help foil a plan to destroy the earth, and all without any adult accompaniment. There's also Bratz fashion, underwear, make-up, stationery, linen, food and furniture – just like Barbie. With all these 'branded' accessories, our children really can be living dolls.

So what values are these dolls, the Barbies and Bratz of the world, teaching our kids?

Message in a Dolly

After swallowing my feelings about Barbies and Bratz, I spoke to dozens of little girls about why they liked them. It was clear that, like anything, there are positives and negatives surrounding these toys; it's up to adults to be informed and weigh the pros and cons in our own minds, not simply cave in to child, peer or corporate pressure. We need to remind ourselves that, for toy companies, 'It is only about profit. The role of children is a clear one – they are cash cows to be milked'.[35]

What was made abundantly apparent to me was that these new dolls, the Bratz, were more interesting, bolder and more assertive somehow than their traditional Barbie counterparts. These sexy, brash and socially sophisticated dolls, rightly or wrongly, speak to this century. They certainly speak to this century's child. They're sassy, not boring; they make a statement and, reassuringly for adults, they're unreal. As Caley (eight) reminded a teacher who complained the Bratz can't spell, 'that's just a marketing strategy!' Caley is a cluey kid. But with those giant bobble heads and feet (which means they can stand by themselves, unlike Barbie – there's a lesson in that alone), they're pure fantasy. And they're a more appealing fantasy than original Barbie.

Are they sexy? Yes. But young girls aren't going to change the way they express sexual curiosity and experiment with ideas and feelings through their dolls just because she has a bigger head, streaked hair or a pierced navel. That will happen regardless. This new breed of dolls resembles the young women our kids see on TV or in films and magazines. Original Barbie is more like Bree from *Desperate Housewives*, a Stepford-type wife and a glaring anachronism, on television and in real life. As much as I expected to be shocked by the sexual look of the dolls and find them highly inappropriate, after playing with them and with the kids, I wasn't as horrified as I thought I'd be. But that doesn't mean I wasn't disturbed by some of the other messages implicit and explicit in the dolls and the brands.

Sometimes, when parents, teachers or family associations express public concern (or, as the media describe it, 'outrage') about toys, critics tell them they're overreacting and, to a degree, discount or silence the unease. However, the new Barbies and the Bratz are dolls that deserve to have adult eyes turned on them and opened. But let's be sensible.

On their own, I've no doubt the Barbies and Bratz would be delightful addendums to the toy box and children's imaginative play. But they're not on their own. They exist in a world of merchandise, advertising, celebrities and other appealing products and ideas. In their heavily made-up eyes, pouting mouths, lingerie-wearing and posed skinny bodies, there's entrée to worldly knowledge that's being replicated in other cultural forms our children are accessing. In the magazines our children read; the TV shows, films and news bulletins they watch, which are all laden with 'celebrity gossip'; and in playground and street talk among friends, there's not only a 'passion for fashion', but one for accumulating things and emulating sexiness. The dolls don't cause this; they're a symptom of everything else out there. As Eric Clark writes:

> Always a selling instrument, sex is now aimed firmly at tweens. It is meant to make them feel older, more empowered, more likely to demand successfully what they want. Toys are not the only villains. The bombardment also comes from the wide range of industries so cleverly linked to them: clothes, video games and music.[36]

We can add to this films, TV shows, books, underwear, furniture, accessories and make-up – all of which Bratz, as an 'industry', have a stake in. The Bratz are the zenith (or nadir) of the saturated sexy market and they reinforce the message that it's how you look and what you own that's more important than anything else. Collect friends like you do things and, through ownership, prove your worth and popularity. After all, possession is nine-tenths of today's social laws.

The name 'Bratz' announces a new way of thinking about children that's evolved in the last few decades. Do you remember when the term 'brats' used to be a pejorative? Used to describe kids who were antisocial and rude, it was criticism and parents were horrified and ashamed if their kids were described this way. Now corporations add a 'z', wrap the notion that all kids love to defy adults into a 'cool', very pretty, feminised and sexy package, and it's suddenly the next great thing. It's has become an honorific, a badge.

Who wants their daughter saying to friends who have been invited to their party, 'No present for me, no cake for you!' This is bad manners being marketed as 'cute', 'fun', 'sassy' and as new-age 'attitude'. No, it's not. It's appallingly rude and shouldn't be rewarded. It's turning what would once have been a huge and embarrassing social faux pas and very much a negative into a positive.

If encouraging our kids to be 'Bratz' is being marketed as empowering our little girls, then I think we need to think again. We're being persuaded to believe that instilling manners and curbing 'attitude' (in the negative sense) is either too hard or old-fashioned. Perhaps this is why we buy Bratz for our girls, to camouflage parental shortcomings or because we've just given up. We've raised brats who demand Bratz and spread attitude through the playground like a virus. But that's okay, the other mums, dads and kids are doing the same thing: they're just like us.

And what about the dolls' signature line – a 'passion for fashion'? On the one hand, we have older kids concerned about global warming and other very important political and social issues, while on the other we have a generation of young kids stressing over what to wear to their primary school dance and what the boys think of them because, as the Bratz website declares as it slowly loads, 'It takes time to look this good'.

The Theory of Natural Collection

Pick up a Bratz in any range and the box reads, 'Collect them all!' with 'collectible mask and cape', 'collectible keychain for you!' and so on. Packaging includes leaflets aimed at the kween and tween demographic announcing 'Superstylin Stuff!' with pages of Bratz products from chairs, clocks, lights and canopies to wrist purses informing kids that there's 'room for your money, credit cards, keys and cell phone'. There are even talking Bratz who, when you press the button, utter deep and meaningful phrases such as 'Have you ever had a bad hair day?' or 'Don't forget, your opinion matters, so say what you feel'. And my personal favourite, 'Don't be afraid to ask for what you want'. These can be interpreted (bad hair aside) as important and empowering statements of self-confidence, yet they can also be construed as encouraging kids to use pester-power to ensure parents capitulate to their demands.

Should we stop buying these dolls? Not necessarily. But when adults purchase these types of toys for their children it should be in an informed way, with the understanding that they too have been lured by corporate promises and with the knowledge that they need to be prepared to undermine the sexual and commercial messages and replace them with positive ones. It also means adults should note the age recommendations that come with these toys (as arbitrary as they might seem), and consider the ways in which our kids project their fantasies and imaginative play onto and through these dolls. Purchasing a teen Bratz for a five-year-old is not recommended by the manufacturer. There are good reasons for this, as appealing and interesting as the dolls seem and as much your child may want them and nag you for one because 'everyone else has one'. Of course, what does not suit one five-year-old may suit another and it will certainly depend on your child's cognitive development: how they play and what imaginary scenarios they project need to be considered as well.

Adults should make sure they talk about the messages on the boxes and those implicit in the dolls' sexy, sassy, street-wise looks, and make sure their children understand them as fantasy and as fun. Unfortunately, there are a number of so-called real people who seem to live by this new Bratitude creed: Paris Hilton, Nicole Ritchie, Britney Spears, Lindsay Lohan (who 'stars' in the My Scene Barbie movie and in 2006 admitted to attending Alcoholics Anonymous meetings at the ripe old age of 20 and in 2007 was admitted to rehabilitation after being picked up for drink driving and being found with cocaine), and a host of others. So long as our kids understand that the lives these stars lead are also unreal (and that they have mums and dads, dreams, hopes, good days and bad, disappointments, pimples, smelly breath and even jail terms), then we'll go a long way to making sure that the lines between fantasy and reality remain clear – not in a way that spoils our kids' fun, but in a way that means their own sense of self won't rely on the values promoted by commercial companies out to take our hard-earned dollars by encouraging our kids to build their identities on what they collect and own.

Imagination Versus Limitations

While Bratz, Barbies and other dolls invite creative play and children certainly use their imaginations when constructing scenarios and relationships between their dolls, the ability for kids to explore ideas through these colourful pieces of plastic is being limited by the numerous other tie-ins, particularly the films, websites, magazines, books and TV shows that accompany these 'branded' products. In many ways, the hour-plus animations (including Polly Pocket) featuring the dolls and their accessories direct and restrict the children's play by bringing these objects to life and giving them characters, voices and emotions. Once, children could project themselves onto and into their dolls, invent their lives and relationships. It's not so easy any more. That important imaginative work is being done for them by yet more branded products that parents and adults are being persuaded to buy, often by children who are desperate to own them. This also happens with popular toys for boys such as figurines, let alone electronic games (more on those in Chapter Nine). I believe this is a concern. Adults should be aware of this and modify how much they let their children access and how much they fall into the trap of buying. Discuss the films and other media with your kids; encourage them to create alternative stories and characterisations for the dolls – above and beyond what the manufacturer imagines. An expert on early years child play, Dr Jennifer Sturgess, warns that some modern toys fail to stimulate children in the right way 'because they are not surprising'. She says that the 'good toys are things that allow kids to construct or make up something for themselves'.[37] Professor Susan Danby from the Queensland University of Technology agrees. She advises parents to ask themselves whether a toy can be used in a problem-solving or creative manner: 'If the toy walks, talks and does everything for them, then you have to ask how that engages the child in an imaginative way'.[38]

The Getting of Collective Wisdom
Another point to consider regarding the Bratz and Barbie brands is that these dolls have no maturation milestones. It may seem odd to worry about this in relation to toys but, in so far as toys prepare kids for the 'real' world, this is important.[39]

In their books, DVDs and embodied in the dolls themselves is eternal youth. There's no sense of generations: of grandmother, mother, daughter or of grandfather, father, son – something other toy lines do address. In stories told about Barbie and Bratz (via the movies and books), these dolls rely on each other – their friends frame their lives and function as role-models, confidants and nurturers. Adults are largely absent from their world or function as either needy or villains. Where are Barbie's or the Bratz's parents? Barbie does have parents: their names are George and Margaret Roberts, but Mattel hasn't manufactured them.[40] Instead, these dolls are surrounded by peers or younger versions of themselves (Skipper, Bratz Kidz, Bratz Babyz and so on). They set their own agendas educationally and socially. In Barbie DVDs, she sometimes cares for groups of young girls, rescuing an entire enchanted forest and kingdom, but only after male intervention (and securing a husband in the process). My Scene Barbies never ask for parental permission or extend the courtesy of telling adults where they are. They appear totally autonomous. This can be reassuring and empowering for young girls who look forward to this time in their lives and, as Jane Smiley notes, 'children can manipulate and control them as they cannot the other adults in their lives'.[41] But as Singer Jones argues:

> By obscuring the boundary between adolescence and adulthood, Mattel makes it irrelevant. If Barbie is both a teen and an adult, but, at the same time, always Barbie, this makes teenager-hood as autonomous and self-sufficient as

> adulthood. Moreover, there's no transformation from one to the other.⁴²

Bratz dolls are also defined by an overwhelming absence of adult guidance and protection. When in trouble, the dolls don't ask the grown-ups for help, they ask each other. It raises the question, does this reflect children's reality today? Or is it childlike wish-fulfilment, as reproduced in many popular children's novels, where kids survive without or despite adults? Or is it simply clever marketing to endorse kids and make the dolls more appealing? I'd say it's all of the above. Naomi Wolf, in her polemic, *The Beauty Myth*, discusses how important it is for younger and older women to have intergenerational contact. She writes, 'Young women are dangerously "unmothered" – unprotected, unguided – institutionally and need role models and mentors'.⁴³

In earlier children's literature (as well as Roald Dahl, and the Lemony Snickett and Harry Potter novels) young, empowered children survive without adult help through their wits and loyalty to each other. However, there are also usually one or two adults who are in the wings, trusting the children and guiding them (often through role-modelling) or from afar (such as Miss Honey in *Matilda* or Professor Dumbledore). In the Bratz and Barbie world, they may be loyal to each other, but it's their popular culture knowledge and style or help from a man, friends or magic that aids them.

The time when wisdom was collected, shared and passed from generation to generation, around kitchens and hearths, appears to be disappearing. It's important that we don't let it vanish completely – we can use the toys we buy for our kids, even the Bratz and Barbies, to open the lines of communication, share important female and male information and discuss emotions and ideas about bodies, relationships and material goods. If these conversations take place around the media room, bedroom or study instead of the hearth, so be it. Just make sure they happen.

Providing we encourage and understand our children's fantasy play and become those much-needed mentors, then their toys will be just that – play things, not role-models for future behaviour. Bratitude, a passion for fashion, style, and other concerns the dolls express have their place, but they need to be placed in a much larger and more important context – by the real adults who define our children's world. That's us.

Remember, as long as we're there and aware of (but try not to interfere with) our children's play-worlds, we'll wield far more influence than a few pieces of plastic and their fantastic and abundant bits and pieces. If there's one thing we don't want to be, it's simply yet another disposable accessory.

chapter five

Boys and Their Toys: Guns, Swords and Testosterone

The Laws of Acquisition

Toys and childhood are like birthday and cake. They have a natural relationship. It's difficult to conceive of one without the other. And who would want to? Since ancient times, adults have invented a variety of toys for children to play with, from yo-yos and dolls to dice, to stimulate their imaginations; teach them physical dexterity, sharing and cooperation; enhance their cognitive abilities; and keep them out from under busy grown-up feet. The giving of toys is an important social ritual, enshrined in holidays, anniversaries and festivities as well as making parents, grandparents and other adults who have children in their lives feel terrific. The look on a child's face when they receive a new and longed for toy is etched in many adult memories. The joy and excitement a child expresses as their wish list is fulfilled … for at least five minutes anyhow … makes those hours of anxiety, queuing and blowing the credit card worth it, doesn't it?

As I said in the last chapter, somewhere along the production line, the relationship between adults, children and toys has irrevocably changed. Call it consumer culture, call it parental guilt or child greed, but something has happened to suggest that toys no longer signify what they used to or serve quite the same purpose. No longer do we talk about our children 'wanting' toys, but rather 'needing' them – and usually a specific brand as well. These days, children 'need' toys, not just for play, but for social currency. Ownership of specific brands of toys bolsters feelings of popularity and acceptance in kid culture. It's clear that the number of toys in many children's lives has outgrown the need. And yet, armed with this knowledge and evidence (spilling out bedrooms into hallways and other rooms), we continue to buy, buy, buy. More is no longer enough.

Today we're nurturing *acquisitive* children as opposed to inquisitive ones. It's as if toys aren't being purchased to be practical or even fun objects so much as 'proof' of love or as substitutes for parental time. But, as we all know, presents never substitute for presence. Nor does being deprived of toys in our own childhoods, trying to prove to other adults that we're good parents or feeling satisfied with our generous selves excuse us for overindulging our children.

In so many ways, buying for boys seems less complex than for girls. There are more choices available, and the toys aren't based on appearance and fashioning a self in the way that girls' toys so overtly are. Yet in other ways, they focus on exactly the same types of things, only the self they invite boys to fashion is more competitive and active than girls while still instructing them to be brand conscious. The pressure for boys to own the 'right' sort of toys is as focused and strong as it is for girls – and with the same sorts of results. Kids who don't have the 'right stuff' can be cruelly ostracised and become social pariahs. This is not only difficult for kids to cope with, but also heartbreaking for the adults in their lives to observe. But instead of standing our ethical ground, shoring up our kids' sense of self and teaching them about values and emphasising what *is* important, we take the easy way out and buy more.

The urge to buy more is not only imprinted in the psyches of children and adults in the age of techno-capitalism, it's a fundamental aspect of the toys themselves.

Planned Obsolescence

The toy and other associated industries are a booming, billion-dollar market – far from having the best interests of our kids at heart, they are only interested in profit margins. As a result, built into a great deal of the objects we buy for our children is what's called 'planned obsolescence'.[1] That means that many dolls, cars and other toys are made with the intention that they'll break quickly or become outdated faster than the mullet. Through vigorous marketing, attention is drawn to the newest, latest and greatest thing, rendering what was bought last month redundant and encouraging parents to keep up with toy trends and spend. Corporations encourage us to stock the toy box like we would the pantry: chuck out and replace any toy that has surpassed its use-by date. And we're persuaded it's in the best interests of our children's social health to replace them. Worse, we're made to feel bad if we can't keep up.

Boys and Violent Toys

Aside from the blatant sexual stereotyping and the buy-more ethos of Pokémon and Yu-Gi-Oh (where to 'duel' or combat monsters you need a selection of different cards – rarely available in the same pack), the greatest worry for many adults is the overtly violent nature of boys' toys. This can even be seen in toy ads, which, as Shirley Steinberg and Joe Kincheloe state, 'have witnessed only minor alterations in the last forty years. The adult male voice-over is gone, but close-ups of the toys, and boys' voices making engine and weapons sound effects, continue uninterrupted. Boys still become one with their toys, whereas girls take care of theirs – ever the adoring spectators of their dolls in girl commercials'.[2]

In a society saturated by violent images, it's understandable we'd be concerned about watching our children, boys in particular, emulating sound effects and 'becoming one' with their toys, incorporating a sense of power and physical actions into their play and friendships through what they own. Despite attempts on behalf of parent and family groups and other experts to reduce the number of 'violent' toys for sale in shops, there are still a great many available. Whether it's the muscle-bound action figurines of the various wrestling series (recommended for ages 12 and over), action heroes, replicas of film characters (*Star Wars*, *Pirates of the Caribbean*, *Transformers*, *Teenage Mutant Ninja Turtles* and so on), electronic games (dealt with in detail in Chapter Nine), or toy weapons and dress-ups, toys for boys are often perceived as encouraging our sons to be aggressive and non-cooperative.

The expert jury is divided on whether or not violent toys and images create violent kids. Some suggest that watching brutal movies and playing blood-soaked electronic games facilitates violence,[3] or that war toys train 'little boys to be cannon fodder and/or gun collectors',[4] whereas others state that there's no real evidence to support this.[5] Examples that are often cited to sustain the vicious imagery and toys-breeding-violence case are the Columbine High School massacre in the US, or the murder of toddler James Bolger by two 10-year-olds in Britain.[6] The media has a field day with these and uses them to link violent material and toys with violent behaviour – especially in boys. What then occurs is a moral panic around anything remotely associated with what in the past would have been termed 'rough play'. These days, make-believe games involving weapons and pretend injuries are construed as aggressive and as something that needs to be quashed, even when there is no physical or emotional harm occurring. Only a few years ago, this type of play would have been understood as natural and even beneficial for young boys.

Testosterone has become a dirty word in this society.

The boys who were responsible for the crimes mentioned above didn't grow up in a vacuum. These boys and young men were members of families, schools and communities both literal and online. Everything around them worked in tandem to produce the type of sad, dysfunctional people they turned out to be when they committed their atrocious acts. It wasn't just the games they played, electronic or otherwise, nor was it the violence they watched on the TV that turned them into killers. It was a combination of a whole range of complex familial, social and psychological factors that exploded the day they killed. Gerard Jones discusses the case of a first-grade child who shot and killed a classmate in 2000. As the community and subsequently the world reeled in shock that someone so young could perpetrate such violence, there were the usual attempts to link the boy's behaviour to his media consumption. What was overlooked in much of the public discussion was the fact the child grew up 'in a crack house full of real guns, surrounded by men who used real violence to settle their disputes ... he didn't have toys or video games or any other safe way to relieve his anxiety or express his aggression'.[7] Forensic psychologist Dr Helen Smith, who has studied and worked with thousands of violent young offenders, administered a national US survey and written a book entitled *The Scarred Heart: Understanding and Identifying Kids Who Kill*, states that, 'Not one young person in my experience has ever been made violent by media influence ... Young people who are already inclined to be violent do feel that violent media speaks to them. A few do get dangerous ideas from it. But more of them find it to be a way to deal with their rage'.[8]

Hundreds upon thousands of boys (and girls) around the world play with the same toys, listen to the same music, watch the same TV shows and play the same games and they grow up functional. This comfortable linking of games, violence and tragic and rare outcomes is used by the media to demonise popular culture and fuel fears around toy guns, weapons, boys, and the types of games they like to play. And it works. It works to punish all boys (and girls) who happily and with well-modulated play enjoy make-believe and fantasy violence.

Guns and Rough Play

These days, parents baulk at buying their kids a toy gun for fear it might turn them into serial killers. Then they watch their sons (and daughters) pick up sticks and shoot their friends with them, or in school playgrounds invent complex scenarios involving heroes and villains and death. Susan Linn uses play as a therapeutic tool for working with children. She writes that:

> It is absolutely clear to me that children are capable of deep fear and great rage. The children I see for therapy have neither guns nor swords nor media-linked action figures when we play together. Nevertheless, they frequently commit terrible acts of fantasy violence. My puppets are routinely eaten by monsters, starved, and abandoned ... Fantasy play is a natural and constructive way for children to not only express their feelings but also to gain a sense of control over an often confusing and frightening world.[9]

Other experts argue that children should be allowed to indulge in scary and 'violent' play, but that the ideas for this should be initiated through the kids themselves, not from a TV program they've watched or a toy bought for them.[10] This is somewhat impractical in this media-soaked world, where TV and toy manufacturers work in tandem to arouse desire for products and then 'show' kids how to play with the products as well through cartoons and films. Adults who refuse to buy a particular toy often find the kids know about it anyway and either play with it at a friend's house or transform their own toys into the one they've been denied (for example, Lego blocks might be put together to be an alien that attacks and destroys the world; a stick becomes a gun; a sister's Barbie might become the victim of a dinosaur monster). Often when adults try to redirect a boy's (or girl's) desire to play superheroes or wars or wield a light sabre into what they deem to be more wholesome or worthy pursuits, they fail and everyone ends up miserable. Adults worry that their kids will appear like maniacs-in-the-making and that the 'violent' play they so enjoy might escalate and the boundaries between fantasy and reality will become blurred. Children are confused as well. They see violence on TV and hear discussions about it (if not actually witness it) but, when they want to play at being 'violent', they're forbidden. We're a culture afraid of our own shadows – ones we've created.

Is it any wonder we see so much actual violence on playing fields around the country? We're so busy repressing supposed violent tendencies in our children, particularly boys, that they have no outlet for what are 'normal' emotional expressions any more. On sporting fields, we try to wrap our kids in cottonwool and then express alarm when a fight breaks out – usually between parents on the side-lines who are so busy suppressing their kids' anger, they've been unable to control their own. We're so scared our children are going to hurt each other, sue each other, or worse, make us look like bad parents, that we don't allow them to express themselves in the best way they know and love: through 'violent' fantasy play. Through make-believe. We have a tendency to link 'violent' play with aggressive tendencies – yet in our children's minds and world, they're not the same thing.

This is why films like *Star Wars*, *Terminator*, *The Matrix Trilogy*, *Pirates of the Caribbean*, *Transformers* and *Spiderman*, electronic games such as *Grand Theft Auto* and *Halo 3*, and so much Japanese anime is popular with boys in particular. They love the make-believe violence. It's cathartic for them. On the screen, in comics and in cyberspace, they get a chance to vicariously experience what is now mostly denied to them: the chance to indulge in some imaginative rough play. As Gerard Jones writes in his book *Killing Monsters: Why Children Need Fantasy, Super Heroes, and Make-Believe Violence*:

> To help our children grow up more effectively as individuals, we need to grow up more as a society ... Instead of reacting to make-believe violence like the nervous kindergartner who yells, 'The boys are fighting again!', we need to accept it as a valuable part of children's emotional make-up and discuss with optimism and acceptance how it can best be used and how we can help children use it.[11]

This is yet another balancing act for parents to master. It means allowing children, boys particularly, to express themselves through make-believe 'violence'. Allow them to don the Superman outfit, to zap people (not whack them) with their Harry Potter wands (a symbolic gun), and to wet friends with their super-soakers (an adult nod to politically correct guns). Allow them to 'duel' with the Yu-Gi-Oh cards they own and remind them that even Yu-Gi-Oh needs his friends and that the

Pokémon monsters only stay with masters who are kind. Look for the good messages in these toys and games (they are there) and reinforce that positive side. Don't be distressed if, despite your attempts to limit your child's exposure to violence in popular culture, they still want, in varying degrees, to experiment with it and ask for specific 'violent' toys and games. As Jones discusses, from the 1960s onwards, millions of professionals and parents swept violence from the education and culture of our kids. We believed that if kids weren't indoctrinated with violence, they wouldn't learn it. But this hasn't worked. Children want 'violence'. And, 'as we removed violence from their officially sanctioned culture – from the classroom, from bedtime stories, from adult-approved play – they were left with no source for it but the commercial entertainment industry'.[12] This is partly why kids are so drawn to these types of games and objects. They desire what the games offer them, a chance to assert themselves in different social groups and try on 'power' for size, even though we're sometimes alarmed by what this suggests. But we have to place our children's interest in and occasional preference for this type of play in a familial, social and cultural context as well. Treat it as part of a balanced diet where all sorts of play and emotional responses to other children, adults, games and toys are expressed and modelled through the behaviour of real and fantasy adults (characters in popular culture) as well. It also means supervising the play that occurs in your child's early years with the toys you buy them and the games they play. But that's what adults are *supposed* to do: we're not supposed to abrogate our responsibility at the checkout, the flick of a remote, the turn of a page. If we deny our kids access to a range of these things, or continue, along with many media outlets, to demonise 'violence' in all forms (except, ironically, in blockbuster movies or current affairs shows), what we end up doing is increasing the 'market for provocative bad taste'[13] and encouraging kids to seek to experiment and communicate with their peers – with little or no adult guidance.

Through make-believe 'violence', children can learn cooperation, about power struggles, about sharing and alliances. They'll make mistakes and they'll learn consequences. Donald Roberts believes that our culture could benefit from showing the consequences of real violence more often and invites adults to occasionally discuss with their kids, for example, what would happen to a character like Wile E. Coyote if he *really* fell off the cliff.[14] If we don't allow our boys and girls the opportunity to engage in a bit of imaginative 'violent' play (within reason) now and then, to build worlds that are black and white, where people live, die and are reborn to die another day, then we'll end up with adults who can't handle their anger or aggression or make movies like *Jackass* and *Jackass 2* for other kids (who never had the chance to indulge in make-believe violence) to laugh at and possibly imitate.

The violence I'm referring to here is not the explicit violence that we see on the nightly news or in Hollywood blockbusters or R- and MA-rated electronic games. I do not condone, in any way, shape or form, that sort of violence (nor do I condone hitting, beating, pushing, punching or any sort of aggressive physical contact, but I do approve of pretend fights and play). It's important to remember that these are produced by adults; they're not generated by children. But neither are they generated *for* children. That's where parental awareness and the setting of boundaries come into play.

We're so nervous about allowing children to play with toy guns or dress up as characters that (to us) represent violence because we're afraid it will turn them into violent adults. We become literal instead of examining the emotional and symbolic power of the imaginary slaps, punches, wands and fights that our children adore making and playing. It's important that we distinguish between reality and fantasy and allow our children to have their fantasies.

This is something that *The Dangerous Book for Boys*, by Conn and Hal Iggulden, has addressed. By writing a manual of (mainly) outdoor and other activities mixed with geography, history and even astronomy, they've created an international bestseller that blends imagination and practicality. Hal Iggulden feels that the book 'restored a little bit of respect in being male, as I think we have for a generation seen the world through a female narrative'.[15] He has a point. There's evidence to suggest that we've 'bubble-wrapped' our children, especially our boys, and at the expense of their emotional, psychological and (with the rise in obesity rates) physical wellbeing too.[16] Boys need male role-models. Australian research has revealed that boys behave better when fathers are involved in their lives while British researchers have shown that, in some ethnic groups, boys are suffering from what's been termed 'father hunger', which leaves young men vulnerable to peer pressure and outside influences.[17] Where there is no father, other males in the family and broader social networks (such as friends and even teachers) can serve a very important purpose; boys need 'real' as opposed to virtual men (film and TV stars and computer-generated versions of masculinity, which are often stereotyped and limited) on which to build their sense of self. This can only happen if the adults in a child's life also understand the role of 'violent' play and fantasy and have a healthy relationship with these.

As Jones persuasively writes, 'Adult anxieties about the effects of entertainment are sometimes the real causes of the very effects we fear most'.[18] This can also apply to the often imagined fears that face our kids if we allow them to play outdoors. Our concerns about the potential dangers lurking in our gardens and on the streets have created a generation of 'indoor' kids and exacerbated a 'disconnection between childhood and nature'.[19] There are even terms for this disconnection: nature-deficit disorder or sensory-deprivation.[20] Richard Louv was so concerned about this, he wrote a book called *Last Child in the Woods*. Experts such as Barry Elvish, CEO of Queensland's Creche & Kindergarten early childhood care network, share this concern. Elvish says that the 'sanitisation of early childhood is an absolute disgrace and the end result is we're going to have children that are sense-deprived and have a limited understanding of the natural environment around them'.[21] Dr June Factor, who examines children's folklore and songs, doesn't understand what has happened to play: 'The question you ultimately have to ask is, do we really have to put so many impediments in [the children's] way? It's a form of disregard, of what children's interests are. It's a form of contempt'.[22]

Children need to be given opportunities to explore their natural environment, feel the dirt (or sand) between their toes, see animals in their habitat, experience the wind on their faces and the sun on their (UV-protected) limbs. To deny kids access to these kinds of experiences is to create problems later in life and set bad examples. As Louv wistfully notes about his childhood experiences: 'Those woods and fields shaped me; they were my Ritalin'.[23]

While we don't want to turn children feral, we do need to strike a balance between indoors and outdoors, screen time and fresh air, and teach our kids that beyond the seductions of film, TV and the computer screen lies a garden, street and world that's worth exploring using all five senses.

Educational Toys

Ellen Seiter, the author of *Sold Separately: Parents and Children in Consumer Culture*, writes that the idea being sold to adults through a variety of media is that play and toys are only worthwhile if they're educational.[24] When Julie Aigner-Clark, mother of a toddler, founded the Baby Einstein Company in 1998, she almost single-handedly concretised the notion that toys and videos, when used correctly (or linked with the name of a historical genius), can boost a baby's brain power. According to Susan Gregory Thomas, this blend of playthings and education 'caused a major shift in the child-rearing style and core beliefs of the majority of American parents, cutting across social and economic boundaries'.[25] In other words, parents across the world were, through clever and relentless marketing, sold the notion that if your baby or toddler (and in some cases, unborn baby) is exposed to everything from classical music to flashcards and specific DVDs, then they were being educated and thus given an advantage over their peers. And it worked. As one mother, who tried to collect every Baby Einstein video for her 16-month-old son, claimed: 'The sooner [children] are stimulated, the more they'll learn in the long run ... It's more about the intellectual foundation he's getting than the entertainment'.[26]

Realising that Aigner-Clark had tapped into a profitable and untapped goldmine, other businesses that focused on pre-schoolers also joined the bandwagon such as Mattel's Fisher-Price and Hasbro's Playskool. Changing their business strategies, they began ensuring that their products wore what's been referred to as the educational 'halo' because, as one marketing executive put it, 'if you can get educational credit, you can pretty much get away with anything'.[27]

We're made to believe that in this fast-paced, cut-throat, competitive world, we need to give our children every advantage we can – even through their toys and play. Whether it's allowing unborn babies to listen to Mozart or strapping a device to pregnant bellies that plays 16 'lessons' of rhythmic sounds (yes, really), or brain-training 'games' by Nintendo, the womb-to-grave push for the consumer dollar now begins before birth. Persuade keen parents that a 'toy' gives their children an edge over others, and it's sold. Add the mystique of electronics and there's an extra incentive.

Dressed as fun as well as educational, techno-toys are hot property. While toys that have flashing lights, play music, teach children to read or advance their maths skills can be very entertaining and educational, they are no substitute for the physical presence, interactions, questions and answers (even wrong ones) of a living, breathing, caring and interested adult. Early childhood specialist Jane Roberts says that in many ways parents use interactive toys to substitute for their own interactions with their children.[28] Dr Michael McDowell of the Royal Australian College of Physicians says that any learning for children under three is 'essentially based around human relationships and through emotional and social connections'.[29]

Even information technology, usually the realm of older kids and adults, became toddler-friendly after Aigner-Clark, and 'lapware' was sold to parents (computers that can be used by kids while they're sitting in adult laps) to introduce kids to screens and, you guessed it, give them another edge. But, as Gregory Thomas points out, while we may believe kids are smarter today because they can push a mouse around or insert a disc somewhere, 'archaeological and anthropological record[s] show that children have always begun using the predominant tools of their culture at around four or five years old'.[30] Just because a child in Lane

Cove, Sydney, or Canning Vale, Perth, can use a computer, it doesn't mean they're smarter or more sophisticated than their ancestors who learned how to use rudimentary tools. Gregory Thomas argues that the 'real change, it seemed, was the influence of marketing: people believed it'.[31]

The word 'educational' on toys (and now TV shows) is a ploy to persuade adults that they're bad and irresponsible if they don't buy or allow their kids to watch them – that somehow adults are denying children a head-start in life, an advantage. It's not true. As Susan Linn states, 'the best toys are inherently educational in that they serve as tools for helping children actively explore, understand, and/or gain mastery over the world. Even if they have multiple parts, they are simple enough to be put to many different uses, and to become different things in a child's imagination'.[32] Gregory Thomas writes that 'Every one of the experts I consulted said that such toys ['educational'] offered no special advantage. They were the products of marketing, not research'.[33] Other research has found that 'educational' toys and DVDs may actually do more harm than good, with one Columbia University researcher suggesting that the reason babies were so mesmerised by Baby Einstein was because they were 'slipping into what could be described as a low-level seizure state'.[34] In buying the 'educational' spin, adults are simply contributing to a $78-billion-dollar market.[35] Another study conducted by the University of Connecticut examined whether or not babies and toddlers could acquire greater vocabularies from watching not only 'educational' TV, but shows specifically designed for them. The researchers concluded that none of the children learned better from television; on the contrary, 'Toddlers do learn the meaning of new words best when taught by an adult caregiver, and they are least likely to learn new words presented via television programs with animated characters'.[36] Using what adults, particularly parents, learn from their children – that repetition, familiarity, friendliness, bright colours, music and soft, sing-song voices get positive responses – educational toys and entertainment have persuaded us that they can replace real-life presence and interaction. They cannot.

Don't be fooled by the description 'educational'; be inspirational instead and your child will thank you.

Toys, Toys, Toys

By now you'll realise that these expensive, cheap and ubiquitous objects that we delight in making and buying for our children, while they may have a long history, are not the simple things we may have believed. Laden with symbolism, criticised, praised, desired, loathed, envied, treasured and destroyed, they're part of the social fabric of every family and community. We live in a material world where we're increasingly being judged by what we have, not what we do or think. While most of us are unhappy with this situation and do what we can to instil different values in our kids, too often we undermine our own best efforts by buying our kids more toys than they can play with, responding to wants rather than needs.

We buy more than we can afford or our children require. A sideeffect of this is that, because we're always buying toys and 'things' for our kids, when it does come to birthdays and Christmas we no longer know what to buy. The number of parents, grandparents, friends and relatives of children I hear crying, 'What do you buy for the kid who has everything?' is ridiculous. In a world stricken by poverty and disease, children in the Western world suffer a different kind of malady: affluenza – the sickness of middle-class affluence. So what do you buy for the kid who has everything? The answer should be nothing. But we don't; we buy more.

Our kids are growing up in a world that, despite the best efforts of concerned adults, continually reinforces the message that what you own is who you are. Even before our kids are born, this message is being instilled in their parents and the other grown-ups in their lives who then seek to provide their kids with the best in life. But the 'best' has become confused with a materialist outlook that also includes the most – the most expensive and the greatest number. Instead of resisting these trends, we're falling victim, believing it's out of our control. Hal

Niedzviecki argues that 'most of us are taking the path of least resistance ... Chat rooms, instant messaging, movies, tunes, TV shows, online video games, an endless array of mall stores. This is the life of our rapidly aging young people. For current and future generations of pop-culture-bred new conformists'.[37]

Our kids trust us to instil in them values and ethics that will help them navigate the difficult terrain of school, friendships and, later, personal and professional relationships. Values that will help them turn out to be well-rounded, functional human beings. To do this, they need to know that material goods, like fashion, do not make a person, they are merely decoration. Things don't solve problems, people do – and it's people skills we have to teach them. Objects, toys and brands might be an adjunct to all this, but how important an adjunct is up to you. Don't believe all the marketing messages that tell you to buy more for your kids or that you can't or shouldn't stop. You can. Don't worship at the altar of materialism and turn your kids into greedy consumers. Resistance isn't futile: it's essential, through communication, subversion and awareness.

Susan Linn writes that 'our job as parents, in addition to nurturing and protecting our children, is to help them learn to live in a civil society by transmitting positive values and standards of behaviour'.[38]

As the cartoon character, the environmental warrior, Captain Planet once said, 'the power is yours'. Use it wisely.

chapter six

The D'oh of Homer: The Questionable Wisdom of the Electronic Babysitter

TV Killed the Radio Star

On 16 September 1956, more than 97,000 Australians gathered in living rooms, clubs and town halls and outside shop windows to watch Bruce Gyngell deliver the first national broadcast on a clunky innovative piece of technology called the television.[1] Though this new-fangled medium had been available in the UK and US since 1928,[2] Australia received it just in time for the Melbourne Olympics. The moment has been mythologised: it didn't just mark the beginning of television but, as Sir Richard Boyer claimed in 1957, it was also the introduction of 'the major single influence upon the generations to come'.[3]

From one lucky household in a neighbourhood owning a TV in 1956, to almost every household possessing multiple TVs and video and DVD players, and continually upgrading them today; from tuning into one grainy channel to having five free-to-air and subscription TV with dozens of channels available, we've become a nation of TV addicts. By 2000, we weren't simply re-organising rooms to accommodate TVs, we were designing houses around them with the inclusion of the all-important 'Media Room' in house plans. TV has become more than an appliance; it has become an essential component of house design, an important member of the household as well as being indicative of a specific lifestyle choice. Owning a TV is equivalent to making a statement – we're a family (or an individual) who likes to watch.

Within education, TV has wielded enormous influence as well. What happens on the TV screen is now incorporated into classrooms and lecture theatres around the country. Our children study the works of Homer beside the words of Homer Simpson, and the relationship between Veronica Mars and Weevil with the same intensity that they study Romeo and Juliet's. TV is, as Canadian cultural critic Marshall McLuhan argued, not simply the medium, it's the message.[4] In other words, TV as a material form and as a vehicle for communication shapes our lives and alters the way we perceive ourselves and the world.

Taking Sir Richard's statement as a starting point, I'm going to examine the influence TV has not only upon us, but on our tots, tweens and teens. In 2006, the average number of television sets per household in Australia was 2.3,[5] suggesting it's an important aspect of our lives that helps to shape particular family and personal dynamics. Our growing fortress mentality, where we lock ourselves away behind closed doors and rely on new technologies to preoccupy and stimulate us, has made TV one of the most attractive and 'safe' entertainment options for many families. Yet, TV has been blamed for everything from Attention Deficit Hyperactivity Disorders (ADHD),[6] the breakdown of social (and sexual) relationships, to childhood obesity, sleep deprivation and poor performance at school, and then in the same breath being praised for educating, engaging and distracting our kids.[7] What's clear is that, love or loathe it, the TV is many things to many people. I'm going to look closely at exactly how much and *what* types of shows our kids are watching in order to make sense of the arguments for and against the role of TV, the 'electronic babysitter', in our lives.

Neither Seen Nor Heard

Debating the value or otherwise of TV has been a favourite pastime. Writing to the *Sydney Morning Herald* in 1951, WA Clarke warned that:

> Television is going to be one of the big menaces of the future ... people are tearing down bookshelves, bureaus; slinging out cocktail cabinets; generally playing havoc with their domestic ensembles so that a 'viewing room' can be created ... Children are refusing to study or eat because taking meals or studying is a waste of good viewing time ... Every night meals are hastily disposed of and the ritual in front of the TV screen commences.[8]

In 1954, Gerry Grant wrote that 'the worst sufferers will be the children, who, unless restrained, will watch TV instead of living and growing normally'.[9] Simon Townsend, the creator of Channel Ten's *Wonder World* series, recalls that throughout the 1950s newspapers produced articles about the way television would alter the shape of children's eyes (square eyes) and ruin their eyesight. He also remembers dentists commenting that television would damage children's jaw lines.[10] Other myths about television included that if you wore dark glasses and watched television you would get a brain tumour and looking at the test patterns was dangerous for epileptics.

The arguments against television haven't changed much in over 50 years and still have the ability to raise moral panics. Psychologist Dr Aric Sigman goes so far as to suggest that 'TV damages people, particularly children, psychologically, politically, neurologically and metabolically'.[11] Many adults and parents still fear the consequences of too much television for their children physically and mentally. While television has become a focal point of many families' lives, with children often lying in front of the set, as Mackenzie Wark describes it, 'basking in its aura',[12] the relationship kids have with TV is far more complicated and less sinister than we've been led to believe.

Despite the pleasure we gain from this convenient and highly entertaining medium, it's often cast as a social villain. But for every research study that holds the TV accountable for something, there's another to suggest it's not all bad – in fact, it can even be very good.[13] While we worry about the amount of violence on TV, we don't seem to be nearly as concerned about that as we do anything remotely related to sex. We might mumble about the grotesque and disturbing images of wounded and dead from war-torn countries, pictures of starving orphans, or even the brutality of popular action films, but we also accept them as part of the language of TV. If images of naked breasts, sexual innuendo or consensual sex between two adults is portrayed, the TV police (in lieu with the Family Association) come out guns blazing.

Music video programs manage to raise the hackles of most adults with children in their lives. These shows, of which there are now many, depict images of highly sexualised young women shaking their booty to get male attention. This generally happens on a Saturday morning – children's peak viewing time – though there are dedicated channels on satellite TV as well. A case in point is the soft-porn clip 'Fergielicious', where an incredibly sensual young woman sings about teasing boys, using her body to excite them and, presumably, the viewers too. While it might be all right for older people to watch, children hearing lyrics like 'I'll be so tasty, tasty, I'll make you crazy', is problematic – particularly when kids choose to publicly repeat them and emulate the moves. Clips featuring a range of familiar artists such as Christina Aguilera, Madonna and the popular Pussycat Dolls are highly sexualised and provocative displays. They reduce girls to little more than objects for boys to ogle and boys as little more than bodies driven by sexual desire and the need to gaze at these objects or completely ignore their presence. So many rap songs refer to girls in a reductive street language, calling them 'bitches', 'skanks' and 'hos'. These songs, and their accompanying clips, suggest that a girl's value is contingent on how her body looks and is used (or is prepared to be used), and how much the boys value both of these things. For boys in these clips, personal worth appears to be contingent on the vehicle they own, the bling they display and the girls prepared to drape themselves over them wearing as few clothes as possible. Older kids understand that this is the fantastical visual language of these songs, as much as we might find them hard to swallow. In their media-savvy way, teenagers know that this is an aesthetic code used to sell the song, not necessarily a lifestyle. For younger kids, however, a constant diet of musical sex without parental explanation (that it's all an act and everyday girls and boys don't behave like that) can be very unhealthy.

We worry about how much the images of sex and violence manipulate our children. The good news is that *our* behaviour, whether we're violent or not in our relationships and how we talk about and enact sexuality, is far more influential than the very narrow representations on TV. We influence kids far more than characters or celebrities, even those featured in steamy music videos, ever could.

Lights! Camera! Action!

While I discussed issues around toys and violence in the last chapter, I do want to briefly address concerns around TV and violence as well. Ever since Fredrick Wertham published his book *Seduction of the Innocent* in 1953, which claimed that reading superhero comics led to delinquent behaviour and called for them to be banned, there has been an almost unhealthy readiness to link children's entertainment to problem behaviours.[14] (Wertham's opinion was actually based on talking to young people in prison and discovering that they liked to read comics – he failed to look at the lack of choices they were given or their level of education, and didn't ask other children, who were *not* in prison, what they read.) Kathleen McDonnell discusses how, from the 1970s onwards, when social scientist Leonard Eron first made the connection between violent behaviour in kids and what was being beamed into homes via cartoons and other kids' shows, there was a plethora of other commentators eager to jump on the 'TV is bad' bandwagon.[15] In the 1980s, there was a groundswell of protests against violent television content and its influence on children, especially boys. These objections were made, ironically, by those who grew up on a TV diet of Fred Flintstone punching Barney Rubble, Daffy Duck having his head blown off by Elmer Fudd and Coyote being squashed by the anvil he always intended for Road Runner. Still, the animated

TV series *Teenage Mutant Ninja Turtles* (based on a comic strip and now a major film), about a group of pizza-guzzling, half-turtle, half-human orphans who lived in the subways of New York and fought crime with martial arts, had adults complaining in droves. This was followed by objections about *Mighty Morphin' Power Rangers*. Kids in playgrounds and lounge-rooms everywhere started trying on the Turtle and Power Ranger moves for style. Irresistibly funny and named after four great Renaissance artists (Donatello, Michelangelo, Leonardo and Raphael), the Turtles were a hit. The *Power Rangers*, which originated from Japanese TV, also used magic and kung-fu fighting mixed with rock music to battle robotic enemies while wearing fabulous costumes. Merchandise linked to both made them hugely popular with kids.

Academic George Gerbner led the push against these types of shows claiming that the cartoons depicted what he called 'happy violence' or 'violence without consequences'.[16] Yet so many of these critics, Gerbner included, failed to look at the context in which kids watched television, what their own family backgrounds and situations were. They also didn't differentiate between slapstick and clearly animated mayhem and real, disturbing violence.

These protests have largely been laid to rest today, with most adults understanding that kids might imitate some behaviours they see on TV, but once it's explained to them it's not appropriate they'll cease or, alternatively, use characters like the Turtles or Rangers to explore their physical world in an empowered way. However, we still occasionally see eruptions of these types of concerns.[17]

Imbued with an Orwellian sensibility, there's a Big Brother feel to many of the negative arguments about the role of TV. But what's sometimes forgotten amid the panic and demonisation is that *we* watch the TV, not the other way around. In other words, we control what we watch, when we watch and how we watch. We can turn the TV off – vote with our remote if we don't like what's on or what our children are being exposed to. And this control can and should extend to those in our care – especially when they're very young.

BabyFirst TV

In 2006 BabyFirst TV, a 24-hour, commercial-free channel dedicated to tots from six months to three years, was launched in the US.[18] Parents were interviewed about the channel and posted comments on its blog, with many adults praising the fact they can 'get a break' and that, through some of the programs offered, they get tips on how to manage their kids as well. Dr Alan Hilfer, a pediatric specialist asked to comment on this new channel, offers words of caution. He says: 'If parents need TV to encourage them to get together with their infants and toddlers, then we have something else we need to be talking about'.[19] He adds that you can't parent by remote control.[20] A Seattle pediatrician, Donald Shifrin, who also chairs the Pediatrics Academy committee that studies television and children, takes it further arguing that '*Sesame Street* has opened a Pandora's box by legitimizing the idea that TV needs to be developed for this demographic ...'.[21] Sue Palmer would agree, stating that our love affair with technology has led us to believe that it can substitute for human relations.[22]

I don't think anyone really *believes* that – not for a moment. TV is like a guilty pleasure that we indulge in for various reasons – both positive and negative. Yet, when it comes to kids, we often choose to ignore the information out there that challenges our viewing habits or those we establish for children in our care. We convince ourselves that these 'experts' who tell us not to let our tots watch TV either haven't seen a kids' show or are out-of-touch, mostly childless academics and scientists preaching from ivory towers with no real-life experience to back their findings, so we tend to brush the information aside or put it in a context that suits our lifestyles. Why? Because changing our TV and other habits when there are kids to raise, work commitments to fulfil and a life to live, can seem too hard.

But habits are made to be broken. Especially bad ones.

How many of us have propped the kids in front of *Play School*, *Sesame Street*, *Teletubbies*, *Boohbah* or *Dora the Explorer*, then rushed around shoving loads of washing in the machine, sat down for a much needed cuppa or attended to work? It's not so much that we're looking for a parental substitute (as some specialists accuse[23]) as we are the space to accomplish other tasks or gain some downtime or a 'sanity-break' for ourselves. Some adults sit with the tots and copy the movements and sing the songs with them, using the TV show in a positive way to facilitate time together and interaction. The shows we're told we can expose our tots to have government approval, are rated appropriately and are enjoyed by our kids – at least they're quiet. The marketing hype tells us these programs benefit our children because they're 'educational'. So what's wrong with a little bit of TV?

Tots and TV

Experts from medicine, pediatrics, sociology, psychology and media who have conducted studies with large and small focus groups over short and long periods of time generally agree upon one thing regarding tots and TV: children under two years of age should not be watching it, *at all*.[24] A study published in 2004 found that children exposed to television between the ages of one and three were more likely to have attention problems by age seven.[25] Another study conducted in New Zealand found a direct correlation between viewing TV in childhood and attention problems in adolescence. Dr Bob Hancox, one of the study's authors, believes that 'parents should take steps to limit the amount of TV their children watch'.[26] The American Academy of Pediatrics released a statement to that effect. They also claim that children over two should only be allowed to watch a maximum of 'two hours educational screen media a day',[27] while an Australian study points to guidelines that clearly state that children two years and over should watch less than two hours of television a day.[28]

There's not much that the TV can offer a child under two that they can't learn in a more appropriate and stimulating fashion from interacting with real people. Despite all the warnings from the experts, 74 per cent of 'all infants and toddlers *watch* TV before the age of two'.[29]

This doesn't refer to simply exposing tots to TV either; this is consciously placing them in front of the screen with the intention that they view what's being broadcast.

In other words, before the age of two, there's nothing that Big Bird, Tinky Winky or Jumbah can teach your child that you can't. The meaningless noises, as cute as they are, that issue from the mouths (or tummies) of Teletubbies and Boohbah aren't nearly as important as the conversation, senseless and otherwise, that *you* have with children – or the periods of silence tots experience in adult company. Not talking to or entertaining young children all their waking hours is perfectly all right as well. Young children need 'downtime', quiet periods where they're not always stimulated. They also need to be allowed to become bored, but that seems to be another dirty word in contemporary society. Recent research even suggests that the current generation of young kids now respond to images on a screen more readily than they do a human face.[30] This is not really surprising as we raise a generation of cybertots and computeens, but it is disturbing.

A 2006 Australian study acknowledges the fact that 'television viewing plays an important role in assisting busy mothers cope with young children, and many value television as a good educational tool, a "babysitter/coping mechanism", and a medium to either stimulate or calm down preschoolers'.[31] The study concludes, however, that there is 'mounting evidence that excessive television viewing among children and adolescents can seriously challenge young people's emotional and physical well-being'.[32] It also recommends that kids under two do not watch TV.

The verdict is in: no TV for tots.

Don't castigate yourself if you've parked your child in front of the TV for a short period of time. There will be few parents and other adults who have not done the same thing and often. Understand that if you still choose to do this, the benefits are extremely limited, if not potentially damaging, despite production company claims to the contrary. What a child gains from interacting with an adult is far greater than anything they pick up from the TV.[33]

Children's viewing habits are created early in their lives and are modelled on those of the grown-ups in their orbit. Studies reveal that 'early childhood exposure to television establishes later television viewing behaviour'.[34]

If you're at home with a tot or pre-schooler, try not to leave the TV on *all* day. To you, it might provide much needed adult companionship and conversation, but it's also a distraction for you and your baby. Limit your viewing during the day. Record the shows you simply can't miss and watch them after your tot has gone to bed. You might think they're too young to understand what *Dr Phil* is talking about or the complexities of your favourite soap – and you'd be right – but tots pick up on our emotional responses and the tones of the voices emanating from the set. These are adult programs that shouldn't be heard or seen by young ears and eyes. They also learn by watching you and *your* reactions to that rectangle in the corner, on the wall or on the kitchen bench. While our kids are little, their minds are those absorbent sponges I mentioned earlier, soaking up the images, messages and ideas in the shows they watch. There's an attitude prevalent in society that, while the kids are glued to the TV, they can't get into trouble. They're at home, under our feet or in another room, safe and sound.

They can't encounter too many problems if we know what they're watching. But not all of us actually watch every single program our kids enjoy. When they're little and chanting the rhymes and singing the songs of *Hi-5*, *Play School*, *The Wiggles* and *Sesame Street*, it might be different. But, as they get older, we tend to drift away from the set, reassured that the G or PG programs our kids know, love and often quote (and that we know other kids are allowed to watch and like) are suitable. The good news is they mostly are. But, as Kathleen McDonnell notes, 'TV ratings have very little impact on kids' real world viewing habits'.[35] So what exactly are our kids are watching and what can they learn from the content?

The Pre-Tween TV Scene

From about the age of three onwards, depending on what they've been exposed to and what other kids they socialise with watch, children have changing and expanding viewing habits. Suddenly, *Bananas in Pyjamas* will be something only 'babies' watch – and this out of the mouth of a four-year-old. Instead, shows with the tween market firmly in their sights will start to appeal to kids as young as four and five. Nickelodeon's clever *Dora the Explorer* on her interactive quest with her monkey friend, Boots, to discover words and places is no longer *de rigueur*. Suddenly, our pre-schoolers and kindy kids love sweet, yellow SpongeBob SquarePants, the savvy *Rugrats*, and Disney's *That's So Raven, Kim Possible, American Dragon: Jake Long,* and *Lizzie Maguire*. And that's before I get to *The Simpsons* – which I will.

There's a lot of good in these programs and their ilk. In fact, many of them are quite saccharine sweet with loads of pro-social meanings. They all emphasise friendship; they have a strong moral code that reflects that agreed upon by the wider world (bad people, from criminals to mean or unjust figures, end up being 'punished'); and they empower young people by placing them at the centre of the story and having them solve mysteries, fix mistakes, learn consequences as well as explore issues around trust, change, families, friends and neighbourhoods. Many of the cartoons also have the young people engaging and being competent with technology – allowing kids to identify with the characters.

In shows directed at the pre-tween market, there's also a conscious effort to represent young people's realities. While many of the characters come from stable homes, like Lizzie Maguire, there are those who are or have experienced marriage breakdowns, loss of a parent or difficulties fitting in, such as Chuckie in *Rugrats*. Certainly, the relationships between siblings explored by so many of the programs hit the mark: whether it be the ongoing battle between Lizzie and her younger brother, Matt; Phil and Lil the twins in *Rugrats*; or *Kim Possible* and her younger twin brothers, Jim and Tim, the interactions between brothers and sisters, and mums and dads depict with accuracy and humour the love-hate relationships kids can have with those who live under the same roof.

Aspirational Casting

Kids today don't want to watch TV shows (or films) that are considered 'suitable' for them. Hence G-rated shows are mainly watched by preschoolers while tweens prefer teen-type shows and teens tune into adult programs. Kathleen McDonnell says that movie producers actively seek PG ratings for their films knowing they appeal to a tween's sense of importance, much more so than a 'sappy-sounding G'.[36] TV shows are the same. Catherine Lumby and Duncan Fine discuss how, from the age of six on, children have quite sophisticated TV viewing skills, which allow them to differentiate between what happens on the screen and in the real world. They also understand genre.[37] No wonder they want more than *The Wiggles*.

Aware of this, producers mostly cast older actors in younger roles. It's called aspirational casting. As the character Dionne quips in the movie *Clueless*, 'in ten years we'll be twenty-seven; almost old enough to play high school students on TV'. There's now also an intensive cross-market of magazine gossip, fashion and accessories attached to the older stars of children's shows that works to influence children's spending habits, sense of self and appearance.

Actor and singer Hilary Duff, who plays the lead in the popular Disney tween show *Lizzie Maguire*, has a fan-base of girls (and boys) whose starting age is four. The show itself is a delightful look at the pitfalls and highs of teenage years and Duff has become a major star with films, CDs, fashion (Duff Stuff) and now perfume to her name. A group of mothers I spoke to in Sydney told me how they took their excited eight-year-old girls to a Hilary Duff concert. The kids not only bought merchandise, but listened raptly as their school-girl idol sang and danced. The problem is, Hilary Duff is *not* Lizzie Maguire. While she plays a much younger role on TV, at the concert she cast off her Lizzie chrysalis and emerged and performed as a late teen, young woman would – as a very, very sexy butterfly. The mums left disturbed, while their daughters lapped it up.

Just as shows aimed at teens are very adult, with older actors playing much younger roles, such as they did in the 1980s with *Beverly Hills*

90210 and now with *The OC* and *Smallville* (Tom Wellings, who plays a teenage Clark Kent, is actually 30 and has been married since 2002), so too tween shows cast actors much older than the roles they're playing. Raven-Symoné Christina Pearman, the lead actor in *That's So Raven*, was 18 when the show started and 21 when production finished in 2006, even though she was playing a 14- to 16-year-old.

While this type of casting may seem harmless, in the world of children's TV it can pose problems. The shows are aimed at kids going through a very important developmental stage, and the casting can make them feel inadequate about themselves; they aspire to look and act older, truncating their childhood. There's a world of difference between an eight-year-old viewer and a 16-year-old actor or, as Hilary Duff overtly demonstrated, between young audiences besotted with who they believe is a tween TV star and an 18-year-old professional performer. This is an enormous gulf that some of these shows, together with marketing, invite kids to bridge. One way to overcome this is to let your kids know exactly how old these actors are and to keep emphasising the differences between what an eight-, 10- and 12-year-old can do and expect and a 16-year-old. Don't deny your kids access to these shows – that just makes them more desirable – but make the programs work for you. Again, it's about knowing what your kids are watching and, by talking with them about it, what they're taking from the shows.

Stereotypes

What should be of concern, and something adults need to address, is the stereotyping many of these shows don't simply depict but positively indulge in. In so many of the Disney shows, for example, especially those that are spin-offs of successful movies such as *The Little Mermaid* and *Aladdin*, girls will be, well, pathetic and in need of rescuing, while boys will be painfully independent and uncommunicative. In the TV shows featuring Barbie or Bratz, the same thing applies. The Bratz, while savvy, wise and loyal to their friends (often the theme of a particular episode), are also wrapped up in appearances and schmoozing with celebrities, albeit under the auspice of grabbing a feature story for their magazine. They also strut around in clothes that Beyoncé wouldn't be seen in and have an endless wardrobe of accessories, which, interestingly, can mostly be bought at a store near you. The Bratz, positive messages aside, emphasise the importance of looks and connections in more ways than one.

Barbie, as we would expect, also deals with issues of friendship, loyalty, trust and faith: all very constructive messages. Undermining these, however, is her never-ending need to be rescued, usually by a very good-looking boy-man. In the Barbie movies, for example *Fairytopia* and *Mermaidtopia*, there are instances where she learns to believe in herself and find inner strength. Her initial status as outsider (she's a fairy without wings) is unfortunately overcome when, as a reward for saving the fairy world, she's given wings and thus accepted by those who formerly tormented her because she is now the same. In the mermaid sequel, she again learns about courage, but is rewarded with an even more glorious set of wings – the best in *Fairytopia*. The underlying message is, look the same or better and you'll be popular and successful – a hero even.

Boys also receive more than a fair dose of stereotypes. In the *Pokémon*, *Yu-Gi-Oh* and *Jake Long* cartoons, for example, the young protagonists always have to prove themselves through competition. While sometimes the message in the cartoons is that not winning is all right, the overall meaning is that to really succeed you have to be the alpha male. In *Rugrats* and *Rugrats Grown Up*, the capable Tommy Pickles, who in many ways is the dominant male in the cartoon, uses pluck, physical ability and intelligence to outsmart adults and other kids alike. He's contrasted to his needy friend, the red-haired, braces-wearing, freckled and spectacled Chucky. As adorable as Chucky might be, he's also the 'loser' of the cartoon and someone kids recognise but don't want to identify with. Interestingly, he's also the one with the single parent – a father. Even shows that satirise elements of boy culture, such as *SpongeBob*, *Yakkity Yak* and *Tutenstein*, fall on dominant male stereotypes such as only offering three types: the aggressor, the victim and the hero. In this way, children's TV reflects what is offered to adults, but it's not an accurate picture of the variety of complex and interesting boys or girls in real life.

This doesn't mean that kids shouldn't watch these shows. What it does mean, however, is that adults should point out the good and bad in these shows to their kids. Highlight the values you want your kids to learn and talk to them about the weaknesses, such as how sad it was that Barbie felt she had to have wings to fit in even though she'd grown so much and was already a lovely person with very loyal friends. Teach them that winning isn't everything, really. It's the trying that's important. Accentuate the value of good friends, of believing in yourself and trying – something the shows do very well.

One aspect of human relationships that many children's shows don't portray well, in that they stereotype them or offer poor role-models, is in the relationships between kids and adults.

Adults on TV

Parents, teachers and other adult characters on children's TV are often depicted as indifferent, stupid, out of touch, mean or absent. They're not to be trusted. While this theme certainly isn't new (it has been in children's literature for centuries, from *The Coral Island* to *Harry Potter*), it's interesting that instead of using TV to bridge the generation gap it's used to maintain it. I'll address children's literature and the positive aspects of empowering kids through absent adults in Chapter Eight, but for now I want to look at the way the relationships children have with adults in children's TV are suffering.

One thing that struck me about the differences between TV for kids 20 years ago and today is how rude the child characters are to the adults in their lives. I'm not talking here about kids who flout rules, rally against adult injustice and try to have their voices heard, nor am I concerned with characters who use their nous to do the right thing against adult advice, such as in *Buffy, The Vampire Slayer* or *Veronica Mars*. Kids are clever and adults can sometimes be very myopic and naïve. What I'm referring to is the number of child characters who seem to go out of their way to disrespect grown-ups; who take great delight in issuing public putdowns and humiliating and stripping adults of dignity (usually teachers). They use patronising tones and generally treat adults as overgrown jokes.

While we all laughed at movies like *Home Alone*, which pitted the left-behind little kid (played by Macaulay Culkin) against burglars in a frenetic slapstick romp, playing on children's fears and overturning them to have the child triumphant – irresponsible, stupid adults who want to hurt children are almost a necessary ingredient in TV as well. Concomitantly, the kids are often mean to the adults. There are so few positive adult characters being offered in children's TV shows, it's not surprising that those who do appear are verbally abused and their dignity is trampled on by kids.

Lizzie Maguire and Kim Possible, both of whom have lovely, caring and mostly responsible parents, are embarrassed by them and quite rude to them, particularly their mothers. Angelina Ballerina is rude to all the grown-ups in her life.

The parent generation tends to get a bad rap, while often the grandparent generation gets a better deal. Jake Long and Yu-Gi-Oh both have grandfather figures who are important and who guide them and function as role-models. The Rugrats' grandparents, while comic foils at one level, also demonstrate love and concern for the children over and over. They also share stories of their own childhood and different cultural experiences, something the kids benefit from in the cartoon. This is both refreshing and essential. The power of stories to shape who we are as an individual and a culture is something I'll deal with the in the next two chapters.

It's highly unlikely that writers and producers will change a successful formula anytime soon, so it's important that adults address all the diverse and not-so-diverse portrayals with kids. Use the shows as educational tools to teach social etiquette: what sort of conversations and tones you approve of and don't approve of and why. Remember this: while you might not mind if your child answers back or adopts a certain tone with you, it's a different matter in the world outside the home. It's important kids understand manners and ways of addressing people with respect even if it's not practised at home. There are different rules for everything and they need to know this. Also point out that not all adults are like those in the TV shows; there are many good, kind and clever ones who can be trusted and relied upon. The lack of communication between generations in these shows is sad and possibly reflects the growing schism between adults and kids in society – one we have to work to overcome.

If we can overlook the stereotypes, modify the sexual ones on so much music TV by discussing them with children[38] and point out the obvious instances of aspirational casting,[39] there is, believe it or not, a lot to be gained from *good* TV in terms of intellectual stimulation. I'm not just talking about documentaries either. Steven Johnson discusses how much more complex mainstream TV has become over the last 20 years. He says that adults have a tendency to compare the shows we watched when we were kids to those screening now and then moan about how much worse they are. In terms of quality, there's no comparison between shows screening 20 or 30 years ago and today. For example, the plot and story lines of *Gilligan's Island* cannot compete with the sophistication of *Seinfeld* just as *The Love Boat* is no match for *The Sopranos* or *Heroes*. Likewise, popular children's shows from decades ago were much simpler than those programmed now. This is because, Johnson says, kids today are much more sophisticated viewers who demand multi-layered storylines and interesting characters from their shows. Compare *He-man* and *Rugrats* or *Smurfs* and *SpongeBob* and you understand what he's talking about. Kids need to know so much more external information to appreciate today's programs – the references to history, other TV shows, books, music, films and celebrities abound. This is what Johnson calls 'supplementary information', some of which arises from within the fictional world of the program for the story to make sense.[40]

The Good, the Bad and the Ugly
Instead of looking at the complexity of a great deal of our children's favourite TV shows, we discuss how 'bad' the programs are. We make

a moral judgement about content rather than commenting on the standard in terms of intellectual stimulation. Early TV programs drew very clear boundaries between good and bad characters, behaviours and values. When we lament the apparent loss of this on TV today, we're not only sentimentalising the past but we're conveniently forgetting that the world is not black and white. Whereas cartoons like *Scooby Doo* and *Josie and the Pussy Cats* had clearly defined heroes and villains, contemporary cartoons like *The Simpsons* and, say, *Fairly Odd Parents,* and even the darker *Batman* cartoon series, which appeal to both adults and children, reveal the multiple shades that colour human nature. While there's still complete rubbish on TV, modern shows often portray the complex reasons underpinning human actions and reveal to us that good people can do bad things and bad people can not only be redeemed, but some even have honourable intentions. Good examples of these kinds of stories can be seen in many popular tween and teen shows such as *Buffy*, *The OC*, *Veronica Mars* and *Blue Water High*. This is also why reality television shows such as *Survivor*, *Big Brother* and the *Idol* franchises are so popular with tweens and teens. They are hierarchical and interactive and capture 'real' moments of raw emotion, anger and drama. They also reflect for young viewers the idea that ordinary people can become extraordinary and those who think they're 'special' can be stripped of their crowns. Reality TV empowers young people by giving them a voice – literally through the voting process, and metaphorically because the characters on the shows *are* them. They talk their language, share their hopes and dreams and have them shattered as well.

Another point Johnson makes is that when we make comparisons between programs like *Big Brother* and a documentary or quality drama like *The West Wing*, or even the older show *M.A.S.H.*, we're comparing apples and oranges. Reality TV should be compared to game or sports shows, while *Big Brother* can never (and nor should it have to) compete with a quality production with professional actors and scriptwriters like *The West Wing* or *Scrubs* and *Arrested Development* for that matter – two other shows that rate well with teens.

One perennial favourite of tweens, teens and adults, which demonstrates how sophisticated yet popular a TV show can be, is the longest running cartoon in history: Matt Groening's *The Simpsons*. Due to its multilayered approach, with stories and dialogue appealing simultaneously to kids and grown-ups but at different levels, it has outlasted, outwitted and out-survived all its competitors in terms of complexity and quality. It's also generated a batch of cartoons with cross-generational appeal such as *Futurama*, *Family Guy*, *American Dad*, *King of the Hill* and *South Park*.

The Simpsons

Screened in over 60 countries, *The Simpsons* is a clever social satire, full of parody, in-jokes and pro-social messages, that has broad cross-cultural attraction. A single episode takes 300 people eight months at the cost over US$1 million to make.[41] In 1998, *Time* magazine voted Bart (an anagram of Brat) Simpson as one of the most influential figures of the last century,[42] and the show itself the best TV show of the 20th century. The *Seattle Times* stated it was one of the '52 works that changed the Millennium'.[43] Boys and girls regularly vote Bart as their favourite cartoon character and the person they most identify with. Homer has been voted 'the greatest American' in a BBC poll in 2003, over and above Abraham Lincoln and Thomas Jefferson,[44] and the greatest TV character of all time.[45] One British professor even went so far as to suggest that Homer was a role-model for contemporary fatherhood.[46]

Adults have often expressed concerns about the material covered in *The Simpsons*. There's no pop culture stone left unturned and no sacred cow that isn't butchered. Kids and adults love the inter-textual references to other films, books, TV shows, celebrities and cultural events.

The characters in the show are recognisable flawed stereotypes, from Apu to Mr Burns, but, whereas TV shows like *Will and Grace* draw on stereotypes and to a degree perpetuate them, *The Simpsons* propagates them to debunk them and draw attention to how limited they are: stereotypes become caricatures. This isn't limited to characters either. The location, Springfield, is also a caricature. At one level, it's a recognisable town and the Simpsons' neighbourhood is a typical suburb but, at another, the world is contracted into its small geographical dimensions. Celebrities, aliens, rock stars, and current and former presidents think nothing of visiting there; it's the epicentre of natural and man-made disasters; and it has a major city up the road, an ocean, a desert, mountains, lakes and every sporting facility, shop and minority enclave you can think of. In fact, no-one needs to ever leave Springfield for the world comes to its doorstep and then wipes its feet all over the place. It's no coincidence that there's a Springfield in every state in mainland US. Springfield and the Simpson family are everywhere, anywhere and everyone. Beneath the humour is a show that critiques the nuclear family, capitalism, stereotypes, bigotry, sexism, racism, homophobia, the education system and disregard for the environment. Yet, for all its apparent naughtiness and challenge to social mores, this show that kids so love and parents are confused about (unless they're fans) is deeply conservative.[47]

Now, don't get me wrong: I love *The Simpsons*. But I also recognise in its format and presentation a celebration of the conventional family model, an emphasis on traditional roles and, ironically, a sort of anti-intellectualism. In every episode, Bart is strangled by his father and sometimes for no reason. This suggests that even a violent father is better than no father. Every episode begins and ends with Marge in either the kitchen or bedroom – regardless of her dreams, desires or attempts to escape her narrow role as wife and mother – emphasising a woman's place. Likewise for Homer. He hates the oppression and lack of challenges provided by the Nuclear Power Plant, but he's locked into the provider role so firmly that even his stints as an astronaut or member of a successful pop group don't offer permanent change. Bart's misbehaviour is celebrated and his poor school performance, deceitfulness and savvy street-smarts are continually rewarded. But Bart is a walking contradiction. He hangs around with the nerdy Millhouse, is loyal to his family when they're in a crisis, clearly adores his mother, and secretly admires and even rallies on behalf of his nemesis, Principal Skinner. Lisa, the blue-stocking and 'brain' of the family, is often the butt of jokes. Her intellect and sense of social justice are undermined by Bart's or Homer's slapstick, physical solutions. Lisa, despite her inner beauty and sense of equity, is one of the least popular characters on the show. And Little Maggie – well, she has no voice and is often overlooked or ignored – sometimes Homer can't even remember her name.

The Simpsons world is definitely one where white, middle-class males rule and where their authority is challenged. This is exactly the reason kids (seven and over) can and should watch it – for that and for its treasure trove of historical, literary and other references. By discussing episodes and what occurs, laughing at the jokes and pointing out the satire and what's problematic to our tweens and teens, we all benefit. Some of the most interesting conversations I've had with tweens, my kids, students and other adults have arisen out of *The Simpsons*. Perhaps one message we can all take from *The Simpsons* is that, while they're a family made for TV, they're also often brought together around the television set, enjoying a program and each other simultaneously.

Watch, Talk and Learn

Where you place the TV and how much emphasis you place on being able to watch a program will also instil viewing habits and attitudes in your child that they'll possibly carry over into adulthood. For example, if you continue to tell your kids to be quiet so you can see how the relationship between Meredith and McDreamy pans out this week on *Grey's Anatomy*, or catch the last innings of the cricket, then you might be suggesting to them that what happens on the screen is more important than what they want to share with you. On the other hand, providing you ask them to wait a moment (until a commercial break, after the show or match) and, as soon as you're ready, find out what they want, you're also teaching them important lessons about patience and respecting adult requests. Despite what some 'experts' say, kids don't have to come first. By waiting to have their wants (as opposed to needs) met, they learn tolerance, cooperation, respect and communication. Like adults, they're part of a larger social group and they need to know their place within that. It's all right to make them wait. Even sometimes for the TV. Just as they once would have had to wait for their fathers to plough the last field, milk the cows, serve a customer, or read the newspaper or for their mothers to beat rugs, knead dough, pick apples, or serve the man of the house first, in this day and age it's the technology that might keep them waiting. It's a sign of the times: just don't make them wait too long.

But if you use the TV to escape from a difficult emotional situation or to avoid communicating, so will your child. This is becoming easier today as so many children have access to not only multiple TVs, but also their very own TV bought for them by adults and located in the worst possible place in the house – their bedrooms.

Bedroom Eyes

Before I discuss the cons of allowing a child to have a TV in his or her bedroom, let's have a look at some of the statistics. A Kaiser Family Foundation Report in the US revealed that 26 per cent of children under two have TVs in their bedrooms – so much for tots and no TV. These statistics increase with age, with 32 per cent of two- to seven-year-olds and two-thirds of children between the ages of eight and 18 having them as well.[48] In Britain, three-quarters of tots and tweens have TVs in their bedrooms.[49] In Australia, the figure of adolescents with TVs in their bedrooms sits around 36 per cent,[50] though one study concluded that, of kids between the ages of eight and 18, 53 per cent had TVs in their bedrooms.[51] Figures for younger kids are currently unavailable but we can assume they would be similar to those in the US and Britain. According to the Australian Bureau of Statistics (2003), 99 per cent of boys and 98 per cent of girls listed TV watching (including videos) as their favourite leisure activity apart from talking to friends.[52]

Most Australian boys and girls spend approximately two hours a day in front of the TV, which matches studies done in the US.[53]

This averages 10 hours a week. This doubles when they co-view with their parents and trebles in families with more than one child.[54] The statistics conclude that children watch an average of between 19 and 20 hours each week.[55] That's before we consider the time spent in front of a computer or electronic games (four hours) or on the phone. In comparison, about three and a half hours a week are spent on reading for pleasure and homework.[56] Interestingly, studies have shown that adolescents with their own televisions don't necessarily view more TV.[57] This is because family viewing habits and other factors have a greater influence on their TV-watching schedules – everything from how much the parents watch to whether or not the family views together.

Nonetheless, giving your angst-ridden, argumentative tween or teen a TV to place in their bedroom creates more problems than it resolves. It's the gift that takes: it takes away your child, it takes away contact and it takes away the ability to work through and resolve problems by providing a convenient escape route.

Experts agree that no child should have a TV in their bedroom.[58] Apart from the TV potentially destroying conversation and general interaction that more traditional activities such as bedtime stories have always provided, when kids are watching TV in their rooms they're unsupervised; adults have no idea about the content of the programs they're accessing or how late they're staying up.

Basically, TVs in bedrooms are an adult prerogative – and they're one that adults need to exercise on themselves, not their children.

TV Dinners

Eating in front of the TV is generally regarded as a no-no. It destroys family conversations, and children who continually eat from their laps on sofas, have their attention seized by an episode of *The Simpsons* or have their parents telling them to be quiet so they can hear the news don't learn table manners. Don't undervalue the importance of table manners. As our kids grow older and are invited into different homes and, later, important social and professional occasions, they need to know basic etiquette and demonstrate their respect for their environment by not eating or talking with mouths full, using cutlery correctly and asking to have condiments passed. They also need to learn the art of conversation: speaking, sharing and listening. Asking to leave the table may seem redundant in this day and age, but it teaches respect for others and sets boundaries around an activity that's meant to be a shared one. After all, teams stick together, through thick and thin. Families are teams as well. To take the analogy further, players who give up or walk off in the middle of a match can lower morale and reduce the team's overall performance. Switching off the TV during dinner means family members get to talk to one another, unpack their day and discover aspects of each other that are important for a healthy family dynamic. It's also been suggested that turning the TV off can reduce the association between TV watching and food. This is something advertisers rely on, hence children's viewing hours (and many adults' ones as well) are saturated with high-fat, high-sugar and vitamin-poor foods.

Advertising

According to the experts, the average child in Australia, the UK and the US views between 20,000 and 40,000 television commercials a year.[59] I've already discussed the fact that some countries prohibit advertising to children under certain ages (see Chapter Two) and, certainly, Australia prides itself on its strict advertising codes that ban commercials in tots' television and allows no more than five minutes of advertisements during school-age children's programming.[60] However, a quick scan of advertisements during prime-time children's TV on Saturday mornings reveals that over a period of two to three hours on two commercial stations, there was a total of over 100 ads. Those 'five minutes' were dominated by, first, snappy 15-second advertisements for toys (approximately 22 in two hours on one channel and between 72 and 90 in three hours on the other), followed by food (one channel had 11 healthy food ads (for dairy, vegemite and breakfast cereals such as Sultana Bran), whereas the other had seven food ads mostly featuring McDonald's). Then there were miscellaneous ads for charities, self-promotion and electronic goods. This suggests that, while we have regulations in place, they are very elastic and don't prevent advertisers reaching and potentially influencing our children, including through product placement and extended advertorials and promotion through competitions and prize packs.

User-friendly Content

While television content isn't as big an issue for older teens as it is for younger kids, it's still there. Introducing kids to different sorts of content as they mature not only sets milestones, but ensures that they're emotionally, psychologically and cognitively ready to deal with the material being screened. And there are some fabulous programs that, when watched together, provide opportunities for frank discussion about topics such as drugs, sexuality, relationships, friendships and school. The prime-time soap operas such as *Neighbours* and *Home and Away* deal with some very topical and meaty issues, from extra-marital affairs and homosexuality to drug-taking. They also deal with concerns close to young people's hearts and realities such as sex, relationships, and parental, school and friendship troubles. So do shows like *Smallville, Buffy, Heroes, Supernatural, The OC, Ugly Betty, Summer Heights High* and *Big Brother*.

Steven Johnson, in his book *Everything Bad Is Good for You*, suggests that while reality TV relies on artificial environments, just like game shows, it possesses an 'emotional authenticity that is responsible for much of [its] appeal'.[61] Tweens and teens relate to this 'authenticity', and they're the main demographic of these shows. Instead of criticising them as innocuous, vacuous tripe, adults should be taking advantage of their kids' interest and, wherever possible, view the shows with them and discuss the issues raised. I'm constantly amazed by the number of people – from the Prime Minister to social commentators – who openly admit to having never watched an episode of reality TV but are ready to decry it all the same. Try to see the shows through young people's eyes. Ask them what they like about them, who they most identify with and who they don't and why. Be prepared to express your ideas about what's portrayed as well – even if you don't like them or are a bit disturbed about the content. Don't be dismissive; really listen and contribute. Don't, whatever you do, condescend.

If these sorts of discussions start in the *Play School* years, they become a good habit, which means when your teens are up late watching *Veronica Mars* and are confronted with date rape or suicide, they know they can talk to you about their concerns around the same issue. Though there might be dark years where communication fails (and it will), the groundwork has been laid. While building bridges can be a daunting and even impossible task, it's much easier to renovate a broken one than start from scratch with building materials that are rusty or eroded.

Global Village

We often hear talk about the 'olden days' and how children were raised by a village. Stacey, a mother of two, feels that there's a sense in which TV functions much like the village used to; it's more than a window on the world. It literally brings different people and ideas into our homes. 'The TV is the village', says Stacey. 'It's the contemporary equivalent of what we used to do – raise kids in a community by concession, passing on values and ideology from person to person, generation to generation. Just as you wouldn't let your child play with everyone in the village, so too you have to be careful choosing which "friends" your kids can play with on TV. There has to be quality control.'

Knowing exactly what and who your child is watching and sharing with in the global village is essential: for tots, tweens and teens. With the ABC introducing another free-to-air channel, ABC3, that caters specifically to the under-15 market, there is a smorgasbord of choice in terms of drama, comedy, animation, education, interactivity and on-demand digital services as well as 50 per cent Australian content.[62] Just because it's denoted as child-friendly, however, doesn't mean that adults should not monitor what their kids are accessing. On the contrary, as Stacey warns, quality control is not only important, it's an adult's duty.

TV Times

Every year since 2000, I've asked my 300 or so first-year students how many TVs they have per household. In 2000, the average was two; this year, it was four. Two students had nine televisions. One student didn't own a TV. I confess to having five TVs – one isn't plugged in, but it's there if we need it. Unless the cricket or the AFL is on, watching TV is very much a whole-family activity.

We now live in households where it's common for children to relax, be distracted, eat and even fall asleep in front of the TV. Far from being the passive interest it was once believed to be (and, according to some, still is), watching TV is an active process. The body may be still, but the mind is busily processing what it sees and hears. This applies to tots, tweens, teens and adults, particularly now as we've become accustomed to television. But just because we're used to it, doesn't mean we should take it for granted.

It seems that, as much as we love the TV and the pleasure it brings, it's also interfering with our family time. Even very young children are watching TV all by themselves, without the usual interactions that occur between adult and child. But so are we. Cheaper technology (and increased access to in-store credit and interest-free purchase plans) has allowed even those of us on low incomes to enjoy the richness of up-to-date electronic appliances – many of them. It's not uncommon anymore for households to own one TV per family member. Whether it's to prevent a war over the remote control, or to be able to watch a favourite program in peace and quiet, what was once a family or group activity has now become a solitary one. One of the negative effects of TV on family life, and children's development in particular, is that it robs us all of family time. But it doesn't have to be that way.

Television needs to be enjoyed together wherever possible and in moderation; it also needs to be monitored. Just as you would never allow your kids to spend hours alone with complete strangers of differing ages, nationalities and personalities, nor should you allow them hours with the TV. Make a point of getting to know the people your kids meet on TV Street.

Cultural commentator Hugh Mackay makes a very salient point when he writes:

> There is a kind of media mania that causes us to feel threatened by the media, as though they have some inherent power over us. The same mania leads us to the dangerous assumption that the media are shaping our society in ways we can neither understand nor control. My message to parents is simple: you have far more influence over your children's attitudes and values than television will ever have ... while the media may change the way we think and communicate, we are still responsible for what we think and what we say.[63]

Once again, it's up to the adults to lead by example and create responsible viewing habits and places for their children. If young kids copy what they see on TV, then it's not the TV's fault – it's ours. It may happen once, but with sensible intervention and explanations, the behaviour shouldn't be repeated – unless, of course, it's good. We have to control, to the best of our ability, what's beamed into our homes and where it's watched. Through discussion and interaction with our children we can use what's screened to create valuable dialogues with our kids. We can also use the TV to facilitate conversations and shared viewing times, making it part of the family instead of another gadget that isolates and separates.

Remember, in and of itself, the TV isn't bad – it's the habits we allow to form around watching it that, like a lousy channel, need to be changed.

chapter seven

Sense and Censorship: Film and the Uncomfortable Question of Parental Guidance

Let Me Entertain You

When French brothers Auguste and Louis Lumiere showed a series of moving images to astonished audiences back in 1886, little did they realise what an impact their technology would have upon the world. Likewise, when Thomas Edison projected his first few metres of film in 1888, he had mainly scientific and educative purposes in mind for this marvellous new invention.[1] Yet, by the second decade of the 20th century, film was acknowledged not so much as a scientific break-through but as a very important storytelling medium. It created monolithic studios, made money for investors, turned those who performed in front of the camera into 'stars' and those behind into 'artistes' but, most importantly and perhaps surprisingly, it entertained adults and children in unforeseen and delightful ways.[2]

Going to see a film became an event and arguably – despite the fact many of us have huge LCD and plasma TV screens at home or can download the latest releases from the internet – it still is. Rarely do people go to see a feature on their own. We tend to organise groups, attend as couples or make it a family occasion. Children, especially, love a trip to the cinema. Despite being in company, there's something wonderfully solitary about sitting in the darkness, enveloped by images and sounds that enable us to lose ourselves in the world and characters being portrayed in larger-than-life dimensions on the giant screen. In an era of digitisation, extraordinary computer-generated imagery (CGI) and special effects, the magic has only increased. Seeing a film has become more than an excuse to get out of the house or amuse the kids, it's become a sensory experience.

Cinema attendance has declined in the last few years because of personal technology and rising costs of tickets and theatre food but, among teens and now tweens, it still retains, as Graeme Turner observes, 'something of its ritual status'.[3] It's important to consider the role of film in children's lives for, as Henry Giroux notes, 'unlike the often hard, joyless reality of schooling, children's films provide a high-tech visual space in which adventure and pleasure meet in a fantasy world of possibilities and a commercial sphere of consumerism and commodification'.[4]

In this chapter, I'm going to discuss the adventurous and pleasurable aspects of films for kids and society generally. I'm also going to consider what responsibilities we as adults have when it comes to our kids (of all ages) and the films they love to watch or are told by outside forces (friends and marketing) they should. Do we employ common sense or rely on censorship? While I'm mainly dealing with big screen films, the ever-turning wheels of big business also mean these features are rapidly accessible through DVD and, later, screened on mainstream and satellite TV. Films aren't exclusively cinematic experiences anymore – they enter our homes. They become part of a DVD collection, are viewed by kids over and over and lodge in their minds and imaginations in particular and meaningful ways. For this reason, it's important to consider what was said in the last chapter about TV and viewing habits when considering film and to read this chapter in relation to the next one as well, which also deals with stories, including Disney films.

Film Collections

Films offer a couple of hours of edge-of-the-seat escapism from a world gripped by terrorism, violence, natural catastrophes and other awful and spectacular realities. In the safety of the cinema, we can boldly go where no-one has gone before; we can embark on dangerous quests with hobbits, discover the magic within with Harry Potter, travel to the future and beyond, kill some 'bad' people with James Bond, fall in love with and be loved by a beautiful star, plumb the depths of despair or vivify our sense of mortality with a slasher flick starring the latest teen sensation. But watching film isn't only about losing ourselves for a brief time. Turner believes that watching 'a popular film is related to a whole range of other desires – for fashion, for the new, for the possession of icons that are highly valued by one's own peers'.[5] Among tweens and teens in particular, seeing and being able to talk about the latest films and the actors starring in them gives them social currency among their friends. It reveals that they're up to date with trends and popular narratives. So does purchasing the associated merchandise that many Hollywood and independent films produce and rely on to keep their films in the cultural eye – from T-shirts, CDs and dolls, to something as simple as a poster tacked on the wall. Many tween and teen bedrooms are shrines to special moments, characters and actors. Taking a cursory glance around my study, I can see memorabilia from *Star Wars, Dr Who, Star Trek: First Contact, Alien, The Wizard of Oz* and *The Lord of the Rings*. Clearly, I'm a fan of science fiction and fantasy or I need to get a life (some would argue both). Take a look at what you've collected or treasured and I'll bet they hark back to your younger years or a favourite film. Look in a tween's or teen's bedroom, and the movie memorabilia they've collected speaks volumes about who they are and what they value in very significant ways.

Similarly, just as CD collections reveal a great deal about the person who owns them, so now do DVD collections. Aware of this, teens particularly are quite self-conscious buyers of films that have significance to them personally or within a specific friendship network. Films are also simultaneously private and public expressions of identity. Before a film can be publicly viewed and enter either our own or the cultural psyche, it first undergoes rigorous evaluation by an appointed committee.

Classifications

Prior to a film entering the public domain, it's scrutinised and reviewed by the Classification Board, which is part of the Office of Film and Literature Classification (OLFC). A government-approved body, members are drawn from all walks of life and are appointed by the Governor-General for a minimum term of three years and maximum of seven. Anyone can apply to be on the Board (whose numbers cannot exceed 20), but they must meet the selection criteria. Every year, they review hundreds of films, books, TV shows and computer games and watch and classify them according to strict regulations.

In Australia, we have one of the most rigorous classification systems in the world. There are six levels of classifications, the first three of which, G, PG and M, denote movies suitable for children of different ages: usually from birth to 15, and are *recommendations* only. Adults can choose to abide by or ignore the classification. G stands for General Exhibition or 'family friendly' viewing and lets adults know the content is very mild – that is, there's likely to be no swearing, violence or sex. PG is short for Parental Guidance and means that the content is mild. Parents or an adult should watch the film with the child, which may have a bit of swearing, possibly some sexual innuendo and a bit of violence, but usually non-gratuitous. M refers to material that is 'moderate in impact' – this is a particularly interesting category and can mean that the film has mild sexual scenes, drug use, violence and swearing – if drug use can be mild. It can also mean that, providing your child is mature (around 15 and accompanied by an adult), then the material is likely to be of a nature that won't offend them or that they've seen before and which an adult can situate in a suitable context.

Beyond the M rating, the classifications change and are legally restricted. MA means the material is 'not suitable for people under 15' and 'Under 15s must be accompanied by a parent or adult guardian'. The content is strong. This infers that the film will contain more than sexual references, possibly some sex scenes that are reasonably graphic. There's likely to be nudity, violence, swearing and drug use. The rating R 18+ refers to movies for those 18 and over and contains what's described as

'High Level Content'. These films are graphic in all regards, though the sex is usually restrained in that, while there might be full-frontal nudity and simulated sex, there's no penetration (though sometimes it's hard to tell the difference). The final category is X 18+ and this is for pornography and explicitly violent films.

All films and other material are judged against the following criteria:

> (a) the standards of morality, decency and propriety generally accepted by reasonable adults
>
> (b) the literary, artistic or educational merit (if any) of the publication, film or computer game
>
> (c) the general character of the publication, film or computer game, including whether it is of a medical, legal or scientific character
>
> (d) the persons or class of persons to or amongst whom it is or is intended or likely to be published.[6]

Censorship

Fundamentally, there are two oppositional ways of thinking about censorship and children. The first relies on understanding it as something imposed by an outside body over which the average citizen has little if any control. The second regards censorship as an internal mechanism that places the individual in charge.

Interestingly, the role of adults, particularly parents, is emphasised in both definitions and their role is represented in quite contradictory ways. On the one hand, adults and parents are perceived as concerned citizens advocating for stricter censorship laws and tighter controls over content in the domestic and public sphere. On the other, when it comes to film and TV, adults are depicted as indifferent carers who abrogate their moral responsibilities and leave it to the faceless, government-endorsed few.

The cases for both interpretations are persuasive and are outlined below. But what we must consider when discussing censorship and what are or are not appropriate films and content is the age of the children. After all, there's a great deal of difference between a tot and a tween and even a tween and someone over 15 years of age. So let's start by discussing children over two and pre-tweens or 'kweens' – tots and little kids.

The Tut-Tut Brigade

There are adults throughout the Western world who express their disquiet over the imagery, suggestive and inappropriate language and behaviour that the censors are allowing to creep into children's TV, films and electronic games.[7] Lobbying various government bodies and institutions, they call for tighter control and stricter regulations. Now, don't make the mistake of believing that these protests are coming from a small group of Harry Potter-hating muggles, religious conservatives or secluded individuals who are being unrealistic as to what material their young children should and shouldn't be exposed to. Former children of the revolution, Baby Boomers, ex-hippies, parents with broad minds and attitudes are among the vanguard of those protesting against the moral liberties being taken in children's film in particular.

Because kids develop cognitively at different rates, some young children are able to cope with complex themes and emotional issues better than others. Jenny, mother of two, says that she had no worries about her son, Max (10), watching the M-rated *Pirates of the Caribbean* series, as he understands the fantasy elements of the film, but she has real problems with him watching a G- or PG-rated American 'cheerleading movie' as she doesn't want him exposed to what she feels are 'shallow American values'. Regardless of what the censors recommend (referring to the first three categories), you're the best judge of what your children should be exposed to – just make sure whatever it is reflects your ethics and their level of understanding.

But it's also important to know that there's a great deal of difference between an M-rated movie and a G-rated one. Just because your six-year-old understands what magic is or appears to be equipped to handle emotional scenes, don't assume they won't be affected by seeing unrelenting on-screen violence or won't respond in some way to turgid undercurrents of sexual tension, all of which can and do appear in M-rated movies. Despite these quite reasonable and clear classification codes, many parents and guardians seem to either be confused as to what children should be allowed to access or, worse, simply don't care.

Parents will often pop a movie on to keep the kids quiet during holidays and get that much needed downtime, or pack them off into the cinema while they shop, relying on the censor's recommendation or being persuaded by their kids and marketing that a certain film is suitable. This is the notion of the electronic babysitter taken to extremes – and it happens every holiday and weekend in cineplexes around the country. But it's not just laziness that drives some adults to make bad choices; some put their own viewing desires above their children's.

For Your Eyes Only

Box office figures attest to the popularity of animated movies during school holidays, but what they don't reveal is exactly for whom the tickets to other less salubrious movies are being purchased. Now, I tend to see a great many movies. Being a teacher of media and popular culture, as well as a social commentator, I need to stay up to date with the latest films. At least that's my excuse. One of my great delights, especially now my children are older, is going to the cinema during the holidays and watching kids in the audience being captivated by the likes of the three *Shrek* movies, *Flicka*, *Flushed Away*, *Night at the Museum* and a host of other fun-filled children's movies – those aimed firmly at the lower and sometimes upper primary market.

My initial pleasure at seeing so many families together fast turned to dismay as I watched some very young children, clutching their grown-up's hand, entering the dark, cavernous spaces of a variety of M-rated movies as well.

That a child of no more than six was sitting behind me during a screening of *Batman Begins* all but spoiled the entire cinematic experience. A dark, clever movie, where the lines between evil and good are blurred, the film explores the depths of the human psyche and uses some deeply disturbing imagery to depict the extent to which the villainous mind will go. A young child, however, does not have the emotional, psychological or social experiences to draw on and make sense of what is ostensibly a creative work, an interpretation of right and wrong, human reaction and intervention. Nor does a child have the capacity to understand social injustice or justice when it is dealt with in such extreme and problematic ways.

Similarly, at a screening of Brad Pitt and Angelina Jolie's *Mr and Mrs Smith*, the potent sexual innuendos and extraordinary violence, which lacked any ethical context, could simply not be processed by youngsters, but they were there – dozens of them with their grown-ups, staring at the bloodshed and violence on the screen. They were also present during *War of the Worlds*, *Star Wars: Revenge of the Sith*, *Fearless*, *Die Hard 4.0* and the James Bond film *Casino Royale*. Propped beside their accompanying adult, their eyes and minds agog at what they bore witness to, these psychologically and socially unprepared youngsters were exposed to a range of ideas, actions and plots that they simply should be protected from, not invited to interact with.

Parental Guidance

Movie makers, game producers and the media do not care about our children – that's *our* job. Every time a child is taken to a movie that's not designed for young minds, we're adding to the corporate coffers, but, worse, we're eroding the magic of childhood.[8]

How can a child chant with Peter Pan that they believe in fairies when they've just seen a man driven insane by a hallucinogenic substance or someone shot to pieces by a beautiful, hard-hearted woman or government-endorsed assassin? How can a child begin to imagine that there is a Santa Claus when the world he or she belongs to is full of such violence and despair?

The censors try to do their job but, in the end, it's up to us. As adults and parents, we create the context in which our children grow and learn. To the best of our ability, we set reasonable limits and boundaries around what they're exposed to. These can and should be flexible and expand with each year and each time our kids prove they're equipped to handle what they see and hear. We should never wrap our kids in cottonwool – that's just stupid and cruel – but, just as we introduce new food into their diets, usually by burying it in more familiar fare, so we should facilitate their introduction to new ideas through our own belief and value systems. Sometimes this is very difficult for adults as ideas and even behaviour that would have been unheard of a few years ago are now frequently shown in children's films.

Likewise, there's a great deal of confusion generated around the release of what, at one level, are marketed very broadly as 'children's films', such as those in the Harry Potter franchise, and the actual content and themes that are depicted. The fourth and fifth films in the Potter series, *Goblet of Fire* and *Order of the Phoenix*, perplexed many adults who understood the books as 'children's literature' but found the films and the visualisation of previously only imagined scenarios confronting. This is where knowledge of both the film's content and an acute awareness of a child's cognitive development must be considered before choosing to see the film. Reading about magic, death and violence are very different to witnessing them, particularly when the details are so explicit. Parents and adults responsible for children need to take all these things into consideration; and sometimes this means making a child wait until they're older before allowing them to see a film, no matter what the peer or social pressure.

Having said that, there are times when no matter what precautions adults might take neither they nor the child are prepared for what they witness on screen.

The Ratings Creep

New Yorker Ellen Goodman writes, 'Parents are forever being told to monitor their children's media without being told how'. She cites the ratings creep as an example – the fact that what was once yesterday's R rating is today's PG.[9] An example of this is the Kennedy-Miller film *Mad Max*. Given an R rating in the 1970s, it would probably be lucky to be classified M today. For contemporary parents, there are no guarantees regarding what's going to be heard or seen under the guise of Parental Guidance or even General Exhibition and we often don't know how to deal with the inappropriate material when it does manifest.

As one culturally astute parent bemoaned, the control of the media is so remote that even the home is no longer sacred when it comes to shielding our children from the negative attitudes, language and images that abound in the world – they are beamed in and around us in ways that lie outside our control or, it seems, our say.

That's because, in many ways, what was once profane is now sacred. Words we never would have dared to utter in front of our parents are now the kinder argot of our pre-schools. And this is all replicated and circulated through children's popular culture. Is this something we should be worried about? There's no simple answer to this. But certainly it's in our control – the only problem is that it's generally after the event. It's unexpected and we're taken off-guard. But that doesn't mean we shouldn't discuss and deal with it, express our disapproval or place it in a broader context to reduce its impact. An example of this is swearing on film. While some adults don't mind kids swearing, I don't think it's a good sound, especially out of the mouths of babes. But kids will copy those words they sense make adults cringe or better still get a response – even an angry one. An effective way to deal with it is to ask them to stop when they're very young but also explain why. They'll stop, providing you don't overreact every time the word is said. That which doesn't attract attention is often abandoned in favour of something that does. So reward good behaviour with positive attention to distract from the swearing. For older kids, explain to them that you don't allow that language in the house and stick to it. Of course they'll use it, but so long as you adhere to the rule as well, you'll find you don't hear it at home. Perhaps you can also suggest to them that when their vocabulary is as good as yours, then they can swear.

But swearing is just the tip of the film iceberg, with parents often feeling like the *Titanic* – they just know they're going to sink, yet they don't want to bring their kids down with them.

No matter how hard some adults try to limit or grade their kids' exposure to adult ideas and words, it's often the commercials and advertisements for forthcoming films that have them shielding their youngsters' eyes and ears in dismay. Where once taking your child to watch the latest animated offering at the cinema was a safe bet, these days it's a psychological and emotional lottery as previews of coming attractions that fall well outside the rating of the feature are displayed. Scantily dressed young women, men (and women) flashing weapons, and high-speed car chases are not really suitable visual epigraphs for *Madagascar* or the movie *Charlotte's Web*.

It doesn't matter whether you've checked the programming and rating of a particular show or film and deemed it suitable for your kids to view. Your child can be comfortably ensconced in front of the TV enjoying a specific film, when advertisements endorsing various products will crop up – often using sex to sell. And just when you've distracted your children long enough to reassure yourself they didn't understand it anyway, commercials advertising the evening's viewing and news bulletins reporting unmitigated violence, racial, religious and sexual hatred, as well as images of global poverty and disease are likely to be shown.

Parental Rights

While I do not want to come over all Mary Whitehouse on you, there's a point at which, with very young kids, we have to say enough is enough. Adults can mostly choose where and when we digest nudity, language, sexual behaviour and violence, and we would like to be able to choose when our children do too – not leave it up to the faceless few who constitute the censorship panel. We can no longer depend upon them to protect our children from what we might consider inappropriate material as the boundaries around proper and improper continue to blur. Social values can and do change to reflect contemporary attitudes: but if the material your children are exposed to doesn't support your values, then you need to know what they have seen so you can discuss the content with them or make the decision to avoid it all together.

The inclusion of sex and violence in various films and TV shows is often defended as a matter of creative freedom. When it comes to adult consumption and choice, the argument is convincing. However, when it comes to our children and what they can access, the claims are a matter of semantics and would be downright offensive if we didn't have control – but we do. Parents who want to create a buffer zone between their children and the rest of the world for a few short years have the right and ability to deny access to or admit into their home certain ideas and images.

Only, in this day and age, there are no guarantees that you'll be successful and that's why it's important to know how to deal with material when it comes into your child's imaginative orbit.

Another growing area of concern regarding the pre-tween and early tween market is the rampant merchandising. When the M-rated movies *Pirates of the Caribbean: Dead Man's Chest* and *Superman Returns* were released in the USA and Australia, they were accompanied by a marketing blitz aimed directly at kids, even though they weren't considered old enough to see the films. T-shirts, dinner plates with skulls and crossbones, collector cards, computer games and dolls resembling the characters hit the shelves and parents' hip pockets.[10] This strategy will continue as long as there's money to be made and pester-power to harness. Furthermore, the rather simple toys and their novelty reduce the significance of the movie's rating and persuade parents that, if their kids are playing with Jack Sparrow or Superman, then they may as well see the film. Whenever this happens, the studios and their merchandising attack have won.

Once again, adults need to be reminded that they can say 'no' – it's not a crime. But allowing your kids to see a movie that you haven't censored, through reading reviews, asking those who have attended and evaluating what you know about the content just might be.

Play It Again ... and Again, and Again

Lots of adults are bemused by the fact that their four- and five-year-olds don't simply watch a film once. Young children are more than capable of viewing a film like *Finding Nemo* 20 times in a row. They can quote almost every line and, despite having seen it yesterday (and the day before), want to watch it again. Part of the reason for this might be the complexity of the narrative, but that's not the only reason – after all, even simple films like *Bambi* capture children's imaginations. Kids love repetition and routine, and not just in films – the same thing happens with bedtime stories, which can also become boring for the adults (there are only so many times you can read the delightful *Who Sank the Boat?* or play the same games). The more familiar something becomes, the more kids love it; it's reassuring for them (as marketers know). There are no surprises (though they'll re-enact the emotions), only known and therefore safe territory. It's only as we grow older that we seek stimulation from something new and different each time. So let your kids watch their favourite (and suitable to you) films over and over. They're exercising their memories, their imaginations and enjoying some much needed escapism – and you get to do something else for an hour or so.

The Sleeper Curve

While there may be more and more 'language' and adult ideas creeping into movies that were once considered the exclusive domain of children, much of it goes over their heads, especially as filmmakers understand that adults take children to the movies and enjoy being entertained as well. Hence we have films like *Shrek*, *Shrek 2* and *Shrek the Third*,

Happy Feet, The Incredibles, Ratatouille, Enchanted and *Shark Tale*, all with layers of meanings aimed at different age groups. Producers now focus on guaranteeing return business by appealing to all age groups in the cinema – even with G and PG films.

As far as older tweens (nine to 12) and teens are concerned, they're more than ready for the layers of meaning and often appreciate what's aimed at the adults more than the grown-ups! They're better educated, particularly when it comes to popular culture and their film expectations. They're sophisticated consumers of animation and other types of movies and therefore get many of the references. Raised on a diet of visual culture, they understand genre and expect to be entertained at the least and challenged at most. While there's no doubt that there are many dreadful films out there in terms of quality of acting and story, the movies that rise to the top of the Hollywood heap do so for a reason.

Steven Johnson, in *Everything Bad Is Good for You*, writes about the 'Sleeper Curve' effect. Applying it to television, video games, the internet and film, he argues that, while we're ready to debunk popular culture and view it all as trashy and unedifying, there's evidence that over the last decade the stories being told on TV and in the movies are growing more complex and sophisticated, thereby demanding more intellectual work of audiences.[11] In the last chapter, I mentioned this in relation to TV, but it's also true of films. Plots are becoming increasingly intertwined and have multiple threads requiring viewers to do a lot of mental work to join the dots. Rampant cross-cultural referencing to other films, TV, music and literature (such as in the *Shrek* films) demands certain knowledge of the viewer for the story to be fully appreciated. One of the examples Johnson uses is comparing the first *Star Wars* movies (episodes IV–VI) to Peter Jackson's *The Lord of the Rings*.

The creator of *Star Wars*, George Lucas, relied upon a fairly traditional good versus evil scenario and based his narrative arc on Joseph Campbell's seminal work *Hero of a Thousand Faces*. Luke Skywalker is the protagonist who denies his birthright, is orphaned, flees his home, takes up the mantle that's offered to him, trains hard to become a warrior, claims his name and finally confronts his internal demons, finds self-belief, challenges his father, gains a sister and emerges a hero. There are other characters who also face personal challenges, such as Leila, Han Solo and even C3PO and R2D2, but they're only a few, and they're mainly sidekicks to enhance Skywalker's journey. Their stories interrelate and come together at the end, emphasising Skywalker's victory. The tale is fairly linear and is almost literally, in terms of costuming, black and white.

Peter Jackson's *Lord of the Rings*, based on the trilogy by JRR Tolkein, is a richer story with a great many more characters, all of whom have their own back-stories and futures that don't necessarily intersect with the hero's (Frodo's) journey, but are important in their own right. A viewer has to balance all these, understand the connections and interplay and fill in the missing links to fully appreciate the story. As Johnson rightly points out, the big movies of the past 10 years – *Toy Story, Shrek, Monsters Inc* (and we can add *Hoodwinked* and *The Simpsons Movie*) – 'build distinct layers of information into their plots, dialogue, and visual effects, creating a kind of hybrid form that dazzles children without boring the grownups'.[12]

He also cites what he refers to as 'mind-bender films' – those movies that 'disorient you … mess with your head'.[13] *Pulp Fiction, Memento, Run Lola Run, Being John Malkovich, Big Fish, The Fountain* and *The Matrix* are just some examples. These films withhold information and force audiences to analyse what's going on, to be active in terms of the film's story and the sense-making process. And we love it. These films were all box-office successes, particularly with the teen demographic who want more viewing pleasure for their dollar.

With an eye to increasing cognitive demands of young audiences, a movie like *Monster House* can be made. At one level, it's a very scary film, but at another it doesn't condescend to either its child or adult audience. It frightens, amuses and intellectually and imaginatively pleases.

By the time our kids leave their tweens and are into their teens, it's a sad truth that there's probably very little in terms of films and content that they won't have seen: drugs, sex and violence are part of a contemporary teenage screen diet.[14] Certainly, adults have a responsibility to make sure that many of the issues in 'teen' films, such as sex, drugs, relationships, peer pressure and the harsher realities of life have been discussed long before their kids 'learn' about them from Lindsay Lohan or Shia LaBeouf. Studies have shown that the 'less people know about an issue, the more likely they are to rely on the media for interpretation of that issue'.[15] Jeanne R Steele writes that 'Teens look to movies (and television too) to understand reality, to understand the world they have inherited. Poised, if not pushed, to break out of the safety net of childhood, they embrace movies as stories about the way the world is, the way they should act as adults'.[16]

The disappointing fact about so many of the films made specifically for the tween/teen market is that they're generally vacuous, stereotyped stories filled with characters who triumph because of how they look or what they own more than through their wits or any sense of consequences or social responsibility.

In her book *Branded: The Buying and Selling of Teenagers*, Alissa Quart discusses the way teen films changed from being about kids uniting against the common enemies of adults 'and a future of soullessness', where the motto was be yourself and discover your inner beauty, to being about kids who 'have it all'.[17] She compares movies that explored teenagers' sense of separation and alienation with horror or humour like *Carrie* or *The Breakfast Club* to some of the recent teen hits. Discussing blockbusters such as *Ten Things I Hate About You*, *Clueless*, *Bring It On*, *She's All That* and *Legally Blonde*, Quart argues that 'it's difficult to feel affection for these studs and sylphs and even harder to pity them; for them, MTV television is akin to the Talmud, and their bodies are so underdressed that they give new meaning to *pretty in pink*'.[18]

She decries the narratives of these films, which focus on makeovers (*Princess Diaries*, *She's All That*), stress the importance of social connections over emotional ones (*Clueless*, *Mean Girls*) and celebrate competition (*Bring It On*, and any teen sport flick).[19] Nowadays, the popular kids are those who wear the right clothes, drive the right cars and display the 'right' brands. 'Winning', whether it's a group of friends or a member of the opposite sex's attention, may not mean having to change who you are on the inside, but it is contingent on changing the way you are on the outside – something Olivia Newton-John's character, Sandy, in *Grease* learned. It's all about looks and facades. Where is Ferris Bueller when you need him?

Oh, that's right; he changed into Napoleon Dynamite …

Brought to You By …

Some of the most popular tween and teen flicks are just one long commercial for specific products – such as *Bratz: The Movie*. Aware of how necessary the tween/teen market is to the financial success of films, the budget allocated to advertising and tie-ins sometimes outweighs the cost of the film itself. Furthermore, 'the filmmakers, [are] well aware of the new law of teen films that says that all main characters must be style influencers …'.[20]

Young, 20-something actors like Keira Knightley, Orlando Bloom, Scarlett Johansson and Kate Hudson, and teen stars like Miley Cyrus, promote brand consciousness as something desirable not only in their films but outside the studio complex as well. The main characters (who, just like on TV, are much older than the characters they're playing) all wear designer clothes, have trendy haircuts and own the latest accessories – they are effectively walking, talking billboards. The companies pour money into the films for the positive associations that will arise out of having their brands and the actor/character appear together. Quart is very worried about the way brands are used in movies, suggesting that it's not only a 'major form of conversation, and whimsy in teen films; it is a symptom, and potentially a cause, of teen culture's growing obsession with acquisition'.[21]

We might think that these are harmless, escapist fantasy films that present young people in a relatively innocent light. Most of the movies portray sound values and ethics – the mean kids are punished and the 'good' (read 'beautiful') kids are suitably rewarded. But these films don't arise in a vacuum and neither are they watched in one. Like everything else discussed so far, they're part of an increasingly complex diet of ideas and notions about the self that young people are being presented with – and at younger and younger ages. Most tweens and teens see these high-school romps for what they are – fantasy versions of the angst-ridden, self-conscious years of adolescence where hierarchies rule and cliques define a teen, such as the movie *Mean Girls*. This is something *Buffy the Vampire Slayer* (the movie and especially the TV series by Joss Whedon) explores with depth and perception by placing the high school at the centre of the story over Hell's mouth and populating Buffy's and her friends' conflicted teen years with vampires, werewolves and other monsters. Slaying the beasts becomes a metaphor for the battle young people face with their own internal demons as they shed the chrysalis of adolescence and take up adult responsibilities. Tweens, however, as savvy as they seem to be, brought up on a diet of the more recent bubble-gum high-school films, could be forgiven for believing that when you wish upon a star (or take out a loan to pay for plastic surgery), your nose, breasts, pecs, teeth, acne and weight are magically fixed and friends flock to your side. They might also be forgiven for believing that they're very special – but more on that in Chapter Ten.

Over Exposure

In 2006, at the Australasian College of Physicians annual scientific meeting, pediatrician Dr Hasantha Gunasekera presented findings based on a study of adolescents and 87 of the most popular films of the last 20 years. Of the movies analysed, 53 had sex scenes but only one of these films had the suggestion of a condom. Most of the movies included smoking, a third depicted intoxication from alcohol and 7 per cent included cannabis use. Dr Gunasekera claimed that 'the average child will spend twice as much time watching the media than they will listening to their teachers in the classroom and ... more time than they will speaking to their parents'.[22]

Instead of being alarmed by these statistics and statements, what adults need to do is take them as an opportunity to act – to talk to young people about the consequences of smoking, drinking and having unprotected sex while being aware that, in modern times, learning, as educator Henry Giroux continually reminds us, is located in the spheres that young people move in: daytime television, film, fanzines, the internet, movies and music.[23] Before we can effectively educate our kids about these kinds of things, we need to understand how the spheres they operate in function.

Out of Sight, Out of Mind

Living in a highly technological society poses a plethora of problems for even the most vigilant of parents. As I discussed in the previous chapter, while the television is a domestic and often shared appliance that enjoys an ambivalent relationship with householders in that it brings the family together while simultaneously alienating them by discouraging interaction, there are increasing numbers of young people with televisions in their bedrooms. In this private space, the concerned eye of the parental 'spy' can't monitor what is being accessed and this includes the films they're viewing (let alone the kids who claim to be seeing one film (DVD, game, internet site) while really viewing another whether at a public multiplex, a friend's house or in their bedrooms).

Out of sight, our children unwittingly and deliberately taste the tempting but forbidden fruits of adult visual culture.

And, like Adam and Eve, these delights will be tasted no matter how often or from whom the warning to be cautious comes. But this doesn't mean that it shouldn't concern us, or that we should reduce our attempts at moral guidance and supervision. Rather, what it does suggest is that censorship should not be left to the few who make decisions about what is and isn't appropriate for our kids but that, first and foremost, censorship should begin at home.

I'm not talking here about only allowing images of kittens and puppies frolicking in a paddock while bees hum around their heads to be seen, nor am I suggesting that only happy thoughts and phrases be uttered. That's both a ridiculous and impractical notion. What I'm talking about is working hard to protect our young children and tweens from unnecessary and frequent images of violence, meaningless and gratuitous sexual encounters, ideologies that spout religious, racial and sexual intolerance or demean one sex to promote the other, and suggestive language. No matter how hard we try, these things will slip through our adult radar and into our children's social and emotional spheres, but what we have to ensure is that they are moderated and explained by our older (and hopefully wiser) interpretations and placed in a broader family and social context. We need to educate our children about what we consider right and wrong and ground them in reality, not some film, televisual or cyberspace fantasy. And, by doing so, we take responsibility for the popular culture and ideologies inherent therein that our kids consume.

This, I'm sad to say, no matter how good and committed our intentions, is not as easy as it sounds. The local video shop with its cornucopia of DVDs and games, the TV, the internet and the local cinema become convenient electronic babysitters that engage the young and satisfy the old. And, in parent land, there's only one rule: if the children are happy, we are too.

We have to be more vigilant than ever about what our tots, tweens and even our teens are exposed to through the films they watch – those exciting visual stories that reflect, critique and explore our society in mostly entertaining ways – and the contexts we, as the adults in their lives, create for them. We can't control everything our children access but, when we can, we have to ensure that it is visually, psychologically and emotionally appropriate. The judgement of the censors is only one step towards knowing, to the best of our ability, the content of the films our tots and tweens long to see. While reviews and personal recommendations can be an important part of our decision-making process, viewing these films with our kids is even more so. If we watch with them, then we can facilitate the ideas and substance of the films. Yet again, we can lead by example, through discussion, behaviour and the wider family and social context we establish. It's up to us, in the first years of a child's cognitive development and for as long as we can afterwards, to foster the type of role-models and identities we want our children to emulate. We have to ensure that the wonder and magic of the world is not extinguished more quickly than it already is; that hopes and dreams are as much a part of their young lives as the less attractive options.

The early years in particular are an all-important time that we should nurture and then encourage our children to hold on to as a talisman throughout their long, scary and often difficult adult future. We must learn to say 'no' to inappropriate material and separate our desires from our children's. This will go a long way towards restoring those brief years of enchantment and developing healthy moral and ethical radars within our children so that, once they reach their teens, they can function as their own censors.

chapter eight

Once Upon a Time: Disney, Harry Potter, Hans Christian Andersen and Other Grimm Tales

Fairytales, Folktales and Other Beloved Stories

Just as toys and children have a natural relationship, fairytales and folktales have always been associated with childhood. Remembering stories known and loved as a child, adults delight in retelling them to suit their own era, sometimes making the hero or heroine resemble their little boy or girl as they outwit big bad wolves, ogres, giants and wicked stepmothers. By firesides and later in dimly lit bedrooms, monsters and villains were quickly and heroically banished with the utterance of a phrase or the turn of a page, but not without appropriate consequences and lessons. Sadly, there's evidence to suggest that fairytales, nursery rhymes and folktales are slowly disappearing from our cultural memory-bank. In Britain, there are calls to establish a 'parenting workforce' where adults are trained to support parents to provide 'good early years education' through, among other things, singing nursery rhymes to kids – a form of folktales in themselves.[1] That this has to happen at all is disturbing, as rhymes, fairytales and folktales play an important role in children's social, emotional and psychological development. In his landmark study on the impact of fairytales on children, *The Uses of Enchantment*, child psychologist Bruno Bettleheim argued that fairytales have a powerful therapeutic value, teaching children 'that a struggle against severe difficulties in life is unavoidable'.[2]

In our contemporary culture, where fairytales either aren't told anymore or have been recast to suit contemporary gender and sexual ideologies, TV and film most often instruct and guide our children as well as first introduce them to the classic stories. As demonstrated in the last two chapters, through their visual narratives, TV and film deliberately and inadvertently provide a moral, ethical and social education. Douglas Kellner suggests that 'media culture has replaced traditional institutions as major instruments of socialisation, and young people often receive role models and materials for identity from media corporations rather than their parents or teachers'.[3]

But whereas fairytales showcase the various difficulties and triumphs that life offers, popular cultural interpretations can often trivialise them, remove the moral message altogether, or suggest that behaving and looking a certain way renders, like a wave of a fairy-godmother's wand, any problems redundant.

The Magic Kingdom

When discussing fairytales, folktales and children's culture, it's impossible not to recognise the legacy left by Walt Disney and his global corporation, nor its omnipresent trademarks. There are the ubiquitous Mickey Mouse ears, one of the most recognisable symbols in the world today – and to think Walt Disney wanted to call him Mortimer. There's also the magic castle, with pennant fluttering, and animated curving rainbow followed by a splash of stars, which precedes some of the most successful movies in cinematic history. We also have the Mickey Mouse Club, responsible for many of the current tween idols such as Britney Spears, Christina Aguilera and Justin Timberlake. You can also experience Disney by visiting one of its five theme parks. There are two in the US (Anaheim in California and Disney World in Florida), and one each in Paris, Tokyo and Hong Kong. In these Disney multiverses, the 'happiest place on earth', imagination and reality converge.

Costumed actors patrol the boulevards, always smiling, possessing no facial hair (which as John Saffron pointed out is odd considering Walt had a moustache), and never once breaking out of character (which is forbidden). In fact, potential actors are told they have to bring 'energy and spirit to the role – make it real' and that they're 'not people dressed up in costumes' because 'anyone can do that'.[4] The streets are free of rubbish, and full of adults and kids having a great time. There's no sign of dirt, distress or injuries (though all these things exist). Inside the Disney gates, it's easy to believe that you're really in a magic kingdom. Certainly, the faces of the children make you feel that way.

The Disney empire isn't restricted to parks alone. Disney owns 18 television stations, the entire US ABC network, six film studios, 65 radio stations, four record companies, three publishing imprints with sub-divisions, and 15 magazine titles, as well as a cruise line, stores, a theatre company, restaurants, educational DVDs, internet holdings and even a specifically designed, quite nostalgic township in Florida called 'Celebration'.[5] This is before we consider the hold Disney has on the public imagination through all of these and thousands of beloved characters.[6]

Relying on its steadfast reputation as a purveyor of family values and wholesome good fun, Disney nonetheless protects its name and image rigorously. When three childcare centres in South Florida used some of the cartoon characters from Disney's animated family album on their exterior walls, legal suits followed.[7] In this instance, property and money were more important than offering kids placed in daycare a few familiar and fun faces to sweeten their time away from their parents.

Criticism of Disney or questioning the meanings behind some of its most popular stories has sometimes led to legal action (by the corporation) or accusations from a loyal public of, yet again, those who dare to challenge Disney being killjoys or left-wing or, worse, trying to destroy goodness and happiness. Critics are rapidly silenced. Henry Giroux stands firm when he says that Disney has a public responsibility to address criticism, not gag those who query its practices, precisely because it provides us all with so much entertainment and pleasure.

He writes, 'Given the influence the Disney ideology has on children, it is imperative for parents, teachers, and other adults to understand how such films influence the values of the children who view them. As a producer of children's culture, Disney should not be given an easy pardon because it is defined as a citadel of fun and good cheer'.[8] Like Giroux, many adults have expressed concern over the sway Disney has over our children's lives as well as the way the corporation sometimes seems to erupt over, and then deflect, the smallest bit of criticism.

Despite the pervasiveness of Disney in so many spheres of not just American life but the global imagination, it's arguably known and loved the best for its animated fairytales and it's these that I want to focus on now to help adults develop what Giroux calls a 'language of pleasure and criticism'[9] so they can discuss Disney products – all of them – as well as those being developed by other companies with their kids.

A Whole New World

Revisiting tales we knew and loved as children, such as *Cinderella*, *Beauty and the Beast*, *The Little Mermaid*, *Aladdin*, *Hercules* and *Chicken Little*, and seeing them reinvented as all-singing and dancing Disney spectaculars can be an uplifting, terrific experience for adults. After all, so many of us grew up with the classical tales as bedtime stories. I was certainly well versed in the Grimm fairytales and those of Hans Christian Andersen and matured with an understanding of the importance they held in my life as moral and ethical touchstones for social and gender relationships.

Initially, I was thrilled each time Disney released an animated version of a fairytale; like most adults and children, I'm excited by the prospect of seeing a visual interpretation of a beloved tale. But every time I watch the colourful Busby Berkeley-style numbers dance across the screen, with their retro look and feel, a tiny voice inside me tolls a warning. What lessons are these sumptuous, happily-ever-after tales of beautiful and very stereotyped boys and girls, ethnicity, love and romance really teaching our kids, if they're teaching them anything at all?

Can we actually overlook the fact that underpinning Disney, like most businesses, is a money-making enterprise? Encouraged to think of Disney in mostly benign and generous ways, we think of the pleasure it brings our children, rather than the lessons its movies teach, the ideologies they espouse or the dollars the corporation is pocketing. It's hard for a parent to deny their child's wishes, not just to be taken to the movie, but to own a three-dimensional replica of Jasmine, Simba, Ariel or Chicken Little, the DVD, computer game, decorated bed linen, pencil cases or a toothbrush, because they're all part of the Disney experience as well.

However, there's a strong argument to suggest that the toys and other tie-ins, examples of the extent of Disney's cultural influence, actually focus more on teaching our children how to be good little materialists in this corporate, consumer-driven world than they do anything else. Let me reassure you that, while I sometimes cringe at what's being portrayed, I've also enjoyed many Disney films on my own and with kids. I believe the Disney universe does some good by providing just the sort of escapist fantasy that it does. But, believe it or not, so do the classical fairytales upon which so many of the most successful Disney movies ever made are based. It is hard not to consider why such well-known and beloved tales are so radically altered by Disney if not to serve some ideological purpose.

In fairness, it's not only Disney that has changed the tales. Designed to be cast in a different light for each generation and culture, fairytales and folktales have always been entertaining, frightening and thinly veiled lessons and warnings about life, people, goodness and evil that were passed down and altered from generation to generation. To look at the way the classic tales have been changed, I'm going to share some of the different versions of the more popular ones, a bit of their history and social context, and the possible meanings we can glean from them before returning to Disney. Then, I'm going to briefly consider the other types of stories our kids are being told by looking at the Harry Potter phenomenon as an example of the power of children's literature to captivate kids' minds and hearts. As fairytale expert Maria Tatar writes,

'It is nothing short of astonishing that we reflect so little on the stories read to our children – stories that so many of us acknowledge as having a profoundly formative influence on our childhood selves'.[10]

A Brief History of Some Classic Stories

Traditional tales, myths and legends have been around since humans first communicated. Many have survived and are still told today, but not nearly as often as they used to be. They're almost always filled with violence, conflict and enchantment. They address all sorts of critical, therapeutic, conservative and challenging issues.[11] The roles of children (naughty and nice), parents (good, weak, foolish, evil, loving and brave), strangers, beasts, biological and social families, class distinctions, work, ethics, dignity, manners and numerous other forms of interaction and emotional and psychological journeys are explored through fairytales and folktales.[12]

Tatar explains that fairytales originated in 'an irreverent peasant culture that arose in conscious opposition to the feudal state's ruling class. By overdoing it in the realm of storytelling, these narrators were able to alleviate – if only temporarily – some of the tedium that marked the daily life of their audience, allowing them to indulge in fantasies of wealth, success and empowerment'.[13]

The Grimm brothers, particularly, edited and rewrote the tales they chose to put in book form at least six times, sanitising and 'cleaning up' the contents of the stories, changing relationships, 'certain conditions' (this refers to pregnancy – Rapunzel and the Prince didn't sit around discussing recipes in that tower), and tidying up the prose until it suited the sensibilities of their times. This was partly because even though initially they had intended the tales to be for an adult audience, they found they actually appealed to a children's market instead.[14] Fundamentally, the moral and ethical meanings of the tales the brothers chose remained and their impact on generations was enormous. Poet WH Auden described the Grimm's collection as ranking 'next to the Bible in importance'.[15]

Cinderella

Arguably one of the most enduring and important of the fairytales is 'Cinderella'. There are many versions of the story about the beautiful young girl cast down in life due to circumstances beyond her control before being 'rescued' by a man of higher social standing, from literal reworkings such as the films *Ella Enchanted, Ever After* and *The Slipper and the Rose,* to contemporary spins such as *Pretty Woman, Working Girl* and *Maid in Manhattan.* There are also the reality TV series based on the tale – *The Bachelor, The Bachelorette, Australian Princess, Joe Millionaire* and basically any reality show that takes a person from obscurity to fame.[16]

Cinderella is a tale that can be traced all the way back to ancient China.[17] In this very early version, a young girl called Yeh-hsien is badly treated by her stepmother but finds the time to feed a huge goldfish that lives in a pond near their home. Jealous of the affection the goldfish bears for her stepdaughter, the stepmother kills it by dressing in Yeh-hsien's clothing, luring it out of the pond and stabbing it to death. Distraught at the loss of her goldfish, Yeh-hsien is told by a man who appears from the sky (this *is* a fairytale) to hide the fish bones in her room and her wishes will be granted. She does this and wishes for gold, jewels, food and clothes, which, as the man predicted, all appear. One day, Yeh-hsien's stepmother and stepsister leave to attend a cave-festival. Once they disappear, Yeh-hsien dresses herself in a beautiful cloak made from kingfisher feathers and tiny gold shoes and attends the festival too. She's recognised by her step-relations and flees, losing a shoe. The shoe is found by a cave person who sells it to the ruler of the island kingdom of T'o-han. The ruler decides he wants to marry the woman who fits the impossibly small shoe and demands that all the women in his kingdom try it on – to no avail. Eventually, he finds Yeh-hsien and makes her his chief wife. She takes her shoe and magical fish bones back to his country. As for the stepmother and her daughter, they're killed by flying stones and are buried in a cave named the Tomb of the Distressed Women. Visiting the cave then becomes part of a mating ritual with locals. The king of T'o-han, however, is greedy with his wishes and basically uses up the magic and then buries the bones on the shore, which are, one day amid a rebellion, washed out to sea.

In the thousands of other versions of the story that exist, the Cinderella character (also called everything from Donkeyskin to Cendrillon, Cennerentola, Mossy Coat, Ash-Girl, Katie Woodencloak, Catskin and Rashin Coatie) is sometimes, as Tatar writes, 'cruel and vindictive ... compassionate and kind ... genteel and self-effacing ... clever and enterprising ... coy and manipulative'.[18] She rarely has a fairy godmother, but relies on her own pluck to save herself from either her stepmother's evil intentions or her father's sexual advances. A great many of the early versions of the Cinderella story had incest as their theme, particularly the Indian version, which is translated as 'The Father Who Wanted to Marry His Daughter'. What these sorts of stories reinforced is that there comes a time when fathers must hand their daughters (and the family name) to another man to ensure the continuation of the bloodline. It also explains the stepmother's jealousy towards her stepdaughter who, as she grows older, attracts the sexual desire of her father. No wonder the stepmother wanted Cinderella out of the way. The shoes (or rings and other objects that often feature) are symbolic of the 'right' or 'wrong' fit or partner.

In many cultures, the Cinderella story ends in bloodshed, with the stepsisters and stepmother being boiled, thrown off cliffs or placed in barrels that have huge nails driven through them and then rolled around town. At the very least, those characters who hindered or hurt Cinderella get their just desserts in a way that makes a child listener deliciously reassured about fairness and good behaviour.[19]

French writer Charles Perrault gave us not only the glass (or fur) slipper but a tearful reconciliation between Cinderella and her cruel stepsisters once she's united with her Prince and the overbearing stepmother is out of the way.[20] In an Armenian version, Cinderella weeps over her stepsisters, promising forgiveness, and in the Disney sequel to the Cinderella story the Princess even finds a husband among the court officials for one of her stepsisters.

My personal favourite is the Grimm version of Cinderella. Initially told to me by my grandmother, I was soon, by the age of six, reading it for myself and over and over. I told it to my children and their friends and now I share it with hundreds of children in schools across Australia and overseas, as well as my students at university. They all thoroughly enjoy it and even prefer it to the Disney version.

In the Grimm rendition, many of the basics remain the same. Cinderella's mother dies and the father remarries. Once Cinder's father passes away, all pretence at caring for Cinderella's welfare is discarded and the sweet orphan becomes her stepmother's and stepsisters' servant. Her one solace is to visit her mother's grave, over which hangs a huge hazel tree, grown from a twig that lodged itself in her father's hat years before on a trip he made to the markets.

In this story, the Prince holds three grand balls on consecutive nights to choose a future wife. The stepmother and her daughters all attend. Cinderella, who is told she can also go providing she finishes impossible tasks, gets supernatural help to complete them but discovers that her stepmother's word is made to be broken. She is forbidden to attend the balls and left at home. Undeterred, she waits until her stepfamily leave and visits her mother's grave, kneeling under the hazel tree and chanting, 'Shiver and shake dear little tree, gold and silver shower upon me'. For three nights, a dress drops out of the tree, each more exquisite than the last. Cinderella dons them and graces the balls with her elegant presence. The Prince has eyes and arms for no-one else and the mysterious beauty earns the envy and admiration of all. Each night, at the stroke of midnight, she escapes the Prince's devout attentions by a hair's breadth, arousing his curiosity and ardour even further. On the third and last night, reluctant to leave, she overstays her time and, on hearing the clock chime midnight, flees. She discards, as opposed to loses, her shoes so she can run faster. The Prince follows her and, after a series of adventures, finds not only a shoe, but where Cinderella lives as well.

The following morning, the Prince and his entourage arrive and ask that the daughters of the house try on the shoe. To deceive the Prince, the stepsisters follow the advice of their mother and cut off their heel or toes to make the small shoe fit. When the Prince rides past Cinderella's mother's grave with first one sister and then the other, the birds in the branches of the tree begin to sing:

> Prithee, prithee, look back,
> There's blood on the track.
> The shoe is too small,
> At home your true bride is waiting thy call.

Disturbed, the prince returns each of the girls. Once Cinderella is revealed, the stepmother is furious, her great social plans for her daughters are destroyed, and her heart bursts and she dies. That was always my favourite bit. The sisters attend Cinderella's nuptials, but on the day of the wedding, as they are being transported to the ceremony, those talkative birds swoop into the carriage (or the steps of the church) and pluck out their eyes. So, for their meanness and cruelty to Cinders, the stepsisters are made lame and blind for the rest of their lives.[21]

Kids (and adults) love the inherent justice in this account. In fact, children have a very strong sense of what's fair and what's not and many of the classic fairytales can reassure them that, if you live according to socially accepted moral codes and are good to people no matter how they might treat you, justice will be served.

The Little Mermaid

Another favourite across the generations is Hans Christian Andersen's 'The Little Mermaid'.[22] An original tale from the imagination of the gentle, asexual and quite eccentric Andersen,[23] it tells of a little mermaid's journey towards spiritual enlightenment and desire for a 'soul' (something that only humans can possess). The youngest of six girls and, since her mother's death, raised by her father and her wise old grandmother, the little mermaid (nameless in the tale) longs to visit the ocean surface – something she can only do on her 15th birthday. In this watery world, it's a significant rite of passage. The heart-wrenching fable tells of her love for a human prince whom she rescues from drowning and how she gives her voice to the sea-witch in exchange for a pair of human legs. In this version, the little mermaid has her tongue cut out with a coral blade. Rendered mute, she also endures physical agony as each step she takes on her human legs feels like knives driving through her body.

At the end of the story, the little mermaid is rejected by her prince who has fallen in love with another woman. Her sisters, who have visited the sea-witch in an effort to save their sister, watch as the little mermaid weeps on the railings of the marriage-ship, aware she must now die. It's at this moment that their shaved heads become apparent. They've sold their beautiful hair to procure a knife that, should the little mermaid plunge it into the heart of the sleeping prince, will free her from the spell and allow her to return to the ocean as a mermaid and live out her years. But the little mermaid refuses. Her love is so great she sacrifices herself and thus earns the right to a soul. Standing on the prow of the ship, she casts herself into the ocean, prepared to die and become foam on the waves. At the last moment, the 'daughters of the air' (or angels) dive down from the sky and save her from this briny fate.

The lesson (religious connotations aside) in this tragic fable is unambiguous. Don't try to change yourself to make someone love you; if they don't love you for who and what you are, then they simply aren't worth it. The Disney version, on the other hand, featuring the quite sexual flame-haired Ariel – described by critics as a cross between rebellious teenager and a model fashioned 'in the editorial office of Vogue',[24] and as a 'sexy heroine' who would have made 'Snow White blush and Belle scorn'[25] or a 'slightly anorexic Barbie doll'[26] – suggests have an extreme makeover and the whole world will love you.

And let's not forget that undulating octopus, the villainous Ursula, who reassures Ariel that losing her voice isn't so bad because men don't like women who talk. This is reinforced when handsome Prince Eric tries to steal the kiss of 'true love' from Ariel, even though she hasn't spoken a word or managed to communicate in any other way, including sign language, other than making eyes at him.

While the stories of Cinderella and the Little Mermaid have been around for centuries, often the only accounts known to our tots, tweens and teens (and even adults) are the Disney ones. Stripped of morals and much of their original meaning, the Disney reworkings follow the 'happily ever after' paradigm. It's certainly true that we can take our children to the cinema knowing they'll leave satisfied with the outcomes and unlikely to be damaged or upset – and that's a great relief for adults. We can generally feel safe taking kids to a Disney movie – they're a known quantity. But just because the children walk away with a smile on their face, a song in their heart and clutching a figurine or toy replica of their favourite character, it doesn't mean we shouldn't look at what else they're taking away from Disney animations.

These films rely on stereotypical presentations of gender, race and culture and therefore any opportunities that may exist to challenge these or introduce kids to new concepts are reduced. In Disney's *The Little Mermaid*, for example, an all-male secondary cast replaces Andersen's female-centred world, something Giroux notes as well.[27] Jack Zipes believes that the Disney films, while transforming the classic tales into entertainment commodities, also celebrate the innocence of male power and the domestication of women.[28]

It's important we don't forget the other renditions of the famous tales and allow the earlier versions to occupy a space in our children's hearts and imaginations, just as the Disney films do. This is why it's important for adults to familiarise themselves with these stories and introduce children to the wonders of them. Just like they did in the past, and Disney does now, adults can modify or exaggerate the content to suit their own agendas.

Aladdin

Disney considerably altered the story of 'Aladdin'. So successful was their version that many people are unaware it *is* an adaptation. The story of the street urchin named Aladdin is one of the many tales purported to be contained within the Persian/Arabic classic *Arabian Nights*. 'Sinbad' and 'Ali Baba and the Forty Thieves' are other well-known ones, but there are many gems in the collection. Actually, Aladdin was a much later addition to *Arabian Nights*; it was not one of the 11 basic stories that formed the original work.[29] It was written in French around the 1700s and translated back into Arabic and then claimed as one of the 'lost tales' from the 14th-century Syrian manuscript.[30] Nonetheless, the tale has come down to us as part of a greater story – or a series of them – that took a thousand and one nights (the one was added by British translators) to tell. The premise behind *Arabian Nights* is told in the Prologue or 'The Story of King Shahrayar and Shahrazad, His Vizier's Daughter'.

This frame narrative tells the tale of the caliph or king, who, having had his trust in women broken, develops a habit of taking a new wife every day. He marries his daily bride in a lavish ceremony, sleeps with her and, in the morning, has her executed by chopping off her head. It isn't long before girls and their families not only try to avoid being chosen, but also are in short supply. Then, along comes the wise and canny Shahrazad, or Scheherazade, who, in the grand tradition of myths and tales, volunteers for the job of wife. Understanding the power of words and stories to instigate change and teach, she spends 1001 nights telling her husband a range of stories, parables and legends about jealousy, greed, stupidity, love, heroism and self-sacrifice. Through her stories, the king comes to recognise the faults in himself, his narrow-mindedness, and discovers ways to change his behaviour. He learns to trust, gains wisdom and falls deeply in love his wife.

The poor boy who finds a magic lamp and, after a series of triumphs and mistakes, transforms from pauper to prince is one of the stories we now accept Shahrazad tells her husband. It also resonates in our culture, because it is a rags-to-riches tale. This is why *Aladdin* is one of Disney's all-time favourites. When, after *The Little Mermaid* was completed, the idea to do a film based on 'Aladdin and his Magic Lamp' was first touted, the then Chief Executive Officer of Disney Enterprises, Michael Eisner, didn't feel that a story set in the Middle East would have mass appeal and instead, encouraged the creative team to concentrate on 'Beauty and the Beast'. It was only after that film had spectacular box-office success that Disney proceeded with *Aladdin*.[31]

Despite the unprecedented commercial success of *Aladdin*, which grossed $502 million worldwide, won two Academy Awards (Best Song and Best Score), five Grammys and critical acclaim (in no small part due to the casting of Robin Williams as the voice of the genie who agreed to do it for a scale wage of less than $500 a day because, according to James B Stewart, he was grateful for the career boost Disney gave him when he was cast in 1989's *Dead Poet's Society*[32]), the film also attracted negative publicity from a number of quarters. Critics expressed concern over the film's racial portrayal of the Middle Eastern characters.

Released in 1992, in the aftermath of the Gulf War, *Aladdin* provided many Americans, especially kids, with their first 'harmless' glimpse of the Middle East post-war. What's highly problematic is that nearly all the 'good' characters, despite being native to the fictional city of Agrabar, have pale skins and Anglo-American accents. The evil characters on the other hand are nearly all swarthy, sharp featured and thickly accented. Though Disney prides itself on creating animated characters that resemble, if somewhat cutely, their real-life counterparts, and spends time and money getting backgrounds correct, the Arabic script that's occasionally seen in the film is a meaningless, if artistic, scrawl and names are mispronounced.[33] The opening song was slightly adjusted after complaints were received regarding the lyrics. The original tune ended with the lines: 'Where they cut off your ear/If they don't like your face/It's barbaric, but hey, it's home'.

Disney executives were aware of the racist nature of the song. The lyricist, Howard Ashman, submitted an alternative set of lines with the first that had no mention of violence, but instead focused on the temperature and landscape. These were substituted after the complaints, though 'It's barbaric, but hey, it's home' remained.[34]

Have you ever noticed how much Aladdin resembles Tom Cruise? That's no accident. Stills from the military recruiting movie *Top Gun* (financed by the navy whose enlistments soared as a result) were used to aid animators in their construction of young Aladdin. Someone who used to represent the all-American, wholesome, good guy was the basis for a Middle-Eastern hero and images of him from what was ostensibly a military-funded movie were used to make a child-friendly animation of a popular folktale.[35]

In light of all this, it's interesting to consider what ideologies the film promotes. On the surface it's harmless, colourful and funny. But this particular interpretation and its songs, characterisations and art took years of planning to bring to the big screen. What was omitted, included and changed, therefore, was absolutely deliberate. Knowing about the exclusions, troubles and complaints, as well as the stereotypes, doesn't mean that viewers have to dislike the film. On the contrary, this awareness simply means that any pleasure is now contextualised and, depending on how you feel about this knowledge, possibly made even richer. I thoroughly enjoy the film, but I also made sure my kids knew about its origins as a tale among many from an old and grand culture. I didn't tell them about the other issues until they were old enough to understand them – there was no point. But at least I viewed the film through eyes that were wide open and with a mind that boggled at what Disney had accomplished – the good and the not-so-good.

Comparing the original or earlier versions of a tale to the movie adaptation and treating it as an imaginative adventure that adults and kids can undertake together really does open up a 'whole new world', and one beyond that which the Disney empire has created.

Motherless Disney

Speaking of Disney-generated worlds, have you ever noticed the absence of mothers in Disney movies? While Disney can be congratulated for exploring all forms of family, it's more than a little peculiar that mainly mothers die or disappear in Disney films. And this is despite the fact that in the classical tales, Disney's source material, mothers and other female role models feature strongly. Cinderella, Ariel (in Andersen's tale her grandmother and sisters are significant and the sea-witch isn't evil), Jasmine, Simba, Mulan, Nemo and Belle are raised without mothers and the list goes on. Patriarchy replaces, oppresses and even elides matriarchy in the Disney galaxy – and we have to begin to consider what this teaches our kids – particularly about family and women's roles (never mind men's as well).

This then brings me to sexual stereotypes and representations of gender. So many critics have a field day with the nostalgic and outdated ways in which males and females are created in the Disney *films*, as well as the animations. All the characters in the cartoons are 'pretty', extraordinarily thin (only comic sidekicks, fathers and villains carry weight) and Anglicised. The girls may start out independent but by the end they need, want and are desired by the central male character. In most of the films, the girls sacrifice their world, their dreams, to 'get the guy' (Ariel, Belle). The man is even rewarded by an elevation of social status, riches (Aladdin), or an obedient wife who has proved herself handy in domestic space (Cinderella), or she civilises the animal in the man (Belle).

To be fair, as Susan Hopkins points out, the racial misrepresentations and white-washing of history aside, in *Pocahontas* and *Mulan*, Disney attempted to offer heroines who would walk their 'own path' and were action-orientated and assertive instead of passive. Though she also draws attention that even these 'kick-butt' girls are still heavily sanitised and can only find their 'true selves' by doing, in terms of the world created, the 'right thing', which means putting themselves before others even though other characters don't.[36] Rebecca-Anne DoRozario believes that the Disney princesses not only embrace their sexuality, but are directed towards self-discovery and self-rule.[37] Deborah Ross disagrees, claiming that Disney is feminism in reverse. After all, Ariel 'gets her legs, she makes her stand, she marches – but only down the aisle to marry some guy named Eric'.[38]

Perhaps Disney should take a lesson from an episode of *Desperate Housewives*. Determined to make a school play 'politically correct' by changing the ending of 'Red Riding Hood', a particularly dominant mother is reminded why these tales have endured. This woman intends to rewrite the story so that, instead of being killed, the wolf befriends Red who extracts a thorn from his paw, until Lynette Scavo (played by Felicity Huffman), mother of four, informs her that the 'original' tale did earlier generations no harm. Changing the ending defeats the entire purpose of the tale, which is to relay an important lesson in an unthreatening and, for children, entertaining way. Maybe we should all listen to Lynette – including Disney.

Fractured Fairytales

Does this mean Disney, with its fractured fairytales, stereotypes and money-driven conscience, is all bad? No, not at all. But what it does suggest is how important it is for parents, adults and teachers to be aware of what their children are consuming. We are encouraged to think of cartoons as 'harmless', but it's often in this guise that a great deal of ideological foundation work is being done. Henry Giroux offers good advice when he suggests that 'parents, community groups, educators and other concerned individuals must be attentive to the diverse messages in Disney films in order to both criticize them when necessary and, more important, to reclaim them for productive ends'.[39]

Discussing the passivity of the females, the narrow and often aggressive representations of the males, ideas of race and gender, and the way families are depicted with kids of all ages is essential. Kids can relate to and understand these tales; they love them. So using them in a constructive way is both easy and necessary to query, challenge or accept the stories.

Disney isn't the only studio to rewrite fairytales for the mass market. Dreamworks has the hugely successful *Shrek* franchise, which not only parodies fairytales (and popular culture) but Disney as well. Some think of it as Jeffrey Katzenberg's (former Disney head of studio and, in many minds, the person responsible for breathing life back into Disney animation) revenge for the shoddy treatment he received when he was forced to leave the company in 1994. Not only was he refused a farewell party, banned from attending the opening of *The Lion King* and allegedly owed millions, Katzenberg went so far as to accuse Michael Eisner of doing an 'assassination job' on him.[40]

Katzenberg, it turns out, didn't need Disney. Kids and adults appreciate *Shrek* and its endless parade of fairytale favourites who, as Hopkins wryly notes, replace 'Disney's earnest predictable world with a world of hip humour, camp contradiction and irony. "We know, you know", the film seems to say, playing to the sophistication of ... audiences'.[41] As studios such as Dreamworks and Pixar rise to the challenge of retelling classical stories (and inventing new ones), such as the noir-ish and independently produced *Hoodwinked* (a remake of 'Red Riding Hood'), Disney now has some serious and healthy competition, including a German/American co-production entitled *Happily Never After*. This film has as its tagline, 'Don't let your hair down; don't go to the ball; don't visit grandma'. Sadly, despite the hype, it was a film that relied not only on fairytale stereotypes, but every contemporary and gender cliché available and was very disappointing as a result.

The Next Chapter

While I've taken Disney to task, I'm also aware of the joy it has brought into people's lives. As I said above, the concern is that so many kids these days (and some adults) only know the Disney version of the fairytales and folktales. They don't know that the Little Mermaid doesn't marry the prince or that Cinderella is capable of subverting her stepmother's ploys and that Aladdin, while now part of *Arabian Nights*, is understood as a Middle Eastern fable (even though it didn't originate from there) and on it goes. We live in a culture where we have so much choice available to us and our kids, but when it comes to stories we seem to always go for the easy one – too often, the Disney film.

This is more than a little disheartening, particularly when such a wealth of imagery and ideas in the classical tales and other narratives have been turned into films. We should seek to link the written and the visual as often as we can – use one to inspire an interest in the other. If a child loves the film, you should encourage them to read the story that inspired it as well. Or, better still, read the story to them.

Some of the fairytales I've relayed above are quite menacing and have a great deal of physical brutality in them. Nonetheless, you shouldn't be afraid of the inherent darkness in the classical fables – after all, kids enjoy and expect it. As Arthur Schlesinger Jr writes, they 'tell children what they unconsciously know – that human nature is not innately good, that conflict is real, that life is harsh before it is happy – and thereby reassure them about their own fears and their own sense of self'.[42]

Watched by children already familiar with the classical versions, the whimsical, musical Disney adaptations can provide an *alternative* viewpoint rather than functioning as the only version children ever know. In that way, the notion that 'dreams come true' becomes a possibility. It's understood as something that comes from within, through hard work, a solid belief in the self and through kindness towards and tolerance of others, rather than from some outside force that subtly dictates conformity and the magical maintenance of sexual, gender and racial divides.

This is also true of other books that, if not already classics, are fast becoming regarded that way. I'm mainly (but not exclusively) referring to the Harry Potter franchise.

Going Potty Over Harry

Early in the novel *Harry Potter and the Philosopher's Stone*, Professor Minerva McGonagall, deputy principal of Hogwarts School of Witchcraft and Wizardry, discusses the infant Harry Potter with Albus Dumbledore, her employer. She exclaims: 'He'll be famous – a legend, there will be books written about Harry – every child in our world will know his name!' Ever since Harry Potter first came out of the closet at 4 Privet Drive and captivated generations of readers, every word, line, chapter and character in the novels has been deconstructed. Metaphors, symbols, similarities to earlier children's tales such as those created by Roald Dahl, Enid Blyton and even TH White (author of *The Once and Future King*, an Arthurian novel upon which the musical *Camelot* was based), links to myths and legends[43] – all have been pored over and the relevance of the stories to readers' everyday lives compared. However you read the Harry Potter novels – whether as a story of one boy's courage and loyalty in the face of great adversity; as rags to riches; as anti-authoritarian; or as contemporary wish-fulfilment in an increasingly alienated and alienating society – almost all the critics agree: JK Rowling got the formula right.

So right, in fact, she's now the richest woman in Britain.

Rowling's books, the most successful children's books ever (and not just in fiscal terms, though her success is also contingent on a global economy and international marketing hype), follow the basic tenets of a great read. As the Deputy Head of Christ Church Primary School, Anne Williams, said, Rowling uses 'the same formula as Shakespeare used – magic, potions and what happens next'.[44] She also doesn't steer away from making her extraordinary magical folk ordinary by depicting them with faults and flaws, a great sense of humour and a strong desire for justice.

Despite the unprecedented success of these books, adults still expressed alarm about the psychological and emotional twists and dangers in them and the use of magic by the characters. When the third book in the Harry Potter series, *The Prisoner of Azkaban*, was published in 1999, it was universally described by critics as the darkest and best novel yet. Likewise, when the film was released, debates over whether or not an M rating should be applied raged. The OFLC gave the film a PG classification, deciding adults could act as their child's 'Patronus' (a spell of protection in the Potter books). The fourth film (and fourth, fifth, sixth and seventh books – in the last, for example, Rowling warned for months that two favourite characters must die) was met with similar worries. The evil explored in all the films to date merely reflects that present in the novels.

In the world of children's literature, enigmatic, evil beings and reader pleasure go hand in hand. Just ask Roald Dahl, Maurice Sendak, JRR Tolkein, Phillip Pulman and other authors and critics such as CS Lewis, John Marsden, Garth Nix, Marina Warner, Lian Hearn and Jack Zipes. Tales of Manichean battles between dark forces and young people upon which the fate of the world hangs are some of the most popular – and with good reason. Even more popular are those stories that refuse to tip-toe around sticky issues such as threats, death and the unpleasant depths to which human nature can descend.

Just as the fairytales of old were beloved by generations, so too are the new breed of children's books that portray the world in realistic shades of grey (offering difficult and sometimes terrible moral choices, but still empowering kids) satisfying readers at deep emotional and psychological levels. This is the reason the Harry Potter books and others written in a similar vein are so popular – they refuse to condescend to their child or adult readers, they acknowledge the complexity and toughness of life, but they also reveal its beauty and the ways in which this can be found as well. As the director of *Pan's Labyrinth*, Guillermo del Toro says:

> I do think there is far more an immoral position in creating a movie like *Free Willy,* where I'm telling a kid, you know, 'If you swim next to a … killer whale she'll become your friend' … no! She will eat your … guts and spit you out![45]

Rowling didn't do anything particularly new with her tales; instead she drew on familiar themes and archetypes to remind young and old about what it means to be human.[46] Mind you, she has still received a fair amount of criticism and had accusations levelled at her, whether it was because of the unpalatable stereotypes or turning our children to the occult. It's a form of justice that the only thing that has happened is that the books (and films) have become more popular. Nonetheless, it's good to be aware of what some of the naysayers are grumbling about.

Gender Stereotypes

Numerous critics have commented on the problematic portrayals of women and girls in the Harry Potter books, stating that they're an amalgam of different and quite negative stereotypes.[47] Hermione starts out as a blue-stocking nag and moral touchstone, only to develop into – as Julia Eccleshare has noted – a 'crusading zealot' in her efforts to create equitable conditions for the House-elves.[48] Rather than being a romantic interest, Hermione functions more like a mother figure (though the changing nature of her relationship with Ron Weasley is resolved in the final book). Similarly, Ginny Weasley, who blushes scarlet any time Harry speaks to her, is rendered victim and needs rescuing in the *Chamber of Secrets*. Though Harry develops an interest in Cho Chang, an older girl from Ravenclaw, it's mainly because she is pretty and shares his enthusiasm for Quidditch.

Older females fare worse. Mrs Weasley is domineering if kindly, but almost asexual despite her six children. Mrs Dursley is plain obnoxious and the Hogwarts' women teachers are all painted, humorously and fondly, as mere variations on schoolmarms. It's fitting, perhaps, in books designed to attract a primarily male readership, as Danielle Crittenden writes, that girls would be reduced to functionaries and stereotypes without disillusioning the female readership.[49]

But is this fair? The girls and women in the novels are also, like the lead boys, loyal, brave, use their intelligence and wits and nurture the best qualities in their friends, children and allies. The boys, particularly Harry, are critiqued for being, well, so boyish. They love their sport and quickly abandon their studies if ever the opportunity for investigation or a quest comes along. Sometimes they're incredibly uncommunicative and prone to mood swings – much like adolescent boys in real life.

Bullying appears to not only happen at the school but be facilitated by the likes of Snape and other teachers, resulting in some of the students having a miserable time or being forced to watch their backs instead of concentrating on learning – another reality of the education system. One aspect of the novels that isn't often noted is the irony of a boy wizard who really doesn't like reading much himself (unless it's a Quidditch book or magazine) actually reminding children and adults of the pleasures of the written word.

There's a moral in that – the success of Harry Potter aptly demonstrates the power of a good story, written and visual, to capture and stimulate minds and hearts and encourage people to think outside the confines of their own world. The Harry Potter books have been so good at this, it's no wonder some people worry that their children have been bewitched.

Magic

Over the years, various fundamentalist groups have denounced the Potter books and films as having a range of insidious intentions behind them. Head of the Sunshine Coast Christian Outreach College, Pastor Chas Gullio banned the Potter books because he judged them anti-Christian. He branded Harry a bad role-model as he had 'no morals, he lies and casts curses'.[50] Nunawading Adventist Primary School in Victoria also prohibited the books at some stage.[51] In the United States, there were accounts of bans and burnings. A veritable witch-hunt unfolded, but it doesn't take a doctorate in the bleeding obvious to know that JK Rowling did not invent magic. Magic, witches and wizards are the stuff that dreams are made of and form the foundation stones of society. From Homer to Virgil, from China to North America, tales of sorcery, intrigue and curses abound. Through the stories of writers such as Longus, Apelius, Mary Shelley, Bram Stoker and, more recently, Enid Blyton, Roald Dahl, JRR Tolkein, Paul Jennings, Susan Cooper, Ursula Le Guin, Emily Rodda, Lian Hearn and Sara Douglass, readers and listeners are given access to worlds, people and powers beyond their realm of experience that nevertheless become a touchstone for morals, attitudes and ethics. In creating Harry Potter, Rowling simply accessed a long line of literary and oral traditions – including the Christian one.[52]

One of the first places I encountered magic was in the Bible. Nothing was as thrilling as Noah constructing the ark, Moses parting the Red Sea or Jonah hitching a ride in a whale's belly – that was until I read about Jesus turning water into wine and dividing the fish and loaves, as well as coming back to life. The Bible was also the first place I read about murder, lust, cowardice, sorrow, passion and greed. Jezebel, Cain, Herod and Judas conjure up a range of behaviours, but I would rather my children model themselves on Harry Potter than on any of the above.

A number of psychiatrists have noted the positive role-model that Harry provides. He is healthy and survives his parents' murder and an abusive upbringing mentally intact.[53] His story follows a tried formula of many tales: a quest (which is a metaphor for the psychological journey), empowerment through magic, battles against evil, self-doubt, betrayal and discovery. Hysteria surrounding the messages and scenes of witchcraft and magic in Rowling's books overlooks the more significant and timeless messages the text and the films offer. Harry is a vulnerable, decent, ethical person who operates according to a strict moral code. He easily recognises the good and bad in people and is loyal to those who abide by the more important rules: stay true to your friends, love unconditionally, always admit (eventually) when you are wrong and be prepared for consequences when you step outside your own moral framework. True courage, the books demonstrate, comes from within.

One doesn't have to dig very deeply into Rowling's stories to find literary treasure. For example, Professor Albus Dumbledore ('outed' as gay by Rowling in 2007), Principal of Hogwarts School of Witchcraft and Wizardry, is reminiscent of Merlin from Arthurian legend and Gandalf from *Lord of the Rings*. His first name means 'white' in Latin. He represents a force for virtue thereby drawing on the positive metaphoric associations of 'white' and 'light'. It's to Dumbledore that Harry turns for guidance and whose goodwill, advice and praise he seeks. Hagrid, the giant groundskeeper, owns a dog named Fluffy who possesses three heads, thus recalling Cerberus, the guardian of the gates of the Underworld in Greek mythology. Hermione, Harry's companion, was also the name of the daughter of Menelaus and Helen of Troy as well as that given to the wife of Leontes in Shakespeare's *A Winter's Tale* – which in turn is based on the Greek myth of Pygmalion. The name of Harry's owl is also the name of the patron saint of orphans, and these are just for starters. Rowling is not the only author to draw on literary and other traditions to write her stories, but she's a fine example of what creators of good narratives do – gesture to others and thereby enrich the tale being told and allow us all, regardless of age, gender and even religion, to dream about what might be. Not an easy task in this day and age.

Consuming Harry

While the Harry Potter books and films offer us and our children respite and adventure, there's no doubt Rowling's success has turned the stories into a consumer nightmare. Instead of just the books or DVDs, there are hundreds of ways that children can access and own parts of Harry's world – and that's before I discuss the interactive nature of many of the websites (I deal with the internet in the next chapter). And there is also a Harry Potter theme park being planned.[54] Again, it's simply a matter of making sure that as the adult you don't buy into the excessive nature of the culture of acquisition and materialism and thereby run the risk of spoiling what's potentially a magical experience. As Jack Zipes argues:

> Phenomena such as the Harry Potter books are driven by commodity consumption that at the same time sets the parameters of reading and aesthetic taste. Today the experience of reading for the young is mediated through the mass media and marketing so that the pleasure and meaning of a book will often be prescribed or dictated by convention.[55]

Award-winning Australian writer Sonya Hartnett expresses her disappointment over the commercial hype surrounding the Potter books. She laments 'this sort of rabid support of Harry Potter to the exclusion of so many other good books of children. It was fine for a couple of years until it crossed the line and became really sickening and stupid'.[56] Zipes and Hartnett make valid points – that's why it's up to adults to help facilitate and maintain children's interest in reading, even if it's generated by commodity and consumer culture and the commercialisation of children's literature. But there has to be both an awareness of what the kids are consuming (or what's consuming them) and limits set. Before you reassure yourself that 'at least the kids are reading', it's important to consider the quality of what children are accessing in terms of books. Some public librarians are expressing concern that, unless a title is based on a licensed character (excluding Harry Potter – they are referring to

TV and film-generated characters whereby the books follow the success of the visual medium), it's almost impossible to get children interested in reading.[57] Tom Engelhardt suggests that this kind of reading may even be harmful to kids as it fundamentally links books to a whole range of merchandise, thus equating the act of reading with shopping.[58] In the US in 2003, a list of the 10 most popular toddlers' books were all based on TV or film characters.[59] While we might congratulate ourselves that our children are reading, as one publishing sales executive warns, 'don't kid yourself too hard – the kids haven't been attracted to a book, they've been seduced by the branding'.[60]

What we need to ensure is that our children are offered choice. Embrace the positive aspects – the kids *are* reading – rather than focusing solely on the negatives. Film, TV and the growing population of licensed characters may have initiated interest in a book, but don't let it end there. Use their enthusiasm for one writer or genre to introduce them to others outside the media and marketing maelstrom. After all, it's still up to us whether or not our kids, through their reading choices, become more than cogs in a monolithic marketing machine.

The Power of Stories

The stories told about and for young people, whether they're in a fairytale, film, novel or a magazine, are almost as diverse as the tots, tweens and teens themselves – but only if we offer our kids a smorgasbord. That's the key to any issues around stereotyping or concerns we have that certain products will instil unhealthy ideas or values in our kids. Disney and the tween/teen magazines mentioned in Chapter Two seem to have a great deal in common: the alluring promise of happily ever after – all it needs is a bit of magic (make-up, accessories, interest from the opposite sex) and you can get whatever or whoever you want.

It's up to us to ensure that our kids get a balance in the stories they're told. In his testimony to a Senate hearing in the US on media violence (in the wake of the Colorado high-school massacre), Professor Henry Jenkins said, 'All of us move nomadically across the media landscape, cobbling together a personal mythology of symbols and stories taken from many different places. We invest all those appropriated materials with various personal and subcultural meanings'.[61] What's also imperative is that among the stories told to our kids by others (through popular culture) and those that they 'cobble together', we include ones about ourselves. Kids love to learn their family history through tales of 'when we [the grown-ups] were young'. What grandma and grandpa did as kids; how mum, dad, their parents' friends, teachers and other adults in their lives coped with the joys and rigour of childhood. Don't rely on stories from other sources alone to shape your child's sense of self. Take advantage of the rich variety of narratives on offer, mix them with your own, and allow them to be both a window to the world and one of the many doors that your child chooses to open.

chapter nine

Give Me Some MySpace: The Cyberlution of Social Networking and Electronic Games

You've Got Mail

If ever an invention changed society, it has to be the computer. After the computer came the internet, then email, Google, chatrooms, sites, blogs, YouTube, MySpace, Facebook, and the list goes on. One of the ironies of computer technology is that it was never designed with public communication in mind. On the contrary, the computer was earmarked for military use and the internet developed in response to Cold War fears over Russia's growing technological superiority after the launch of the first sputnik in 1957.[1] What wasn't expected was that the internet would also allow instant and extremely accessible communication outside the military-industrial complex.

From the personal email sent to keep in touch with partners, children, friends and lovers, to being able to call up information and entertainment at the movement of a cursor, to mobile phones, these technologies have enabled us to stay in touch and share almost anything with anybody and everybody, instantaneously and often. On the positive side, they allow us to feel connected, even when physically distant, and to keep relationships flourishing. On the negative, they've opened the door to spam, stalking and a sense of obligation to respond. They've left our children open to potential abuse as cyberstalkers roam virtual reality, visiting chatrooms and various sites in the hope of snagging a child and, through email, reeling them in hook, line and sinker. They've also been overused and misused with kids and adults fretting and becoming anxious if they're separated from their computers or phones for more than a few minutes.

Rather than worrying what our over-reliance on technology signifies, much media attention and the hype around technology focuses on how distracted our kids have become: that they're less book-literate, unable to have functional physical relationships, obese and have the attention span of a gnat. Of all the negative press that the developing affiliation our kids have with technology receives, the possibility of our kids being exposed to a sexual deviant takes precedent. This means that other dangers and, indeed, the positives of cyberspace are often lost in all the panic.

In this chapter, I'm going to explore our children's relationship with the medium they're now born knowing how to use – the internet and other digital devices such as computers, mobile phones and electronic games – and discuss the social and personal significance of these. It's a relationship that often leaves adults confused, wary, alarmed and excited as we try to balance our own growing dependency on computer and digital technology and the rapid way it's changing life – but not as we know it – for us and our kids.

Change for the Better

How we speak about technology, whether it be an LCD TV, a computer, a mobile phone or the latest gaming device from Nintendo, reveals a great deal about us as a society and as individuals. Whereas our children are mostly excited and unthreatened by technology and the increasing role it plays in our lives, adults are mostly suspicious and very cautious about it, particularly when it comes to the younger generations. Despite the fact we welcome washing machines, vacuum cleaners, microwaves and countless other time-saving or entertainment-based technological devices into our homes, we have an ambivalent relationship with computers, mobile phones and electronic games. We continue to view them with a jaundiced eye, moaning about the way our lives have changed because of them – and, generally, for the worse. But is this really true? We are able to communicate with friends, business colleagues and strangers on the other side of the world (or over the divider) in nanoseconds through the internet or with mobile phones; to obtain information about almost anything with only the touch of a button; and to be entertained and stimulated by games and a variety of data streams by professionals and amateurs – our lives have never contained so many options. Yet we remain mostly negative about these amazing gadgets and the alternative perspectives and opportunities they offer.

I'm going to deal with the last point first in an effort to understand why this ambivalence about technology exists. I'll do this by going back in time and taking a look at one very scary and misunderstood literary monster.

Monstrous Technology

Ever since Mary Shelley penned her masterly novel *Frankenstein* in 1818, at the age of 18, humans have been hesitant and more than a little afraid of technology. Shelley's story, which has gripped the imaginations of generations, centres on the scientist Dr Viktor Frankenstein and his monster. Frankenstein makes a being from the body parts of dead people, brings it to life by harnessing electricity and, after seeing the abomination he has produced, turns his back on his creation. In effect, he abrogates his responsibility, ignoring the consequences of what he has made.

Rejected and neglected, this 'child' of Frankenstein's experiments, is confused and lonely. Learning language through books (Goethe's *Sorrows of Young Werther*, Milton's *Paradise Lost* and a volume of Plutarch's *Lives*) and listening to a family in whose barn he hides for months, the monster tries to make his way in the world, but his horrifying appearance means that he is continually abused and hurt. The creature tracks down Dr Frankenstein, who is haunted by what he has done, and begs him to make him a female partner. If Frankenstein does this then, the monster promises, he'll disappear. Frankenstein agrees, only to rescind his word just as the female is close to being brought to life. Worse, he dismembers her, tearing her limb from limb. Distraught and furious, the monster then seeks vengeance, killing Frankenstein's younger brother (implicating a beloved female servant – Justine – who is subsequently killed); his best friend, Clerval; and his bride, Elizabeth, on their wedding night. The book (which was rewritten in 1831) has the monster die in a huge fire or disappear into the Arctic's icy wastelands after his creator, father and nemesis, Frankenstein, who is very sick, dies remorseful.

The moral of the story is complex, but centres around two notions: first, that humans have no right to play God; and, second, that they must take responsibility for what they've created. Frankenstein, by literally taking life into his own hands, plays God. By refusing to be accountable for what he has made, he suffers terrible psychological, emotional and physical consequences – and so do those he loves. These themes feature in so many of our science-fiction movie classics that explore our fears around technology, the power it can wield and just who controls what we create and the consequences of this. Examples include the *Terminator* and *Matrix* trilogies, *2001: A Space Odyssey*, *Blade Runner*, *War Games*, *Star Trek* (the Borg particularly), *Robocop*, *Minority Report*, *I, Robot*, and *Existenz*. Novels such as William Gibson's classic *Neuromancer*, Neal Stephenson's *Snow Crash* (which inspired the formation of the online virtual world, Second Life[2]), and Tad Williams *Otherland* quartet, and TV series such as *Lost in Space*, *Dr Who*, *Stargate: SG 1*, *Atlantis*, *Lexx* and *The Twilight Zone*, among many, all explore our fears that one day the 'creature' we invent will rise up and take over, and we may not accept liability. Even movies such as the *James Bond* franchise and the TV series *Alias* depict technology that can be harnessed for evil or virtuous intentions (depending which side you're on). The relationship humans have with technology has become a contemporary morality tale, but it's the ways in which our children interact with it that causes the greatest concern.

Good or Bad

Instead of accepting that the world is different now, we couch so much of our language about the changes that technology has wrought on our lives in terms of 'good' or 'bad', particularly when we consider the influence and 'power' it has over our children. We bemoan the fact that kids sit in front of screens, have phones or iPods glued to their ears, or have deteriorating language skills because of SMS and email.

Sonia Livingstone explains this dichotomy, stating that through technology 'optimists foresee new opportunities for democratic and community participation, for creativity, self-expression and play, for the huge expansion of available knowledge, thereby also supporting diversity, difference and debate. Pessimists lament the end of childhood, innocence, traditional values and authority'.[3] The adage 'things were so much better then' has become a contemporary mantra, especially for those with selective memories and those rose-coloured glasses I mentioned in the Introduction.

What concerns me about these sorts of statements is that they appear to suggest that we have no control over what's happening. It's as if technology acts upon us and we're helpless to resist – it's the Big Brother and TV paradigm all over again. Yet, while I can't deny it's hard to professionally (and personally) function these days without a computer or phone, we can still *choose* when to sit in front of it, type, surf the net and play games, or whether to answer the ring, return the SMS or not. We're not 'punished' (except perhaps by an unreasonable employer, exasperated clients or frustrated friends and family) if we don't and neither are our lives radically altered (more on that shortly). More importantly, we can *choose* whether or not to purchase these gadgets for our kids (or ourselves) in the first place and, when we do (because we almost always do – and that's okay), we can also set rules and boundaries about how much we buy, the type of technology, where and when our kids get access, time spent on it and where the technology is located.

However, to read reports in the media and listen to adults discussing computers, phones, tweens and teens, it's as if they're talking about Frankenstein's monster – these things have suddenly developed a life of their own. No, they haven't. Like the misguided doctor, we breathe life into them and fail to take responsibility, thus turning them rabid and losing control over what, ultimately, we choose to bring into our lives. Henry Jenkins believes that much of the rhetoric around digital and electronic media springs from 'our fears of adolescents'; in a sense, they're the monsters we, like Dr Frankenstein, have created. It's also due to the fact that adults live in an era where 'the dominant forms of popular culture … now reflect their children's values rather than their own'. Jenkins also writes about the way teens in particular invest in symbols and various popular culture forms (such as electronic games and the internet) as a way of expressing their burgeoning autonomy from the adult generation. This can be quite threatening for parent culture. As Jenkins states, 'The intentionally cryptic nature of these symbols [we can include here the truncated language that's used to SMS and email] often means adults invest them with all of our worst fears, including our fear that our children are breaking away from us'.[4]

Kids, however, seem to have a much healthier and functional relationship with technology. They instinctively understand the way it can be used (and yes, abused). For many young people, especially savvy tweens and teens, it validates their sense of self. This is particularly evident through the growth of shared electronic sites such as YouTube, MySpace, Facebook, Xanga and Flickr, where anyone can upload video footage of themselves or someone else; display their artwork, music, sense of humour, desires, thoughts, songs, photos and clips from favourite TV shows and films; and interact with each other in the limitless worlds of cyberspace.

Down(loaded) in History

Historians will one day mark March 2002 as the year social relationships were irrevocably altered. For in 2002 some young internet entrepreneurs developed an original but straightforward notion. Recognising the fundamental need people have to connect with each other, they designed virtual spaces on the world wide web that would satisfy this. Then they gave them simple but alluring names such as Friendster,

MySpace, YouTube and Flickr, and invited anyone with an internet connection and the desire to link up with other people via cyberspace to 'come on download'. Word spread faster than a virus.[5]

Just over three years and millions of people and dollars later, there are hundreds of sites and the list of viable spaces to visit and places to stake a claim are growing. With some attracting up to 270,000 new visitors a day, they're very lucrative for their owners. In 2005 Rupert Murdoch spent US$580 million to purchase the MySpace Company, while in 2006 Yahoo bought the photo-sharing site Flickr for an estimated US$35 million.[6]

But what are these 'sites' exactly and how do they function? And, more importantly, how have they revolutionised social relationships, particularly with young people?

The (Virtual) Reality of It All

Instead of celebrating the democratic and mostly benign nature of the material on these sites, the media reproduces stories about 'hoon' videos, violence, stupidity and the sexual nature of some of the uploads and then generalises, implying that everything on the internet is bad and all those who access it are heading down a dangerous path. These sorts of notions are confirmed when a tragedy, such as the suicide pact between two teenage girls, Stephanie Gestier and Jodie Gater, who were found dead in the bush, is uncovered. One of the girls posted at least three odes to suicide on her site, while the other articulated her despondency with life.[7] In the aftermath of the girls' suicides, the media appeared to disregard that the same medium that was condemned for facilitating their deaths was also used by many people, young and old, as a source of solace and an outlet for expressing their grief. What is also overlooked in the wake of shared mourning is that these types of incidences are by far the exception rather than the rule. Instead of heeding these terrible outcomes as warnings to monitor our children's web use, there's a tendency to blame the technology and the impenetrable angst of teens and regard both as beyond adult power to change.

A closer inspection of a variety of internet sites reveals that while there are some disturbing pages, these are in the minority. Overwhelmingly, there's some excellent, very funny and satirical material being uploaded from across the world and shared in a domain where everyone knows your (fake) name and where a select number get, for a few minutes at least, a taste of 'fame'. In the relative security of cyberspace, strangers and friends get to access user-generated content (UGC) and see and talk to each other. Also, depending where they log onto, they are given a yard-stick by which they can measure their own lives, culture, tastes, sex, age, dreams and aspirations – including dark thoughts and intentions.

Instead of gathering at the local shopping mall, park or someone's home and occupying the same physical space, tweens and especially techno-competent teens (and many older people too) are opting for the internet and 'meeting' their friends there. The choices for socialising are enormous: from Flickr to the business Linkedin; from Facebook to MySpace and YouTube or the popular kids' site ClubPenguin; and to more thematically focused sites built around sex, romance or fandom. Around the globe, people are clicking on and zoning out, creating what have been described as 'online mirrors of their circle of real-life acquaintances'[8] in the process. In other words, for those with the technology, know-how and inclination, these spaces offer the internet consumer, especially those aged between 15 and 35, a central, cohesive point from which to share personal information and to engage in some online socialisation.

MySpace

For example, MySpace, an interactive web community described as attracting '16-to-34-year-old hipsters',[9] is one cyber alternative. Launched in Australia in 2006, within two months it had over one million local users. Worldwide it's estimated that there are 100 million users.[10] A May 2007 Hitwise survey shows that MySpace holds a 79.7 per cent share of the worldwide online market.[11] A person can log on for free and create what's called a 'treehouse' or profile of information about themselves with either private or public access: everything from photos, to favourite movies and songs, to video clips and artwork, to blogs or journals about how they spend the day. From there, the person can invite others into their 'treehouse'. The visitor is able to read and view the material and get to 'know' the treehouse creator. What they can learn is only limited by how much the creator wants to share. A visitor can also notify another like-minded person about what they've found and the list of visitors and 'friends' to the original treehouse grows.

Described as a 'Living Web',[12] it's built from the inside out, by millions of little spiders – the users – who weave 'nodes' of information about themselves and the world they live in. It takes the notion of networking and makes it both literal and metaphorical: like a web, it expands from a point of origin, yet it's also intangible because it exists only in the cyber-realm. But it's weaving its way across the globe, joining countries, cultures, religions, genders and people in a way that's only limited by the imagination.

When News Corp bought MySpace in 2006, they introduced some restrictions. Kids under 14 are banned, and 14- and 15-year-olds can only reveal their full profile to people who appear on their list of 'friends'.[13] Ask your teen if they have built a treehouse in MySpace (or another shared site). I'll bet they have or they know someone who has. I was surprised to discover both my children had and, when I logged on and was invited 'inside', I was delighted and a little perplexed about what they'd uploaded and shared with others. But it was personal, warm and entirely appropriate for them. I then spent the next few weeks visiting the treehouses of many others and, apart from one or two, the overwhelming majority were interesting, funny and occasionally boring. They were testimonies to 'me', the creator; public displays of the self that exposed varying degrees of insight, talent, pathos, absurdity and narcissism. News Corp's MySpace has also introduced a tool that allows parents to monitor, in a very minimal way, what their kids are doing on the site. It doesn't reveal the user's password or communications, but it does let parents know their child's username, age and location they list on their profile and whether or not they have multiple ones (one for family, another for friends). After all, you don't want your 10-year-old pretending to be 14, or your 14-year-old pretending to be 18 in this domain or any other for that matter.

There have been five legal suits brought against MySpace in America by parents whose kids became victims of cyber-predators. Basically, their children created profiles and were contacted.[14] One of the children involved was 13 and had his own webcam – in his bedroom. He was persuaded to perform sexual acts in front of the camera by his virtual 'friends'.[15] While the families are anxious to blame someone, attributing responsibility to a carrier is hardly the place to start. What is a 13-year-old doing with an internet connection in his bedroom, let alone a webcam, in the first place? The fact is, suing MySpace and its parent company News Corp does not change the conditions in which these kinds of terrible events can happen. That has to occur within families, through education and communication. But more on this shortly.

Danah Boyd, a PhD candidate from the University of California's School of Information conducting research into the social significance of these sites to young people, is reassuring about both the dangers of the net and the ways in which young people use these sites. She claims that the 'data shows pretty conclusively that predators as we imagine them are not a significant threat'. Boyd has also discovered that 'most young users of MySpace do not surf to strangers' profiles and instead engage with their known friends and acquaintances'.[16] Research conducted by criminology professor Sameer Hunduja, who examined adolescents' pages on MySpace, found that 90 per cent of the 1475 teenagers in the study, whose pages were public, 'did not disclose their full name in their personal profiles', while '40 percent of teenagers … kept their pages completely off-limits to everyone but their friends'.[17]

Making a Connection
The popularity of these new cyberspaces may be hard for older generations to fathom: after all, how can viewing a screen or tapping away at a keyboard compensate let alone replace the benefits and hazards of

face-to-face communication? Can these people really be 'friends' when our kids don't know them except the selective material they read or see about them on the net? Has the notion of friendship changed so much that you can call a person one without ever having met them? I think it has. But this isn't new; it's merely an evolution – a rapid one, from how business and other relationships are being formed and sustained and have been ever since technology entered our lives. We're almost as quick to make connections as those high-speed cables under our floor.

'Friend' is a word laden with meaning in our culture. Cyberspace has, to a degree, relegated it to what we once used to call acquaintances. Perhaps this is why physical friends now have more elaborate monikers, with the term 'best' being added or a pseudo-blood relationship being embraced, defined by the description sister/sista or bro/brother, all of which help to separate the 'real' friend from the 'virtual' one. 'Best mates' or 'mate' is also common in Australia and establishes not only a hierarchy of friendships but the degree to which interaction and sharing take place. 'Best' also suggests physical knowledge of each other – a relationship beyond cyberspace.

Nonetheless, it's uncommon for tweens and even teens to enter into internet dialogues with people they don't already know (which supports Boyd's research, mentioned above) – though it can happen. Jessica (16), from Sydney, never invites anyone into her cyberspace without having already made physical contact. Jordan (nine) is the same, as his mother watches with whom and when he connects. This is, of course, what adults should be doing: monitoring their children's online (and offline) connections. The older they are, however, the more kids need to be allowed the independence to choose with whom they want to communicate in the real world and in virtual reality.

MeSpace
Many of us resent the fact that, while we sit in our offices, the person in the next cubicle, across the hallway or in the next building will email rather than phone or leave their desk and talk to us about a matter. We

vacillate between enjoying our mobile phone and its convenience to resenting its intrusion into our personal lives; this ambivalence and the sense that our kids are going to have even more complicated relationships with technology colour our perspective. These relationships are only as complex as we allow them to become.

For our teens (and those savvy tweens who may have built treehouses and familiarised themselves with various cyber-sites), this is about more than simply socialising or getting and staying connected. These interactive social spaces have made the internet the new place to 'be', for young people particularly but for many older ones too. It's a means of forging a sense of self, of creating a distinct identity and promoting a 'me' outside the usual strictures of family, peers, school, work and colleagues.

Information placed on a website creates a certain impression and will either attract or repel potential visitors and therefore 'friends'; this limits and certainly influences what a person chooses to reveal. Teens and now tweens understand this and are very good at fashioning a version of themselves that often bears little if no resemblance to them in reality. Starting with false names, tags or whatever else we want to call them (though most often real names are used), as well as ages, the elaborate and often fun disguises start there – but they don't generally go much further. Often the cyber-name and possibly age are the only false elements of a young person's on-line identity. Other aspects may be part of a fantasy identity without real intent to deceive, rather just to experiment in what's perceived as a safe environment and in an unthreatening way.

Whereas once girls in particular would pour their innermost thoughts and feeling into a diary, keeping it under lock and key, the internet has become a new public private testimony. The blog (weblog) has become a form of confessional where anyone and everyone spills the beans on their work, relationships, schoolteachers, parents and themselves. Jenkins describes them as 'more private and personal than traditional journalism, more public than diaries'.[18] Newspapers encourage readers to blog about articles and respond to columnists;

celebrities, scientists, secretaries, soldiers, mothers, fathers, lovers, everyone, it seems, blogs. Why should our kids be any different? The false name offers both protection from unwanted attention and censure in real life, but can also become a defence against provoked or unprovoked attack. There are quite a few cowards and bullies on the net who relish the disguise of a different name and use it as a launch pad for criticism and vitriol – sometimes at our children's expense. The majority of people do not abuse the system this way and, overwhelmingly, the internet is still a medium through which ideas and information can be exchanged. It's no wonder young people relish the blog – reading and creating them. Their growing popularity undermines the idea that reading and writing are dying. They're not; it's just the way we do these things is changing.

YouTube

In 2006 YouTube, a video-sharing website, was named *Time* magazine's Invention of the Year.[19] Started by young entrepreneurs Steve Chan, Chad Hurley and Jawed Karim, it was initially intended as a site where people could share their travel videos. Instead, users appropriated it for their own use, uploading footage of their home movies, spoofs, injuries, drunken behaviour and musical abilities as well as eyewitness footage from disaster and war zones. People, especially young people, seem to love looking at other ordinary people doing their 'thang'. The more amateur and grainy the video, the better. Lev Grossman believes it's YouTube's authenticity that has made it so successful. 'Slick is overrated. Slick is 2005', he writes. He also calls it a 'self-stoking mass collaboration'[20] that works better the more people use it. And they do: 'streaming more than 200 million videos a day'.[21]

Corporations like Nike, NBC, CBS, Universal Music, Sony BMG and Warner Music have also invaded the site, developing partnerships, understanding that users not only willingly click on ads, but also enjoy sampling new release singles, episodes of TV shows and anything else the companies care to throw out there.

In 2006 YouTube was sold to Google for $1.65 billion.[22] As universities recognise, with the offering of degrees in computer design and games, there's a lot of money to be made through this technology. But it's not only a money-making enterprise, it's a community where people are known and visited and where some even become famous.

It should be no surprise that teens and older people also upload information about themselves and examples of their talents in the hope that their 15 minutes of cyber-fame will provide some longevity and also a real, money-making career. The fact that this has happened to a number of individuals who flaunted their creative abilities on the net has not gone unnoticed. The Australian group Sick Puppies gained notice after their single 'All the Same' was attached to Juan Mann's 'Free Hugs Campaign' and uploaded onto YouTube. It has since been viewed approximately nine million times. Rock bands Jet and Arctic Monkeys have used MySpace to announce private concerts, while new talents such as US comedian Dane Cook and British songstress Lily Allen were 'discovered' in the same virtual domain. The *Britain's Got Talent* winner in 2007, humble opera singer Paul Potts, received worldwide fame mainly through the dissemination of his audition and later, heat performances, on YouTube. This increased his fan base as people from around the world logged on, watched and appraised his voice (and more). Since his victory, he's toured the globe and, thanks to YouTube and later media support, he is both known and admired – which doesn't hurt sales of his CD either. If people like Allen, Potts and the Sick Puppies can gain fame, then for young people, there's no apparent risk and, like winning the lottery, your ticket to the stars may be drawn.

High-school year-books and photo albums, prone to gather the dust of neglect once the initial excitement of recall and reflection passes, are now also being uploaded for general consumption and potential alteration by internet users. The photo-sharing site Flickr, and Facebook and MyYearbook.com are examples. New generation software has meant that photos, once permanent impressions of a moment, can be digitally changed, transforming the notion of collective memory into individual taste. Described as an 'infinite scrapbook',[23] these sites have also resulted in professional work for some members: their photography making impressions in the right places.

This sharing of images, or 'culture of generosity' as Caterina Fake, one of the minds behind Flickr, calls it, has also led to the advent of a new kind of citizen journalism.[24] For example, when the Australian Embassy in Jakarta was bombed in 2004, the first photos of the devastation were posted on Flickr, bypassing the usual news networks and offering multiple versions of a dreadful reality. Fake calls her site the 'eyes of the world',[25] but these spaces could also be described as sensory and auditory epicentres too: there's a sense in which they have their finger on the global pulse, and it's the younger generations, our kids, at the vanguard.

The Validation of Computation

What makes cyberspace an attractive place to be in a world that most often criticises and invalidates our tweens and teens and tells them they're not as smart, polite, kind or socially conscious as previous generations is the fact that in the cyber realm they're legitimated. More than that, they're taken seriously and have a 'voice' that is listened to – whether it's through their pictures, videos, written word and revelations or because of something as simple as finding their tastes in popular culture shared with another user. Boyd believes that 'young people who use MySpace are trying to map out a public territory for themselves, removed from the adult world'.[26]

Henry Giroux sums up the excitement young people feel about the internet when he writes that:

> popular culture is not just an enormous site of contradiction but also a site of negotiation for kids, one of the few places where they can speak for themselves, produce alternative public spheres, and represent their own interests. It's also one of the most important sites for adults to learn how

childhood identities are produced, how effective investments are secured, how desires are mobilized, and how learning can be linked to progressive social change.[27]

Teens (and some tweens) aren't only building 'treehouses', they're building a sense of themselves as individuals and trying on a variety of identities for size. We don't give kids much credit, for all that we are fiercely protective of them and talk loudly about their 'rights'. In cyberspace, recognition comes in other significant forms. Kids get to tell their stories, explain who they are and how they come to be in a particular personal and cyber-realm. In virtual reality, there is always someone who will listen; it only becomes a concern when the adults in their real life won't or can't. But that's our problem, not theirs – kids find, in cyberspace, someone *will* hear them scream, usually 'friends' who understand them and their needs.

We do need to be aware that some of the people who listen aren't our children's friends and may make an effort to contact them, play on their vulnerabilities and exploit them. If our children are informed internet users who can communicate with their parents and understand they must let the adults know if they're contacted in an inappropriate way, this won't be a problem. These types of people aren't going to go away. The point is not to punish our kids by denying them access to virtual reality; it's about educating them about the risks and, to the best of our ability, being aware of where they're going while they're there.

Private Property

It's not just the endless opportunities for friendships and information that virtual reality can offer that make it so appealing. By playing electronic games and listening to a personalised music selection via MP3s, as well as corresponding online, kids can create private spaces within the public world of home, school and life. It seems like a contradiction in terms, but through these mediums tweens and teens are able to contract the world into their own shape and time and interact with it on their terms, shutting off the outside world and concentrating on something that makes them feel in control for a change. Able to manipulate two, three or more pieces of technology at once, they divide their attention, communicating with their voices and fingers, sharing and being intensely private at the same time. Our teens are not only accustomed to performing like this, they prefer these multi-interactions that traverse public and private domains. It's hard for adults to understand this, particularly when the music is loud, the game violent and colourful, the site laden with images and chatter, and our kids claiming they're doing their homework, but we do need to make the attempt. We tend to judge how kids do their school work, chores, relax or switch off by our pre-technology or quite primitive standards and find children's choices wanting. We compare and decide the choices our kids have available to them or are making are not as good as the choices we made. It's not worse for kids, it's just different.

By demeaning the media through which our kids validate and empower themselves (like any other medium that does that for them, such as comics, TV, film or music), we're denigrating the young person as well. And let's not forget that for children with disabilities or learning difficulties, or those who are struggling socially, sexually and emotionally, in the democratic regions of cyberspace, where all you need is a computer and keyboard skills, any inequalities are often rendered redundant and kids can 'play' without fear of being seen, bullying, repercussions or discrimination.

While some people are bemoaning the loss of physical communication brought about by our dependence on new technology such as mobile phones and the internet, others are celebrating the positive applications of these cyber-realms and the social networking they encourage, suggesting they harness 'collective intelligence'. Critics are more likely to call it a pooling of ignorance and caution users.

As I mentioned before, where consumers, particularly younger ones, need to be warned is around issues of cyberstalkers – those adult predators who lurk on sites popular with kids and use the animation and child-friendly graphics as a disguise to advertise a product, an idea or, worse, themselves. This is where parents and carers need to educate and familiarise themselves about the realities of virtual space and what their children are accessing and sharing with other users. While it may seem an infinite task, it's only limited by the 'history' recorded in your computer's database or, better still, by what your child tells you. For all that we're experiencing a cyberlution, not even the internet can replace the benefits of face-to-face discussion – about the potential positives and negatives of cyberspace, how information is a powerful tool that can be used in ways it was never intended, and the pros and cons of social networking – with your child.

The Digital Divide

In this Microsoft-eat-Apple world, we're disadvantaging our kids if they don't have access to a computer and, as they get into their mid- to late teens, preferably possess their own computer. It's a truism that while books, TV and film open a window on the world, with a computer the window's left wide open for the world to enter us, through our homes, kids' bedrooms and our minds.

Aware of the potential dangers, even if they're overstated, parents nonetheless feel perplexed by the new technologies. This has created what's been termed the 'digital divide' between adults and kids – where kids feel at home with techno-gadgets and adults are either rushing to catch up or happy to sit back and let the children take charge. Marc Prensky describes it nicely when he calls kids 'Digital Natives' and adults 'Digital Immigrants'.[28] Overwhelmed by what our kids take for granted, adults, as immigrants in Technology-land, sometimes find it so hard to learn the language of IT (Information Technology), they rely on young people to translate for them. Just think of how many high schools employ the services of a savvy teen when a data projector is needed or a computer problem arises or how often kids teach their parents how to use new technologies in the home. While it's important we provide kids with the technology, it's even more important that we set rules and regulations around access and usage. We can use the technology to open up lines of communication instead of allowing them to become a barrier that means natives and immigrants won't understand each other let alone speak the same language. Being a Digital Immigrant is no excuse for not making an effort. This is particularly true in relation to the abbreviated language being used by kids to communicate with each other across all forms of digital technology – from mobile phones, SMS, email to chatrooms. Acronyms are becoming increasingly popular as a means of swiftly getting points across and/or being able to discuss or warn friends that adults are lurking. For example, there are the harmless LOL (Laugh Out Loud), BTW (By The Way), to MOS (Mum's Over my Shoulder), NIFOC (Naked in Front of Computer), and the alarming LMIRL (Let's Meet in Real Life).[29] It's important we try to familiarise ourselves with the language our kids use to bridge the growing techno-gap.

The Digital Divide also refers to the separation that has occurred on another social scale: between the 'information rich' and the 'information poor' – that is, those who have the financial means and access to new technologies and those who don't. Interestingly, those who are considered 'information poor' are also those who are likely to possess fewer books and watch less TV. In a country like Australia and other Western centres, we can bridge this divide through the education system by ensuring that those children without the financial means to own a computer can at least be assured of access while at school. It's also through education that we can guarantee that our kids are made savvy and literate users of all forms of technology. This means incorporating not just how to use the technology into the classroom, but also teaching ways of being critical consumers who are visually and textually literate and able to make wise choices. This is the only way to manage and feel confident about the influx of new technologies into society.

We live in exciting times, where knowledge and ideas are at our children's fingertips. But if we don't know what those fingertips are tapping, then we also don't know how our kids are mentally travelling. This is why, up until mid-teens at least (again, it will differ from child to child), it's important that children don't, under any circumstances, have internet-ready computers in their bedrooms.

Strange Bedfellows

While so many adults are wary of the internet, they're still prepared to buy their kids computers and then put them in their children's bedrooms, often with a wireless connection and even a webcam. Yet, these same people wouldn't leave their kids in an unlocked house or take them to the other side of the world and desert them in the middle of a busy road. I know these are extreme examples, but allowing kids as young as six to have computers with internet access in their bedrooms is inviting trouble – no matter how savvy or 'digitally native' you think your child might be. Reasons for giving tweens their own computers are often couched in well-meaning terms. Whether it's to give them their own space to do their homework or quiet time away from the TV and their siblings so they won't be disadvantaged in the school rat-race, or to get them out of adult hair, no reason is good enough: we're talking about tweens and young teens. Their time on computers should be supervised, even if it's from a distance. Experts agree that, while kids are still in primary school and the early years of high school, computers with internet access should be in a family space.[30] Putting young kids with the internet in bedrooms not only splinters the family (just as personal TVs do), it also increases the risk of them being exposed to adult concepts, ideas and attentions – and those damned marketers – before they're anywhere near ready to understand what they are and how to cope with them. This is not about how much you trust your children; it's about recognising they don't have the life-skills to cope with some of the people or material they may encounter. As for a webcam – they don't need it. It's yet another piece of technology that we, and our kids, have been persuaded we need. We don't – we merely want it.

Another reason for reconsidering placing any electronic gadget in your child's room is sleep deprivation. This applies to computers, mobile phones, gaming systems and, of course, television sets as well. It has been proven that these items function to keep kids awake, especially teens who seem to delight in SMSing each other at all hours of the night. In fact, according to Michael Carr-Gregg, 80 per cent of kids stay up too late precisely because of the wonderful technological gadgets housed in their bedrooms.[31] Belgian research has found that an awareness of incoming phone messages has meant that, because young people have different levels of sleep patterns, many of them fail to fall into the much needed deep sleep as they lie in anticipation of receiving a message. This affects long-term memory, because it's during REM (Rapid Eye Movement or deep sleep) that we process what we've learned and transfer it to our memory. A British survey discovered that more than half of the tween population had mobile phones (a quarter of these under eight), so it's not just a teen problem.[32]

While your child might whinge that they can't fall asleep without the TV on, according to Sue Palmer American research has shown that 'bright lights on television sets and computers can reset the circadian clock, changing the sleep-wake cycle'. Italian scientists have found that 'these lights block the secretion of the sleep hormone, melatonin, which usually begins when it gets dark outside'.[33]

Even so, warn psychologists, it's important adults know that, because of the wiring of adolescent brains, the melatonin that floods our systems and makes us want to fall asleep takes two hours longer to kick in with teens than with younger kids or adults. So staying up late is, in a way, a natural state for our adolescents. Because they often can't sleep in, having to get up for school or work, they endure the day tired and 25 per cent less alert than they would be if they had the sleep they need, which is ideally around 10 hours.[34]

A study of Belgian adolescents found that two out of five teenagers watched TV to try to help them fall asleep. Instead of working, they found the TV kept them awake longer. More than 20 per cent of kids in the survey played computer games and 60 per cent listened to music to help them fall asleep.[35] Dr Michael McDowell, a developmental pediatrician at Brisbane's Mater Children's Hospital, in response to this study, emphasised the need for rules around bedtime, 'rather than just letting the kids find their own solutions'.[36]

There are ways of helping teens overcome their technological dependency.

Computers, until your child is about 15, need to be in shared spaces. If your teen has a mobile phone, then make sure it's taken out of the bedroom and recharged every night in a communal spot, like the kitchen. Put his or her phone with your phone, turn them off and ignore them until morning. That way, there's not only down time for everyone, it removes the temptation to check for messages.[37]

Lack of sleep doesn't only affect academic performance; it affects mood, appetite and interpersonal relations – particularly with family members. A grumpy child impacts upon the whole household and, as Palmer notes, generates a vicious cycle.

Technology Etiquette

It's easy to address etiquette and the other problems associated with personal technology including MP3 players. Just as we teach our kids about good and bad behaviour, so too we have to teach them how to include technology in their lives in a way that is inoffensive and as unobtrusive and socially friendly as possible. We also have to lead by example. While we might all be able to multitask, there are downfalls to this. Parents arrive home from work in the evenings and are ignored by children busy monitoring their various electronic devices; but, possibly worse, parents are also retreating from interacting with their kids as they find it difficult to penetrate their children's universe.[38] A 2005 survey conducted by the Kaiser Family Foundation in the US found that kids were, due to media-multitasking, engaging with the media up to 8.5 hours a day. This means that downtime away from all this is reduced, and therefore the ability to relax and ponder minimised. More important, as psychiatrist Edward Hallowell notes, is to consider what 'you are *not* doing if the electronic moment grows too large'.[39] In other words, if you're not communicating as a family and sharing important discussions about holidays, sex, each other, personal problems and so on, then it won't be an electronic game, mobile phone or TV program that will 'rot your brain, it's what you're not doing that will rot your life'.[40] Family dynamics are created; it's the interactions between the family that you establish early on that will become habitual as your children mature. Spending more time with technology than each other is not the way to raise a happy family.

While kids are still tweens, lay the ground rules for the use of computers, mobile phones, MP3 players and video games. First, as suggested above, create a space, even a small one, in a communal room within the house that's dedicated to the computer and games. Set time limits and, without being intrusive, check that your child is actually searching the sites, talking to the friend they claim to be or playing an age-appropriate game. It's not that you don't trust them; the net can be unwieldy to navigate and it's easy to stumble upon unsuitable sites or be contacted by someone you didn't invite. Likewise, just because a game is rated PG, unless you keep an eye on it, how do you know that everything contained within it meets *your* standards? Checking is just a way of safeguarding your child and, while they're still young, someone has to take responsibility for this. As Jenkins notes, while there were numerous complaints about children accessing the potentially violent game (potentially, in that a player can choose the level of violence he or she engages with) *Grand Theft Auto 3*, which had an MA rating in the US, a Federal Trade Commission study found that 83 per cent of all video game purchases were 'either made by parents or by parents and children together'.[41] This suggests that parents wittingly bought games for their children that were not age-appropriate. They most likely did this with no awareness of content; either they succumbed to pester-power or, possibly, they were meeting their own desires and using the children as an excuse. We need to know what we're buying our children and understand the consequences of our choices.

As kids get older, you can increase the time they spend with various media, up the rating and content that they access, and be less vigilant, particularly if you've communicated with them about inherent dangers or problems and how to deal with these.

While internet-censoring devices are all right for the computer, they're not foolproof. They also remove so much useful information that can contribute to your child's knowledge that the learning experience is sometimes compromised. Yet again, what's appropriate for some kids and families won't be for others – that's why it's important for parents to know what their children are doing and be responsible for setting the limits.

Once kids hit their teens and enter the middle years of high school, then it's time to rethink net usage and other technologies and whether or not to give your child a personal computer. By the age of 15 or 16, a child who knows that an adult has been looking over their shoulder, and who has been made computer and internet literate, will be more than capable of managing on their own. Will they access violent and sexual imagery? Probably. But ask yourself, what would you have done at that age? Viewing this type of material, in context with their usual home, school and general life, is also a normal way of exploring the big, wide adult world of which they're soon to become a part. They know it's naughty (hence it will be done behind closed doors) but, hopefully, if anything really disturbs them, they'll discuss it with you as well. In their mid-teens, it's unlikely that they'll suddenly adopt a whole new set of values or attitudes on the basis of a website or image they've seen. While their own perceptions of the world and people may alter through the media they use and interact with, the changes are unlikely to be radical – if they are, then it's probably because they were established on shaky and contradictory foundations in the first place. As Mission Australia's National Survey of Young Australians revealed in 2006, what young people value most are their family and friends and that includes the influence these people have on their belief systems and morals as well.[42]

Personal technology like MP3 players, laptops and mobile phones are, in the scheme of things, still relatively new, so it's not surprising that etiquette around their use has developed slowly. The number of letters to editors complaining about people answering their phones in the cinema, at weddings and funerals and at other very inappropriate times is astonishing. It's not surprising that, if adults don't know how to use these gadgets appropriately, chances are a young person might not either.

As a society, we need to talk about what's acceptable and unacceptable in terms of mobile phones and MP3 players. For example, in schools, mobile phones have been banned because kids were SMSing in class. At university, the same thing occurs, with students who are merely a few seats away or across campus seemingly unable to concentrate for an hour or two – instead they want to set up a meeting or to and fro about an issue or friend. Being seen to be part of a network gives them social cache, and the 'beep' that tells them they have a message also signals popularity and acceptance, but we also need to explain what's appropriate and inappropriate. Taking calls or SMSing during classes or any formal function is not good manners. It also means that kids aren't learning how to be patient or pay exclusive attention to something or someone. Explaining to teachers, lecturers, hosts or employers that your phone is switched on because of an important call (an emergency) is, of course, different. We need to educate kids that it's all right to have downtime, to escape the frenetic 'wired' lifestyle of our 24/7 pace. Being out of the loop doesn't mean the end of the world. Switching off our own phones or giving priority to family and kids will also help our children understand the role the mobile phone plays in life. It's important, but not that important.

Likewise, MP3 players need to have codes established around their use. When someone is talking to you, it's downright rude to keep listening – even with one ear-piece in. Just as kids want our full attention, it's not wrong to expect them to give us theirs as well.

Mine's Bigger Than Yours

Technology has made our lives simultaneously easier and more complicated. Caught in a never-ending communication loop that prevents us from completely escaping work (or anyone for that matter), we've also become obsessed with owning the latest and greatest in terms of the technology available. So much technology, such as fridges, freezers and washing machines, is designed to have a shorter shelf-life, yet too often computers, phones and other personal electronic devices barely get time to sit on the shelf let alone break. It takes nanoseconds for computers, phones and other devices to become outdated.

Instead of accepting that what we do have is adequate for our purposes, we become caught in a competitive cycle where, yet again, the technology we own – like the clothes we wear, food we eat and shows we watch – reflects the type of person we are.

The number of very young children with mobile phones is growing. One study found that in the UK a quarter of all seven-year-olds had mobile phones. This figure rose to 89 per cent in children aged between 11 and 12.[43] An Australia Institute paper in 2007 revealed that mobile phone companies were increasingly targeting the tween demographic, producing 'child friendly' phones using familiar brands such as Mattel, Disney and Nickelodeon, mainly because the adult market is saturated. This campaign is working because, as Roy Morgan research data revealed, almost one-quarter of Australian tweens (increasing to two-thirds with girls aged 12–13) own phones.[44] Eager to have the latest fashion statement and associated kudos, they flash them around the playground and text each other instead of talking. School Lost Property bins all around Australia and the Western world are groaning under the weight of misplaced phones. Kids don't understand or respect the expense or intention behind the phones – and what is that? Parents are buying them in the hope that a little piece of metal and plastic will keep their kids as close as an umbilical cord, especially when they feel guilty about their long hours and after-school care. For those parents who don't buy pre-paid, hefty bills are usually just around the corner. Parents are sometimes persuaded that buying a mobile phone for their tot or tween will protect them. No, it won't. It might make you feel better and therefore assuage guilt but, in a really dangerous situation, your child will be unlikely to have the chance to use the phone; teaching them other survival skills may work much better.

Buying the sales pitch and clever marketing, our kids also fall into the trap. Not content with what they have, they compare theirs with others and start in with the pester-power. In our desperation to find a good present or eagerness to placate our kids, we either buy a phone or upgrade their existing one. In doing this we inculcate just the right kind of consumer values that capitalism needs to flourish. Perfectly useful technology sitting in recycling and lost property bins, slim pay packets, high credit-card bills and continuous guilt are just some of the consequences.

Playing Games

The final technological breakthrough I want to discuss is electronic games. This includes those you can load onto the computer and those you can play on the internet or on dedicated machines such as Nintendo, PlayStation and Xbox. Bond University academic Jeffrey Brand claims that 79 per cent of Australian households have a form of computer gaming device and likens this statistic to TV ownership in the 1970s.[45]

The history of electronic games is a fascinating one. According to Aphra Kerr, digital games, whether on home consoles, PCs or in arcades, wouldn't have been possible without transistors, the cathode ray tube and integrated circuits.[46] While they were never intended to be developed as commercial enterprises, their emergence in the 1960s, when the Space Race, Cold War and rock and roll were on everyone's minds and hearts, created the environment in which they would flourish – so did a change in work patterns. The influx of women into the workforce meant that there was a rise in demand for time-saving domestic appliances. With more time on their hands, people looked to be entertained: enter the digital game.[47]

The first games to be developed and mass produced were funded from scientific research institutes. Founded on sporting principles, tennis, hockey and a ping-pong style game were released on two different platforms: the tennis/hockey games were designed for home while 'Pong' was for arcades.[48]

In 1981 Nintendo and Sega began exporting arcade games to America. In 1986 both companies launched two home-console systems. Steve Poole describes them as 'the Beatles and Rolling Stones of the late 1980s and early 1990s. Nintendo was the Beatles; wholesome fun for all the family. Sega, on the other hand, were the snarling, street-smart gang, roughing it up for the hardcore videogame fans'.[49]

The marketing of digital games, while always appealing primarily to a young, male audience, began to change in the 1990s. Sony, instead of launching their PlayStation 2 console as a game-only device, sold it as an 'entertainment system'. This shift was copied by other companies that understood parental concerns about games as well as the need for families to justify the expense for what had once been merely a platform for electronic games. PlayStation 3, Nintendo Wii and other consoles now move between trying to go for broader appeal or simply grabbing the ever-increasing gamers' market.

Violence in Games

With the growing popularity and consumption of digital games came the critics. Games have been linked to violence (particularly after the Columbine High School massacre), negative attitudes and behaviours, obesity, poor health generally and shorter attention spans – much like TV. In discussing the negative attitudes to games, Aphra Kerr defers to David Marshall who suggests that 'while computers are associated with work and education, videogames are seen as a waste of time and a waste of human resources'.[50] This could go some way to explaining a lot of the bad press they get. Jenkins reminds us that:

> every storytelling medium in the history of mankind has included violent themes and stories, because we depend on stories to help us sort through our conflicting values and mixed feelings about aggression. We turn to violent entertainment ... because it gives us a sense of order in a world that otherwise can seem totally chaotic. We fantasize about a lot of things we'd never want do in real life, and through fantasy we bring those impulses momentarily under control.[51]

Jenkins wisely reminds us that 'if you look at the personal background of those kids who have been involved in school shootings, you will find a history of real-world aggression and violence. They don't need games to teach them to hate and hurt; they learned that at home or at school'.[52] The same can be said for young people with sexual problems.

Even that which makes so many adults shake their head in disbelief has its champions, and digital games are no exception. In *Everything Bad Is Good for You*, Steven Johnson devotes a great deal of space to discussing the virtues of electronic games. One of the funniest and perhaps most surprising points he makes is that a great many gamers spend a lot of time *not* having any fun. He says that, while games will never equip young players with the benefits a 'good' book might, you can 'judge games by the criteria designed to evaluate novels: Are the characters believable? Is the dialogue complex?'[53] He also argues that it's not 'what you're thinking about when you're playing a game' that counts, it's 'the way you're thinking that matters'.[54] In games, there are often puzzles to be solved, and multiple threads of narrative and characters to tie together to create sense and meaning. There are rewards to be gained by moving logically from one phase or level to another. He compares the structure and mode of thinking required to play games (even the violent shooting ones) as equivalent to word or logic puzzles. While they don't offer much in the way of psychological or moral depth, or lessons in how to communicate, they do provide those who try them with certain competent technical skills. They 'teach abstract skills in probability, in pattern recognition, in understanding causal relationships that can be applied in countless situations, both personal and professional'.[55] He then cites the popular game *Zelda* as an example of all of this.

Columnist and essayist Lev Grossman would likely agree with Johnson. Writing in *Time* magazine in 2004, he responded to the panic about games like *Grand Theft Auto: San Andreas* by acknowledging that it,

> sounds like a game that glorifies delinquency, juvenile and otherwise. And it does. But it's also an extraordinary experiment in interactive storytelling. You play a playa, a

> Snoop-style gangbanger wandering a vast, absurdly detailed version of California. There's no hard and fast narrative. You go where you wish and do what you like, and the game makes things interesting accordingly. This is something that's possible in no other medium. San Andreas combines the richness of art with the freedom of real life to create something entirely new, totally unclassifiable and really, really cool.[56]

Grossman has also alluded to something else that makes games attractive entertainment and relaxation options for kids. They're a form of digital dress-ups, where kids can play 'cops and robbers', girls can be boys and boys can be girls. Action heroes, warriors, thugs and fantasy figures and stories about them are only a controller away. Games are another means through which kids can explore a range of identities, safely and with adult supervision. It's no wonder adults also enjoy the flexibility and freedom of these kinds of games, not just on a console but online as well. They must, as there are over 800 million online gamers registered.[57] It's an opportunity to walk in someone else's shoes for a while, even if your own are perfectly comfortable. This is why the alternative virtual world *Second Life* is so appealing as well.

Used in moderation, balanced by other stimuli and played at an age-appropriate level, games teach our kids more than hand-eye coordination. The increasing reliance we have on technology has given us all the ability to have what Linda Stone refers to as 'continuous partial attention'[58] – that is, we're able to watch the TV, talk on the phone and play Solitaire on the computer at the same time. This is a superficial skill that requires us to give the three or four things we're doing our continuous but only partial attention simultaneously. Those much maligned Xbox, Nintendo, PlayStation and computer games, on the other hand, require children's full attention to make order out of chaos and therefore complete the challenge. Concerns around this continuous partial attention or multitasking, however, suggest that 'the mental habit of dividing one's attention into many small slices has significant implications for the way young people learn, reason, socialize, do creative work and understand the world'.[59] The quality and depth of what young people do suffers.

Again, moderation is the key. Just as in the past we would criticise kids for having their nose in a book all day, so too we don't want to see kids glued to the screen – computer, TV, mobile phone – or attached to a game console for hours on end either.

Cyberspace: The Final Frontier

Current and emerging technologies have revolutionised social interactions, but that doesn't mean more traditional forms of learning or meeting people will be replaced, not by us or our children. Rather, the old and the new will have to learn to work in tandem, in public and personal lives, allowing people, young and old, to connect and disconnect as their age, preferences, mobility, technological access and abilities allow. After all, the reality is that even in cyberspace, we're still only human.

For something that's only been around for just over three decades, the impact of cyberspace is not only enormous, but it's still to be properly assessed. How will historians of the future reflect on these times, the moments when, in terms of technology, we were all babes in the virtual woods? How will history itself be recorded? Will emails fill the cyber-tomes of years to come and the professional and personal exchanges of the public speak to our descendants? Hopefully, if they do, it will be to recognise us as discerning and capable users, not whingeing, technology-addicted victims.

We've created the 'monster' of technology and now it's virtually our responsibility to ensure it doesn't destroy our children.

chapter ten

My Little Prince/ss: Why Kids Don't Always Have to Feel 'Special'

Anything But Ordinary

If ever a term has changed meaning over time, it has to be the word 'ordinary'. According to the *Oxford Dictionary*, when applied to people it can mean, 'regular … or the usual kind, not singular or exceptional'. There was a time when 'ordinary' also inferred reliable, comfortable and unlikely to cause offence. These days, however, as an adjective 'ordinary' is not only likely to offend, it's considered negative. Describe someone as 'ordinary' and you may as well stamp 'failure' on their forehead. Call a child 'ordinary' and, if you're not physically or verbally abused, then you'll probably witness the child being wheeled into a doctor's surgery and given massive doses of Prozac while the parents go to counselling and/or court.

When did this change? When did being 'ordinary' become a synonym for 'loser'? It happened the moment the importance of being an individual or 'special' entered our collective psyche.

Standing out from the crowd has now become a life-ambition, particularly for younger generations brought up on a pop culture diet of makeovers and reality television.[1] Through these shows we're invited to champion an Idol, a Survivor, the 'Next Top' model or a *Big Brother* housemate. We watch in fascination as people shed kilograms, have plastic surgery, encounter law enforcement or cheating partners and view their 'natural' responses. These once 'ordinary' people are beaten with the celebrity stick and after exposing themselves, literally and emotionally on television, having their story told and retold in gossip mags and their image circulating in public, transform into 'special'. They're somebody. Why? Because they were prepared to be 'themselves' and endure ritual humiliation in the hope of emerging triumphant, as the most 'special' – the winner, the one on top, the 'survivor', the 'idol' and any other word we can think of to acknowledge their 'specialness'. Added to the allure of this is the fact that some 'idols' and 'survivors' have gone on to lucrative careers and fame. In 2007 Jennifer Hudson, runner-up in a series of *American Idol*, won various awards, including an Academy Award, for her performance in the movie *Dreamgirls*. This is the exception more than the rule with most of the participants having their 15 minutes and then sinking without a trace. Even so, these people usually have very healthy notions of self long before they ever appear on TV.

The attribute of being 'special' is linked not only to how well you're known, but to how you feel about yourself. Self-esteem and 'specialness' appear, in our society, to go hand in hand. This is why parents and other adults who work with kids try hard to make all kids feel 'special', through gifts, verbal and physical rewards, and careful use of language in the home, at childcare and at school. As a culture, we strive to ensure children's egos are healthy. Except sometimes we lose sight of what constitutes 'healthy' when it comes to self-perceptions and end up creating ego-maniacs.

While we can reason that kids need to feel 'special', particularly in a world that's generally geared to remind them they're not, there are many experts who argue that by over-emphasising our children's most trivial accomplishments we're doing them more harm than good. Social commentator Hugh Mackay makes a very interesting observation about self-esteem. Describing it as 'the simpering twin of happiness', he asks:

> Where did this lopsided emphasis on self-esteem – self-regard, self-importance – come from? When did we decide it would be a good idea for children to take themselves so seriously, to believe everything they do is wonderful, and never a word of criticism or correction to be heard? 'Brilliant,' we cry, at the drop of a hat, 'gold stars all round!'[2]

Stroking our children's egos gives them an unrealistic view of themselves in relation to the rest of the world. American psychiatrist Robert Shaw argues that 'if we lavish pointless praise and empty pats on the back to children, we're doing them a disservice'.[3] There's a great deal of truth in this. By constantly telling our kids, those little people we love, that they're special, wonderful, brilliant, beautiful, clever and talented, we're often setting them up to fail. In using hyperbole to give them an over-inflated idea of themselves and their abilities, we can potentially damage future relationships they might have by instilling in them a belief that they're too good and foster within them unrealistic expectations about life. We can make it difficult for them to conduct themselves in a professional manner in a workforce that doesn't constantly remind you how valued you are as a person or shower praise on its staff – except when it's really deserved. We can also make it very difficult for them to have meaningful personal relationships, particularly if they believe they're too good for anyone or that no-one's good enough for them.

A US report called 'Egos Inflating Over Time' suggests that the undue emphasis on the positive, such as 'tot-level self-esteem boosting, luxury-as-necessity entitlement, and what one calls "instant fame-ification"', in contemporary parenting and educative techniques has led to a rise in narcissism and lack of resilience in younger generations. At the same time, this generation is also recognised as very hardworking and able to critically reflect upon and disapprove of the narcissism within its own ranks.[4] If kids are indeed becoming more egocentric, then it's clear that not only did the adult generation contribute to (if not cause) this, but also we can do something about it – the earlier in a child's life, the better.

That's not to say that we shouldn't praise and encourage our kids when it's appropriate. But they're the key words: *when appropriate*. The very politically correct notion of 'positive reinforcement' has meant that whenever kids do anything, from the simplest chore such as placing dishes in the sink, completing their homework, answering a question or tying their shoelaces, even when it's done badly, they're told how amazing they are and bells and whistles sound. A growing trend in schools is for teachers to give out certificates of 'achievement' to every child in the class. I spoke to one 10-year-old, Jayden, who, over the years, has been given many certificates. A clever child, he is dismissive of his accomplishments. 'Everyone gets them', he said. 'They don't mean anything.' Jayden's not alone with these thoughts. Nearly every child I spoke to who had been 'awarded' certificates felt they were just bits of paper. Not at first, of course; their disillusionment set in later when they realised that being praised and recognised happened to everyone – even those who did virtually nothing to earn it. Some of the certificates my children received were 'Excellence in: Individual Skills', 'Teamwork Award', 'Commendation Award' and, for my daughter, a 'Special' award for 'Being quick and accurate with maths calculations'. Both kids received 'Participation Awards' for various school cross-country runs, even though they came last – the same award that the winners received. British social commentator Melanie Phillips once referred to this as the 'all must have prizes' ideology.[5] The repercussions of constantly telling at least one generation of kids that they're special and can do and be anything they want, and giving them prizes for everything, is only now being felt.

In 2004 *American Idol* judge Simon Cowell, the dyspeptic Englishman, had a glass of water thrown in his face by 18-year-old contestant Jonathan Rea. Cowell had basically told Rea, in his dry and direct way, that his performance was dreadful. Refusing to believe Cowell, Rea argued with him. Then he reacted to the criticism by dousing Cowell with water.[6] The story went global and Cowell, who'd been portrayed as a cultural villain for bruising so many young people's egos over the years, was hailed a hero. Suddenly, he was praised for 'telling it like it is'. Commentators said the incident was evidence that 'the most coddled generation in American history had come of age'.[7]

As a result, many discussions in the public press and around water-coolers ensued. At the heart of these was the identification of a syndrome called 'Too Much Positive Reinforcement'. In a very interesting article published in 2004, journalist Sue Corrigan explores the meaning and evidence behind this 'syndrome':

> Since the 1970s, the dominant ideology has been that children must be praised at every possible opportunity, never criticised or chastised, to boost self-esteem and protect their supposedly fragile egos. [The result of this has been that] we've produced a generation of pompous, self-important youngsters with a massively over-inflated view of their talents and abilities, unable to conceive of themselves as fallible and, therefore, unable to cope graciously [if at all] with life's harsher realities.[8]

In 1997 British broadcaster Jenny Murray warned that kids were being over-indulged and growing into adults who believed their every whim would be sated.[9] Not supposed to raise our voices to kids, meant to turn every single situation into something positive, told we're all lousy, absent, indifferent or smothering parents, adults are confused. Then, to add to this, we're told that our children are all precious and special and that we should be grateful for every single minute we get to spend with them, even if sometimes we don't like them very much. This is especially true when our little tween 'princesses' morph into what psychologist Michael Carr-Gregg calls 'Princess Bitch-Face'. Carr-Gregg describes Princess Bitch-Face as the pre-pubescent 'chore dodger', who has to keep abreast of whatever her peers are doing, divides her parents and family and rules the roost, makes outrageous requests to reach a well-orchestrated 'compromise', distracts to get her own way and threatens self-harm or absence when she doesn't.[10]

Psychologist Carol Dweck, from Columbia University, studied the effect of praise on more than 400 fifth-grade kids in a dozen New

York schools. She found that praise backfires with kids who are used to receiving it constantly for every effort, as they emotionally buckle at the first sign of failure. Interestingly, when her results were explained to parents, the response from one was, 'I don't care what the experts say … I'm living it'. Despite the evidence that constant praise would not benefit her children, this woman was determined to continue. This is because, Dweck believes, 'Offering praise has become a sort of panacea for the anxieties of modern parenting … In a similar way we put our children in high-pressure environments, seeking out the best schools we can find, then we use constant praise to soften the intensity of those environments'.[11] Those environments don't only refer to schools, but to all the other structured and 'beneficial' ones in which we place our children in the belief that we're giving them an advantage – athletically, artistically or academically. Sometimes, however, our reasons for placing them there can be found by looking at our own insecurities and sense of inadequacy, many of which spring from our childhood or feelings of opportunities lost – something, with the best of intentions, we don't want our children to suffer.

Dr John Irvine provides some timely advice when he warns parents not to live life through their children. He writes that 'So many parents put enormous stress on children to perform the best so that they can glean some of the reflected glory. Although parents get away with it when the kids are young (when they idealise their parents), later on these kids tend to burn out, or; later still, walk out to escape the pressure'.[12]

Not Very Constructive Criticism

Trying to discuss the role adults play in shaping kids and the ideas around this sensibly is very difficult. When it comes to children, the adults responsible for them tend to take a defensive posture. Criticism, constructive or otherwise, stirs our emotions and guilt. Irregardless of whether we're at home with children or work and place our kids in care, we personalise the debate and bring our own experiences to bear upon it. But as Carr-Gregg wisely states, while this might seem like 'parent-bashing', 'we have an obligation to make healthy choices that will guide our daughters [and sons], socialise them and eventually teach them to be independent. If we don't perform this role, who will?'[13]

If we're overindulging our kids and couching useful advice and criticism in such saccharine sweet and politically correct language that it has become detrimental to their sense of self, then we need to be talking about this, as individuals, as families and as a society. As Shaw noted and Boston-based media critic Dr Jean Kilbourne confirms, children might have more these days in terms of possessions and be told they're fabulous, but they look more moody and miserable than ever.[14]

Instead of dealing with bad behaviour and attitudes towards adults, peers, teachers and society, we pathologise it – send the kids to the doctor and get a diagnosis or blame an outside influence (friends, teachers, school or work culture). There's a great deal of comfort in this, but also an abrogation of responsibility. If we can attribute the behaviour to something else, then we can assuage our guilt and don't have to re-evaluate our child-rearing practices. We argue with the teacher who says our child is misbehaving in class or is a bully in the playground, even when the evidence is indisputable.[15] We sneer and become angry with other parents who dare to suggest that our child misbehaved in their house or hurt their child. In short, we become emotional and don't want to listen to anything negative about our child, only the positives, thank you very much! But the offshoot of this is that not only do we fail to teach our kids that they're not always right or terrific and that some behaviour (language and attitude) is absolutely unacceptable, we also make the child a victim of something that, at times, is well within their control and ours to change. We fail to teach them to take personal responsibility for their actions and accept consequences. Now, while the fault doesn't always lie at our children's feet, we seem to be losing rationality and perspective. Unable to tolerate the smallest criticism, we refuse to listen or see and persist in looking at our kids through some very dirty rose-coloured glasses.

Another popular way of managing problematic behaviours is to label them. Shaw argues that 'a host of new clinical diagnoses have been invented to explain away spoilt and antisocial behaviour ... we used to be clearer about the importance of parenting, but we've forgotten what children require to grow into happy, responsible adults'.[16]

But does one glass of water in the face from an overwrought teenager really signal a generation of molly-coddled kids reaching adulthood and not coping? And, if it does, what does that promise for the future of our tweens and teens?

The Princess Syndrome

Not only has 'special' become a very popular word in today's society, but the terms 'princess' and 'goddess' are widely used as well – and not just in the way Carr-Gregg deploys them. As Peggy Orenstein wryly notes, 'To call princesses a trend among girls is like calling *Harry Potter* a book'.[17] Princesses used to belong in the realm of fairytales, at least they did until Diana came on the scene. Princess Diana, the 'Queen of People's Hearts', made being a princess real and accessible as well as hard work. She was the embodiment of all those childhood fables – beautiful, kind and humble – though she didn't get to live happily ever after. Australia now has a former Taswegian, Princess Mary, to admire and look to as a role-model for young girls wishing to meet a socially superior man and be elevated. Whereas fathers would once speak lovingly of their 'little girl' or 'daddy's girl', now it's their 'little princess'. While it might just be a term of endearment to some adults, the fact that it has been hijacked by marketing forces to sell products and usage in popular culture gives it a much more significant meaning.

Seen printed on T-shirts, in magazines, on DVDs, at parties, as the basis of films, and as an expression of desire, it seems that anyone can become a princess or be treated like one. Not only do little girls want to be princesses, so do tweens and teens, whereas grown-up 'princesses' often claim 'goddess' status.

These days, being an everyday princess means being showered

with attention and things and having a sense of entitlement. It's also being used as a marketing ploy to advertise a range of toys, beauty products, clothing and other merchandise designed to make kids and their parents feel 'special'. Even young men, our tortured male teens, talk about treating their girlfriends like 'princesses' as a way of romancing and wooing them. Likewise, turn on the TV or read teen (or adult) magazines and girls either declare their desire to be treated like a princess or gush over the man in their life who does treat them that way. But there is a downside to this. A survey by American youth organisation Girls Incorporated, released in October 2006, revealed 'school-age girls overwhelmingly reported a paralysing pressure to be "perfect": not only to get straight As and be class captain, but also to be kind and caring'.[18]

The Grimm brothers and Hans Christian Andersen would be rolling over in their graves. Disney has done its work well. So much for feminism – forget equality, just give the girl some adulation.

Tiaras have become more than something that might occasionally appear in a dress-up box or perched on the heads of royalty; they're now fashion statements.[19] Give it to Paris Hilton to wear and, it seems, tweens and teens will follow. Tiaras are common accessories at school dances, kids' birthday parties and hens' nights. Just as everyone can be 'special', in the realm of public space everyone – boys too – can be a princess.

Kids' birthday parties are often themed around being 'princess' for a day (more on parties shortly). Instead of teaching kids that those who treat others nicely usually find this reciprocated, little girls (and some older ones) are almost encouraged to be aloof, bitchy, unsociable and demanding and then they're rewarded for it with faux-friendships, gifts and the adoring comments and looks of proud parents. Shaw argues that the 'whole issue of confidence or self-esteem has attained a trendy, almost cult-like status. It should be a natural product of a healthy productive life lived by fully developed children',[20] not construed as a short-cut for time-deprived parents to make their kids feel worthy.

Anyhow, what's cute in a precocious five-year-old is anything but that in a 15- or 25-year-old.

The Goddess Within

Too old to be a princess is no deterrent to special-hood. Teens and adults graduate from 'princess' status to that of 'goddess' and wait to be worshipped. I find this language, often spelled out in self-help books and again marketed back to vulnerable women and girls, quite off-putting. First, the goddesses of early Greek and Roman myths are often spoiled, arrogant, unfaithful, indifferent to the pain they cause, and basically incredibly flawed. It's part of their appeal – but usually as moral lessons in how *not* to behave, not templates for modern living. In other cultures, goddesses are the well-spring of life and nurturing. They are wise, capable and earn the respect and trust of those who worship them. They receive, but they also give back in abundance. They deserve the loyalty and faith of their followers.

Today anyone can call themselves a goddess. Buy a sticker, a book, burn some incense, demand attention and claim yourself worthy of devotion – but without earning it. I find this sad that we so readily grasp labels and concepts to make ourselves feel better, tell ourselves we're beautiful, kind and good. Instead of modifying our behaviour and earning love and, if we must, devotion, we slap on a bumper sticker, read how great we are simply because of our sex, and chant mantras to persuade ourselves that we really do deserve the attention/man/luck/friends/love that we just don't seem to be getting. And then we wonder why we're so unhappy.

Children are emulating this sense of entitlement as well. Language is such a powerful tool. While the intention behind the positive words and the culture of 'all kids are special all the time' may have been to make them feel important, confident and valued, the constant reiteration of specialness through terms like 'hero', 'princess' and 'goddess' renders these significant terms meaningless. It empties them of emotion and power.

Again, the experts aren't suggesting for a moment that kids shouldn't be told what they're doing is good or their actions worthy – they're saying it should only happen when they actually accomplish something. If you choose to call your daughter a princess and want her to feel like one, then make sure it's when she deserves to be – not regardless. Until that point is reached, kids should be encouraged and nurtured, but not flattered. Remember, princesses grow up into queens – just what sort of queen is up to you. I'd rather my children were members of my family, not heads of a pseudo-royal one.

So what happens when everyone is special?

We're *All* Special!

The interesting thing about being 'special' in this day and age is that it's an attribute we all seem to possess. It just needs to be bought, uncovered, claimed or discovered. Just as we can find that unique quality that makes us stand out, more than ever before we're wearing and desiring the same brands, clothes, food, gadgets, technology and music. We're buying or remodelling the same sorts of houses; taking the same holidays; admiring or loathing the same celebrities, politicians and other public figures; and recording our lives on the net for everyone to gawp at. At the same time, we pride ourselves on our individuality. We wear it like a badge.

In Monty Python's *The Life of Brian*, the main character speaks to the adoring crowds gathered beneath his windows, telling them they don't have to be followers. He shouts, 'You're all individuals!' So, when everyone's an individual, what do we call someone who's not? Hal Niedzviecki, in his book *Hello, I'm Special: How Individuality Became the New Conformity*, argues that those who work hard to proclaim their difference from the pack are simply demonstrating their conformity to a pack-mentality. He writes that in contemporary times, this so-called 'individuality' is 'part sociological phenomenon, part (pop) cultural practice, part challenge to old orthodoxies of institutional expertise, and part expansion of a me-first agenda long promised by the abundances of techno-capitalism'.[21] In other words, we're good little consumers persuaded to believe we're somehow unique and that through our purchasing power we can proclaim this to the world.

But the sad truth is, we've never been more alike.

We're *all* special.

Slogans, many lifted straight from popular culture and the advertising world such as 'Just do it', saturate the modern imagination. 'Believe in yourself', 'You can be anything you want', 'Because you're worth it' (and the L'Oreal kids slogan, 'Because we're worth it too'), 'Reach for the stars', and 'The sky's the limit' are no longer simply testimonies of inner strength and fortitude; they are announced as if they're a God-given right. The right to be special. All we have to do is buy the product, watch the show, jump onto the latest trend, talk about the latest hit song, movie, celebrity or ourselves, and we stand out from the crowd – we're 'in the know' – we're special. We can even buy cards that tell us how wonderful and unique we are – they're in every store that sells stationery.

When Will I Be Famous?

Ask kids what they want to be when they grow up and many declare 'famous' without understanding the concept but knowing that it signifies them as somehow extraordinary. Caught up in this, parents do everything they can to get their children to the top of the heap, give them a head start in life – from endowing them with 'special' names (I'll get to those shortly), to forking out $1800 and lining up for hours at a models casting call to give their kids a 'shot at stardom',[22] or spending $45 on a designer dummy for a baby.[23]

All it takes to move from 'normal' to 'special' is a 'look', a video on YouTube, a treehouse on MySpace, a name, a designer outfit, a party, an expensive object and constant reminders from those who love us. Anything that makes us, as Niedzviecki writes, 'a more and better you'. He discusses the phenomenon of the reality TV show *Idol* as contributing to this, describing the young hopefuls who wait in queues for days and hours on end in an effort to get on air as wanting to partake in this 'I'm Special' sameness:

> Here are thousands of young people planning on singing interchangeable pop songs, and they all share the same

> dreams: Each believes that he or she is a unique individual soon to be singled out and led to the altar of stardom. This is the new-conformist coming-out party, a where-were-you-when moment for a generation of perpetual teens searching for that elusive feeling of specialness.[24]

Businesses have, by recognising parents' insecurities about the kind of childhood and, therefore, life that they're providing for their kids, discovered a niche market. By designing and marketing a whole range of products and experiences to anxious parents, businesses have created a veritable industry around making kids (and thus parents) feel 'special', and ensuring they have an advantage in the race towards adulthood.

Educational and athletic DVDs as well as an assortment of structured activities involving sport, craft and music are available for tots in most capital cities. In an effort to socialise and give their kids a developmental headstart, many parents are embracing a range of expensive options – from 'sensory motor work' classes for tots six weeks and older, to singing and dancing lessons for toddlers. Hugh Mackay refers to this as the 'Little Emperor' syndrome, where life revolves around the every whim of a child who has power and yet, ironically, no control over him or herself.[25] He argues, 'We're tending to overindulge and over-parent the current crop of babies and toddlers, simply because they're in short supply'.[26] With the birth rate at an average of only 1.7 children per woman, Mackay has a point. Experts would also support his cynicism about these types of ventures, particularly when longitudinal studies suggest that there are absolutely no long-term advantages for kids in these types of activities – except, possibly, social. It's testimony to our Protestant work ethic–based society that we prefer structured activity to unstructured. It gives us a sense of achievement and purpose to not only timetable our lives, but also those of our children – from tots to teens with extra classes, music, sport, language and art tuition – thus making ourselves and our kids feel worthy or 'special'. Time to ponder, reflect and dream is being eaten away – so is downtime with the family. Dr John Irvine says that kids need play 'where there's no structure, no one telling them what to do … It helps them work through conflicts. And they need to be able to see us at play too, and parents can learn from kids how to do downtime'.[27] We don't think of the fact that, when we load our kids' lives with activities and structure, it might be because we're being lulled with big promises and assurances. If we do acknowledge this, and still proceed, all well and good. At least it's with open eyes. Consider this: if you make sure your children have plenty of time to P.A.R.T.Y. – that is, Ponder, Absorb, Reflect, Think and Yearn – then they're less likely to turn into kids who have to be Stimulated, Occupied, Distracted and Scheduled – that is, little S.O.D.S. But there are many other ways to make kids feel special these days – whether it's on the sporting field or in the beauty salon.

A Sporting Chance

I believe in children participating in sport – it teaches cooperation, how to be part of a team, patience and, if taught properly, how to be a gracious loser. So often, however, kids are encouraged or forced into sport so adults can live their own lives vicariously through their children and thus feel 'special' themselves. This is why there's so much bad behaviour at children's sporting events. The media, parents' groups, schools and society are rife with gossip and stories about adults losing control at matches. There's talk about off-field violence, abuse (physical and sexual), malnutrition, excessive training and substance abuse. It's become so common that the United Nations has warned pushy parents to stop forcing their kids into sporting success.[28]

Why do parents and other adults push their kids into arenas they have very little desire to enter? What I'm referring to here is different to those instances where adults try to encourage their kids into teams and classes for short-term gains, or those kids who love what they're doing and feel stimulated and challenged. I'm referring to what we call 'stage' mums and dads – the unreasonable and demanding parent who forces their kids to participate and compete and then consistently finds fault with their efforts.

The reasons for this are complex. While these parents appear to be the opposite of those who dote and praise, in many ways they're the same; the methods are different but the intention is identical – to make their kids and themselves feel 'special'.

The violence that erupts off the sporting field can happen when the adult feels overwhelming and uncontrollable disappointment that their kids (or his or her team) didn't perform – they didn't shine. The failure is taken personally, as a reflection of the adult. Instructions, coaching and refereeing decisions and even the championing of kids by other adults all become distorted through the lens of perceived failure, and abuse and anger spill over. Yet, as Dr Joe Tucci, Chief Executive of the Australian Childhood Foundation, says, 'When you pressure your children beyond their capacity you are affecting their self-esteem and development … Parents who berate their kids and start fights with the coach and other parents have really got to look at themselves and see what they are doing is not helpful to their children'.[29]

There are also the adults who become enraged because their child doesn't win a trophy, whether it be from a sporting, drama, academic, chess or dance competition. All the effort and expense of lessons, ferrying kids around in cars, tantrums, inconvenience, time wasted, sewing costumes and having to endure countless rehearsals or rounds appear to have amounted to nothing. Your 'special' child doesn't win. Instead of taking it in his or her stride, understanding that there can only be so many winners, the adult and, subsequently, the child, falls apart. Instead of being rational, so many adults become enraged at judges, referees, other competitors and even the child victors. Pent-up anger and frustration bubble over with a sense of injustice that all the weeks of effort, of promised glory, have been worthless.

Irate, disillusioned adults often do one of two things – sometimes, both. First, the adult will buy a substitute 'prize' for the disappointed boy or girl, trying to compensate for what they didn't win (or for the hurt caused to the child by the parent expressing their own anger and disappointment), thus ensuring the child still feels 'special'. One has to wonder what this is teaching. Second, particularly among female-dominated sports or arts, a slander campaign against the triumphant kids and their parents (and judges, referees, coach or instructors), begins – often conducted in front of the unsuccessful child. Diminishing the accomplishments and talent of others seems to have become, sadly, a way of bolstering our own and our kids' self-esteem. But again, what values is this instilling in our children? If they're taught to understand that not everyone's special and that it's perfectly all right not to win or be in the limelight all the time, they would be able to handle defeat with the minimum of despair and sense of personal failure. We need to teach our kids to move on to the next venture without dwelling on the last and becoming despondent and resentful.

As parenting expert Jane Barry says, 'Two of the greatest attributes we can encourage in our kids are a healthy self-esteem and self-confidence. One of the ways to achieve this is for kids to solve problems successfully and for them to be able to master skills independently'.[30] This includes how to be a dignified loser, which is much preferable to the arrogant winner – the one who runs around making noises, thrusting arms up in the air and pulling aggressive faces.

All in a Name

In a desperate effort to make their kids stand out in the crowd, some parents go to great lengths to pick unforgettable names, not realising that the handle they've just bestowed is also attached to some very heavy baggage. Naming a child is a huge responsibility that some adults don't seem to take seriously. They give their kids names they would have liked or that reflect their tastes, hobbies, celebrities or popular culture and then wonder why their children are teased in the playground.

When Gwyneth Paltrow named her child 'Apple', everyone's first thought was that she had a grudge against Bill Gates. The jokes were endless. But spare a thought for the poor kids who were named Gandalf, Snoop, Superman and Arsenal. One child was even lumbered with the name 'Harry Potter' – even though Potter is not his surname. Tiger is also popular with over 100 kids in Britain being given that moniker and a few were even called Adidas and Reebok – the offspring of consumer culture indeed.[31]

While we can bless our kids with original names, we also have to think long and hard about the repercussions of them and sacrifice special for understandable or beyond ridicule if we can.

It's My Party

Children's birthday parties are another booming business spawned from the need to make our kids feel 'special'. Often claiming to save adults' time (and they do), party businesses offer parents themed parties for their kids (for the big bucks), with face painting, craft, games and prizes – and that's just for first course. You can also order magicians, clowns, fairies – pay for it and it's yours. One business even states that 'every show is individually personalised!' And that 'the birthday child is the true "STAR" of the show!'[32] There are also gift boxes to match the theme and reduce parent workload. Many of these party places also make the birthday cake and other foods. Depending on how much you want, it's not cheap. Seven-year-olds can have disco karaoke, pirate, girlfriend, superhero, fairy or King Arthur parties. Dream it and be it.

In an effort to give their kids something special (and, let's face it, impress other adults), more and more parents are opting for these party plans. Happy to exchange wads of cash and be spared organisation and effort, parents glow in the aftermath of their booking accomplishments.

One Sydney mother, who organised her own party for 21 children, moaned about the expense. Despite budgeting for food and activities, she overspent buying every visitor a gift – a movie ticket. After all, she explained, 'they'd all spent so much money on Kyle, I didn't want to look like a cheapskate'. I thought the point was for guests to buy gifts for the birthday boy or girl. There's also the story of the children who attended a birthday party and found an iPod in their goody bag. I'm sure it's an urban myth, but one of our times if it is. The British supermarket chain Tescos 'found the demand for goodie bag contents had risen 12-fold in the past three years'.[33] Many parents feel pressured to place more elaborate treats in their child's party bags with the average take-home party bag for Australian kids costing the hosts $20 each – whether the celebration occurs at home or somewhere else.[34] This tends to make the colouring book and beautifully wrapped pencils bought as a birthday present horribly inadequate. But perhaps that's the point.

Again, that ugly spectre of competition and comparative parenting rears its head.

Another trend that has emerged with children's parties is that, instead of leaving their kids at the host's house, parents are opting to stay. Columnist Frances Whiting humorously despaired when attending a friend's child's birthday party that not only did the mothers remain, but the fathers did too. She added, 'I'm told by several mothers I know that this sort of behaviour is becoming the norm and that mums and dads everywhere, instead of doing what normal parents would, which is, of course, to see the children's birthday party as the glorious gift of free babysitting that it is, are actually choosing to stay'.[35] Smothering, overprotective, or just responsible?

Beauty at a Cost

Children's birthday parties are only the icing on the cake of special-hood. Another business that has boomed in the last few years, as mentioned in Chapter Three, is the tween and teen beauty salon visit. Kids as young as six are being taken to beauticians for facials, manicures, pedicures and, once in their tweens, for waxing and plucking as well.[36] In an effort to make them feel special, kids are literally getting the treatment. It seems to be working. Next to the sexualised images and products aimed at pre-schoolers and tweens are real-life kids and their parents purchasing and using them. Six out of 10 girls aged seven to 10 wear lipstick and more than two in five wear eyeshadow or eyeliner; a quarter wear mascara; and three in five wear perfume.[37] Fake tans have also become very popular with the under-12 market.[38] From an image of stolen childhood to the recipe for a lost one: all you need is the wave of a mascara brush, a squirt of perfume and some artificial colouring.

Catering to this desire to look older and engage in activities once the exclusive realm of older teens and adults, salons are skewing their business to capture this new market. Salon birthday parties are not uncommon – in either hairdressing or beauty.[39] While salon owners defend their decision to pander to this burgeoning youth market saying that they're simply meeting a demand, we have to ask who is creating it? If a seven-year-old asks for a facial, how hard is it for a parent to say no? All it takes is one mother to take her child for 'special' treatment, to talk about it and others will follow. But if we're giving six-year-olds manicures, we have to consider what they have to look forward to when they're older. This drive to make our kids feel special also truncates their childhood and consumes their innocence by exposing them to rituals and sensations that haven't been earned, yearned for or reached; they are simply wanted – usually by parents keen to be seen as 'hip' and 'trendy' but also as doing something meaningful and 'special' with their kids.

Many tweens would be happy bonding over anything with their mothers or fathers, not necessarily a beauty treatment or fashionable hairdo. Of course, doing what mum does is going to make them feel special – but not if it keeps happening. Baking a cake together, having a picnic or looking through photos and talking can also inspire the same type of 'warm and fuzzies' that a visit to the hairdresser might. It will also be cheaper and, when the child wants to do it again, it's easy to think of alternatives.

Beauty treatments should be reserved for older kids. They're a special experience all right, but not if you've been having them since you left nappies. In catering to our children's every whim, we're making life boring and removing the sense of wonder at teen and adult rituals and rites. We're taking away the accomplishment our kids need to feel when they've strived for something, behaved in a mature manner and, through hard work and perseverance, made their own dreams come true.

By indulging our children in these kinds of treatments, we're teaching them to focus on the surface, to privilege their appearance and to judge others this way as well. The cost of this superficial trend is already very high. A survey done by Dove's Campaign for Real Beauty discovered that girls between 10 and 17 years of age had the poorest body image and very low self-esteem. The study also found that a third of the girls aged 15–17 rate their mothers as the most powerful influence.[40] In other words, if mum doesn't feel good about herself, or judges herself in accordance with others, then it's likely her daughter will as well.

Ordinary *Is* Extraordinary

The truth is most of our kids are going to be, in the great scheme of things, ordinary. And that's perfectly all right. Not everyone can be top of the heap, a star or 'special' – at least, not all the time. To play at being a princess or superhero is fine, but believing you should be treated like one in everyday life and all the time is conceited and downright impractical. You won't get very far in life demanding respect – like everything else, it has to be earned.

While the last thing a parent apparently wants is an 'ordinary' child, I believe we need to rethink exactly what we mean by this. There's nothing wrong with ordinary, particularly if it also implies well-balanced, content and comfortable in their own skin. Parents may want an individual who will stand up and be counted, show some 'bratitude', but there are ways kids can do this without buying into the culture of 'special'.

Deep down, we all know this but, instead of accepting it, we decry ordinary and feel a little ashamed. We place our kids under a cruel microscope to discover what it is that makes them different and sets them apart, and then try to enhance this. If there's nothing remarkable, we find a common attribute and try to go through the painful process of making it uncommon. Sometimes it's good to be a part of a greater whole, to not stand out. But because we've been taught to believe that being 'special' means a bright future, when it comes to our kids we want nothing less.

This drive to be special, to stamp individuality and thus difference on everything from people to places, permeates a culture that is, in many ways, becoming a conformist nightmare. The irony is that the more we focus on 'me' and attempt to meet the standards of a limited corporate, political and distorted ideological blueprint, the less we think about 'we', and what really matters. We also set our kids up to fail.

Jane Barry believes that 'a strong sense of "I can do this" and "I'm a good person" for a child, whether they are five or 17, is a great barometer for parents to feel confident that they've done a pretty decent job'.[41]

By focusing on the individual and what makes us 'special', we create an 'us' and 'them' mentality. Instead of looking for what makes us the same, ideologically, morally and ethically, we search for that which distinguishes us as different. We exaggerate the little things (often superficial or external only) to make them count and miss that which we can delight in sharing – with each other and our children.

And in doing so we forget that without 'we', there's no community.

conclusion

The Parent Trap

Overrated Childhood

We live in a contradictory era where, on the one hand, we place too much emphasis on childhood and, on the other, we take it for granted and assume that kids are kids and will cope no matter what. It's not that simple. I don't mean to suggest for a moment that childhood is unimportant – it's very important – but we appear to have lost sight of the bigger context. Childhood is but the beginning and a very short period of an individual's life. Thomas De Zengotita believes that 'No society in history has ever sanctified children the way we do ... Just think of the specific resources in time, energy, and material that we collectively invest in children, real and imagined. Think of the political rhetoric about families, of the way kids get sentimentalized in journalism, in movies, and TV shows and commercials. Children are icons of the media age'.[1]

What we seem to have overlooked in our push to romanticise, sentimentalise and, as Daniel Donahoo suggests, idolise our children[2] is the fact that, while childhood might be the foundation stone on which a person's life is built, it's not definitive. Some adults try to pack everything into those few short years, truncating or erasing the wonder and catapulting their kids into a future that they haven't yet begun to live, while others follow every kiddie trend, listen to and follow the latest advice, take their kids to the 'right' films, buy the 'right' toys, clothes and gadgets; or they over-protect their kids, shielding them from everything including normal risk-taking behaviours and consequences that teach us about boundaries and how to interact with each other in the physical and human environment, and from ideas and concepts that teach them to question and to learn.

It's not up to anyone else to create our kids' childhood – that's our responsibility: at an individual, family and social level. While we worry about the people who come into their orbit, the childcare we'll give them, their education, the type of house they'll live in and the neighbourhood, the friends they'll make, any medical problems they'll have and a range of other issues, we don't tend to think long and hard about the popular culture aimed at and for our kids or their access to it. Or, if we do, we're influenced by damning media reports that make us anxious, or by hyper-positive marketing that reassures us and persuades us to relax and buy. It's confusing. Yet we should be thinking about popular culture. We should be striving to understand the multiple roles it plays in shaping our kids' sense of self, our sense of self, our culture, other cultures and the future. Kathleen McDonnell believes that kids 'crave the menu pop culture has to offer, and it's up to adults to try and discover why this is ... children are not a critical audience in the same sense adults are'.[3] Very young children rely on adults to do the thinking for them – they require us to reflect and make decisions based on information and some foresight and then pass on our knowledge so we can teach them to think for themselves and make wiser consumption choices. But we can only do this successfully and weigh up the consequences if we know what it is we're allowing our kids to access and how this can potentially affect them – in good and bad ways. And this includes the popular culture that both we and our kids consume.

Childhood: A Giant Step Towards Adulthood

I was talking to a 42-year-old father of two, Tim, who is also an uncle. He said something to me that I thought very profound. When asked how his 12-year-old nephew had behaved while he was visiting him, he found himself having to defend Aaron to the grandparents who claimed that, in their experience, they felt the tween was aloof, rude to his parents and selfish. Tired of having to explain that he found Aaron perfectly 'normal' for his age, Tim finally said, 'Look, I don't think there's a problem. God, he's 12. He's also confident, self-assured and good at talking to other people outside the family. In fact,' he continued, 'I told my mother that while Aaron may not be much of a kid, in that unrealistic and idealised sense that so many have, I felt he had the potential to be a fine adult. Isn't that a good thing? Childhood is so short. It used to be that our life expectancy was 33, now it could be 133. We spend such a brief time as kids. Our job as parents, as adults, is to make sure that those being raised now turn into good ones'.

Tim also made the point that sometimes adults put enormous expectations on children, wanting them to behave in ways that few ever did, except perhaps in Enid Blyton books. When it comes to childhood, we can be quite myopic, but at the expense of the younger generations. Looking at their childhood, we judge it as wanting. This is ironic considering that, as I said above, it's up to us, in league with the other social, cultural and human forces around us, to construct it. Yet, instead of being active in childhood formation, we often leave it to outside forces alone – especially popular culture. Then we whinge about what we sense occurring – that our kids' childhood is being stolen and their innocence consumed. And it is for some kids. But whose childhood are we really talking about? Our children's, based on a dim and reconstructed memory of what we experienced? Or, as Tim says, an idealised version possibly created by a combination of Disney and a host of parenting books and TV shows that offer happily-ever-after finales or endless advice and warnings?

Childhood and 'innocence' will only disappear completely if *we* let them. If we choose to keep our lives separate from that of our kids, to treat them as the 'enemy' in a generational war that's been raging for centuries, then it could well vanish and very quickly.

I feel it's time to call a truce.

Through popular culture, and an awareness of the role it plays in all our lives, we can do this.

Infotainment Rich

Information about the tiniest aspect of popular culture – how it's produced, marketed, altered and designed to appeal – is not only interesting, but lessens the power the popular culture has to persuade, shape and potentially change people, except when they choose to let that happen. For so long, adult culture has been swept along in a tide of disenchantment and disempowerment that tells us, like Dr Frankenstein, we can't control the technology, TV, films, music, fashion and so on that our kids watch, listen to, use or wear. This is utter rubbish. We can and, when it's within our homes, families, schools, communities and countries, we must. That's not to say that we become censorship vigilantes. On the contrary, it means we have to start engaging with the forms our kids know and love to understand what kinds of information and entertainment they're being fed – how they are processing the infotainment and what ideas they're receiving. How it's shaping their sense of self. We then need to use this to open the lines of communication. With just a little bit of effort on our parts, we can deploy all the different elements of popular culture as tools that will help us raise healthy and wise adults who understand that being 'sexy' is not something you can buy, wear or own, nor is it intrinsic to meaningful relationships. It will help us raise kids who are 'savvy' about how corporations, marketers and the media work and for whom being 'tortured' or trying to conform to a narrow template of 'sexiness' or a generational template was a self-inflicted and brief pastime.

Selling Sexiness

British sociologists David Buckingham and Sara Bragg explain our discomfort around 'sex' and children when they write that 'Children's sexuality – or in their knowledge of sexuality – may be becoming visible to adults in a way that it was not in the past, or at least the recent past. It is not so much that children have suddenly become sexual, more that adults are now being forced to recognise it'.[4] This is why we don't like it. Children aren't supposed to sexy. They're supposed to be cute and sweet and naïve – like a May Gibbs gumnut baby. Not a Britney Spears, 'hit me one more time' sort. While both are unrealistic, we allow the Britneys of this world to flourish.

Kids *are* sexual beings, and that includes tots. Corporations, advertisers and the media generally use this fact to sell products and notions to adults, only they turn a biological and cognitive reality into an adjective – they turn sexuality into 'sexy' – through fashion, advertising, music, celebrity endorsements and even through toys. This appeals to our very savvy tweens who know the word 'sexy', have a sense of what it means and, seeing the way it makes adults react, want to get in on the act. That's all it is at this age, an act. If, however, this pretence, this corporate-driven construct, isn't exposed, then by the time kids become teens, they'll have adopted it as a legitimate identity and torture themselves if they fail to rate on the sexy radar.

Given too much currency in this day and age, sex doesn't just sell, it's come to define a way of being for young and old that accrues rewards – popularity, recognition and kudos. Afraid of what will happen if they don't jump on the 'sexy' bandwagon, many adults and, in turn, tots, tweens and teens, are being forced to embrace 'sexiness' as a concept to sell merchandise, ideas and even themselves. Businesses aren't going to stop doing this as long as we keep buying 'it'. Again, the power lies with us to make changes and those changes can begin at home. Monitoring what elements of popular culture, whether it's TV, film, the internet, fashion or toys, enter the door and discussing them with children can reduce the power they have to convince us all to adopt, watch and use them. Laughing aloud at the 'sexy' music videos, revealing the ages of the 'teens' in movies and TV shows, explaining that Barbie and Bratz are fantasy figures – even in the 'real-life' films – and making sure that relationships, emotions and feelings between people are discussed and emphasised goes a long way to creating a healthy context for 'sexiness'.

Savvy Kids

'Savvy' is a great word. It means to know or understand, but also connotes a shrewdness or worldliness that comes with experience. At a superficial level, our tweens appear just so savvy. They seem to understand concepts and adopt mannerisms and language well beyond their chronological ages, evoking pride and alarm in equal measure among adults. Certainly, when it comes to interacting with popular culture, particularly technology, they have a know-how and ability that belies their age. Yet, before we become too comfortable with this or reassure ourselves that they're still very young and therefore naïve, we need to remind ourselves that just because so many of these kids can 'talk the talk' doesn't mean they're ready to 'walk the walk' and step into the adult world. They'll try. Through nagging, demanding and an uncanny ability to argue logically and persuasively, they'll try to get adults to relent and allow them to stomp around in grown-up shoes too fast and too soon.

The point is, as mature as they seem and often look, they're not. It doesn't matter if tweens have been surfing the net since they were two or wearing make-up and travelling since they were five, they still have a very limited experience of life, situations and other people to draw upon. They might remonstrate and beg to be allowed to paint their faces, watch a certain movie or stay up to catch a TV show all their friends view or attend a concert, but the adults in their life need to consider what it is *they* want for their tweens. If that is for them to engage in adult experiences through films, the internet, how they style themselves or perform in public, even though they might not be cognitively ready, then be prepared to deal with the consequences of this. Permission for tweens to play in the adult world should only be given if grown-ups are there to guide, contextualise and reassure. Personally, I think tweens can wait a few years, but not everyone feels that way and certainly, as I've said, children develop differently. But we also need to be aware that if we allow our tweens to become savvy about teen and even adult experiences, what sort of experiences will they seek when they reach those ages?

Savvy tweens are both a reality and a fantasy. In terms of fantasy, they belong to the digitised and plastic world of Bratz and other popular toys and celebrity icons. Remember, so many of the famous tweens are actually teens, just as the teens are sometimes adults. Being aware of this and the ways in which the corporate and entertainment industries market to us and our children, making us believe that behaving like an adult is 'normal' for a tween these days, can go a long way to helping us say 'no' and 'not yet'. It's not 'normal', not in our world. Savvy tweens are only a reality in the corporate world – where 'knowledge' and the desire to possess this in all sorts of inappropriate ways sells.

The Tortuous Years

We often hear how hard it is for teenagers these days – and I believe it is. Popular culture bombards young people, from tots to adults, with unrealistic and narrow concepts of beauty, gender and accomplishments. Through films, TV shows, magazines, books, fashion and advertising, our teens are being sold a blueprint for success in this world and it's so reductive. It's no wonder they get depressed and anxious, and suffer low self-esteem (particularly regarding their bodies). Assailed by so many notions of who they should be and how they should look, given a bunch of vacuous celebrities or buffed and rich athletes as role-models, they're flung into a whirlpool of emotions, aspirations and ideas. Told they're 'special' and amazing and can do anything they want, they get to their late tweens and early teens believing this and then look in the mirror (stare, compare and despair), or get honest or unkind feedback from a peer group, don't do so well in a subject at school, or fail to win a trophy, and come to the unwarranted conclusion that their entire life and goals are a sham if not a shambles. They might never look like Jesse Metcalf (from *Desperate Housewives*), possess the beauty of Cameron Diaz or, despite uploading dozens of their own songs onto MySpace or YouTube (songs that their family told them were amazing), have the internet and subsequent global success of Sandi Thom or make the cut in the *Idol* auditions. Instead of taking it in their stride and telling themselves it doesn't matter, not everyone can be the 'best' but what they do is terrific nonetheless, they view themselves as 'losers', as having let everyone down and torture themselves over their looks, style and lack of talent. If, however, they've been made aware of how constructed all the images circulating in popular culture are, how so many of them are designed with the intention to part consumers with their money and instil in them a desire for more, more, more, they might not be so distressed. Similarly, if the great internal qualities they have are nourished and any abilities they possess are appreciated, they'll gain a strong sense of achievement, personal satisfaction and self-respect.

Of course, even the most savvy and aware of kids will go through those angst-ridden years where self-doubt and negative thoughts about everyone and everything threaten to swallow them. But if, through popular culture, adults have an ongoing dialogue with their children (through popular culture, we can speak the same language as our children and get a sense of them and they us), then it's possible that those grim years may be abridged.

As I said earlier, understanding something reduces its power. That's why I'm a firm advocate of including popular culture in the classroom – not at the expense of the classics, but alongside them. Educating ourselves and our children about how images, toys, fashions, celebrities and stories are created and circulated through all sorts of different media undermines the power they have to influence and shape our society, us and our children, except in the ways we want them to. It turns the entertainment culture of our times into an edutainment culture by placing it within a broad social and historical context. Popular culture becomes enriched with meaning beyond the trivial and superficial (which is how we tend to dismiss it to our own detriment), and a part of our lives that we control and, importantly, enjoy. And so can our children. It's also important to remember that as much as it's ubiquitous, 'popular culture is only one influence on our children's imaginations. Real life triumphs media images every time'.[5]

Parents Are *Not* a Child's Best Friend

Parents should never try to be their tot's, tween's or teen's friend. That's not their job. Sharing and understanding the popular culture kids engage with does not mean becoming their best buddy. There are other people in their lives, mainly their peers, who function in that way. The role of a parent is to prepare their child for the adult world. Setting boundaries and rules that are flexible, that adjust according to age and behaviour; teaching respect for the self and others; providing a safe emotional, physical, psychological and imaginative environment; and, above all, engendering in your children both trust in your judgement but also in your ability to acknowledge when you're wrong and say sorry is paramount. Creating a culture within the home whereby tots, tweens and teens understand what will and won't be tolerated is also the key to good parenting.

It won't always be rosy or easy. Teens tend to become angst-ridden no matter what interventions or safety nets we put in place. But if they know that when they're ready they can come to talk to you, then their escape into the dark places of their mind will hopefully be temporary. Give them space, respect their need for friends outside the home and, like the butterfly that's set free, they'll return. Even if it's only to sit down and watch an episode of *Family Guy* with you. Laughter can be the best parent-child, cross-generational medicine.

Guilt, Glorious Guilt

No matter what we do, whether we protect, neglect, indulge or deprive our children and their childhood, or manage a wonderful balancing act of all these, we're never going to feel good about what we do with our kids 100 per cent of the time. As Gwyneth Paltrow confessed to Oprah Winfrey, the one emotion no-one warned her to expect on the birth of her first child was guilt (and that was before she named the baby!). Welcome to the Parent Trap – *guilt*.

Raising kids is like baking a cake. We follow one of the many recipes available (usually passed down through the family), adding our own touches here and there. We mix it together and place it in the oven.

We may have followed all the directions down to the last letter, but if the temperature is off even slightly, the power fails, one ingredient isn't quite measured correctly, or we leave it too long or take it out too soon, the cake will have flaws. If we're lucky, it may look good, but until we slice and try it, put it to the test, we won't really know. But one thing you can bet your money on is that someone will always have a better recipe. They'll even share it with you whether you want them to or not.

It's not until our kids are adults and enter the big wide world that we know if we've done our job successfully. What's more important, however, is that you prepare your kids to leave childhood. We all have to – overindulging, spoiling and even over-structuring your kids' childhood just makes them unable to cope in the adult world. While we may be responsible for 'baking' our kids, what we have to provide them with is the emotional, psychological and imaginative ingredients to take on, survive and thrive in the real world. While we may have created a child who looks good on the outside, like a cake, it's what's on the inside that really counts. Dr John Irvine tell us that one of the most important things a parent must do is attend to their child's needs not wants. He writes:

> Many parents fail to meet their child's needs for soft and firm love, boundaries, respect, love, trust, time to share and encouragement. Instead, they substitute needs for materialistic wants, but as this fails to satisfy the aching need within, the child craves more and more wants as a substitute for unmet needs.[6]

Popular culture and the various marketing and other forces that support its maintenance focus on these wants and try to persuade us and our kids that they are actually needs. They're not. Through a bit of balance, wisdom and consistency, we can restore the difference. If childhood *is* being stolen from our kids, if their innocence is being consumed, then we have only ourselves and our lack of skills or effort to blame – this is the message that we're getting from popular culture and a barrage of experts. And, in part, they're right. We all wish that when our children were born we'd been given a handbook or list of instructions that told us how to assemble and maintain our child – from tot to teen. Sad fact is, though we often resort to professionals and help books, we generally fly blind and pretty much scared and feeling like the world's biggest failure. Despite what we're being told, we haven't lost the ability to acquire those skills – we've just been led to believe we have.

Developing Skills

Kids develop at different rates and the adults they live with know this better than any expert and certainly better than some marketer. In so many ways, however, instead of empowering adults to make intuitive and wise decisions, the information in the public realm does the exact opposite by telling us what our children should be like at certain ages and how they should be behaving; what milestones they should have reached; what they should own, wear; how they should behave; and what they should have accomplished. When our kids don't measure up to these quite arbitrary standards, we feel we've failed – so do they. So, when the experts tell you that children under the age of two shouldn't watch TV, it's important that you know that and the reasons why. But if you make the decision that it's okay for your tot to view TV, it's with full knowledge of the possible consequences and the ability to overturn any negative ones.

We aren't born knowing how to parent – we only learn to do this once we have children. Just as we teach children life-skills, they teach us parenting ones. Similarly, though all adults were once children, they often don't know how to relate to or communicate with kids. While there are so many different ways we can learn parenting skills and how to talk to kids, the popular culture they invest in provides us with an easy, accessible and often interesting way of doing this. But instead of utilising it, we've allowed it to become an obstacle between us and the children in our lives. It doesn't have to be. The good news is we already possess the basic skills to break down this diverse, fun-filled and sometimes quite problematic barrier.

It's About Time

In the first chapter, I explained the way children were viewed in history. One of the most prevalent representations was the child as a miniature version of an adult. In dress, behaviour, work and play, there was little to distinguish children and adults. There's a sense in which we've returned to these notions, but in a way that makes many of us deeply uneasy. Having swung the pendulum in a direction that almost erased children as people, silencing their voices, ignoring their rights, we've swung so far the other way that we've not only embraced them as individuals in contemporary times, but allowed them to access the adult world and even exploited their attempts to do so. We feel we've lost control. It has either been handed over to our kids, who don't know how to manage, or we're allowing other forces to have far too much say in how our kids should be raised.

They shouldn't – they don't care.

Children, whether tots, tweens or teens *are* miniature adults, in the sense that they're all in the process of becoming. They're growing into the world, their bodies and their minds. While still very young, kids are adaptable. They adjust to their environments and are shaped by the attitudes of the adults and other kids around them, including those represented in various forms of popular culture. They modify their behaviours accordingly and they develop ideology that they'll carry with them into adulthood.

By allowing our children to access popular culture from a very young age in a balanced and educated manner, we can offer them an exciting and amazing array of choices. A bit of TV, film, some books thrown in, magazines, toys, an occasional trend indulgence, access to the internet and time with electronic games, music and, when they're older, a mobile phone should all be enjoyed along with physical activities, outdoor play, games, conversation-filled meals with family and friends, and lots of time to dream and ponder. Teaching children to understand the role popular culture plays in their lives; discussing celebrities, advertising and the way images are circulated and the meanings that accompany them; and setting boundaries, rules and safety nets against misuse will help give them proportion and a sense of balance in their lives.

Popular culture should be a smorgasbord of delights that forms part of a healthy emotional, physical, psychological and imaginative life. We may occasionally over-indulge, but so long as we don't continually binge we'll have a healthy relationship with it – and so will our children. Film, TV, music and all those other technological and creative wonders that form popular culture alone don't make our kids sexy, savvy or tortured, nor do they alone erode our children's innocence and childhood. Understanding the role they play at a personal, family and social level ensures that they never will.

We're all worried about our children and their rapidly disappearing childhoods and not without some reason. By working together, first as a family unit, whatever its composition, then as a society, and that means with the media and corporate and popular culture, we can protect childhood and ensure it isn't stolen or consumed – not in a maudlin or unrealistic way, but in a manner that our children deserve and need. This means not being afraid to question various forms of popular culture, the legislation governing it or the way it's being taught (if it is) in schools. It requires us to speak about what may concern us or what we want to applaud and accentuate. Learning about our children and the popular culture they access means we're learning not just about our kids, but about their culture and ours. Knowledge about popular culture breaks down generational walls, and when used correctly creates a level playing field, allowing us to speak a shared language and therefore communicate with each other. Through understanding the everchanging landscape of popular culture, creating a context in which it can be read, used and enjoyed, we can make childhood loving and challenging but also real. Together we can construct a solid foundation upon which our children can build meaningful, functional and compassionate adult lives – lives that aren't dictated by corporate interests or superficial trends, but ones that place them in control of their identity, thus creating a brighter future for them and the generations that will follow.

Notes

introduction The Toxic 'Truth' About Our Tots, Tweens and Teens

1 Pakula, K. (2006). 'OMG! You're such a chatterbox', *Sydney Morning Herald*, 1–2 July, p. 21. In 2005, according to market research company, GfK Australia, two million Bratz dolls were sold (see Gregg, N. (2006). 'Ken to the rescue to save Barbie from Bratz', *Courier-Mail*, 11–12 February, p. 11).
2 Parkin, J. (2007). 'Childhood trash or treasure?', *Courier-Mail*, 21 March, p. 47.
3 Zurbriggen, E. L. et.al. (2007). '*Report of the APA Task Force on the Sexualization of Girls*', APA Online. Washington, American Psychological Association. www.apa.org/pi/wpo/sexualizationrep.pdf, retrieved 18 September 2007.
4 Barrientos, T. (2006). 'Gender rap for fairy in training', *Courier-Mail*, 2–3 September, p.15.
5 Clark, E. (2007). *The Real Toy Story: Inside the Ruthless Battle for Britain's Youngest Consumers*. London, Black Swan, p. 10.
6 Australian Bureau of Statistics (2006). *Children's Participation in Cultural and Leisure Activities*, Canberra. Children spend more time watching TV (videos and DVDs too) than any other activity. An estimated 90% of 12–14-year-olds access the internet, 68% emailing or messaging, 52% for leisure, 43% gaming and 40% downloading music. Also, 18% of 9–11-year-olds and 10% of 5–8-year-olds access the internet daily.

chapter one Back to the Future: Childhood Through the Ages

1 Postman, N. (1994). *The Disappearance of Childhood*. New York, Vintage; Heywood, C. (2001). *A History of Childhood: Children and Childhood in the West from Medieval to Modern Times*. Cambridge, Polity. See also Andersen, J. (2005). *Hans Christian Andersen: A New Life*. New York, Woodstock, pp. 235–6; Kociumbas, J. (1997). *Australian Childhood: A History*. St Leonards, NSW, Allen & Unwin, p. xiv. See also the poetry of William Wordsworth, William Blake and Samuel Taylor Coleridge. For example, Wordsworth's *Prelude*:

'Introduction – Childhood and School Time', 'Three Years She Grew in Sun and Shower', 'Ode: Intimations of Immortality from Recollections of Early Childhood' and 'To H. C. Six Years Old'; Coleridge's 'There was a Boy'; and William Blake's *Songs of Innocence* and *Songs of Experience*, among many others.

2   See Andersen, *Hans Christian Andersen*, who cites John Locke in the 1690s and French philosopher Jean-Jacques Rousseau as among the first to take an interest in child-rearing and acknowledging childhood as a distinct stage (pp. 232–4). In the introduction of Kociumbas, *Australian Childhood*, the influence of Locke and Rousseau is also noted. Both men understood childhood as a time when the future adult was formed. Children were 'like empty vessels, easily filled with desirable aspirations and values' (p. xiii).

3   Fox, R. L. (2006). *The Classical World: An Epic History of Greece and Rome*. London, Penguin, p. 39.

4   Ariés, P. (1962). *Centuries of Childhood*. Harmondsworth, Penguin, pp. 31–47.

5   Ariés believes that, up until the 12th century at least, 'there was no place for childhood in the medieval world' (p. 31). As well as discussing various artistic representations of children (tied to the Christian religion particularly), he also examines the limited vocabulary to describe children, concluding that 'Language did not give the word 'child' the restricted meaning we give it today: people said 'child' much as we say 'lad' in everyday speech' (p. 125). In his chapter, 'The Evolution of Childhood', in deMause, L. (ed.) (1974). *The History of Childhood*. New York, Harper Torchbooks, Lloyd deMause disagrees with Ariés's contention about the dearth of representations of children in medieval art (see pp. 7–8). He also discusses the language (and clothing) used to define children and notes the similarity of terms for grandmother and baby (pp. 18–19).

6   Ariés, *Centuries of Childhood*, p. 59.

7   Ibid.

8   Postman, *The Disappearance of Childhood*, p. xi.

9   Hanawalt, B. A. (1993). *Growing Up in Medieval London: The Experience of Childhood in History*. New York, Oxford University Press, p. 7.

10 Heywood, *A History of Childhood*, p. 12.

11 See Hanawalt, *Growing Up in Medieval London*. Also, Jenks, C. (2005). *Childhood* (2nd edn). London, Routledge; Waller, M. (2000). *1700: Scenes from London Life*. London, Hodder & Stoughton, particularly Chapter 8; McDonnell, K. (2005). *Honey, We Lost the Kids: Re-thinking Childhood in the Multimedia Age* (rev. edn). North Melbourne, Pluto; Heywood, *A History of Childhood*; Andersen, *Hans Christian Andersen*, specifically pp. 231–7; Kociumbas, *Australian Childhood*.

12 Hanawalt, *Growing Up in Medieval London*, p. 6.
13 Ibid., p. 8.
14 See also Postman, *The Disappearance of Childhood*.
15 Hanawalt, *Growing Up in Medieval London*, p. 6.
16 Kociumbas, *Australian Childhood*, p. xii.
17 Quoted in Postman, *The Disappearance of Childhood*, p. 43.
18 McDonnell, *Honey, We Lost the Kids*, pp. 33–4.
19 Ibid., p. 33.
20 Quoted in Waller, *1700: Scenes from London Life*, p. 67.
21 See also Stearns, P. N. (2006). *Childhood in World History*. New York, Routledge.
22 Hoyles, quoted in Jenks, *Childhood* (2nd edn), p. 53.
23 We also have to be mindful that much of what we understand about children and childhood, through their games, toys and the way they have been described in literature and art, still reflects what adults thought about children rather than expressing the voices of kids themselves, as Kociumbas, *Australian Childhood*, notes on p. xvi.
24 See Hanawalt, *Growing Up in Medieval London*; Jenks, *Childhood* (2nd edn).
25 Jenks, *Childhood* (2nd edn), p. 53.
26 Holland, T. (2003). *Rubicon: The Triumph and Tragedy of the Roman Republic*. London, Abacus, p. 111.
27 Tucker, M. J. (1974). 'The Child as Beginning and End: Fifteenth and Sixteenth Century English Childhood', in deMause, L. (ed.) *The History of Childhood*, pp. 229–57, argues the opposite in relation to Breughel's paintings. He writes that Breughel's work shows 'men and women besotted with drink, groping each other with unbridled lust … children eating and drinking with the adults … doing the same things' (p. 251). In Andersen's *Hans Christian Andersen*, Andersen argues that in the work of Breughel 'children are depicted in more or less merry situations, but it's not always easy to distinguish between what are games and what are assaults' (p. 233).
28 Ariés, *Centuries of Childhood*, pp. 48–59.
29 Odysseus is one of the heroes of the 10-year-long Trojan War. When the war concluded, he and his men set sail for home with the booty they had collected. However, the gods conspired against them and it was another 10 years and after many tribulations (which included, among other things, sojourning with goddesses, being threatened by a Cyclops, Polythemus, his men being murdered or drowned, and surviving Scylla and Charybdis (clashing rocks and a whirlpool)), as well as having marvellous gifts bestowed upon him, before Odysseus, the sole survivor, returned home.
30 Homer. (1991 ed.). *The Odyssey*. London, Penguin, p. 348.

31 See Ovid's *Metamorphoses* and Robert Graves's *Greek Myths* for more information.
32 Losing one's parents was a harsh reality for many children and, as Maureen Waller notes, in London during the 1700s, 'hybrid' families (with step-parents and children) were not uncommon due to the high mortality rates. She also notes that, 'unfairly or otherwise, the notion of the wicked stepmother was current' (Waller, *1700: Scenes from London Life*, p. 68).
33 Andersen, *Hans Christian Andersen*, p. 232.
34 Shakespeare (1866). *Shakespeare's Works*. New York, D. Appleton. *As You Like It*, act II, scene vii, p. 312.
35 Jens Andersen believes this is because *The Divine Comedy* 'only has room for and takes into account fully developed human souls' (Andersen, *Hans Christian Andersen*, p. 233). But the point here is that Dante *does* distinguish between child and adult.
36 Ford, B. (ed.) (1982). *Blake to Byron: The New Pelican Guide to English Literature*. London, Penguin, pp. 40–2; also McDonnell, *Honey, We Lost the Kids*, pp. 42–4. McDonnell argues that 'So many of our beliefs about children's innocence are tied up [with] the necessity of keeping them in the dark about sexuality and the harsher aspects of life' (p. 44).
37 See Andersen, *Hans Christian Andersen*, and Butts, D. (1997). 'How Children's Literature Changed: What Happened in the 1840s?', *The Lion and the Unicorn*, 21(2): 153–62.
38 Hanawalt, *Growing Up in Medieval London*, p. 9.
39 Ibid., pp. 10–12.
40 Ibid., pp. 205–6. Kociumbas argues that girls were little more than a 'decorative ornament and plaything of her husband ... a miniature model of femininity' who also had to be a 'responsible and prolific mother' (Kociumbas, *Australian Childhood*, p. xv).
41 Hanawalt, *Growing Up in Medieval London*, p. 131. Hanawalt also notes that most apprentices were males and that during the 14th century, the average age to enter an apprenticeship was 14 but, by the end of 15th century, kids were aged 16 or older. Apprenticeship was considered so important that in the 1500s, right up until the 1800s, orphans between the ages of 5 and 14 were collected and apprenticed in unskilled jobs. See also Tucker, M. J. (1974) in deMause (ed.) *The History of Childhood*, p. 250.
42 Postman, *The Disappearance of Childhood*, pp. 13, 43.
43 Alchin, L. K. 'Nursery Rhyme Lyrics and Origins', retrieved 7 June 2007.
44 Jenks, *Childhood* (2nd edn), p. 57. Lloyd deMause also notes that 'Children have always taken care of adults in various concrete ways. Ever since Roman times, boys and girls waited on their parents at table, and

in the Middle Ages all children except royalty acted as servants, either at home or for others, often running home from school at noon to wait on their parents.' (deMause, *The History of Childhood*, p. 20).
45 Heywood, *A History of Childhood*, see particularly pp. 121–34. Heywood also makes the point that poor families often had to decide whether it was worth their while educating their children or putting them to work – not both (pp. 138–40).
46 Mackay, H. (2007). *Advance Australia ... Where? How We've Changed, Why We've Changed and What Will Happen Next*. Sydney, Hachette, p. 185, makes the point that the Liberal government's 2005 financial incentive to families to have an extra child: one for each parent and 'one for the country', 'bore shades of the old "populate or perish" slogan of the 1950s'. The government's promise of extra cash also revealed their awareness and fears about Australia's declining birth rate, and the role of children in guaranteeing a future for everyone.
47 Quoted in Heywood, *A History of Childhood*, p. 9.
48 Ariés, *Centuries of Childhood*, p. 125.
49 deMause (ed.), *The History of Childhood*, p. 42.
50 Ibid., p. 40. Lloyd deMause also notes that these children in turn grew up to batter their own children (p. 41).
51 See Waller, *1700: Scenes from London Life*, pp. 68–9; Grille, R. (2005). *Parenting for a Peaceful World*, Alexandria, Longueville Media, p. 55. Grille says children as 'young as four were forced up chimneys for hours at [a] time ... Starting at four years of age, children worked 16-hour days in coal mines or textile mills', p. 55.
52 McDonnell, *Honey, We Lost the Kids*, p. 35.
53 Briggs, A. (1990). *Victorian Cities*. London, Penguin.
54 Andersen, *Hans Christian Andersen*, p. 353.
55 In his biography of Andersen, Jens Andersen loosely draws the parallel between the Match Girl and prostitution and relates the circumstances to Hans Christian Andersen's own upbringing where his grandmother had three children to three different men (and served some time in prison), while his neglected mother was also sent to beg with groups of children. See ibid., pp. 353–4, 377.
56 See Tatar, M. (ed.) (1999). *The Classic Fairy Tales*. New York, W. W. Norton for more information.
57 Stoffel, S. L. (1997). *Lewis Carroll and Alice*. London, Thames and Hudson, p. 40. Stoffel also notes that to interpret Dodgson's interest as entirely sexual is to place a contemporary and salacious understanding upon his intentions.
58 Ibid. pp. 40–8.
59 deMause (ed.), *The History of Childhood*.

60 See ibid., specifically pp. 43–51. See also Finch, L. (1993). *The Classing Gaze: Sexuality, Class and Surveillance*. St Leonards, NSW, Allen & Unwin, for a fascinating discussion of child prostitution in Australia and England and the 'Age of Consent' law which made sex with girls under the age of 16 illegal. These laws were passed due to the campaigning of feminists and evangelists who sought to stop child rape and prostitution (pp. 74–5). However, as Finch notes, there were arguments to lower the age to 14 because it was considered that 'in Australia, a girl over twelve years was not necessarily a child as in many cases her sexuality was already well advanced beyond innocence and she was, in fact, often a dangerous sexual disrupter of moral order ...' (p. 81). Furthermore, the southern hemisphere was thought to advance a girl's puberty to at least 14 (p. 80). These arguments were, Finch argues, tied up with notions of convict immorality and misguided middle-class attitudes towards the working classes.
61 McDonnell, *Honey, We Lost the Kids*, pp. 37–9.
62 Giroux, H. A. (2000). *Stealing Innocence: Corporate Culture's War on Children*. New York, Palgrave, p. 5.
63 See Ariés, *Centuries of Childhood* and deMause (ed.), *The History of Childhood*.
64 Hanawalt, *Growing Up in Medieval London*, p. 11.
65 See also, Brooks, K. (2003). 'Nothing Sells like Teen Spirit: The Commodification of Youth Culture', in Mallan, K. and S. Pearce (eds), *Youth Cultures: Texts, Images, and Identities*. London, Praeger, pp. 1–16.
66 Giroux. *Stealing Innocence: Corporate Culture's War on Children*, p. 19.
67 McDonnell, *Honey, We Lost the Kids*, p. 63.
68 Cadzow, J. (2007). 'The parent trap', *Good Weekend Magazine*, 3 February, p. 21.
69 Mackay, *Advance Australia ... Where?*, p. 202.
70 Ibid.
71 Ibid.
72 Ibid., p. 24.
73 Readfearn, G. (2007). 'Status symbol toddlers', *Courier-Mail*, 14 March, p. 51. Dr Prue Aherns, a lecturer in art history at the University of Queensland who specialises in children's fashions, argues that 'Children's wear has come almost full circle since the Victorian era, where they were dressed as miniature adults'. She adds that 'really, it's only a superficial resemblance' (p. 51).
74 In her 2004 book, *Born to Buy: The Commercialized Child and the New Consumer Culture*, Juliet B. Schor, who conducted a study on children's participation in consumer culture over a three-year period, writes that 'Higher levels of consumer involvement result in worse relationships

with parents, which also leads to increased depression, anxiety, lower self-esteem and more psychosomatic complaints'. Quoted in Gregory Thomas, Susan. (2007). *Buy, Buy Baby: How Big Business Captures the Ultimate Consumer – Your Baby or Toddler*. London, Harper Collins, p. 13. This is supported by Gregory Thomas, who when interviewing a marketing executive for her book, *Buy, Buy Baby*, records that he said 'the moment a baby can see clearly, she becomes a consumer' (p. 2).
75 Quoted in Giroux, *Stealing Innocence*, p. 57.
76 Hanawalt, *Growing Up in Medieval London*, p. 11.

chapter two 'Bling, Bling, Why Don't You Give Me a Ho?': The Commercial Theft of Childhood

1 Lindstrom, M. (2004). *Brand Child: Remarkable Insights into the Minds of Today's Global Kids and Their Relationships with Brands*. London, Kogan Page, pp. 1–2; Palmer, S. (2006). *Toxic Childhood: How the Modern World Is Damaging Our Children and What We Can Do About It*. London, Orion Books. Palmer writes that 'brand loyalty can be encouraged in children as young as two through exposure to brand logos and mascots on screen and on products they enjoy. Three-year-olds can be influenced to ask for brands by name.' (p. 232)
2 Gregory Thomas, S. (2007). *Buy, Buy Baby: How Big Business Captures the Ultimate Consumer – Your Baby or Toddler*. London, Harper Collins, p. 80.
3 Linn, S. (2004). *Consuming Kids: The Hostile Takeover of Childhood*. New York, The New Press, p. 1. See also, Burke, E. (2007). 'Teens in the money as state booms', *Sunday Mail*, 11 February, p. 3, who reports that in Queensland 'Youngsters aged 10 to 17 have an average of $110 a week to spend on themselves'. This is $20 more than in other states with the exception of Western Australia, where the gap is only $10. So young people are also targeted for their capacity to directly spend as well.
4 Editorial Australasia (2006). 'Sizzle: How Big Brands Steal Children's Hearts', *New Internationalist*, September, p. 14.
5 Quoted in ibid., p. 15.
6 Lindstrom, *Brand Child*, pp. 46–7.
7 Gale, J. (2007). 'Kids Free 2B Kids'. www.kf2bk.com, retrieved 6 May 2007.
8 Adams, P. (2006). 'Corporate Pedophilia', *Weekend Australian*, 18 November, p. 62.
9 Gregory Thomas, *Buy, Buy Baby*, p. 20.
10 Linn, *Consuming Kids*, p. 5. See also Palmer, *Toxic Childhood*, p. 230. Palmer states that 'the average child in the US, UK and Australia sees between 20,000 and 40,000 commercials a year'. See also Centrella, A., S. Gray-Murphy, S. Morfidis and E. Sommerville (2003). 'Globalization,

Sex & Profits'. www.lilithgallery.com/articles/feminist/Globalization-Sex-Profits.html, retrieved 30 November 2006. The documentary by Goodman, B. (2001). *Merchants of Cool*. Frontline, USA, PBS, identified that US teenagers view 3000 discrete advertisements a day 'and 10 million by the time they're 18'.

11 Linn, *Consuming Kids*, p. 42. See also Gregory Thomas, *Buy, Buy Baby*, p. 5.
12 Linn, *Consuming Kids*, p. 24; see also Chapter 3. See also Madden, C. S. (1991). 'Marketers Battle for Mind Share', *Baylor Business Review*, 9 (Spring): 8–9. According to Dinyar Godrej, neuroscientists and psychiatrists are searching for what's been called the 'buy button' in the brain. This has created a new buzzword – 'neuromarketing' (Godrej, D. (2006). 'Captive – How the Ad Industry Pins Us Down', *New Internationalist*, September: 3).
13 Gregory Thomas, *Buy, Buy Baby*, p. 87.
14 Ibid., p. 13.
15 Ibid.
16 Lindstrom, *Brand Child*, p. 13.
17 Haig, M. (2004). *Brand Royalty: How the World's Top 100 Brands Thrive & Survive*. London, Kogan Page, pp. 2–3.
18 Editorial Australasia, 'Sizzle', p. 20.
19 Lindstrom, *Brand Child*, p. 196.
20 Quart, A. (2003). *Branded: The Buying and Selling of Teenagers*. London, Arrow. Quart cites a number of examples, but see in particular pp. 30–1.
21 Quoted in Burke, E. (2007). 'Teens in the money as state booms', *Sunday Mail*, 11 February, p. 3.
22 Gregory Thomas, *Buy, Buy Baby*. See p. 50 and Chapter 2.
23 Linn, *Consuming Kids*, p. 45.
24 Gregory Thomas, *Buy, Buy Baby*, p. 57.
25 Goodman, *Merchants of Cool*.
26 See Clark, E. (2007). *The Real Toy Story: Inside the Ruthless Battle for Britain's Youngest Consumers*. London, Black Swan, pp. 114–15.
27 Goodman, *Merchants of Cool*, defines 'cool hunters' as being 'structured around, really, a search for a certain kind of personality and a certain kind of player [they mean a dominant child] in a given social network'. One teen market researcher, Dee Dee Gordon, admits that 'cool hunters' look for kids who 'are ahead of the pack because they are going to influence what the other kids do. We look for the 20 per cent, the trendsetters, who are going to influence the other 80 per cent.'
28 See Quart, *Branded*, pp. 54–9; Linn, *Consuming Kids*, pp. 110–11. Linn also refers to 'Alpha' kids who adopt trends and make them 'cool'. Australasia, 'Sizzle', p. 20, discusses the psychology of parental disapproval which encourages marketers to create an outrageous campaign and image and thus make products 'cool'.

29 Viswalingam, P. (2006). *Decadence: The Meaningless of Life*. SBS.
30 Totaro, P. (2006). 'Silk and lace turn little girls into eye candy', *Sydney Morning Herald*, 18 February, p. 5.
31 Quoted in Koha, N. T. (2007). 'Aguilera set to launch the raunch', *Sunday Mail*, 15 April, p. 9. See also Levy, A. (2005). *Female Chauvinist Pigs: Women & the Rise of Raunch Culture*. Melbourne, Schwartz, for an interesting polemic on sex, gender and raunch.
32 Lamb, S. and L. M. Brown (2006). *Packaging Girlhood: Rescuing Our Daughters from Marketers' Schemes*. New York, St Martin's Press, p. 107.
33 Ibid., pp. 107–8.
34 Ibid, p. 1.
35 See Wiseman, R. (2002). *Queen Bees & Wannabes*. London, Piatkus, for a fascinating discussion on the pecking orders in tween and teen female social groups.
36 Margo, J. (2004). 'The secret life of teens', *Weekend Australian Financial Review*, 20 February, pp. 14–15.
37 Brooks, K. (2003). 'Nothing Sells like Teen Spirit: The Commodification of Youth Culture', in Mallan, K. and S. Pearce (eds), *Youth Cultures: Texts, Images, and Identities*. London, Praeger, p. 3.
38 Linn, *Consuming Kids*, p. 4.
39 Mackay, H. (2007). *Advance Australia ... Where?* Sydney, Hachette, p. 192.
40 See Lumby, C. and D. Fine (2006). *Why TV Is Good for Kids: Raising 21st Century Children*. Sydney, Pan Macmillan, p. 260 specifically, but also Chapter 6 generally.
41 See Giroux, H. A. (2000). *Stealing Innocence: Corporate Culture's War on Children*. New York, Palgrave.
42 Adams, 'Corporate Pedophilia', p. 62.
43 Brooks, K. (2005/2006). 'Corporate Kidnapping', *Melbourne's Child*, 13: 16–18. See also Brooks, K. (2005). 'Who are we kidding?', *Courier-Mail*, 31 January, p. 11.
44 See, for example, the well-known chain B & T (Bras and Things), as well as the relevant section in most department stores.
45 Gregory Thomas, *Buy, Buy Baby*, pp. 148–50, 150–3.
46 See Peretti, J. (1998). 'Middle Youth Ate My Culture', *Modern Review*, 5: 15–19; Lloyd, S. (2000). 'Big Kids, Big Money', *Business Review Weekly*, 28 January, pp. 50–7. These writers mainly refer to older people trying to maintain the illusion of youth by buying products and maintaining lifestyles more suited to younger people. They are called 'middle youth' and 'adulescence'. Susan Linn, on the other hand, refers to 'age compression', where older actors play younger parts in TV shows, advertisements and other media created for and aimed specifically at children (see Linn, *Consuming Kids*, pp. 18–19).

47 See Grose, M. (2005). *XYZ: The New Rules of Generational Warfare*. Milsons Point, NSW, Random House, for an interesting discussion of what it means to be part of a specific generation and how to work within and outside the stereotypes imposed by our year of birth. Kate Crawford, however, in her 2006 book, *Adult Themes: Rewriting the Rules of Adulthood*, Sydney, Pan Macmillan, offers a scathing critique of generational categories. She writes that the 'Multinational recruitment company Hudson conducted a survey to reveal the difference in attitudes between generations X and Y. Unsurprisingly, what they found were consistent similarities ... conclud[ing] that while generational groupings may be engaging, entertaining and intuitively appealing they offer little more than caricature, exaggerated and distorted to engage popular interest'(p. 11). Her book is well written and insightful and examines just who is included and who is absent from discussions about 'adulthood'.
48 Mackay, *Advance Australia ... Where?*, p. 205.
49 Gregory Thomas in *Buy, Buy Baby* cites Nickelodeon Jr's top executive, Brown Johnson, who develops shows for toddlers, despite recommendation and evidence from numerous professionals and bodies, that children under two should not watch TV (more on this topic in Chapter 6). When asked about the programs on his channel he reveals that they're there because 'it's about building allegiance to a brand' (p. 10).
50 Linn, *Consuming Kids*, p. 32.
51 See ibid., pp. 34–5.
52 Ibid., p. 32.
53 Ibid.
54 MarketingSherpa Inc, (2006). 'How to improve your campaigns targeting kids ages 4–7 and "tweens" ages 8–12'. www.sherpastore.com/Kids-Market-Tween-Buying-Machine.html, retrieved 13 November 2006.
55 Ibid. See also www.youthintelligence.com. (2006). 'The Intelligence Group: Trend School', retrieved 13 November 2006.
56 Lindstrom, *Brand Child*, p.193.
57 Ibid., p. 211.
58 Linn, *Consuming Kids*, p. 43.
59 (2006). *Little Friends*, Issue 8, ACP Magazines.
60 Quart, *Branded*, p. 66.
61 Linn, *Consuming Kids*, p. 6.
62 Wenham, M. (2006). 'Mums the real heroes', *Courier-Mail*, 1 August, p. 15.
63 Editorial Australasia, 'Sizzle', pp. 14–15. This article also points out that in France some people believe that commercials prepare kids for the reality of the world, while in Britain attempts to ban junk-food advertising to kids would have meant an annual loss of revenue to the tune of £441 million. For all the concern various governments

express about childhood obesity and general health, surely they could compensate broadcasters for taking a firm stance.

64 Zurbriggen, E. L. et al. (2007). *'Report of the APA Task Force on the Sexualization of Girls'*, APA Online, Washington, American Psychological Association. www.apa.org/pi/wpo/sexualizationrep.pdf, retrieved 18 September 2007.
65 www.commercialexploitation.org. (2007). 'Campaign for a Commercial-Free Childhood', retrieved 20 June 2007.
66 Palmer, S. (2006). *Toxic Childhood: How the Modern World Is Damaging Our Children and What We Can Do About It.* London, Orion Books.
67 Linn, *Consuming Kids.*
68 The Parents Jury exists in Australia (www.parentjury.org.au) and focuses on issues such as obesity and marketing to kids.
69 Gale, J. (2007). 'Kids Free 2B Kids'. www.kf2bk.com.au; Young Media Australia also supports kf2bk.
70 Gale, J. (2007). Interview with Karen Brooks, 13 September 2007.
71 Palmer, *Toxic Childhood*, p. 296.
72 Puente, M. (2006). 'From the sandbox to the spa', *USA Today*, 1 August, retrieved 30 November 2006.
73 Ibid.
74 MarketingSherpa Inc. (2006). 'How to improve your campaigns targeting kids ages 4–7 and "tweens" ages 8–12'.
75 Lindstrom, *Brand Child*, p. 61.
76 Ibid., specifically, p. 92, but also Chapter 5.
77 Quart, *Branded*, p. 69. Quart discusses the marketing conferences she attended and reveals the language (which borrows from psychology) that is used by marketers. She also reveals that Sabino gave a series of alarming (for parents) statistics to her listeners: '100% of tweens watch TV, 87% listen to radio, 85% play video games. The median age for a first solo purchase is eight years old. The average ten year old has memorized from 300–400 brands; 92% of kids request brand-specific products' (pp. 68–9). See Linn, *Consuming Kids*, Chapter 1, for more information on what goes on at tween and teen marketing conferences. Linn, a psychologist, also refers, quite despondently, to the psychobabble used and the fact that trained psychologists deploy their skills to aid marketing firms.
78 Cavett, D. and S. R. Geary (1999). *Sell and Spin: The History of Advertising.* New Video Group.
79 Quart, *Branded*, p. 5.
80 Ibid., p. 6.
81 Steinberg, S. R. and J. L. Kincheloe (eds) (1997). *Kinderculture: The Corporate Construction of Childhood.* Boulder, Westview, p. 153.

82   Rush, E and A. La Nauze (2006). *Letting Children Be Children: Stopping the Sexualisation of Children in Australia*, Australia Institute.
83   Devine, M. (2007). 'Kids exposed to sex too soon', *Sydney Morning Herald*, 15 April, p. 15.
84   Hopkins, S. (2002). *Girl Heroes: The New Force in Popular Culture*. Annandale, NSW, Pluto, p. 189.
85   Ibid., p. 88.
86   Lamb and Brown (2006). *Packaging Girlhood*, p. 189.
87   Alarcon, C. (2005). 'A girl's new best friend'. *B &T*, www.bandt.com.au/news/18/0c031518.asp, retrieved 5 July 2007.
88   Ibid.
89   Alarcon, C. (2005). 'Smells like teen spirit'. *B & T*, www.bandt.com.cu/news/10/0c02c510asp, retrieved 23 June 2007.
90   Ibid.
91   Holroyd, J. (2005). 'The tweens are in vogue', *Age*, 10 April, p. 3.
92   Quart, *Branded*, p. 6.
93   Alarcon, C. (2004). 'New survey reveals the power of being teen'. *B & T*, www.bandt.com.au/news/64/0c026864.asp, retrieved 22 June 2007.
94   Quart, *Branded*, p. xxiv.
95   Ibid.
96   Alarcon, C. (2005). 'New magazines on market'. www.bandt.com.au/news/64/0c026864.asp, retrieved 22 June 2007.
97   Hartley, J. and C. Lumby (2003). 'Working Girls or Drop-Dead Gorgeous? Young Girls in Fashion and News', in Mallan, K. and S. Pearce (eds), *Youth Cultures: Texts, Images, and Identities*. London, Praeger, especially pp. 52–6.
98   Rush, E. (2006). 'Adult world must let girls be girls', *Sydney Morning Herald*, 10 October, p. 13.
99   Quoted in Pryor, L. (2007) 'A treat for tweens as twins hit town', *Sydney Morning Herald*, 20 February, p. 3.
100 Carr-Gregg, M. (2005). *Surviving Adolescents: The Must-Have Manual for Parents*. Camberwell, Vic., Penguin, p. 117.
101 Allen, E. (2007). 'Talking about sex, baby', *Courier-Mail*, 27–28 January, p. 57.
102 Ibid.
103 Ibid.
104 Linn, *Consuming Kids*, p. 66.

chapter three Fashion Victims: The 'Celebrification' and Sexualisation of Children Through Clothing

1   Finkelstein, J. (1994). *Slaves of Chic: An A–Z of Consumer Pleasures*, Kew, UK, Minerva, p. 120.

2   Calefato, P. (2004). *The Clothed Body*. Oxford, Berg, pp. 78–81.
3   Entwistle, J. (2000). *The Fashioned Body: Fashion, Dress and Modern Social Theory*. Cambridge, Polity Press.
4   Finkelstein, *Slaves of Chic*, p. 119. Finkelstein repeats this important notion in Finkelstein, J. (1996). *After a Fashion*. Carlton South, Vic., Melbourne University Press.
5   Brooks, K. (2006). 'Comfortably Numb: Young People, Drugs and the Seductions of Popular Culture', *Youth Studies Australia*, 2(2): 9–16.
6   Finkelstein, *Slaves of Chic*, p. 127.
7   Niedzviecki, H. (2006). *Hello I'm Special: How Individuality Became the New Conformity*. San Francisco, City Light, p.19.
8   Tucker-Evans, A. and K. Patterson (2006). 'Big prices for little fashion', *Sunday Mail*, 26 March, p. 24, pictures a girls' size 3–4 jacket for $195 and a white tank top for $117. These are by no means top of the range. In Readfearn, G. (2007). 'Status symbol toddlers', *Courier-Mail*, 14 March, p. 51, he discusses toddler fashion and the fact that Australians are estimated as spending 2 billion dollars annually on clothing for their tots.
9   Lurie, A. (1981). *The Language of Clothes*. New York, Henry Holt & Co., p. 46.
10 Danaher, C. (2007). 'Racy wear for kids under fire', *Herald Sun*, 16 June, p. 21. See also www.news.com.au. (2007). 'Kylie's knickers put in knot', retrieved 18 June 2007.
11 Danaher, 'Racy wear for kids under fire'.
12 Ibid.
13 Carr-Gregg, M. (2006). *The Princess Bitchface Syndrome: Surviving Adolescent Girls*. Camberwell, Vic., Penguin.
14 Needham, Kirsty (2002). 'Baby dolls', *Sydney Morning Herald*, 30 November, p. 29.
15 Hutchinson, J. (2006). 'Bringing up Barbie', *Sunday Herald Sun*, 12 November, pp. 35–8.
16 Rhone, N. (2006). 'Style ideas a good fit for tweens', *Atlanta Journal Constitution*, 21 October, p. FE1.
17 Ibid.
18 Carr-Gregg, *The Princess Bitchface Syndrome*, p. 14.
19 Aedy, R. (2006). 'The Death of Childhood?', *Life Matters*, ABC Radio National, 27 September 2006.
20 McDonnell, K. (2005). *Honey, We Lost the Kids: Re-thinking Childhood in the Multimedia Age* (rev. edn). North Melbourne, Pluto, p. 101.
21 Totaro, P. (2006). 'Silk and lace turn little girls into eye candy', *Sydney Morning Herald*, 18 February, p. 5.
22 Ibid. Also cited in Bantick, C. (2006). 'Too much too soon', *Sunday Mail*, 13 August, p. 54.

23 Tirman, J. (2006). *100 Ways America Is Screwing Up the World*. New York, Harper, p. 240.
24 Rush, E. and A. La Nauze (2006). 'Corporate Paedophilia: Sexualisation of Children in Australia', Discussion Paper No. 90, Australia Institute.
25 See, for example: Johnston, C. (2006) 'Corporate pedophilia' or are some seeing too much in the marketing?', *Age*, 14 October, p. 11, and Pracy, M. (2006). 'Let's look at the bigger picture', *Australian*, 12 October, p. 10, along with the stance of people such as Duncan Fine who, on the *Insight* program 'Bras, Bratz and Tweens' (aired SBS, 17 April 2007), argued (as he has elsewhere), that the concerns being expressed over the sexualisation of children reminded him of repressive regimes such as the Taliban. See also, Fine, D. (2006). 'Parenthood', *Sunday Mail*, 8 October, p. 17.
26 For example: Conway, A. (2006). 'Young ones won't be young for long', *Australian*, 12 October, p. 10, and a letter to the editor, Cartmill, I. (2006). 'Advertisers must accept some responsibility', *Australian*, 13 October, p. 19.
27 Rudd, J. (2001). 'Oops ... childhood's vanished', *Courier-Mail*, 26 March, p. 11.
28 See www.cbc.ca/consumers/market/files/money/sexy/marketing.html. (2006). 'Sex Sells: Marketing and 'Age Compression', retrieved 18 January 2006.
29 McDonnell, *Honey, We Lost the Kids*, pp. 58–9.
30 See Hayne, J. (2004). 'Real Life: Would you let your 8-year-old look like this?', *Sunday Mirror*, London, 23 May, pp. 1–2, and Chester, R. (2003). 'Dollies one minute, dolled up the next', *Courier-Mail*, 12 August, p. 13, for a sample of some of the reportage on not only Morgan, but the potential impact of images like those for which she posed.
31 Hayne, 'Real Life: Would you let your 8-year-old look like this?'.
32 Stolz, G. (2007). 'Family calls in star handler', *Courier-Mail*, 17 September, p. 18.
33 Stolz, G. (2007). 'Too young?', *Courier-Mail*, 14 September, pp. 1–2.
34 Ibid. The judging panel was comprised of a media representative, a fashion photographer, a fashion design academy representative, a designer and a Gold Coast Titans rugby league player, who were 'not made aware of the contestants' ages'.
35 Weston, P. (2007). 'Teen reigns on birthday parade', *Sunday Mail*, 16 September, p. 15.
36 See Paolo Santonastoaso, S. M., Angela Favaro (2002). 'Are Fashion Models a Group at Risk for Eating Disorders and Substance Abuse?', *Psychotherapy and Psychosomatics*, 71(3): 168–72; Knight, I. (2005). 'Bad girl', *Times Online*, London, 25 September.

37 See Stolz, 'Too young?'; Stolz, 'Family calls in star handler'; Sweetman, T. (2007). 'Sending a girl to do a woman's job', *Sunday Mail*, 16 September, p. 63.
38 Ibid.
39 See Chester, 'Dollies one minute, dolled up the next'.
40 John Bastick, the then editor, included this statement by way of apology to his readers for not including a photo of Webster in that issue. In 2006, Webster also posed for *Zoo* magazine, dressed in a bikini with a military helmet on. The picture's shout line read: 'For the Boys: Anzac Special' and featured a black and white montage of war photos behind her.
41 See Giroux, H. A. (2000). *Stealing Innocence: Corporate Culture's War on Children*. New York, Palgrave, pp. 39–64, for an excellent and quite confronting discussion of the subculture of kids' beauty pageants.
42 Ibid., quoted on pp. 50, 39.
43 For more commentary on the JonBenet Ramsay case, see ibid., pp. 44–64, and McDonnell, *Honey, We Lost the Kids*, pp. 55–61.
44 Quoted in Readfearn, 'Status symbol toddlers'.
45 Humphreys, D. (2003). Book Clubbin', *Absolutely Fabulous*. UK.
46 Rushby, A. (2006). 'Desperate housewife', *Courier-Mail*, 12 December, p. 33.
47 Finkelstein, *Slaves of Chic*, p. 118. See also, Bellafante, G. (2003). 'The littlest clotheshorse', *New York Times*, 4 November, p. B11.
48 See Tucker-Evans, A. (2007). 'Stunning cost of formal gowns', *Sunday Mail*, 6 May, p. 11, and Quart, A. (2003). *Branded: The Buying and Selling of Teenagers*. London, Arrow, pp. 82–7, for some examples.
49 'Is your 7-year-old wearing lipstick, too?', *Sunday Mail*, 12 September 2004, p. 41.
50 Ibid.
51 Puente, M. (2006). 'From the sandbox to the spa', *USA Today*, 1 August, retrieved 30 November 2006.
52 See Bantick, 'Too much too soon', p. 54.

chapter four Toy Stories: Growing Up in a Material World
1 Douglas, S. J. (1995). *Where the Girls Are: Growing Up Female with the Mass Media*. New York, Random House, p. 295.
2 Readfearn, G. (2007). 'Pots of fun', *Courier-Mail*, 12 September, p. 45.
3 Quart, A. (2003). *Branded: The Buying and Selling of Teenagers*. London, Arrow, p. 18.
4 Ibid.
5 Clark, E. (2007). *The Real Toy Story: Inside the Ruthless Battle for Britain's Youngest Consumers*. London, Black Swan, pp. 116–17.
6 Quoted in Niedzviecki, H. (2006). *Hello I'm Special: How Individuality*

Became the New Conformity. San Francisco, City Light, p. 142.
7   Inness, S. A. (1999). 'Barbie Gets a Bum Rap: Barbie's Place in the World of Dolls', in McDonough, Y. Z. (ed.), *The Barbie Chronicles: A Living Doll Turns 40*, New York, Bantam; Inness, S. A. (2004). *A Girl Thing: Tough Female Action Figures in the Toy Store*. New York, Palgrave Macmillan.
8   Linn, S. (2004). *Consuming Kids: The Hostile Takeover of Childhood*. New York, The New Press, p. 68.
9   Shields. C. (1999). 'I Believe in Dolls' in McDonough, *The Barbie Chronicles*, p. 187.
10 Clark, *The Real Toy Story*, p. 105.
11 See McDonough (ed.), *The Barbie Chronicles*.
12 Steinberg, S. R. (2004). 'The Bitch Who Has Everything', in Steinberg, S. R. and J. L. Kincheloe (eds) (2004). *Kinderculture: The Corporate Construction of Childhood* (2nd edn). Boulder, Westview, pp. 150–63.
13 Dubin, S. (1999). 'Who's That Girl? The World of Barbie Deconstructed', in McDonough (ed.), *The Barbie Chronicles*, p. 37.
14 Ockman, C. (1999). 'Barbie Meets Bouguereau: Constructing an Ideal Body for the Late Twentieth Century' in ibid., p. 79.
15 Clark, *The Real Toy Story*, p. 105.
16 There are many histories of Barbie available. I used the following to provide this version: McDonough (ed.), *The Barbie Chronicles*, especially Steve Dubin's and Carol Ockman's chapters; Steinberg's chapter on Barbie in Steinberg and Kincheloe (eds), *Kinderculture*; and Clark, *The Real Toy Story*, Chapter 4, 'Barbie Goes to War: Battle of the Dolls'.
17 Clark, *The Real Toy Story*, p. 122.
18 Ibid., pp. 212–20.
19 Ibid., p. 106.
20 See Dubin, 'Who's That Girl?', p. 26.
21 Lovell, J. (2006). 'Barbies go under the hammer', *Courier-Mail*, 27 September, p. 14.
22 Quoted in Bantick, C. (2006). 'Too much too soon', *Sunday Mail*, 13 August, p. 54.
23 Carr-Gregg, M. (2006). *The Princess Bitchface Syndrome: Surviving Adolescent Girls*. Camberwell, Vic., Penguin, p. 17.
24 Clark, *The Real Toy Story*, pp. 118–19.
25 Ibid., p. 121.
26 See Hamer, M. (2002). 'Barbie's got competition', *Age*, 12 December, p. 3.
27 Gregg, N. (2006). 'Ken to the rescue to save Barbie from Bratz', *Courier-Mail*, 11–12 February, p. 11.

28 Quoted in Reed, M. (2005). 'Ho Ho Ho: It's the Bratz Pack', *Age*, 17 December, p. 14.
29 Gibbs, N. (2006). 'The Secret of Barbie's Rivals', *Time*, 20 February, p. 64.
30 Clark, *The Real Toy Story*, p. 125.
31 Reed, 'Ho Ho Ho'.
32 McNamara, S. (2007). *Bratz: The Movie*. USA. In the official *Bratz Magazine Movie Issue*, one of the stars of the film was asked would there be more live-action Bratz movies in the future. Her response was: 'Definitely!! Everyone can look out for Bratz 2! We're gonna dominate movie screens around the world so everyone will know how to show their BRATITUDE!!' ((2007). *Bratz Magazine: Official Bratz Movie Issue*, p. 4). Reviews of the movie are scathing. Jeannette Catsoulis writes that 'this be-yourself message would be more convincing if it weren't so mixed; applauding athleticism while coaxing female jocks into stiletto heels is hardly the height of girl power.' She also notes that 'in human form, however, their craniums appear normal, giving no indication of the acres of retail space within' (Catsoulis, J. (2007). 'Tender Hearts and Lip-Gloss Dreams', *New York Times*, 3 August). John Anderson describes the movie as possessing a 'symphonic awfulness'. Both Lisa and I (we attended a screening the second day of its release) found it exceeded what I confess were low expectations. It was stereotyped, focused on looks and possessions as a form of empowerment and ticked every feminine-equals-manufactured-appearance-and-passivity as well as popularity-is-your-ticket-to-success box.
33 After seeing the movie, I interviewed two young girls, both aged 13, and asked them if they enjoyed the film. They enthusiastically responded 'Yes!' When I asked what messages they felt the film relayed, they were thoughtful for a moment. Taylor said, 'Learn to be friends with everyone and you don't have to be mean', while Elise felt the movie said, 'Don't judge people by what they look like on the outside'. The girls didn't admit to having the dolls, but they had seen the shorts of the movie and felt it 'looked really cool'. They reiterated that they loved the film. Admittedly, I was surprised, but also pleased that the girls took such positive messages away from what I felt was a very ordinary film by any standards, although, at 13, the girls are just outside the Bratz target demographic. Inside the cinema, there were mothers with girls ranging in age from four to late tweens. One mother complained about the movie's superficial content to the usher.
34 See back of packaging.
35 Clark, *The Real Toy Story*, p. 212.
36 Ibid., p. 133.
37 Readfearn, 'Pots of fun', p. 45.

38 Ibid. This article also suggests a variety of alternate forms of play, depending on a child's age, that aren't expensive, such as turning chores into a game, filling a bottom kitchen drawer with non-sharp items, cubby-building, dress-ups (a perennial favourite), and keeping a supply of cardboard boxes for kids to turn into cars, boats, TV sets, rockets etc. Sturgess, who is quoted in Readfearn (p.45), also stresses that parents need to be aware that there's a difference between 'child-minding toys and toys to play with. If parents just keep buying those toys to buy themselves another 10 minutes, then those are not the best sort of toys.'
39 See Jones, Wendy Singer (1999). 'Barbie's Body Project', in McDonough (ed.), *The Barbie Chronicles*, specifically, pp. 98–104, for a discussion of how Barbie promotes a lack of mentoring between generations.
40 Ibid. I found this little gem in the footnotes, p. 220.
41 Smiley, J. (1999). 'You Can Never Have Too Many', in ibid., p. 191.
42 Jones, 'Barbie's Body Project', p. 99.
43 Wolf, N. (1991). *The Beauty Myth: How Images of Beauty Are Used Against Women*. London, Vintage, p. 283.

chapter five Boys and Their Toys: Guns, Swords and Testosterone

1 Linn, S. (2004). *Consuming Kids: The Hostile Takeover of Childhood*. New York, The New Press, p. 67.
2 Steinberg, S. R. and J. L. Kincheloe (eds) (1997). *Kinderculture: The Corporate Construction of Childhood*. Boulder, Westview, p. 25.
3 See Lumby, C. and D. Fine (2006). *Why TV Is Good for Kids: Raising 21st Century Children*. Sydney, Pan Macmillan, Chapter 3, for a discussion about 'Media Violence Panics'.
4 Douglas, S. J. (1995). *Where the Girls Are: Growing Up Female with the Mass Media*. New York, Random House, p. 299.
5 See, for example, arguments presented by Jones, G. (2006). *Killing Monsters: Why Children Need Fantasy, Super Heroes, and Make-Believe Violence*. New York, Basic Books; Linn, S. (2004). *Consuming Kids: The Hostile Takeover of Childhood*. New York, The New Press; and specifically Chapters 7 and 2 of Lumby, C. and D. Fine, *Why TV Is Good for Kids*.
6 See also Jones, *Killing Monsters*, particularly pp. 55–6; and Brooks, K. (2003). 'Nothing Sells like Teen Spirit: The Commodification of Youth Culture', in Mallan, K. and S. Pearce (eds), *Youth Cultures: Texts, Images, and Identities*. London, Praeger, pp. 1–2.
7 Jones, *Killing Monsters*, p. 55.
8 Ibid., quoted on p. 28.
9 Linn, *Consuming Kids*, p. 106.

10 Ibid., pp.106–7. Linn discusses the opinions of child development specialists, professors Diane Levin and Nancy Carlsson-Paige, who argue that 'the impetus for healthy, adaptive war play – or any kind of play with scary and/or violent themes – should come from the children themselves and not from the toys we give them or the media to which they are exposed'.
11 Jones, *Killing Monsters*, p. 225.
12 Ibid., p.132.
13 Ibid., p. 142.
14 Ibid., quoted on p. 195.
15 Bantick, C. (2007). 'Just jolly good fun for boys', *Courier-Mail*, 18–19 August, p. 25.
16 Condon, M. (2007). 'Toys in the attic', *Q Weekend*, p. 20, cites a 2006 Diabetes Australia Report which reveals that 280,000 young people between five and 19 are obese.
17 Ibid.
18 Jones, *Killing Monsters*, p. 16.
19 Condon, 'Toys in the attic', p. 20.
20 Ibid.
21 Ibid., p. 20.
22 Ibid.
23 Ibid., p. 22.
24 Seiter, E. (1995). *Sold Separately: Parents & Children in Consumer Culture*. New Brunswick, New Jersey, Rutgers University Press.
25 Gregory Thomas, S. (2007). *Buy, Buy Baby: How Big Business Captures the Ultimate Consumer – Your Baby or Toddler*. London, Harper Collins, p. 8.
26 MacDonald, J. (2003). 'Smarter Toys, Smarter Tots?', *Christian Science Monitor*, p. 12.
27 Gregory Thomas, *Buy, Buy Baby*, p. 9.
28 Molloy, F. (2006). 'Can High-Tech Toys Make Kids Smarter?', *LiveWire, Age*, 23 November.
29 Ibid.
30 Ibid., p. 15.
31 Ibid.
32 Linn, *Consuming Kids*, p. 67.
33 Gregory Thomas, *Buy, Buy Baby*, p. 20.
34 Ibid., p. 216.
35 Molloy, 'Can High-Tech Toys Make Kids Smarter?'.
36 Gregory Thomas, *Buy, Buy Baby*, pp. 98–100.
37 Niedzviecki, H. (2006). *Hello I'm Special: How Individuality Became the New Conformity*. San Francisco, City Light, pp. 230–1.
38 Linn, *Consuming Kids*, p. 33.

chapter six The D'oh of Homer: The Questionable Wisdom of the Electronic Babysitter

1. Hall, S. (1976). *Supertoy: Twenty Years of Australian Television*. Melbourne, Sun Books, pp. 28–9.
2. See Curthoys, A. (1986). 'The Getting of Television: Dilemmas in Ownership, Control and Culture 1941–1956', in Curthoys, A. and J. Merritt (eds), *Better Dead than Read: Australia's First Cold War 1945–1959*, vol. 2. Sydney, Allen & Unwin, pp. 123–54.
3. Boyer, S. R. (1957). 'Television in Perspective', *Australian Quarterly*, 26: 15–21; quote from p. 17.
4. McLuhan, M. (1964). *Understanding Media: The Extension of Man*. London, Routledge, pp. 7–23.
5. Tom Loncar, P. F. and Julie Dalziel (2005). *Digital Media in Australian Homes*. Sydney, Australian Communications and Media Authority.
6. Christakis, D. A., F. J. Zimmerman, D. L. DiGuiseppe and C. A. McCarty (2004). 'Early Television Exposure and Subsequent Attentional Problems in Children', *Pediatrics*, 113: 708–13.
7. See Rideout et al. (2003). 'Zero to Six', *The Henry J. Kaiser Family Foundation*, Fall: 2–36; Linn, S. (2004). *Consuming Kids: The Hostile Takeover of Childhood*. New York, The New Press; Palmer, S. (2006). *Toxic Childhood: How the Modern World Is Damaging Our Children and What We Can Do About It*. London, Orion Books; Barker, R. (2004). 'TV and Your Child', *The Australian Women's Weekly*, June, pp. 145–6; Collins, R. L., M. N. Elliott, S. H. Berry, D. E. Kanouse, D. Kunkel, S. B. Hunter, A. Miu (2004). 'Watching Sex on Television Predicts Adolescent Initiation of Sexual Behavior', *Pediatrics*, 114: 280–9; Lumby, C. and D. Fine (2006). *Why TV Is Good for Kids: Raising 21st Century Children*. Sydney, Pan Macmillan.
8. Quoted in Curthoys, 'The Getting of Television', pp. 123–54, 135.
9. Grant, G. (1956). 'Television and Us', *Overland*, July: 7–8.
10. (1995). *Glued to the Television*. Melbourne, Vixen Films.
11. Quoted in Fynes-Clinton, J. (2006). 'The kids are all right', *Courier-Mail*, 15–16 July, p. 51.
12. (1995). *Glued to the Television*.
13. See Lumby and Fine, *Why TV Is Good for Kids*, particularly Chapter 2, 'TV Panics: Media Villains', which provides a discussion of studies that argue in favour of (moderated and moderate) TV viewing.
14. See McDonnell, K. (2000). *Kid Culture: Children and Adults and Popular Culture*. Toronto, Pluto; Lumby and Fine, *Why TV Is Good for Kids*, pp. 58–9.
15. McDonnell, *Kid Culture*, p. 14.
16. Gerbner, G. (1994). 'TV Violence and the Art of Asking the Wrong

Question', Centre for Media Literacy, www.medialit.org/reading_room/article459.htm
17 See Mackay, H. (2002). *Media Mania: Why Our Fear of Modern Media Is Misplaced*. Sydney, University of New South Wales Press. The chapter entitled 'What Kind of Violence' provides a discussion of media violence.
18 See (2006). 'www.babyfirsttv.com', retrieved 7 December, for some examples of programming and testimonies on the blog from 'happy' parents.
19 Quoted in Brzezinski, M. (2006). 'Baby's First TV Channel', retrieved 11 May 2006.
20 Ibid.
21 Press, A. (2006). '24-hour baby channel debuts to gurgles and a few groans', retrieved 11 May 2006.
22 Palmer, *Toxic Childhood*. See also Gregory Thomas, S. (2007). *Buy, Buy Baby: How Big Business Captures the Ultimate Consumer – Your Baby or Toddler*. London, Harper Collins. In Chapter 4, Gregory Thomas discusses the difference between 'foreground' and 'background' TV and its impact on babies and toddlers. Foreground TV is that which is designed specifically for kids in these age groups (e.g. Baby Einstein videos and anything on BabyFirst TV), while background television refers to anything else (p. 94). Research concludes that the target audience gain nothing from foreground TV except 'strong character recognition'; in other words, inculcation in a brand. As for background TV, it not only reduces adult/child interaction (by 22 per cent), but distracts kids from focused play (pp. 94–8).
23 See Palmer, *Toxic Childhood*, p.114.
24 See ibid., p. 255; Linn, *Consuming Kids*.
25 Christakis, D. A., F. J. Zimmerman, D. L. DiGuiseppe and C. A. McCarty (2004). 'Early Television Exposure and Subsequent Attentional Problems in Children', *Pediatrics*, 113: 708–13. See p. 710 specifically.
26 Landhuis, C. E., R. Poulton, D. Welch and R. J. Hancox (2007). 'Does Childhood Television Viewing Lead to Attention Problems in Adolescence? Results from a Prospective Longitudinal Study', *Pediatrics*, 120(3): 532–7.
27 See Rideout et al. 'Zero to Six', pp. 2–36, p. 5.; Linn, *Consuming Kids*, p. 55; Palmer, *Toxic Childhood*, p. 255.
28 See Hardy, L. L., L. A. Baur, S. P. Garnett, D. Crawford, K. J. Campbell, V. A. Shrewsbury, C. T. Cowell and J. Salmon (2006). 'Family and Home Correlates of Television Viewing in 12–13 Year Old Adolescents: The Nepean Study', *International Journal of Behavioural Nutrition and*

Physical Activity, 3(24), pp. 1–8 published online; Marsden, S. (2007). 'Kids hurt by TV diet', *Courier-Mail*, 20 February, p. 14; Rideout et al., 'Zero to Six', pp. 2–36, p. 5.
29 Rideout et al. see graph p. 5.
30 See Lister, D. (2006). 'Lure of television is stronger than a smile', *The Times*, London, 7 November, p. 9, who quotes Martin Doherty, a lecturer in psychology and co-author of the study with Dr Markus Bindemann, who says: 'How a child has been socialised in the first few years of life will seriously affect whether he or she engages with people or engages with a television screen'.
31 Hardy et al., 'Family and Home Correlates of Television Viewing in 12–13 Year Old Adolescents', p. 2.
32 Ibid.
33 ABC Radio National's *Life Matters* program, hosted by Richard Aedy, dedicated a show to children's TV (21 September 2007) and its worthiness, whether we, as adults, care about what our children watch and the relevance of kids' TV in the age of downloading and other digital technology. Patricia Edgar, founder of the Australian Children's Television Foundation, said: 'Good TV is good for kids', acknowledging that some TV fare is very mediocre. Other guests were Duncan Fine (co-author of *Why TV Is Good for Kids* and kids' tv writer, for example, *High-5*) and Jenny Buckland (Chief Executive, Australian Children's Television Foundation). Callers admitted both their reliance on TV to entertain and distract their children, but also their concerns about content – violence and sexism. Some callers also expressed their appreciation of the sophistication and humour of some kids' shows.
34 Ibid.
35 McDonnell, K. (2005). *Honey, We Lost the Kids: Re-thinking Childhood in the Multimedia Age* (rev. edn). North Melbourne, Pluto, p. 71.
36 Ibid., p. 83.
37 Lumby and Fine, *Why TV Is Good for Kids*, p. 73.
38 See Collins et al., 'Watching Sex on Television Predicts Adolescent Initiation of Sexual Behavior', pp. 280–9; Martino, S. C., R. L. Collins, M. N. Elliott, A. Strachman, D. E. Kanouse and S. H. Berry (2006). 'Exposure to Degrading Versus Nondegrading Music Lyrics and Sexual Behavior Among Youth', *Pediatrics*, 118: 430–41, for interesting and disturbing discussions.
39 Linn, *Consuming Kids*, p. 111, gives an example of 'aspirational' in regards to marketing, explaining that it's when 'teens are seen as aspirational twentysomethings and twelve-year-olds are described as aspirational seventeen-year-olds'.

40 Johnson, S. (2005). *Everything Bad Is Good for You: How Popular Culture Is Making Us Smarter*. London, Allen Lane, pp. 62–115.
41 Irwin, W., M. T. Conard and A.J. Skoble (eds) (2001). *The Simpsons and Philosophy: The D'oh! of Homer*. Chicago, Open Court, p. 1.
42 Corliss, R. (1998). 'The Cartoon Character: Bart Simpson', *Time*, 8 June, pp. 204–5.
43 Bargreen, M., M. M. Bayley, M. Berson, J. Harti, P. MacDonald, K. Mcfadden, M. Upchurch, R. Updike, D. Kim (2000). '7 Works That Changed the Millennium', *Seattle Times*, 2 January, p. E1.
44 Daily, W. (2003). 'Simpson, eh? Homer voted world's greatest American', retrieved 28 June 2007.
45 Online, B. N. (2001). 'Homer voted top TV star', retrieved 25 June 2007.
46 Network, B. O. (1999). '"Top Dad Homer "Icon for Blair"', retrieved 25 June 2007. The same article also cites Adrienne Burgess, author of the book *Fatherhood*, who warns against praising Homer too much as he is also 'a fool, reinforcing cultural stereotypes of fathers as buffoons'.
47 For lively discussions on *The Simpsons*, see Irwin et al. (eds), *The Simpsons and Philosophy*. For a fan's very informative perspective on the show, see Turner, C. (2004). *Planet Simpson*. London, Ebury.
48 Rideout et al., 'Zero to Six', pp. 2–36.
49 Palmer, *Toxic Childhood*, p. 257.
50 Hardy et al., 'Family and Home Correlates of Television Viewing in 12–13 Year Old Adolescents'.
51 See Royal Australasian College of Physicians: Paediatrics and Child Health Division (2004). 'Children and the Media: Advocating for the Future'. ww.racp.edu.au/hpu/paed/media.
52 Australian Bureau of Statistics (2003). *Children's Participation in Cultural and Leisure Activities*. Canberra.
53 See Rideout et al., 'Zero to Six', pp. 2–36.
54 Hardy et al., 'Family and Home Correlates of Television Viewing in 12–13 Year Old Adolescents', p. 5.
55 Sargent, J. D. and I. Sharif (2006). 'Association Between Television, Movie and Video Game Exposure and School Performance', *Pediatrics*, 118(4), pp. 1061–70. According to a newspaper report from Scotland, another study found that the average British child aged four to six watches 16 hours of TV a week and by their teens, 'four out of five have a television in their bedroom'. See Lister, D. (2006). 'Lure of television is stronger than a smile', *The Times*, London, 7 November, p. 9.
56 See Sargent, 'Association Between Television, Movie and Video Game Exposure and School Performance', pp. 1061–70; Australian Bureau of Statistics, *Children's Participation in Cultural and Leisure Activities*.

57 Hardy et al., 'Family and Home Correlates of Television Viewing in 12–13 Year Old Adolescents', p. 5.
58 See Palmer, *Toxic Childhood*; Rideout et al., 'Zero to Six', pp. 2–36.
59 See Linn, *Consuming Kids*, p. 5; Palmer, *Toxic Childhood*, p. 230.
60 Lumby and Fine, *Why TV Is Good for Kids*, pp. 94–5. Note also that Associate Professor Lumby is a member of the Advertising Standards Bureau.
61 Johnson, *Everything Bad Is Good for You*, p. 97.
62 See 'Aunty targets kids with own channel', *Courier-Mail*, 24 September 2007, p. 19.
63 Mackay, *Media Mania*, p. 15.

chapter seven Sense and Censorship: Film and the Uncomfortable Question of Parental Guidance

1 Turner, G. (1999). *Film as Social Practice* (3rd edn). London, Routledge, p. 1.
2 See ibid., pp. 1–32.
3 Ibid, p. 113.
4 Giroux, Henry (1997). 'Are Disney Movies Good for Kids?', in Steinberg, S. R. and J. L. Kincheloe (eds), *Kinderculture: The Corporate Construction of Childhood*. Boulder, Westview, p. 54.
5 Turner, *Film as Social Practice*, p. 8.
6 Office of Film and Literature Classification, 'The Classification Board/National Classification Scheme', retrieved 15 May 2007.
7 Johnson, S. (2005). *Everything Bad Is Good for You: How Popular Culture Is Making Us Smarter*. London, Allen Lane, p. 12.
8 See also Michael, P. (2007). 'Screens top fear factor', *Courier-Mail*, 6 September, p. 17. This article discusses a study conducted by Dr Jocelyn Gordon of Monash University that examined the impact that scary films and TV shows have on children's sleep. The study reported that 87 per cent of eight- to nine-year-olds suffered night-time fears, while 55 per cent of 15- to 16-year-olds still had anxieties. Gordon argues that 'there is a need for parents to supervise the viewing habits of their children, in particular, younger children, and to be selective and discerning about their children's television and movie exposure'.
9 Goodman, E. (2005). 'Parents at a loss when it comes to editing kids media', *Desert News*, Salt Lake City, 5 August, p. E1.
10 Partridge, D. (2006). 'Swashbucklers plunder box office records', *Courier-Mail*, 11 July, p. 11.
11 Johnson, *Everything Bad Is Good for You*, pp. 9–12, 62–115, 131–6.
12 Ibid., p. 127.
13 Ibid., p. 129.

14 See Collins, R. L., M. N. Elliott, M. N. Elliott, A. Strachman, D. E. Kanouse and S. H. Berry (2004). 'Watching Sex on Television Predicts Adolescent Initiation of Sexual Behavior', *Pediatrics*, 114: 280–9, for a discussion of sex on TV and adolescent sexual experience. See also the contributions by Carol J. Pardun ('Romancing the Script: Identifying the Romantic Agenda in Top-Grossing Movies' and Jeanne R. Steele, 'Teens and Movies: Something to do, Plenty to Learn') in Brown, J. D., J. R. Steele and K. Walsh-Childers (eds) (2002). *Sexual Teens, Sexual Media: Investigating Media's Influence on Adolescent Sexuality*. Mahwah, Lawrence Erlbaum Associates. For example, Pardun writes that 'Bachen and Illouz (1996) found that 94% of the young people in their study looked to television and 90% to movies for love stories. In contrast, only one third said they looked to their mothers and only 17% looked to their fathers to learn about romantic love. Pierce (1993) has argued that teen girls look to magazines to understand their love "script".' (p. 213)
15 Pardun, 'Romancing the Script', p. 213.
16 Steele, 'Teens and Movies', p. 249.
17 Quart, A. (2003). *Branded: The Buying and Selling of Teenagers*. London, Arrow, p. 101.
18 Ibid., p.102.
19 See ibid, pp. 102–25.
20 Ibid., p. 114.
21 Ibid., p. 118.
22 Miles, H. (2006). 'Dangerous exposure', *Courier-Mail*, 16 May, p. 19.
23 Giroux, H. A. (1997). *Channel Surfing: RaceTalk and the Destruction of Today's Youth*. London, Macmillan, p. 31.

chapter eight Once Upon a Time: Disney, Harry Potter, Hans Christian Andersen and Other Grimm Tales

1 'The singing detectives', *Sunday Mail*, 19 November 2006, p. 46.
2 Linn, S. (2004). *Consuming Kids: The Hostile Takeover of Childhood*. New York, The New Press, p. 107.
3 Kellner, D. (1997). 'Beavis and Butthead: No Future for Postmodern Youth', in Steinberg, S. R. and J. L. Kincheloe (eds), *Kinderculture: The Corporate Construction of Childhood*. Boulder, Westview, p. 85.
4 Stewart, J. B. (2006). *Disney War: The Battle for the Magic Kingdom*. London, Pocket Books, p. 11.
5 Giroux, H. A. (1999). *The Mouse That Roared: Disney and the End of Innocence*. New York, Rowman & Littlefield, pp. 67–79; Allman, T. D. (2007). 'The Theme-Parking, Megachurching, Franchising, Exurbing, McMansioning of America: How Walt Disney Changed Everything', *National Geographic*, March: 96–115.

6   See Giroux, *The Mouse That Roared*; Stewart, *Disney War*.
7   Giroux, *The Mouse That Roared*, p. 86.
8   Ibid., p. 90.
9   Ibid., p. 110.
10 Tatar, M. (1992). *Off with Their Heads: Fairytales and the Culture of Childhood*. Princeton, New Jersey, Princeton University Press, p. xxvii.
11 Tatar, M. (ed.) (1999). *The Classic Fairy Tales*. New York, W. W. Norton, pp. xi–xix.
12 See particularly, Tatar, M. (1987). *The Hard Facts of the Grimms' Fairy Tales*. Princeton, New Jersey, Princeton University Press; Warner, M. (1995). *From the Beast to the Blonde: On Fairy Tales and Their Tellers*. London, Vintage; Zipes, J. (1999). *When Dreams Came True: Classical Fairy Tales and Their Tradition*. New York, Routledge.
13 Tatar, M. (1997). 'Introduction', in *Grimm's Grimmest*. San Francisco, Chronicle Books, p. 9.
14 See ibid. and Zipes, *When Dreams Came True*, pp. 61–79, for his chapter on the Grimm brothers.
15 Tatar (ed.), *The Classic Fairy Tales*, p. xii.
16 Other fairytales have also influenced reality TV. For example, *The Swan* and *Extreme Makeover* are thinly disguised versions of 'The Ugly Duckling' by Hans Christian Andersen; while *What Not to Wear* and *How to Look Good Naked* can be interpreted as either 'The Ugly Duckling' or even 'The Emperor's New Clothes'.
17 Tatar (ed.), *The Classic Fairy Tales*, pp. 107–8.
18 Ibid., pp. 101–7.
19 See ibid., for an excellent summary of the variations of the Cinderella story.
20 See Perrault's version in Tatar, M. (2002). 'Introduction', in *The Annotated Classic Fairy Tales*. New York, W. W. Norton, pp. 28–43.
21 A version like this can be found in Tatar (ed.), *The Classic Fairy Tales*, pp. 117–21.
22 Andersen, H. (1968). *Hans Andersen's Fairy Tales*. Prague, The Hamyln Publishing Group, pp. 139–58.
23 For more information, see the fascinating biography by Andersen, J. (2005). *Hans Christian Andersen: A New Life*. New York, Woodstock.
24 Giroux, *The Mouse That Roared*, p. 96.
25 Cox, J. L. (1995). *Fairytales and their Functions: The Study of Three Tales in their 'Original' and 'Disney-fied' States*. Faculty of Humanities thesis, Griffith University.
26 Giroux, H. A. (2002). *Breaking into Movies: Film and the Culture of Politics*. Maiden, Blackwell, p. 114.
27 Ibid., pp. 106, 114.

28 Zipes, J. (2002). *The Brothers' Grimm: From Enchanted Forests to Modern World.* New York, Palgrave Macmillan, p. 60.
29 Mahadi, M. (1990). *The Arabian Nights.* New York, W. W. Norton, p. xiii.
30 Ibid.
31 Stewart, *Disney War*, pp. 106, 123–4.
32 Ibid., p. 123.
33 Giroux, *The Mouse That Roared*, p. 105. Giroux quotes Yousef Salem, a former spokesperson for the South Bay Islamic Association, who says that 'All of the bad guys [in *Aladdin*] have beards and large, bulbous noses, sinister eyes and heavy accents, and they're wielding swords constantly. Aladdin doesn't have a big nose; he has a small nose. He doesn't have a beard or a turban. He doesn't have an accent. What makes him nice is that they've given him this American character … I have a daughter who says she's ashamed to call herself an Arab, and it's because of things like this.' (p. 194)
34 Ibid., pp. 104–5. See also Stewart, *Disney War*; Giroux, H. (2004). 'Are Disney Movies Good for Kids', in Steinberg, S. R. and J. L. Kincheloe (eds), *Kinderculture: The Corporate Construction of Childhood* (2nd edn). Boulder, Westview, p. 174.
35 See Phillips, J. and I. Wojcik-Andrews (1996). 'Telling Tales to Children: The Pedagogy of Empire in MGM's *Kim* and Disney's *Aladdin*', *The Lion and the Unicorn*, 20(1): 66–89. See p. 82.
36 Hopkins, S. (2002). *Girl Heroes: The New Force in Popular Culture.* Annandale, NSW, Pluto, pp. 141–2.
37 DoRozario, R.-A. (2004). 'The Princess and the Magic Kingdom: Beyond Nostalgia, the Function of the Disney Princess', *Women's Studies in Communication*, 27(1), p. 49.
38 Ross, D. (2004). 'Escape from Wonderland: Disney and the Female Imagination', *Marvels and Tales*, 18(1), p. 61.
39 Giroux, *The Mouse That Roared*, p. 108.
40 See Stewart, *Disney War*, for an interesting discussion of the relationship between Disney CEO Michael Eisner and Jeffrey Katzenberg and the films that were produced under their creative influence.
41 Hopkins, *Girl Heroes*, p. 143.
42 Schlesinger Jr, A. (2001). 'What Great Books Do for Children', *The American Enterprise*, 12(5), p. 47.
43 See Eccleshare, J. (2002). *A Guide to the Harry Potter Novels.* London, Continuum; Nel, P. (2002). *J. K. Rowling's Harry Potter Novels.* New York, Continuum.
44 Bouquet, T. (2001). 'The Wizard Behind Harry Potter', *Reader's Digest*, April: 71–8. pp. 76–7.
45 Quoted in Nuckols, B. (2007). 'Mining the imagination', *Courier-Mail*, 18 January, p. 37.

46 See Eccleshare, *A Guide to the Harry Potter Novels*, Part 1.
47 See, for example, Zipes, J. (2002). *Sticks and Stones: The Troublesome Success of Children's Literature from Slovenly Peter to Harry Potter*. New York, Routledge, pp. 170–2.
48 Eccleshare, *A Guide to the Harry Potter Novels*, p. 85.
49 Crittenden, D. (1999). 'Boy meets book: How to get a boy to read? Try risk, derring-do (No vacuum cleaners, please)', *Wall Street Journal*, 26 November, p. 13.
50 'Morals and the trouble with Harry', *Courier-Mail*, 29 January 2001, p. 8. Furthermore, Gullio remarked after reading that there were four murders in the first chapter of the fourth book, 'he did not need to read any more of the books to know they should not be in his school library'. An educator should be in the business of understanding something by 'knowing' it to the best of his ability; that is, reading the books in their entirety before making a judgement call.
51 'What's wrong with a little Harry magic?', *Herald Sun*, 4 July 2003, p. 16.
52 This has been noted by many critics, see particularly Eccleshare, *A Guide to the Harry Potter Novels*; Nel, P. (2002). *J. K. Rowling's Harry Potter Novels*; and Zipes, *Sticks and Stones*, pp. 170–89.
53 See Brooks, K. (2001). 'Children's classic invokes pagan hope', *Courier-Mail*, 10 November, p. 23.
54 See Cleary, S. and S. Taylor (2007). 'Pure Magic'. *Sixty Minutes*. Australia. Reporter Tara Brown spoke of the marketing spin-offs based on the Harry Potter series, including a proposed theme park.
55 Zipes, *Sticks and Stones*, p. 172.
56 Quoted in Neill, R. (2007). 'Strangled by success', *Weekend Australian*, 30 June – 1 July, p. 6.
57 Gregory Thomas, S. (2007). *Buy, Buy Baby: How Big Business Captures the Ultimate Consumer – Your Baby or Toddler*. London, Harper Collins, p. 165.
58 Engelhardt, T. (1991). 'Reading may be harmful to your kids', *Harper's Magazine*, 282: 55–62.
59 Gregory Thomas, *Buy, Buy Baby*, p. 172.
60 Ibid., p. 177.
61 Jenkins, H. (2006). *Fans, Bloggers and Games*. New York, New York University Press, p. 195.

chapter nine **Give Me Some MySpace: The Cyberlution of Social Networking and Electronic Games**

1 Kerr, A. (2006). *The Business and Culture of Digital Games: Gamework/Gameplay*. London, Sage, pp. 13–14.

2   Lalor, P. (2007). 'Game on', *Weekend Australian*, 15–16 September, pp. 4–5. Second Life is a fantasy/sci-fi world where users can 'build' or adopt an 'avatar' (a two-dimensional representation of themselves; there are a number of standard models available). You register a name, usually nothing like your own, and then you join this ever-expanding world. You can either explore and interact with the population (at a basic level, you type conversation in real time, much like MSN chat), and wander or 'teleport' from location to location. If you are really keen, and many users are, you can spend money (Second Life has its own currency but you must buy it with real credit!), and update your avatar, that is, personalise it – buy it new clothes and change its appearance. This is very tempting, as I found when I joined, as it is quite disconcerting to wander around this new world and continually bump into a being who looks exactly like you. You can also purchase real estate, shop, and perform both mundane and extraordinary tasks in this digital universe.
3   Livingstone, S. (2002). *Young People and New Media*. London, Sage, p. 2.
4   Jenkins, H. (2006). *Fans, Bloggers and Games*. New York, New York University Press, p. 196.
5   Grossman, L. (2006). 'The people's network', *Time*, 20 November, pp. 44–7.
6   Levy, S. and B. Stone (2006). 'The new wisdom of the web', *Newsweek*, April, p. 47.
7   See, for example, Schliebs, M. and AAP (2007). 'Police investigate MySpace "RIP"', News.com.au, 23 April; Oakes, D. (2007). 'MySpace link to teens found dead in bush', theage.com.au, 23 April.
8   Rush, W. (2005) 'Social Networking 3.0.' *Technology Review*, 18 November, p. E1.
9   Wood, M. (2005). 'Five reasons social networking doesn't work', CNet.com.
10 Rose, K. (2006). 'MySpace the place to land Jet', *Herald Sun*, 15 August, p. 7.
11 Dudley-Nicholson, J. (2007). 'A new guest book for all your friends', *Courier-Mail*, 5 September, p. 4.
12 Levy and Stone, 'The new wisdom of the web'.
13 See Jesdanun, A. (2007). 'MySpace offers a watchful eye', *Courier-Mail*, 24 January, p. 47; Hansell, S. (2006). 'MySpace to add restrictions to protect younger teenagers', *New York Times*, 21 June, p. C2.
14 See 'MySpace faces legal action over sex abuse claims', www.independent.ie, 19 January 2007, and Cashmore, P. (2007). 'MySpace sued by parents who don't keep an eye on their kids', www.mashable.com, 18 January, p. E1.

15 Eichenwald, K. (2005). 'Through his webcam, a boy joins a sordid online world', *New York Times*, 19 December, p. A1.
16 Hintz, P. (2007). 'Safest space for children to play', *Courier-Mail*, 5 September, pp. 4–5.
17 'Teens show they can look after themselves online' *Courier-Mail*, 5 January 2007, p. 12.
18 Jenkins, *Fans, Bloggers and Games*, p. 179.
19 See Cloud, J. (2006–2007). 'The Youtube gurus', *Time*, 25 December – 1 January, pp. 46–52.
20 Grossman, 'The people's network', pp. 44–7.
21 Press, A. (2007). 'Empowering people one YouTube clip at a time', retrieved 19 May 2007.
22 Cloud, 'The Youtube gurus'.
23 Levy and Stone, 'The new wisdom of the web.'
24 Ibid.
25 Ibid.
26 Hintz, P. (2007). 'Safest space for children to play', *Courier-Mail*, 5 September, pp. 4–5.
27 Giroux, H. A. (2000). *Stealing Innocence: Corporate Culture's War on Children*. New York, Palgrave, p. 13.
28 Prensky, M. (2006). *'Don't Bother Me Mom – I'm Learning!'*, St Paul, Paragon House, p. xx.
29 See Clark, L. (2007). 'Predators unmasked', *Courier-Mail*, 8 February, p. 32.
30 Palmer, S. (2006). *Toxic Childhood: How the Modern World Is Damaging Our Children and What We Can Do About It*. London, Orion Books, pp. 259–60. Palmer also discusses the 'Digital Divide'.
31 Carr-Gregg, quoted in Critchley, C. (2007). 'Schools cave in to sleepy teens', *Herald Sun/Adelaide Now*, Melbourne/Adelaide, 4 May.
32 Palmer, *Toxic Childhood*, p. 94.
33 Ibid., p. 93.
34 Carr-Gregg, M. (2005). *Surviving Adolescents: The Must-Have Manual for Parents*. Camberwell, Vic., Penguin, pp. 97–8; Fallik, D. (2006). 'Too wired for 40 winks', *Courier-Mail*, 29 March, p. 16; McLean, T. (2006). 'Bedtime TV spells trouble for teens', *Courier-Mail*, 27 July, p. 31; Carr-Gregg, M. (2007). 'Sweet dreams make better teens', *Herald Sun*, 18 January, p. 18; Edwards, H. (2006). 'Exhausted students tap in to SMS instead of REM', *Sydney Morning Herald*, 5 February, p. 16.
35 See Eggemont, S. and J. Van den Bulck (2006). 'Nodding Off or Switching Off? The Use of Popular Media as a Sleep Aid in Secondary-School Children', *Paediatrics and Child Health*, 42 (7–8), pp. 428–33.
36 McLean, 'Bedtime TV spells trouble for teens', p. 31.

37 Dr McDowell recommends this as well to prevent disruption to kids' sleep patterns.
38 Wallis, C. (2006). 'The multitasking generation', *Time*, 10 April, pp. 46–53.
39 Ibid., pp. 49–53.
40 Hallowell, quoted in ibid., p. 53.
41 Jenkins, *Fans, Bloggers and Games*, p. 202.
42 Wenham, M. (2006). 'Mums the real heroes', *Courier-Mail*, 1 August, p. 15.
43 Palmer, *Toxic Childhood*, p. 263.
44 Bunce, J. (2007). 'Phone firms target kids', *Courier-Mail*, 19 February, p. 8.
45 Lalor, 'Game on', pp. 4–5.
46 Kerr, *The Business and Culture of Digital Games*, p. 13.
47 Ibid., pp. 14–15.
48 Ibid., p. 15.
49 Ibid., p. 18.
50 Ibid., p. 19.
51 Jenkins, *Fans, Bloggers and Games*, p. 203.
52 Ibid., p. 207.
53 Johnson, S. (2005). *Everything Bad Is Good for You: How Popular Culture Is Making Us Smarter*. London, Allen Lane, p. 21.
54 Ibid., p. 40.
55 Ibid., p. 59.
56 Grossman, L. (2004). 'The art of the virtual: Are video games starting to – gasp! – mean something?', *Time*, 8 November, p. 64.
57 Lalor, 'Game on', pp. 4–5. There is also the growing popularity of the Massive Multi-Player Online Role-Playing Games (MMPORGs) to consider. Some, such as World of Warcraft (WoW), have about 8.5 million players worldwide (see Readfearn, G. (2007). 'Games ate my life', *Courier-Mail*, 25 July, pp. 45–6).
58 See Johnson, *Everything Bad Is Good for You*, p. 61.
59 Wallis, 'The multitasking generation', p. 49.

chapter ten My Little Prince/ss: Why Kids Don't Always Have to Feel 'Special'

1 An adjunct to this whole notion is what US academic Naomi Wolf calls the 'beauty myth' (see Wolf, N. (1991). *The Beauty Myth: How Images of Beauty Are Used Against Women*. London, Vintage). She discusses how, since the 1980s, 'beauty' has given women power in much the same way that money provides that status for men. But she also talks about the hollowness of being hailed as an object of beauty for those who seek fulfilment through aesthetics. Another interesting analysis of the effects of what is now a beauty industry can be found in Kuczynski, A. (2007). *Beauty Junkies: Under the Skin of the Cosmetic Surgery Industry*.

London, Vintage. Kuczynski not only reveals the marketing that goes on behind the scenes of cosmetic surgery (including labelling a particular brand of post-surgery bandages as 'sexy'), but discusses how beauty is a contemporary currency that women and men, from increasingly younger ages, are being persuaded they have to invest in. Ageing is now treated like a disease that can be cured.
2. Mackay, H. (2006). 'So much love, but sadly it's the wrong kind', *Sydney Morning Herald*, 16 December, p. 36.
3. Corrigan, S. (2004). 'Now it's OK to be cruel to be kind', *Courier-Mail*, 24 April, p. 31.
4. Collins, C. (2007). 'Self-esteem overdose', *Courier-Mail*, 5 March, p. 39.
5. Corrigan, 'Now it's OK to be cruel to be kind'.
6. See Bredemeyer, L. (2004). 'Student finds fame at Idol audition'. *ACUoptimist.com*, 11 February, p. E1.
7. Corrigan, 'Now it's OK to be cruel to be kind'.
8. Ibid.
9. Ibid.
10. Carr-Gregg, M. (2006). *The Princess Bitchface Syndrome: Surviving Adolescent Girls*. Camberwell, Vic., Penguin.
11. Bronson, P. (2007). 'Why it's wrong to praise your kids', *Weekend Australian*, 28–29 April, pp. 14–19. See also Horin, A. and A. Patty (2006). 'Stop doing the homework, overzealous parents warned', *Sydney Morning Herald*, 23 September, p. 1; Williams, D. (2005). 'Parents behaving badly', *Time*, 16 May, pp. 44–51.
12. Irvine, J. (2005). 'Top 10 parenting mistakes', *Sunshine Coast Daily*, 28 December, p. 32.
13. Carr-Gregg, *The Princess Bitchface Syndrome*, p. xv.
14. Aedy, R. (2006). 'The Death of Childhood?', *Life Matters*, ABC Radio National, 27 September.
15. See Harris, S. (2006). 'Nasty little angels', *Sunday Mail*, 14 May, p. 35.
16. Quoted in Corrigan, 'Now it's OK to be cruel to be kind'.
17. Orenstein, P. (2007). 'Litte Miss Cliche', *Courier-Mail*, 28–29 April, pp. 22–5.
18. Ibid., p. 22.
19. There is also a series of books called *The Tiara Club*. The boxed set includes a small doll complete with tiara.
20. Corrigan, 'Now it's OK to be cruel to be kind'.
21. Niedzviecki, H. (2006). *Hello I'm Special: How Individuality Became the New Conformity*. San Francisco, City Light. p. 5.
22. Davies, H. (2006). 'Model-hunter in tax strife', *Sunday Mail*, 5 November, p. 37.
23. Tucker-Evans, A. (2006). 'The $45 dummy', *Sunday Mail*, 14 May, p. 40.
24. Niedzviecki, *Hello I'm Special*, p. 66.

25 Mackay, H. (2007). *Advance Australia ... Where? How We've Changed, Why We've Changed and What Will Happen Next*. Sydney, Hachette, pp. 191–7. The 'Little Emperor Syndrome' gestures to the fact that most families in the Western world are having less children. Just as China's one-child policy meant that the only child born to the family was cosseted and fussed over, so too this tendency to idolise, adore and provide in abundance for the 'only' child has spread to other countries, including Australia.
26 Mackay, 'So much love, but sadly it's the wrong kind', p. 36.
27 Horswill, A. (2007). 'Kids need "down time"', *Courier-Mail*, 2 July, p. 33.
28 Metlikovec, J. (2006). 'Kids hurt by sports monster', *Herald Sun*, 13 October, p. 17.
29 Ibid.
30 Barry, J. (2004). 'Building a healthy self-esteem', *Courier-Mail*, 31 January, p. 5.
31 Hamilton, A. (2006). 'Gandalf, Arsenal, it's dinnertime', *Weekend Australian*, 18 November, p. 17.
32 'Partee Petite: Big Parties for Little People', www.parteepetite.com.au, retrieved 18 December 2006.
33 Collins, M. (2007). 'Party bags are a contest for Mum', *Sunday Mail*, 15 April, p. 59.
34 Ibid.
35 Whiting, F. (2006). 'Parents crash the party', *Sunday Mail*, 3 December, p. 16.
36 See Foster, K. (2005). 'Would you let your 4-year-old go for a makeover?' *Scotland on Sunday*, 24 June; Hill, A. (2005). 'Why beauty spas thank heaven for little girls', *The Observer*, 1 May, retrieved 1 July 2007.
37 Foster, 'Would you let your 4-year-old go for a makeover?'
38 Aedy, R. (2006). 'The Resilience of Children's Culture'. *Life Matters*, ABC Radio National, 20 February. Dr Jean Kilbourne discusses the incidence of the growing popularity of fake tans with tweens, as well as that 70 per cent of seven to 10-year-olds in the UK are now wearing make-up. This program was repeated on 16 January 2007.
39 Byrnes, H. (2005). 'Beauty myth ... 68% of girls think they're not pretty enough', *Sun Herald*, 15 May, p. 9; Hall, L. (2006). 'Wax works for bullied girls', *Sun Herald*, 17 September, p. 36.
40 Weaver, C. (2007). 'Women ashamed of bodies', *Sunday Mail*, 6 May, p. 19.
41 Barry, 'Building a healthy self-esteem'.

conclusion The Parent Trap

1 Zengotita, T. D. (2007). *Mediated*. London, Bloomsbury. pp. 41–2.
2 Donahoo, D. (2007). *Idolising Children*. Sydney, University of New South Wales Press.

3 McDonnell, K. (2000). *Kid Culture: Children and Adults and Popular Culture*. Toronto, Pluto, p. 19. McDonnell adds that while children are not the 'critical audience in the same sense adults are. Neither are they mere dupes and robots blindly following the dictates of pop culture moguls, as so many adults maintain.' I agree. She also recognises that it is essential for adults to educate kids about the 'economic clout' of pop culture and the values contained therein (p. 20).
4 Buckingham, D. and S. Bragg (2004). *Young People, Sex and the Media: The Facts of Life?* New York, Palgrave Macmillan, p. 4.
5 Jenkins, H. (2006). *Fans, Bloggers and Games*. New York, New York University Press, pp. 195–6.
6 Irvine, J. (2005). 'Top 10 parenting mistakes', *Sunshine Coast Daily*, 28 December, p. 32.

Select Bibliography

(2006). 'Clothes make the kid', *Australian*, 12 October, p. 11.
(2006). 'Cotton-wool kids', *Sunday Mail*, 17 September, p. 40.
(2006). 'How gaming is all work and no play', *BBC News*, 14 March, http://news.bbc.co.uk/go/pr/fr/-/2/hi/technology/4774534.stm.
ABC Radio (2006). *Life Matters: The Death of Childhood?*, hosted by Richard Aedy, 27 September, ABC Radio, Australia.
ABC Radio (2006). *Life Matters: The Resilience of Children's Culture*, hosted by Richard Aedy, 20 February, ABC Radio, Australia.
ABC Radio (2007). *Life Matters: Children's Television*, hosted by Richard Aedy, 21 September, ABC Radio, Australia.
Adams, Phillip (2006). 'Weekly column', *Weekend Australian*, p. 62.
Agence France-Presse (2006). 'Columbine video game defended', *Courier-Mail*, 22 May, p. 15.
Alderman, Kellie (2007). 'Fashion balancing act for tweens', *Sunday Mail*, 1 April, p. 18.
Allman, T. D. (2007). 'The Theme-Parking, Megachurching, Franchising, Exurbing, McMansioning of America: How Walt Disney Changed Everything', *National Geographic*, March, pp. 96–115.
American Academy of Pediatrics Committee on Communications (1996). 'Impact of music lyrics and music videos on children and youth', *Pediatrics*, no.RE9144.
Andersen, Jens (2005). *Hans Christian Andersen: A New Life*, Woodstock, New York, London.
Anderson, John (2007). 'The film based on the TV series and toy line is a high school nightmare', *Los Angeles Times*, 3 August.
Ariés, Phillipe (1962). *Centuries of Childhood*, Penguin, Harmondsworth.
Ashcroft, James (2007). 'Gene to blame for kids' conduct', *Courier-Mail*, 6 February, p. 11.
Atfield, Cameron, Chalmers, Emma and Lion, Patrick (2006). 'Safety net for grief', *Courier-Mail*, 21 November, p. 9.
Awad, Amal (2006). 'Saccharine, sex-laden lyrics bound for oblivion', *Sydney Morning Herald*, 28 August, p. 18.

Barker, Robin (2004). 'TV and Your Child', *Australian Women's Weekly*, June 2004, pp. 145–146.
Barnard, Malcolm (2002). *Fashion As Communication* (second edition), Routledge, London.
Bauman, Valerie (2006). 'Web generation preserves memories online', *USA Today*, 25 June, www.usatoday.com/tech/news/techinnovations/2006-06-25-yearbook-online_x.htm.
Behr, Rafael (2006). 'Sex lives and the internet', *Courier-Mail*, 4 November, pp. 19–23.
Bell, David and Hollows, Joanne (eds) (2005). *Ordinary Lifestyles: Popular Media, Consumption and Taste*, Open University, New York.
Bellafante, Ginia (2003). 'The Littlest Clotheshorse', *New York Times*, 4 November, p. B11.
Bettelheim, Bruno (1987). *A Good Enough Parent*, Thames and Hudson, London.
Bogart, Leo (2005). *Over the Edge: How the Pursuit of Youth by Marketers and the Media Has Changed American Culture*, Ivan R Dee, Chicago.
Bravehearts Pty Ltd (2003). *Ditto's Keep Safe Adventure*, Computer Software.
Brody, Michael (2004). *Kid's Popular Culture: The Selling of Childhood*, retrieved 14 September, http://www.commercialexploitation.org/articles/seduction_of_toys.htm.
Brooks, Karen (2001). 'Children's classic invokes pagan hope', *Courier-Mail*, 10 November, p. 23.
Brooks, Karen (2003). 'Nothing Sells like Teen Spirit: The Commodification of Youth Culture' In *Youth Cultures: Texts, Images, and Identities* (Mallan, K. and Pearce, S., eds). Praeger, London.
Brooks, Karen (2005). 'Who are we kidding?' *Courier-Mail*, 31 January, p. 11.
Brooks, Karen (2005/2006). 'Corporate kidnapping', *Melbourne's Child*, December/January, pp. 16–18.
Brooks, Karen (2006). 'Comfortably Numb: Young People, Drugs and the Seductions of Popular Culture', *Youth Studies Australia*, vol. 2, no. 2, pp. 9–16.
Brown, Jane D., Steele, Jeanne R. and Walsh-Childers, Kim (eds) (2002). *Sexual Teens, Sexual Media: Investigating Media's Influence on Adolescent Sexuality*, Lawrence Erlbaum Associates, Mahwah and London.
Buckingham, David and Bragg, Sara (2004). *Young People, Sex and the Media: The Facts of Life?*, Palgrave Macmillan, Houndmills and New York.
Calcutt, Andrew (1999). *White Noise: An A–Z of the Contradictions in Cyberculture*, Macmillan, London.

Calefato, Patrizia (2004). *The Clothed Body*, Berg, Oxford and New York.
Carne, Lucy (2006). 'These jeans would fit a child of 8', *Sunday Mail*, 27 August, p. 23.
Carne, Lucy and Blake, Sarah (2006). 'Music video anger: Kids watching rock 'n' raunch clips at breakfast', *Courier-Mail*, p. 41.
Carr-Gregg, Michael (2005). Interview on *Sunrise*, Channel 7, 10 December.
Carr-Gregg, Michael (2005). *Surviving Adolescents: The Must-have Manual for Parents*, Penguin, Camberwell.
Carr-Gregg, Michael (2006). *The Princess Bitchface Syndrome: Surviving Adolescent Girls*, Penguin, Camberwell.
Carr-Gregg, Michael (2007). 'Sweet dreams make better teens', *Herald Sun*, 18 January, p. 18.
Catsoulis, Jeannette (2007). 'Tender hearts and lip-gloss dreams', *New York Times*, 3 August.
Chalmers, Emma (2006). 'Families far less care-free', *Courier-Mail*, p. 7.
Children's Society (2007). *Childhood Friendships at Risk Reveals a New Survey*, retrieved 7 June, www.childrenssociety.org.uk.
Christakis, Dimitri A., Zimmerman, Frederick J., DiGiuseppe, David L. and McCarty, Carolyn A. (2004). 'Early Television Exposure and Subsequent Attentional Problems in Children', *Pediatrics*, vol. 113, pp. 708–13.
Christiansen, Melanie (2007). 'Youth start early', *Courier-Mail*, 16 February, p. 11.
Clark, Eric (2007). *The Real Toy Story: Inside the Ruthless Battle for Britain's Youngest Consumers*, Black Swan, London.
Clark, Laura (2006). 'Pushy parents lose the plot', *Courier-Mail*, 5 December, p. 28.
Clark, Laura (2007). 'Fearful parents deny life lessons', *Courier-Mail*, 7 June, p. 25.
Clark, Laura and Dolan, Andy (2007). 'Bleak picture of modern childhood', *Courier-Mail*, 2 July, p. 39.
Coleman, Oliver (2006). 'Kids prefer tube to you', *Courier-Mail*, 6 November, p. 18.
Collins, Jim (ed.) (2002). *High-Pop: Making Culture into Popular Entertainment*, Blackwell, Malden and Oxford.
Collins, Rebecca L., Elliott, Marc N., Berry, Sandra H., Kanouse, David E., Kunkel, Dale, Hunter, Sarah B. and Miu, Angela (2004). 'Watching Sex on Television Predicts Adolescent Initiation of Sexual Behavior', *Pediatrics*, vol. 114, no. 3, pp. 280–89.
Condren, Bernadette (2006). 'Singing a song of child development', *Courier-Mail*, 4–5 November, p. 72.

Cox, Janelle Leigh (1995). *Fairytales and their Functions: the Study of Three Tales in their 'Original' and 'Disney-fied' States*, Faculty of Humanties thesis, Griffith University, Brisbane.
Critchley, Cheryl (2007). 'Schools cave in to sleepy teens', *Herald Sun/ Adelaide Now*, 4 May.
Critser, Greg (2003). *Fat Land: How Americans Became the Fattest People in the World*, Penguin, London and New York.
Curthoys, Ann (1986). 'The Getting of Television: Dilemmas in Ownership, Control and Culture 1941–1956', in *Better Dead Than Read: Australia's First Cold War: 1945–1959 Volume 2* (Curthoys, A. and Merritt, J., eds), Allen & Unwin, Sydney, pp. 123–154.
Danesi, Marcel (2003). *Forever Young: The 'Teen-Aging' of Modern Culture*, University of Toronto, Toronto.
Davies, Hannah (2006). 'The deadly search for "thinspiration"', *Sunday Mail*, 16 July, p. 24.
Davies, Hannah (2006). 'Sorry ... but you can't say "no" to a child', *Sunday Mail*, p. 4.
Davis, Glyn and Dickinson, Kay (eds) (2004). *Teen TV: Genre, Consumption and Identity*, British Film Institute, London.
Davis, Mark (1997). *Gangland: Cultural Elites and the New Generationalism*, Allen & Unwin, Sydney.
deMause, Lloyd (ed.) (1974). *The History of Childhood*, Harper Torchbooks, New York.
Desjardins, Doug (2004). 'Kids TV Surpasses Film as Source for Branded Merchandise', *DSN Retailing Today*, vol. 43, no. 11, pp. 47–48.
DoRozario, Rebecca-Anne (2004). 'The Princess and the Magic Kingdom: Beyond Nostalgia, the Function of the Disney Princess', *Women's Studies in Communication*, vol. 27, no. 1, pp. 34–60.
Douglas, Susan J (1995). *Where the Girls Are: Growing Up Female with the Mass Media*, Random House, New York.
Dudley, Jennifer (2004). 'Fame just a blog away', *Courier-Mail*, 11 December, p. 31.
Dudley, Jennifer (2006). 'Disconnection anxiety', *Courier-Mail*, 19 July, p. 5.
Dudley, Jennifer (2006). 'Married to the mobile', *Courier-Mail*, 19 July, pp. 4–5.
Duffy, Michael (2004). 'Once upon a time, children looked forward to growing up', *Courier-Mail*, 8 May, p. 30.
Eccleshare, Julia (2002). *A Guide to the Harry Potter Novels*, Contemporary Classics of Children's Literature, Continuum, London and New York.
Edensor, Tim (2002). *National Identity, Popular Culture and Everyday Life*, Berg, Oxford and New York.
Eggemont, Steven and Van den Bulck, Jan (2006). 'Nodding off or switching off? The use of popular media as a sleep aid in secondary-school children', *Paediatrics and Child Health*, vol. 42, no. 7–8, pp. 428–33.

Ellis, Stephen (2006). 'Google gets some home video truths', *Australian*, 12 October, p. 23.
Engelhardt, Tom (1991). 'Reading May Be Harmful to Your Kids', *Harper's Magazine*, June, pp. 55–62.
Englund, Vicki (2006). 'Play time', *Courier-Mail*, 29 November, p. 45.
Entwistle, Joanne (2000). *The Fashioned Body: Fashion, Dress and Modern Social Theory*, Polity Press, Cambridge.
Etcoff, Nancy (1999). *Survival of the Prettiest: The Science of Beauty*, Abacus, London.
Finch, Lynette (1993). *The Classing Gaze: Sexuality, Class and Surveillance*, Allen & Unwin, Sydney.
Finkelstein, Joanne (1994). *Slaves of Chic: An A–Z of Consumer Pleasures*, Minerva, Kew.
Finkelstein, Joanne (1996). *After a Fashion*, Melbourne University Press, Melbourne.
Firth, Maxine (2007). 'Keeping up with the Jones kids', *Sydney Morning Herald*, 10 September.
Fiske, John (1989). *Reading the Popular*, Routledge, London and New York.
Freydkin, Donna (2006). 'MySpace finds room for split', *USA Today*, 15 August, www.usatoday.com/life/people/2006-08-15-barkers-myspace_x.htm?POE=LIFISVA.
Furlong, Andy and Cartmel, Fred (1997). *Young People and Social Change: Individualization and Risk in Late Modernity*, Open University, Buckingham and Philadelphia.
Fynes-Clinton, Jane (2006). 'It's time to value not criticise our teens', *Courier-Mail*, 23 November, p. 35.
Gale, Julie (2007). Interview with Karen Brooks, 14 August.
Gale, Julie (2007). *Kids Free 2B Kids*, http://www.kf2bk.com.
Geller, Martinne (2006). 'Dressed and wired', *Courier-Mail*, 2 August, p. 5.
Gilbert, Rob and Gilbert, Pam (1998). *Masculinity Goes to School*, Allen & Unwin, Sydney.
Giroux, Henry A. (1997). *Channel Surfing: RaceTalk and the Destruction of Today's Youth*, Macmillan, Houndmills and London.
Giroux, Henry A. (1999). *The Mouse That Roared: Disney and the End of Innocence*, Rowman & Littlefield, New York and Oxford.
Giroux, Henry A. (2000). *Stealing Innocence: Corporate Culture's War on Children*, Palgrave, New York.
Giroux, Henry A. (2002). *Breaking into Movies: Film and the Culture of Politics*, Blackwell Publishers, Maiden.
Giroux, Henry A. and McLaren, Peter (eds) (1994). *Between Borders: Pedagogy and the Politics of Cultural Studies*, Routledge, New York and London.

Goode, Erica (2003). 'Babies pick up emotional clues from TV, experts find', *The New York Times*, 21 January, p. F5.
Gray, Keturah (2005). 'Quarterlife Crisis Hits Many in Late 20s', *ABC New Internet Ventures*, 21 April, http://abcnews.go.com/Business/Careers/story?id=688240&page=1.
Green, Glenis (2003). 'Online for a reality check', *Courier-Mail*, 4 October, pp. 4–5.
Gregory, Jason (2006). 'Die-hard players shoot for international gaming fame', *Courier-Mail*, 21 August, p. 14.
Gregory Thomas, Susan (2007). *Buy, Buy Baby: How Big Business Captures the Ultimate Consumer – Your Baby or Toddler*, Harper Collins, London.
Groot, Vanessa De (2007). 'Reading's right for kids', *Courier-Mail*, 18 January, p. 13.
Grose, Michael (2005). *XYZ: The New Rules of Generational Warfare*, Random House, Sydney.
Grossman, Lev (2004). 'The age of doom', *Time*, 9 August.
Grossman, Lev (2004). 'Blogs have their day', *Time*, 19 December, pp. 68–71.
Grossman, Lev (2004). 'Meet Joe Blog', *Time*, 21 June, pp. 43–46.
Grossman, Lev (2005). 'J.K. Rowling Hogwarts and all', *Time*, 18 July, pp. 60–65.
Grossman, Lev (2005). 'Out of the XBox', *Time*, 23 May, pp. 38–47.
Guthrie, Susan (2006). 'Caring for the cursor kids', *Courier-Mail*, 14 June, p. 46.
Haig, Matt (2004). *Brand Royalty: How the World's Top 100 Brands Thrive & Survive*, Kogan Page, London and Philadelphia.
Hall, Sandra (1976). *Supertoy: Twenty Years of Australian Television*, Sun Books, Melbourne.
Hamilton, Anita (2005). 'Video vigilantes', *Time*, 10 January, pp. 58–59.
Hanawalt, Barbara A. (1993). *Growing Up in Medieval London: The Experience of Childhood in History*, Oxford University Press, New York and Oxford.
Harding, Anne (2007). 'TV Link to Attention Difficulties', *Courier-Mail*, 10 September, p. 12.
Hardy, Louise L., Baur, Louise A., Garnett, Sarah P., Crawford, David, Campbell, Karen J., Shrewsbury, Vanessa A., Cowell, Christopher T. and Salmon, Jo (2006). 'Family and Home Correlates of Television Viewing in 12–13-year-old Adolescents: The Nepean Study', *International Journal of Behavioural Nutrition and Physical Activity*, vol. 3, no. 24.
Harrington, C. Lee and Bielby, Denise D. (eds) (2001). *Popular Culture: Production and Consumption*, Blackwell, Malden and Oxford.

Hartley, John and Lumby, Catharine (2003). 'Working Girls or Drop-Dead Gorgeous? Young Girls in Fashion and News', in *Youth Cultures: Texts, Images, and Identities* (Mallan, K. and Pearce, S., eds), Praeger, London.

Hassed, Craig (2006). 'Tuning in to Pandora's Box', *Weekend Australian*, 12–13 August, p. 10.

Henke, Jill Birnie and Umble, Diane Zimmerman (1999). 'And She Lived Happily Every After … The Disney Myth in the Video Age', in *Mediated Women: Representations in Popular Culture* (Meyer, M., ed.). Hampton Press, Cresskill.

Herde, Chris (2007). 'Mighty growth in mags', *Courier-Mail*, 13–14 January, p. 64.

Heywood, Colin (2001). *A History of Childhood: Children and Childhood in the West from Medieval to Modern Times*, Polity, Cambridge.

Heywood, Lachlan (2006). 'Retailers "eroticise" children in ads', *Courier-Mail*, 10 October, p. 2.

Higgins, Ean (1998). 'Spice trade', *Weekend Australian*, 6–7 June, p. 21.

Higson, Rosalie (2006). 'Out of the mouths of babes', *Weekend Australian*, 18–19 November, pp. 16–17.

Holland, Patricia (1992). *What Is a Child? Popular Images of Childhood*, Virago, London.

Holmes, Robyn M. (1998). *Fieldwork with Children*, Sage, London.

Hopkins, Susan (2002). *Girl Heroes: The New Force in Popular Culture*, Pluto, Annandale.

Horin, Adele and Patty, Anna (2006). 'Stop doing the homework, overzealous parents warned', *Sydney Morning Herald*, 23 September.

Huntley, Rebecca (2006). *The World According to Y: Inside the New Adult Generation*, Allen & Unwin, Sydney.

Hutchinson, Jane (2006). 'Bringing up Barbie', *Sunday Herald Sun*, 12 November, pp. 35–38.

Illouz, Eva (2003). *Oprah Winfrey and the Glamour of Misery: An Essay on Popular Culture*, Columbia University, New York.

Inness, Sherrie A (2004). 'It's a Girl Thing: Tough Female Action Figures in the Toy Store', in *Action Chicks: New Images of Tough Women in Popular Culture* (Inness, S. A., ed.), Palgrave Macmillan, New York.

Irwin, William, Conard, Mark T. and Skoble, Aeon J. (eds) (2001). *The Simpsons and Philosophy: The D'oh! of Homer*, Open Court, Chicago.

Jacobson, Maria (2005). *Young People and Gendered Media Messages*, International Clearinghouse on Children, Youth and Media, Goteborg.

Jakobsson, Mikael and Taylor, T. L. (2003). 'The Sopranos Meets EverQuest: Social Networking in Massively Multiplayer Online Games', paper presented at the Digital Arts and Culture Conference, Melbourne, 2003.

Jeffery, Nicole (2007). 'Young, gifted and stressed', *Weekend Australian*, 27–28 January, p. 24.
Jenkins, Henry (2006). *Fans, Bloggers and Games*, New York University Press, New York and London.
Jenks, Chris (2005). *Childhood* (second edition), Routledge, London and New York.
Johnson, Steven (2005). *Everything Bad Is Good for You: How Popular Culture Is Making Us Smarter*, Allen Lane, London and New York.
Johnston, Chris (2007). 'Brave new world or vitual pedophile paradise?', *Sydney Morning Herald*, 10 May.
Jones, Eurfron Gwynne (1973). *Children Growing Up*, Penguin, Harmondsworth.
Jones, Gerard (2006). *Killing Monsters: Why Children Need Fantasy, Super Heroes, and Make-Believe Violence*, Basic Books, New York.
Jones, Steven Swann (1995). *The Fairy Tale: The Magic Mirror of the Imagination*, Routledge, New York and London.
Kahney, Leander (2005). *The Cult of iPod*, No Starch Press, San Francisco.
Kasser, Tim and Kanner, Allen D. (eds) (2003). *Psychology and Consumer Culture: The Struggle for a Good Life in a Materialistic World*, American Psychological Association, Washington.
Kaveney, Roz (2006). *Teen Dreams: Reading Teen Film and Television from Heathers to Veronica Mars*, I. B. Tauris, London and New York.
Keane, Colleen (2006). 'A childhood reconciled', *Age*, 16 October, p. 10.
Keillor, Garrison (2004). 'Daughter dearest', *Time*, 30 August, p. 76.
Kelly, Tom (2006). 'Boys will be boys again', *Sunday Mail*, 18 June, p. 25.
Kerbaj, Richard (2005). 'The turbulent twenties', *Age*, 21 January.
Kerr, Aphra (2006). *The Business and Culture of Digital Games: Gamework/Gameplay*, Sage, London.
Kinzer, Stephen (2003). 'Dolls as role models, neither Barbie nor Britney', *New York Times*, 6 November, p. E1.
Kirkegaard, Matt (2005). 'Music to be anxious to', *Voyeur Magazine*.
Kirwan-Taylor, Helen (2006). 'Sorry, but my children bore me to death', *Sunday Mail*, 6 August, p. 48.
Kluger, Jeffrey (2001). 'The quest for a super kid', *Time*, 30 April, pp. 50–55.
Kluger, Jeffrey (2006). 'Taming wild girls', *Time*, 1 May, pp. 50–51.
Knowledge Networks Statistical Research (2003). *How Children Use Media Technology*, retrieved 5 July 2006, www.sri.knowledgenetworks.com.
Kuczynski, Alex (2007). *Beauty Junkies: Under the Skin of the Cosmetic Surgery Industry*, Vintage, London.
Lamb, Sharon and Brown, Lyn Mikel (2006). *Packaging Girlhood: Rescuing Our Daughters from Marketers' Schemes*, St Martin's Griffin, New York.
Landhuis, Carl Erik, Poulton, Richie, Welch, David and Hancox, Robert John (2007). 'Does Childhood Television Viewing Lead to Attention

Problems in Adolescence? Results from a Prospective Longitudinal Study', *Pediatrics*, vol. 120, no. 3, pp. 532–37.
Langford, Rachael (2006). 'Addicted to shopping', *Sunday Mail*, 30 November, p. 37.
Langford, Rachael (2006). 'Gen Y speeds up life', *Courier-Mail*, 23 October, pp. 37–38.
Laughey, Dan (2006). *Music & Youth Culture*, Edinburgh University Press, Edinburgh.
Laurie, Victoria (2006). 'Urge to Splurge', *Weekend Australian*, 9–10 December, pp. 16–22.
Lawlor, Ali (1998). 'When teens are cool they're hot', *Courier-Mail*, 14 September.
Lawrence, Jessica (2004). '$100 a week in pocket money boom', *Sunday Mail*, 8 February, p. 40.
Learmonth, Eleanor (2006). 'They'll grow up soon enough', *Sydney Morning Herald*, 22–23 April, p. 21.
Legge, Kate (2005). 'Upwardly mobile', *Weekend Australian*, 28–29 May, pp. 28–31.
Leith, William (2006). 'Growing pains', *Courier-Mail*, 25–26 November, pp. 34–37.
Lemonick, Michael D (2005). 'A teen twist on sex', *Time*, 26 September, p. 46.
Levitt, Steven D and Dubner, Stephen J (2005). *Freakonomics: A Rogue Economist Explores the Hidden Side of Everything*, Allen Lane, London and New York.
Lindstrom, Martin (2004). *Brand Child: Remarkable Insights into the Minds of Today's Global Kids and their Relationships with Brands*, Kogan Page, London and Sterling, VA.
Linn, Susan (2004). *Consuming Kids: The Hostile Takeover of Childhood*, The New Press, New York and London.
Livingstone, Sonia (2002). *Young People and New Media*, Sage, London.
Livingstone, Tess (2006). 'New chapter in childhood', *Courier-Mail*, 15 May.
Lowe, Barry (1995). *Media Mythologies*, University of New South Wales Press, Sydney.
Lumby, Catharine and Fine, Duncan (2006). *Why TV Is Good for Kids: Raising 21st Century Children*, Pan Macmillan, Sydney.
Lurie, Alison (1981). *The Language of Clothes*, Henry Holt and Company, New York.
Mackay, Hugh (2002). *Media Mania: Why Our Fear of Modern Media Is Misplaced*, University of New South Wales Press, Sydney.
Mackay, Hugh (2006). 'So much love, but sadly it's the wrong kind', *Sydney Morning Herald*, 16 December.

Mackay, Hugh (2007). *Advance Australia ... Where?*, Hachette Australia, Sydney.
Mahadi, Muhin (1990). *The Arabian Nights*, Haddawy, H., W.W. Norton and Company, New York, London.
Mallan, Kerry and Pearce, Sharyn (eds) (2003). *Youth Cultures: Texts, Images, and Identities*, Praeger, London.
Marsden, Sam (2007). 'Kids hurt by TV diet', *Courier-Mail*, 20 February, p. 14.
Marszalek, Jessica (2006). 'Beauty can't get a look-in: just give us love and sex', *Courier-Mail*, 29 November, p. 14.
Martin, Jane (2006). 'Forever young', *Sunday Mail*, 12 November, pp. 2–3.
Martino, S. C., R. L. Collins, M. N. Elliott, A. Strachman, D. E. Kanouse and S. H. Berry (2006). 'Exposure to Degrading Versus Nondegrading Music Lyrics and Sexual Behavior Among Youth', *Pediatrics*, vol. 118, pp. 430–41.
Masters, Clare (2006). 'Junk food ads aimed at children', *Courier-Mail*, 27 July, p. 16.
Matchett, Stephen (2006). 'Y I'm not buying it', *Weekend Australian*, 27–28 May, p. 40.
Maugeri, Melissa (2006). 'A more familiar face at home', *Courier-Mail*, 21 July, p. 7.
Maushart, Susan (2007). 'Weekly column', *Weekend Australian*, 25–26 August, p. 9.
McCormick, Moira (1998). 'Mom's "Baby" vids sharpen new minds', *Billboard*, vol. 110, no. 40, pp. 72–73.
McDonnell, Kathleen (2000). *Kid Culture: Children and Adults and Popular Culture*, Pluto Press, Melbourne.
McDonnell, Kathleen (2005). *Honey, We Lost the Kids: Re-thinking Childhood in the Multimedia Age* (revised edition), Pluto Press, Melbourne.
McDonogh, Yona Zeldis (ed.) (1999). *The Barbie Chronicles: A Living Doll Turns 40*, Bantam, New York.
McElgunn, Jim (2004). 'Child's Play', *Canadian Business*, vol. 77, no. 6, pp. 42–45.
McGrath, John E. (2004). *Loving Big Brother: Performance, Privacy and Surveillance Space*, Routledge, London and New York.
McLean, Sandra (2006). 'TV keeps packing on the weight shows', *Courier-Mail*, 29–30 April, p. 24.
McLean, Sandra (2006). 'Under the radar', *Courier-Mail*, 21 December, p. 57.
McLuhan, Marshall (1964). *Understanding Media: The Extension of Man*, Routledge, London and New York.

McNair Ingenuity Research (2003). *Kids, Pastimes and Media Use*, Sydney, retrieved http://www.mcnairingenuity.com.
McNamara, Mary (2004). *The Princess Principle*, retrieved 14 September, www.freenewmexican.com/artsfeatures/3568.html.
McRobbie, Angela (1994). *Postmodernism and Popular Culture*, Routledge, London and New York.
McWilliam, Erica (2006). 'School's out on mumbo-jumbo', *Courier-Mail*, 24 May, p. 22.
Meryment, Elizabeth (2006). 'Retro rodent returns in 3-D', *Weekend Australian*, 6–7 May, p. 26.
Metcalf, Fran (2006). 'A slight hope of success', *Courier-Mail*, 29–30 April, pp. 50–51.
Metcalf, Fran (2006). 'Rewarding the patient child', *Courier-Mail*, 29 November, p. 47.
Miles, Janelle (2007). 'Study to check how the computer generation ticks', *Courier-Mail*, 20 February, p. 7.
Milliner, Karen (2006). 'Telly tubbies', *Courier-Mail*, 22–23 July, pp. 23–25.
Moran, Albert (1985). *Images and Industry: Television Production in Australia*, Currency Press, Sydney.
Morris, Desmond (2004). 'Fathers: the insidious lie', *Sunday Mail*, 8 February, pp. 60–61.
Murdoch, Alex (2006). 'Has the net killed the music video star?', *Courier-Mail*, 26–27 August, pp. 54–55.
Murray, Susan and Ouellette, Laurie (eds) (2004). *Reality TV: Remaking Television Culture*, New York University Press, New York and London.
Murtagh, Caitriona (2006). 'End of line for queue hogs with mobiles', *Sunday Mail*, 3 December, p. 32.
Nahrung, Jason (2006). 'Phone to make parents and kids happy', *Courier-Mail*, 11 October, p. 6.
Nel, Philip (2002). *J.K. Rowling's Harry Potter Novels*, Continuum, New York and London.
Niedzviecki, Hal (2006). *Hello I'm Special: How Individuality Became the New Conformity*, City Lights, San Francisco.
O'Connor, Mike (2006). 'Fast track to success', *Courier-Mail*, 29 March, p. 38.
O'Connor, Mike (2006). 'Testing times for a good educator', *Courier-Mail*, 25 October, p. 26.
Orecklin, Michele (2004). 'Stress and the Superdad', *Time*, 23 August, pp. 40–41.
O'Regan, Tom (1993). *Australian Television Culture*, Allen & Unwin, Sydney.
Overington, Caroline (2006). 'There's life, mum, but not as we know it', *Weekend Australian*, 21–22 October, p. 30.

Palmer, Sue (2006). *Toxic Childhood: How the Modern World Is Damaging Our Children and What We Can Do About It*, Orion Books, London.
Palmer, Sue (2006). 'Toxic generation', *Sunday Mail*, 14 May, p. 54.
Papadakis, Mary (2006). 'New push for law against smacking', *Sunday Mail*, 10 September, p. 16.
Papadakis, Mary (2006). 'Teens' world is techno heaven', *Sunday Mail*, 19 November, p. 18.
Partridge, Des (2006). 'Coming out of a screen near you', *Courier-Mail*, 16 August, p. 13.
Passmore, Daryl (2006). 'Our guru called to help UK parents', *Sunday Mail*, 3 December, p. 45.
Passmore, Daryl (2007). 'A world that shuns children', *Sunday Mail*, 16 September, p. 66.
Passmore, Daryl (2007). 'Child carers ban book', *Sunday Mail*, 1 April, p. 24.
Passmore, Daryl (2007). 'Here, now be a good little child', *Sunday Mail*, 14 January, p. 48.
Patterson, Kate (2006). 'Debt generation risks early ruin', *Sunday Mail*, 21 May, p. 71.
Patterson, Kate (2007). 'Brain boost for babies', *Sunday Mail*, 7 January, p. 31.
PBS, USA (2001). 'Merchants of Cool', *Frontline*, PBS, 27 February, directed by Barak Goodman.
Pearce, Kerry Mallan and Sharyn (eds) (2003). *Youth, Culture, Identity*, Greenwood Press, Connecticut.
Pearson, Allison (2003). 'A working mother's day, from A to Z', *Time*, 12 May, p. 72.
Pereira, Joe (2002). 'Parents turn toys that teach into hot sellers', *Wall Street Journal*, 27 November, p. B1.
Poniewozik, James (2004). 'The same young story', *Time*, 11 August, p. 65.
Postman, Neil (1994). *The Disappearance of Childhood*, Vintage, New York.
Prensky, Marc (2006). *Don't Bother Me Mom – I'm Learning!*, Paragon House, St Paul.
Pribram, E. Deidre (ed.) (1988). *Female Spectators: Looking at Film and Television*, Verso, London and New York.
Pryor, Lisa (2007). 'Teenagers beware: domesticated sex threatens your independence', *Sydney Morning Herald*, 17 March.
Quart, Alissa (2003). *Branded: The Buying and Selling of Teenagers*, Arrow, London.
Quigley, Marian and Blashki, Kathy (2003). 'Beyond the Boundaries of the Sacred Garden: Children and the Internet', *ACCE Journal*, vol. 11, no. 1, pp. 70–77.

Ravitch, Diane and Viteritti, Joseph P. (eds) (2003). *Kid Stuff: Marketing Sex and Violence to America's Children*, John Hopkins University, Baltimore and London.
Rideout, Victoria J., Vandewater, Elizabeth A. and Wartella, Ellen A. (2003). 'Zero to Six: Electronic Media in the Lives of Infants, Toddlers and Preschoolers', *The Henry J Kaiser Family Foundation*, Fall 2003, pp. 2–36.
Riley, Susan (2006). 'Too few animated women break the Disney mold', *Ottawa Citizen*.
Robertson, Josh (2006). 'Good rap for grime genre', *Courier-Mail*, 17 November, p. 53.
Robotham, Julie and Lee, Julian (2006). 'Fat chance of avoiding the hard sell', *Sydney Morning Herald*, 27 July 2006.
Robotham, Julie and Lee, Julian (2006). 'Shocking truth of childhood obesity', *Sydney Morning Herald*, 22–23 April, pp. 1, 8.
Ross, Deborah (2004). 'Escape from Wonderland: Disney and the Female Imagination' *Marvels and Tales*, vol. 18, no. 1, pp. 53–67.
Royal Australasian College of Physicians: Paediatrics and Child Health Division (2004). *Children and the Media: Advocating for the Future*, retrieved 14 July, www.racp.edu.au/hpu/paed/media.
Rush, Emma and La Nauze, Andrea (2006). 'Corporate Paedophilia: Sexualisation of children in Australia', *Discussion Paper Number 90*, Australia Institute, http://www.tai.org.au/.
Salamon, Winnie (2007). 'The motherhood statements of feminism ring a bit hollow', *Sydney Morning Herald*, 2 January, p. 9.
Salmon, Jacqueline L (2004). 'Gen X moms put emphasis on fun toys', *Oakland Tribune*, 29 February.
Santonastoaso, Paolo, Mondini, Silvia and Favaro, Angela (2002). 'Are Fashion Models a Group at Risk for Eating Disorders and Substance Abuse?', *Psychotherapy and Psychosomatics*, vol. 71, no. 3, pp. 168–172.
Sargent, Iman Sharif and James D. (2006). 'Association Between Television, Movie and Video Game Exposure and School Performance', *Pediatrics*, vol. 118, no. 4.
Schirato, Tony and Webb, Jen (2004). *Reading the Visual*, Allen & Unwin, Sydney.
Schlesinger Jr, Arthur (2001). 'What Great Books Do for Children', *The American Enterprise*, vol. 12, no. 5, p. 47.
Schlosser, Eric (2002). *Fast Food Nation*, Penguin, London and New York.
Schultz, Julianne (ed.) (2004). 'Addicted to Celebrity', *Griffith Review*, vol. 5, Spring.
Schuman, Michael and Ressner, Jeffrey (2005). 'Disney's great leap into China', *Time*, 18 July, pp. 44–46.

Seiter, Ellen (1995). *Sold Separately: Parents & Children in Consumer Culture*, Rutgers University Press, New Brunswick, New Jersey.
Sell and Spin: The History of Advertising (1999). New Video Group, directed by Dick Cavett and Sean R. Geary, The History Channel.
Shanahan, Angela (2006). 'Family fix for fat children', *Weekend Australian*, 26–27 August, p. 25.
Sinclair, Lara (2006). 'Google sets its sights on video ads', *Australian*, 12 October, p. 14.
Sivulka, Juliann (1998). *Soap, Sex and Cigarettes: A Cultural History of American Advertising*, Wadsworth, London.
Skelton, Tracey and Valentine, Gill (eds) (1998). *Cool Places: Geographies of Youth Cultures*, Routledge, London and New York.
Song, Sora (2005). 'The power of make-believe', *Time*, 14 February, pp. 52–53.
Sourris, Marie-Christine (2006). 'Designer children', *Courier-Mail*, 2 November, pp. 41–42.
Spiller, Emily (2006). 'Generation iPod not ready for the ballot box', *Age*, 16 October, p. 10.
Stanley, Fiona (2006). 'Vision to prevent violence against children', *Australian*, 13 October, p. 18.
Stearns, Peter N (2006). *Childhood in World History*, Routledge, New York and London.
Stein, Joel (2004). 'Goddess of the geeks', *Time*, 26 April, p. 64.
Steinberg, Shirley R. and Kincheloe, Joe L. (eds) (1997, 2004 second edition). *Kinderculture: The Corporate Construction of Childhood*, Westview, Boulder and Oxford.
Sternheimer, Karen (2003). *It's Not the Media: The Truth About Pop Culture's Influence on Children*, Westview, Boulder and Oxford.
Stewart, James B. (2006). *Disney War: The Battle for the Magic Kingdom*, Pocket Books, London.
Sweetman, Terry (2007). 'Sending a girl to do a woman's job', *Sunday Mail*, 16 September, p. 63.
Tatar, Maria (1987). *The Hard Facts of the Grimms' Fairy Tales*, Princeton University Press, Princeton, New Jersey.
Tatar, Maria (1992). *Off With their Heads: Fairytales and the Culture of Childhood*, Princeton University Press, Princeton.
Tatar, Maria (1997). 'Introduction', in *Grimm's Grimmest*, Chronicle Books, San Francisco.
Tatar, Maria (ed.) (1999). *The Classic Fairy Tales*, W.W. Norton & Company, New York and London.
Tatar, Maria (2002). 'Introduction', in *The Annotated Classic Fairy Tales*, Maria Tatar (ed.), W.W. Norton Company, New York.

Thomas, Hedley (2006). 'Disorderly conduct', *Courier-Mail*, 7 April, pp. 14–15.
Tirman, John (2006). *100 Ways America Is Screwing Up the World*, Harper, New York and London.
Torpy, Kathryn (2001). 'Virtual Lolitas', *Courier-Mail*, 10 November, pp. 4–5.
Trites, Roberta (1991). 'Disney's Sub/Version of Andersen's The Little Mermaid', *Journal of Popular Film and Television*, vol. 18, no. 4, pp. 145–52.
Tucker, Sarah (2006). 'Mummy mafia', *Sunday Mail*, 26 November, p. 55.
Tucker-Evans, Anooska (2007). 'Secret of teen talk', *Sunday Mail*, 27 May, p. 20.
Turner, Chris (2004). *Planet Simpson*, Ebury, London.
Turner, Graeme (1999). *Film as Social Practice* (third edition), Routledge, London and New York.
Turner, Graeme (2004). *Understanding Celebrity*, Sage, London.
Turner, Graeme, Bonner, Frances and Marshall, P. David (2000). *Fame Games: The Production of Celebrity in Australia*, Cambridge University Press, Cambridge and New York.
Von Feilitzen, Cecilia (ed.) (2004). *Young People, Soap Operas and Reality TV*, International Clearinghouse on Children, Youth and Media, Goteborg.
Wallis, Claudia (2004). 'The case for staying home', *Time*, 22 March, pp. 50–57.
Wallis, Claudia (2004). 'What makes teens tick', *Time*, 24 May, pp. 46–53.
Wallis, Claudia (2006). 'The multitasking generation' *Time*, 10 April, pp. 46–53.
Warner, Marina (1995). *From the Beast to the Blonde: On Fairy Tales and their Tellers*, Vintage, London.
Weitz, Rose (2005). *Rapunzel's Daughters: What Women's Hair Tells Us About Women's Lives*, Farrar, Straus and Giroux, New York.
Wenham, Margaret and Lill, Jasmin (2004). 'Parents warned of net hunting ground', *Courier-Mail*, 14 February, p. 5.
Whelehan, Imelda (2000). *Overloaded: Popular Culture and the Future of Feminism*, Women's Press, London.
White, Susan (1995). 'Split Skin: Female Agency and Bodily Mutilation in "The Little Mermaid"', in *Film Theory Goes to the Movies*, J. Collins, H. Radner, H. and A. P. Collins (eds), Routledge, New York and London.
Whiting, Frances (2003). 'The children who never were', *Sunday Mail*, 17 August, pp. 58–59.
Williams, Daniel (2005). 'Parents behaving badly', *Time*, 16 May, pp. 44–51.
Williams, Daniel (2006). 'School's out forever', *Time*, 9 April, pp. 48–53.

Williams, Daniel (2006). 'With best intentions', *Time*, 13 February, p. 56.
Wilson, Peter (2006). 'Britain's Lord of the Flies generation', *Weekend Australian*, 4–5 November, p. 17.
Wilson, Rae (2006). 'Is music too sexy for our kids?', *Sunshine Coast Daily*, 14 August, p. 4.
Wiseman, Rosalind (2002). *Queen Bees & Wannabes*, Piatkus Books, London.
Wiseman, Rosalind (2006). *Queen Bee Mums & Kingpin Dads*, Piatkus Books, London.
Wojcik-Andrews, Ian and Phillips, Jerry (1996). 'Telling Tales to Children: The Pedagogy of Empire in MGM's "Kim" and Disney's "Aladdin"', *The Lion and the Unicorn*, vol. 20, no. 1, pp. 66–89.
Wolf, Joan M. (1997). *The Beanstalk and Beyond: Developing Critical Thinking Through Fairy Tales*, Teacher Ideas Press, Englewood.
Wolf, Naomi (1991). *The Beauty Myth: How Images of Beauty Are Used Against Women*, Vintage, London.
Woodward, John (ed.) (2005). *Popular Culture*, Thomson Gale, Farmington Hills.
Zablit, Jocelyne (2006). 'Nature at its breast offends US readers', *Courier-Mail*, 5–6 August, p. 45.
Zengotita, Thomas De (2007). *Mediated*, Bloomsbury, London.
Zipes, Jack (1999). *When Dreams Came True: Classical Fairy Tales and their Tradition*, Routledge, New York.
Zipes, Jack (2002). *The Brothers' Grimm: From Enchanted Forests to Modern World*, Palgrave Macmillan, New York.
Zipes, Jack (2002). *Sticks and Stones: The Troublesome Success of Children's Literature from Slovenly Peter to Harry Potter*, Routledge, New York and London.

Acknowledgements

Books are never written in isolation, but are always a group effort. This book is no exception and would never have been written except for the tireless support and enthusiasm of a number of people to whom I owe an enormous debt of gratitude.

First and foremost, my family – in particular my partner, Stephen, whose quarter of a century of experience in mental health and dealing with people of all ages has been absolutely invaluable. He participated in hours of analysis and endless discussions about young people and popular culture and always offered terrific insights and challenged my assumptions with patience and humour, even when I'd wait until he was almost asleep to begin a conversation.

Second, I want to thank my research assistant, Lisa Hill, for her conscientiousness, efficiency, humour and wisdom (and great coffee). She's a researcher and critic par excellence whose presence in my life has made writing this book an even greater pleasure.

I also want to thank the University of Queensland, in particular the Centre for Critical and Cultural Studies for providing me with an office as well as internet and library access for six wonderful months. I want to thank the staff there, especially Professor Graeme Turner, my mentor, for his enthusiasm, advice and support. I look forward to my next stint there as a Visiting Fellow.

My own institution, Southern Cross University, must also be thanked for embracing the concept of this book so wholeheartedly and for making me feel so welcome. Thanks must also go to my fabulous former students from the University of the Sunshine Coast, past and present, and my colleagues nationally and internationally whose knowledge, research and words have been drawn upon.

I also want to thank my agent, Selwa Anthony, for her unflinching support and belief and for her endless patience and good humour. If only all authors could be so lucky as to have a muse like Selwa. I also want to thank my marvellous commissioning editor, Alexandra Payne, for her passion for this project and wise advice, and all the wonderful people at UQP – you are such a delight to work with.

This book would not have been possible without the understanding and guidance of Dennis Atkins, Geoffrey Shearer and Sean Mooney, all of whom gave me the opportunity to test my ideas in other forums – my sincere thanks.

Finally, I want to thank all the willing mums, dads, grandparents, aunts, uncles, brothers, sisters, teachers and other professionals, tots, tweens, teens and interested adults, including my much put upon friends and family, who so willingly shared their experiences and ideas with me. While my research provided the bones, your contributions have given them flesh. Thank you. Also to the children who shared their views, toys, comics, films, TV shows, books, magazines and computer games with me and tolerated my incessant questions and clumsiness, thank you so much – it was great fun.

Of course, any mistakes and oversights are my own and, as much as I would like to blame any or all of the above, or suggest you speak to them, I can't. This book is my baby, and responsibility for any of its flaws rests with me: its parent.

Index

A

Abby Cadabby 2, 5
Absolutely Fabulous 79–80
acquisition 58, 110
acronyms 218
Adams, Phillip 38, 46
ADHD 125
'adulescence' 48
adult matters 15, 70
Aeschylus, *The Orestian Trilogy* 19
affluenza 97, 122
age compression 37
Aguilera, Christina 42, 127, 174
Aherns, Prue 78
Aigner-Clark, Julie 119, 120
Aladdin/*Aladdin* 20, 67, 136, 176, 184–187, 190
Alba, Jessica 59–60
Alias 203
Alice 26–27
Alice in Wonderland 26
Alien 154
Alighieri, Dante, *The Divine Comedy* 21
Allen, Lily 213
American Academy of Pediatrics 38, 130, 131
American Dad 42
American Dragon: Jake Long 134, 137, 139

American Idol 232, 234
American Psychological Association 2, 52, 99
Andersen, Hans Christian 20, 22, 25, 176, 182, 239
Andersen, Jens 20
apprentices 23
Arabian Nights 184–185, 190
Arctic Monkeys 213
Aries, Phillippe 12, 13, 16, 19, 24
Aristotle 17
Arrested Development 141
As You Like It 20
Ashman, Howard 186
aspirational casting 135–136, 140
Australia Institute 46, 57, 73
Australian Childhood Foundation 30
Australian Family Association 2
Australian Princess 179

B

baby bikinis 78–79
Baby Einstein 119, 121
BabyFirst TV 130–131
Bambi 20, 164
Bananas in Pyjamas 134

Barbie 2, 58, 67, 87, 89, 92–97, 100–101, 106–107, 136–137, 183, 256
Barbie Magazine 7, 63
Barrie, JM 27
Barry, Jane 246
bat/bah mitzvahs 82
Batman (Bruce Wayne) 20
Batman 141
Batman Begins 59
Beauty and the Beast 176
beauty industry 83–85, 248–250
beauty salons, tweens and teens 248–250
Beckham, David 39
Being John Malkovich 66
best friends 260
Bettelheim, Bruno 173
BFF (best friends forever) 58
Bible, The 195
Big Brother 141, 148, 231
Big Fish 166
Bild Lilli 94
birthday parties 238, 239, 247–248
Blade Runner 203
Blake, William 21
blogs 130, 200, 211–212
Blue Water High 141

Blyton, Enid 191, 195, 254
Bond, James 154, 159, 203
Brand Child 39, 50
brands 37, 39, 49–51, 54, 89–91, 93, 95, 98, 100, 110, 168–169, 198, 241
'bratitude' 98, 104, 250
Bratz 2, 58, 67, 79, 87, 92, 95–108, 136–137, 256
Bratz Babyz 1, 2, 5, 99–100
Bratz Kidz 99
Bratz: The Movie 98, 168
Bring It On 167
Brueghel, Pieter, *Children's Games* 18
Buffy, the Vampire Slayer 138, 141, 148, 169

C
Campbell, Joseph, *Hero of a Thousand Faces* 165
Carr-Gregg, Michael 43–44, 71–72, 95, 99, 219–220, 235, 237
Carrie 167
Carroll, Lewis 26–27
celebrity culture 20, 47, 57–58, 67–68, 72, 80, 84–85, 97, 102
censorship 152–172
Centuries of Childhood 12
Charlotte's Web 162
chatrooms 200, 201
Chicken Little 176
child labour 22
child prostitution 26
childhood 11, 12, 264
history of 11–29, 263
protection of 35–36
children's lingerie 70, 71, 78–79
children's names 246–247
children's rights 27–28
Christianity 22, 27
Cinderella 20, 67, 176, 179–182, 190
cinema 152–164, 168–170
Clark, Eric 95, 102
class 83
Classical times 17
classification
electronic games 222–223
film 155–156
Cleo 61
clothing 66–72
ClubPenguin 207
Clueless 135, 167
Coleridge, Samuel Taylor 21
collective wisdom 106–108
commercial messages 38–56, 67–70, 88, 89–91, 104, 119–122, 197
commodification 73, 153, 197
computers 7, 146, 222
in bedrooms 219–221
consequences 85, 134, 203, 222, 226, 253, 257, 262
consumer culture 83, 109, 153, 197–198, 226, 241
continuous partial attention 229–230
Cook, Dane 213
cool hunters 41
Cooper, Susan 195
corporal punishment 25
corporate paedophilia 46–47
corporatisation 37–38, 47, 51–52, 72, 256
Cosmopolitan 10, 61
Cowell, Simon 234–235
cradle-to-grave consumerism 49–50
criticism 236–238
Cruise, Tom 186
cultural paedophilia 47–48
cyber-predators 209, 216
cyberspace 201, 205, 214–215, 230
and disabilities 215
and friendship 209–210

D
Dahl, Roald 107, 191
Dangerous Book for Boys 117–118
David Copperfield 20
David Jones 73
de Berulle, Pierre 24
de Toro, Guillermo 193
Dead Poets Society 186
deMause, Lloyd 24, 27
Desperate Housewives 4, 101, 144, 188, 258
Dickens, Charles 22
Die Hard 4.0 159
digital divide 217–218
Disney 41, 153, 174–178, 183–191, 225, 239
criticism of 175–176
empire 175–178, 183–191
ideology 174–176
Disney Adventures 57
Disney Girl 57
Disney, Walt 174–175
Disneyland 39

Dolly 44, 59, 61, 63
Dora the Explorer 130, 134
Douglas, Susan J 89
Douglass, Sara 195
downtime 244
Dr Who 154, 203
Dreamgirls 232
Dreamworks 189–190
dress-ups 73–75
Duff, Hilary 43, 51, 67, 135, 136
Dumbledore, Professor 107, 191, 96
DVD 7, 152–172

E
Edison, Thomas 152
education 259
educational products and toys 119–122, 243
ego 233
Eisenstein, Elizabeth 15
Eisner, Michael 185, 189
Electra 20
electronic babysitter 125, 132, 171
electronic games 7, 112, 146, 201, 202, 222, 226–230
Ella Enchanted 179
email 200, 204, 205
empowerment 60, 103, 104, 106, 107, 129, 134, 141, 193, 196, 262
Enchanted 165
Entwhistle, Joanne 68
Ever After 179
Existenz 203
exploitation 24, 25–27, 76, 78
extended family homes 15

F
Facebook 200, 205, 207, 213
Fairly Odd Parents 141
fairytales 20, 68, 80, 173–174, 178, 238
Fairytopia 137
fake tans 248
fame 242–244
Family Guy 142, 260
fashion 66–86
fathers,
   absent 19
   hunger for 118
Featherstone, Morgan 75
Finding Nemo 164
Finkelstein, Joanna 67, 68, 69, 80
Flicka 158
Flickr 205, 206, 207, 213, 214
Flushed Away 158
folktales 20, 173
Frankenstein, Dr 202–205, 255
Frankenstein 202–203
Free Hugs Campaign, Juan Mann 213
friendship 210, 260
Friendster 206
Futurama 142

G
GI Joe 89, 95
Gabriel, Maddison 75–76, 78
Gale, Julie 52–53, 99
gender 88–89, 188, 189, 190, 191, 258
generational blurring 48
Gerbner, George 129
Ghirlandaio, Domenico, *An Old Man and His Grandson* 18
Gibbs, Nancy 97–98

Gibson, William, *Neuromancer* 203
Gilligan's Island 140
Girl Power 57
Girlfriend Magazine 59–63
Giroux, Henry 28, 29, 153, 175–176, 189, 214–215
goddesses 240–241
Google 8, 200, 213
gossip 58
Grand Theft Auto 3, San Andreas 115, 222, 228–229
Grease 168
Greek mythology 66, 196, 240
Grey's Anatomy 144
Grimm fairytales 66, 176, 178, 180–182, 239
Grose, Michael 72
Grossman, Lev 228–229
Growing Up in Medieval London 14

H
Halo 3 115
Hamlet 20
Hanawalt, Barbara 13, 14, 21, 23, 28–29, 33
Handler, Ruth 94
Hansel and Gretel 20
Happily Never After 190
Happy Feet 165
Harnett, Sonya 197
Harry Potter 20, 107, 115, 138, 154, 157, 160, 177, 191–197, 238, 246
Hartley, John 62
He-man 140
Hearn, Lian 192
Hercules 176
Heroes 140, 148

heroes/heroines 67, 113, 137, 165–166, 173, 186, 188, 240
Hesiod 17, 18
Heywood, Chris 14
Hi-5 50, 133
Hilton, Paris 2, 39, 52, 57, 85, 88, 104, 239
Holland, Tom 18
Hollywood 117, 165
Home and Away 148
Homer 17
Honey, We Lost the Kids 15
Hoodwinked 166, 190
Hopkins, Susan 58–59, 188, 189
Hoyles, Martin 16
Hudson, Jennifer 232

I
I, Robot 203
Idol 141, 231, 242, 258
Iliad 17
imaginative play 105–106
imperfect adults 11
imprinting 50
Industrial Revolution 15, 25
infant mortality 24, 25
infotainment 255–256
Inness, Sherri A 91
innocence 22, 46, 65, 75, 254, 261, 264
instant gratification, culture of 40
internet 7, 201
iPod 204, 247
Irvine, John 236, 243–244, 261

J
Jackass 2 117
James Bond 154, 203

Jenkins, Henry 198–199, 205, 211–212, 222, 227–228
Jenks, Chris 16, 21
Jesus 12
Jet 213
Joe Millionaire 179
Johnson, Steven 140, 148, 165, 228
Jones, Gerard, *Killing Monsters* 113, 115–116, 118
Jones, Wendy Singer 106–107
Josie and the Pussy Cats 141

K
K-Zone 57
Katzenberg, Jeffrey 189
Kellner, Douglas 174
Ken (doll) 94–95
KGOY (kids growing older younger) 5
Kids Free 2B Kids campaign (KF2BK) 52, 99
'kidults' 20
Kilbourne, Jean 42, 64, 72, 84, 99, 237
Kim Possible 134, 139
King Arthur 20
King of the Hill 142
Kociumbas, Jan 15
kweens 157

L
LaBeouf, Shia 167
Lamb, Sharon and Lynn Mikel Brown 42, 43, 60
Larian, Isaac 97
law 24
Le Guin, Ursula 195
Lego 114

Lewis, CS 192
Lexx 203
licensed characters 197–198
Lindstrom, Martin 39, 55
Linkedin 207
Linn, Susan 44, 49, 50, 51, 52, 65, 92, 113–114, 121, 123
Little Angel 57
Little Emperor syndrome 243
Little Match Girl 20, 25–26
Little Red Riding Hood 20
Livingstone, Sonia 204
Lizzie McGuire 92, 134, 135, 139
Locke, John 16
logos 39, 68, 242
Lohan, Lindsay 2, 57, 104, 167
Lord of the Rings 154, 165, 166, 196
Lost in Space 203
Lucas, George 8, 40
Luke Skywalker 20
Lumby, Catharine 62 and Duncan Fine 135
Lumiere, Auguste and Louis 152

M
M.A.S.H. 141
McDonald's 39, 47
McDonnell, Kathleen 15, 29, 72, 74, 128, 133, 135, 253
Mackay, Hugh 30, 44, 48, 151, 232–233
McLuhan, Marshall 125
Mad Max 161
Madagascar 162

magazines, tween/
    teen 56–63, 67, 84,
    198, 238–239
magic 195–196
Maid in Manhattan
    179
make-believe 114–119
make-up 55, 84
marketers 3, 37, 55,
    71, 90, 165, 219, 262
marketing 87, 153,
    239–240, 253
Marsden, John 192
Marshall, David 227
Matilda 107
Mattel 41, 90, 92–96,
    120, 225
Mean Girls 167, 169
media 113–115, 124–151
    education 125
    room 124
medieval art 14
Memento 166
Merchants of Cool 41
Mermaidtopia 137
MGA Entertainment 2,
    90, 99
Mickey Mouse 174
Middle Ages (medieval
    period) 12, 13, 14
*Mighty Morphin' Power
    Rangers* 129
milestones 54–56, 81,
    82, 148, 262
miniature adults 11, 263
mind share 38, 49
mini-me 31, 78–80
Minogue, Kylie 51, 71
Minority Report 203
mobile phones 7, 201,
    202, 204, 221, 222,
    223–224, 225
    and safety 226
    in schools 224
models 75–76, 78, 231,
    242

Monster House 166
Monsters Inc 166
moral panic 112, 126
Moss, Kate 76
mothers, absence of 187–
    189
Mozart 120
MP3s 215, 222, 224
Mr & Mrs Smith 159
Mulan 188
Muppets 2, 3
music video 127–128
My Scene Barbie 96–97,
    106
MySpace 200, 205, 206,
    207–209, 214, 242, 258
myths 19, 178, 240
MyYearbook.com 213

N
nag factor/pester
    power 40, 49, 81, 90,
    104, 163, 222, 225
Napoleon Dynamite 168
natural
    environment 117–119
nature-deficit
    disorder 118
Neighbours 69, 148
'newstalgia' 48
Nickelodeon 225
Niedzviecki, Hal 69,
    122–123, 241, 242–243
*Night at the
    Museum* 158
Nintendo 226, 229
Nix, Garth 192
nursery rhymes 23–24,
    173

O
Odyssey 17, 19
Office of Film
    and Literature
    Classification 155, 192
Oliver Twist 20, 25

Olsen twins (Mary-Kate
    and Ashley) 67, 85
oral sex 64
ordinary 231–232, 250
Orestes 20
orphans 20

P
paedophiles 44–49
Palmer, Sue 52, 53, 220
Paltrow, Gwyneth 246,
    260
parental anxiety 44
parental guilt 260–262
parenting 29–30
    skills 262
Parents Jury 52
'passion for fashion' 97,
    102, 103, 108
peer groups 33, 106
Perrault, Charles 180
Peter Pan 20, 74, 159
Peter Pan 27
*Pirates of the
    Caribbean* 112, 115,
    157
*Pirates of the Caribbean:
    Dead Man's Chest* 163
Pixar 190
planned
    obsolescence 111
Play School 130, 133, 149
Playboy 60
PlayStation 226, 229
Pocahontas 188
Pokémon 92, 111, 116,
    137
Polly Pocket 88, 105
positive
    reinforcement 234
Postman, Neil 13, 16, 22
Potts, Paul 213
puberty 72
praise 234–236
Pretty Woman 179
Princess Diana 238

Princess Diaries 167
Princess Mary 238
princesses 67, 71, 99, 188, 238–239, 250
Prisoner of Azkaban 192
prizes 245–246
puberty 22–23, 84
public space 40
Pulman, Philip 192
Pulp Fiction 166
Pussycat Dolls 127

Q
Quart, Alissa 51, 56, 62, 90, 167, 168

R
Ramsey, JonBenet 1, 76–77
Ratatouille 165
ratings creep 161–162
Raven-Symoné 85, 136
reality television 20, 141, 231, 242
Renaissance 18
repeat viewing of TV shows/films 164
resilience, lack of 233–234
resistance conformity 69
Ritchie, Nicole 104
rites of passage 82
Robocop 203
Rodda, Emily 195
role models 52, 106, 107, 118, 172, 174, 195
Roman mythology 66, 240
Romantic era 18
romanticising childhood 11, 21–22
Romeo and Juliet 21
Rowling, JK 8, 192–193, 195, 196
Rugrats 134, 137, 139, 140

Run Lola Run 166
Rush, Emma 46, 63, 73
Rushby, Alison 80

S
Santa Claus 160
Sauers, Joan 64–65
savvy 257–258, 259, 264
school formals 81–83
Scooby Doo 141
Scrubs 141
Second Life 203, 229
Sega 226, 227
Seinfield 140
self-esteem 84, 232, 245, 250, 258
self-image 62, 249–250, 258–259
Sendak, Maurice 192
Sesame Street 2, 50, 130, 133
sex 22, 23, 41, 42, 63–65, 93, 102, 127, 128, 163, 191
  in movies 169–170, 188
sexual panic 45, 71, 88
sexualisation 44, 46, 72–73, 77–78, 99, 100, 248, 255–256
sexuality 71, 72–73, 87, 93, 99, 101, 188, 255–256
sexy/sexiness 41, 43, 74–75, 77, 92, 99, 100, 101, 102, 104, 255–256, 264
Shakespeare 20, 21, 22, 192, 196
Shark Tale 165
Shaw, Robert 233, 238, 239
Shelley, Mary 195, 202–203
She's All That 167
shopping 40

Shrek, Shrek 2 and *Shrek the Third* 158, 164, 165, 166, 189
Sick Puppies 213
Simpson, Ashlee 74
sleep deprivation 125, 219–221
Sleeping Beauty 20
Smallville 136, 148
SMS 204, 205, 219
Smurfs 140
Snickett, Lemony 107
Socrates 17, 18, 22
South Park 142
Spears, Britney 8, 74, 85, 104, 174, 256
special 69, 82, 231–238, 241–242, 250–251, 258
Spiderman (Peter Parker) 20, 50, 115
SpongeBob Squarepants 137, 140
sport 244–246
stage parents 244–245
Star Trek 203
Star Trek: First Contact 154
Star Wars 40, 112, 115, 154, 159, 165–166
Stargate: Atlantis 203
Stargate: SG1 203
Steinberg, Shirley 93
Steinberg, Shirley and Joe Kincheloe 111
Stephenson, Neal, *Snow Crash* 203
stereotypes 43, 70, 79, 111, 136–138, 142–143, 167, 184, 187, 188, 189, 190, 193–194, 198
Stoffel, Stephanie Lovett 27
Stoker, Bram 195
structured activities/ lessons 243–246

sugar and spice 1–2
Summer Heights High 148
superheroes 92, 114, 128, 163
Superman 115
Superman Returns 163
Supernanny 3
Supernatural 148
Survivor 141, 231

T
2001: A Space Odyssey 203
T-shirts 80, 83, 98
Tarde, Gabriel 91
Tatar, Maria 177–178
technology 124, 134, 145, 150, 152, 153, 170, 201, 203–205, 217–218, 224–227, 230
  etiquette 221–224
  in bedrooms 219–221
Teenage Mutant Ninja Turtles 89, 112, 129
teenagers 42, 55, 56, 62, 69, 72, 80, 82, 92, 125, 127, 135, 141, 144, 145–146, 148–149, 153, 154, 165, 166–169, 171, 204, 205, 206, 209, 210, 211, 213, 214–215, 217, 220, 221, 223, 238, 240, 243, 248–250, 258–259
Telemachus 19
Teletubbies 130, 132
television 7, 112, 113, 114, 124–151
  adults portrayed on 138–140
  advertising 147–148
  and babies/ toddlers 130–133
  and education 125
  and physical effects 125–126

and sexual imagery 127
in bedrooms 145–146
ownership 125, 150
viewing habits 131–133, 146–147
Ten Things I Hate About You 167
Terminator 203
That's So Raven 134
The Bachelor 179
The Bachelorette 179
The Breakfast Club 167
The Coral Island 138
The Enlightenment 14
The Fountain 166
The Incredibles 165
The Life of Brian 241
The Lion King 189
The Little Mermaid 20, 136, 176, 182–184, 185, 190
The Love Boat 140
The Matrix 115, 166, 203
The OC 136, 141, 148
The Simpsons 8, 49, 134, 141, 142–144, 146
The Simpsons Movie 166
The Slipper and the Rose 179
The Sopranos 140
The Veronicas 58
The West Wing 141
The Wiggles 50, 133, 135
Thom, Sandi 258
Thomas, Susan Gregory 37, 38, 119, 120
tiaras 239
Timberlake, Justin 174
Tolkein, JRR 195
too much positive reinforcement syndrome 235
Top Gun 186

Total Girl 57
Toy Story 166
toys 39, 87–123
  collecting 103–105
  guns 92, 112, 113–117
Transformers 87, 89, 112, 115
Tucci, Joe 71, 245
Turner, Graeme 153, 154
Tutenstein 137
tweens 32, 38, 39, 50, 55, 56, 62, 69, 70–71, 72, 79, 80, 82, 83–85, 90, 102, 125, 134–135, 141, 144, 145–146, 148, 149, 150, 153, 154, 165, 168–169, 171, 204, 205, 207, 210, 211, 214–215, 219, 220, 222, 225, 235, 238, 248–250, 257–258
Twilight Zone 203

U
Ugly Betty 148
unrealistic expectations 233
user-generated content (UGC) 207

V
van Gennep, Arnold 22–23
Veronica Mars 138, 141, 149
victims 62
violence 88, 111–119, 128–129, 160, 164, 244, 245
  fantasy 113–119
  and television 112, 114, 126–129
violent images 112
violent play 111–119
violent toys 111–119
Vogue Girl 61, 63

W

War Games 203
War of the Worlds 159
Wark, Mackenzie 126
Warner, Marina 192
Webster, Nicky 52, 77, 85
Wertham, Frederic 128
White, TH 191
Whiting, Frances 248
Wile E Coyote 117, 128
Will and Grace 142
Williams, Robin 186
Williams, Tad, *Otherland* 203
Winfrey, Oprah 260
winning 232
Wolf, Naomi, *The Beauty Myth* 107
Wordsworth, William 21
workhouse children 25
Working Girl 179
World Wide Web 205–206

X

Xanga 205
Xbox 226, 229

Y

Yakkity Yak 137
Yeh-hsien (Chinese Cinderella) 179–180
YouTube 200, 205, 206, 207, 212–214, 242, 258
Yu-Gi-Oh 87, 92, 111, 115, 137, 139

Z

Zelda 228
Zipes, Jack 184, 192, 197